Images in Mind

Images in Mind

STATUES IN ARCHAIC AND CLASSICAL GREEK LITERATURE AND THOUGHT

Deborah Tarn Steiner

PRINCETON UNIVERSITY PRESS

PRINCETON AND OXFORD

Second printing, and first paperback printing, 2003
Paperback ISBN 0-691-09488-8

The Library of Congress has cataloged the cloth edition of this book as follows

Steiner, Deborah, 1960–
    Images in mind : statues in archaic and classical Greek literature and thought /
Deborah Steiner.
        p. cm.
    Includes bibliographical references and index.
    ISBN 0-691-04431-7 (alk. paper)
    1. Greek literature — History and criticism.   2. Statues in literature.   3. Art
and literature — Greece.   4. Sculpture in literature.   5. Aesthetics, Ancient.
    6. Statues — Greece.   7. Sculpture, Greek.   I. Title.

PA3015.S82 S74 2001
880.9′357 — dc21

                                                                    00-057463

British Library Cataloging-in-Publication Data is available

This book has been composed in Sabon

Printed on acid-free paper. ∞

www.pupress.princeton.edu

Printed in the United States of America

10 9 8 7 6 5 4 3 2

Contents

List of Illustrations

Preface

I SET OUT to write a book about how archaic and classical Greek poets, philosophers, dramatists, and historians introduce statues as cognitive and hermeneutic devices in their texts, using the artifacts as objects "good to think with." But the more I looked at the written sources, the more I was directed back to the statues themselves: it proved impossible to understand why an author inserted a work of art at a particular point in his composition without knowing something of the nature of contemporary images, what they looked like, how they functioned, what they were credited with doing. The result is a book that aims to tell two stories, one about objects, the other about texts, and to show how each proves crucial to the other.

First the objects, and the huge gaps in the material record. For all Greece's assumed influence on later western art, the images that stand at the head of that tradition are largely lost to us, or are extant only in the form of fragments or Roman copies of variable accuracy and quality. While some of the architectural and funerary works still remain, all but a handful of the bronze statues that later ancient viewers particularly prized and chose to copy in marble form have long since disappeared (many melted down, or still buried somewhere in the Mediterranean seabed). So, too, while art historians and aestheticians from the Renaissance on have drawn on the accounts of ancient images given by authors of the imperial age, no extant archaic or classical author includes a direct or unmediated description of a contemporary work of art, or straightforwardly documents an individual or collective response.

But if the vast majority of statues are lost to us, plentiful evidence of another kind remains. As traces in the ground, inscriptions on bases, sacred laws, and the many literary pointers to the ritual practices and events surrounding images amply attest, the objects were deeply embedded in the social, political, and religious fabric of archaic and classical Greece. In fifth-century Athens, a citizen might go from the agora, which had at its center images emblematizing the ten Kleisthenic tribes, through the city streets where herms occupied the crossroads, and into his workshop where a depiction of Hephaistos presided over his kiln; a contestant at the Olympic games could wander through the sacred precinct of the Altis, where statues of former winning athletes stood, wonder at the vast image of Nike, which the Messenians had set up to mark their victory in battle, and be cautioned by an array of bronze effigies of Zeus, figures fashioned from the fines inflicted on those who had deliberately broken the rules of the competitions. More generally, parents mourning the death of a child might set a carved image or stele at his grave, and a fisherman celebrating a successful haul might dedicate a *korē* to commemorate his luck and guarantee that divine favors would continue in future times. As key artifacts in this cultural landscape, images also evolved along with shifts and developments in time and place: modes of commemoration appropriate during the reign of sixth-century tyrants were deemed unacceptable under the radical Athenian democracy, while fresh attitudes toward eros and its legitimate objects could generate new modes of depicting the male and female form.

Setting images within this broader context also allows us to recover many of the attitudes and beliefs surrounding them and some of the responses that they would have garnered. As the examples already cited suggest, no sculpture was erected without a function to perform. Whether apotropaic, talismanic, monitory, consolatory, votive, or commemorative in intent, statues were first and foremost regarded not as representational or aesthetic objects (although their beauty and highly crafted quality were often crucial to their fulfillment of their designated role), but as performative and efficacious agents, able to interact in a variety of ways with those who commissioned, venerated, and even on occasion defaced them. Proof of their dynamic and responsive properties comes from many different domains; inscriptions record that statues were fashioned in order to drive off a havoc-wreaking ghost or hostile spirit sent by an enemy, and in Attic comedy and on painted pots at least, herms react and reply to those who address them with petitions and prayers. Additional evidence belongs to the myths and episodes that archaic, classical, and later authors narrate, some charting the objects' miraculous provenance, discovery, and checkered histories, others imagining their startling displays of potency: statues turn their heads to deny a prayer or register divine displeasure, come possessed with the capacity for speech and song, and disappear from the pedestals where they are placed. No less remarkable is the impact that sculpture may have on the viewer, and the affective properties that it regularly manifests. The artifacts are quite literally transfixing, able to paralyze and madden those who engage with them and to provoke emotions that can run the gamut from erotic delight to despair.

For the recovery of these actions and beliefs, we are chiefly dependent on the literary sources, which introduce statues into their works in a large variety of contexts, sometimes just glancing toward them, sometimes integrating them more centrally into a text. But when an archaic or classical author notes the activities surrounding an ancient image and alerts us to the ways in which his fellow Greeks approached, viewed, and handled the object, he generally does so as the chance by-product of a more self-interested enterprise. As the second story included in this study looks to demonstrate, the real and much more frequently notional images that appear in works of poetry and prose are above all rhetorical and illustrative devices, designed to cohere with the themes and arguments of the surrounding piece.

As vehicles for the exploration of the author's or speaker's prime concerns, images prove endlessly versatile. When the drunken Alcibiades wants to describe that most curious of individuals, Socrates, to his fellow guests, he likens him to a statue of the misshapen and lascivious Silenus, which, when opened up, reveals exquisite divine images concealed behind its crude exterior (Pl. *Symp.* 215a–b). Where Alcibiades deploys statues to figure the split between external appearance and internal reality, other speakers use them to articulate and explore relations between representations — whether artistic, verbal, or dramatic — and originals, the problem of nomination, the possibility of accurate perception through the senses. In search of the properties that distinguish the living from the dead, a writer may cite a statue by way of simile or foil; seeking to evoke the vain nature of the lover's quest, he imagines the beloved in the form of a plastic image; and eager to declare the enduring and highly crafted quality of his own composition, a poet describes his song in the terms that the artifact supplies. In each of its five central chapters, this book treats one of these and the related notions that the sources most frequently address by means of statuary, and traces how the art of the age affects the literary and philosophical imagination.

The innovations in sculptural style and technique that marked the late archaic and classical ages and that constitute the more properly "art historical" dimension that my discussion seeks to incorporate feed directly into the questions sounded by the texts, and prove critical to deciphering their tropes and conceits. Even as sculptors create more naturalistic accounts of their subjects and devise ways of giving their works a heightened emotive and persuasive appeal, poets, dramatists, sophists, and philosophers look to statues when they wonder about the proper use and ethical charge of *apatē*, which all works of mimesis involve, and when they question whether physiognomy and outward demeanor can reflect the inner person. Fainter, but no less suggestive overlaps indicate other crosscurrents. Might the young, graceful, and even seductive victor statues now appearing at Olympia and elsewhere cohere with Pindar's contemporary accounts of the athlete as an *erōmenos* and object of desire, and do the *trompe l'oeil* works fashioned by the artists of the late fifth and early fourth century inform Plato's strictures against representations and his preoccupation with achieving the correct vantage point, which frees the viewer from the distortions that the senses impose?

As this brief overview makes clear, texts are necessary to images because only the contemporary literary sources allow us to apprehend how the Greeks of the archaic and classical ages conceptualized sculpture; and images are necessary to texts, because without them we cannot understand the role of sculpture — both as a class of objects and in particular instances — as a literary device used in poetry, rhetoric, and philosophy. But the exchanges also go beyond this obvious form of reciprocity, and the presence of a statue informs the nature of the surrounding literary construct in more subtle fashion, too, as it imports into the text all the powers, properties, and associations that it possesses in the lives of the audiences. And although some of these same arguments could be made for painting, sculpture stands very much in a class of its own; the image's three-dimensionality, its frequent occupation of the same real space that the viewer inhabits, and its central place within the social, political, religious, and magical practices of the age endow it with facets unique to itself.

A word about organization, methodology, and my use of sources. The book does not aim to provide a comprehensive treatment of archaic and classical statuary, nor a documentation of every instance in which an ancient author cites an image. Instead, its chapters are designed as selective treatments of some of the questions that the objects generated, and as discussions of the preoccupations that sculpture helped contemporary artists, writers, and viewers to articulate. For some readers, my use of both the visual and the textual evidence may seem idiosyncratic. Although the book restricts its scope to the archaic and classical periods, I have on occasion included material from much later authors, who not only describe works no longer extant, but also supply much of our information concerning the ritual practices and anecdotal traditions surrounding the earlier images. I have tried to use this additional evidence only where it supplements or fills out suggestions and implications in the earlier sources, and to bear in mind the very different mentalities and agendas shaping the later texts. So, too, Roman copies of lost Greek originals figure in the argument, but once again come surrounded with the necessary caveats. While the thinking about images set out above informs all the chapters, the discussions can also be read as freestanding essays grouped around a central theme, and each may appeal to a different audience. But if the book aims to accommodate a selective reading, it is also my hope that the overlaps and connections between its several parts will encourage a more comprehensive approach, and that the whole will generate a fuller, more cohesive account of the role of statues in the daily lives, thoughts, and practices of ancient viewers.

Acknowledgments

THIS BOOK has been long in the writing, and it is a pleasure to thank those many individuals whose time and knowledge I have taxed along the way. I owe particular gratitude to Miranda Marvin, Suzanne Saïd, and Froma Zeitlin, all of whom read and offered detailed comments on a still more unwieldy version of the work, and who have all supported this project from its very early stages. I hope that none will be too disappointed with the result. Conversations with Carole Straw and Bettina Bergmann did much to help me first conceptualize the topic, and Lauren Osborne encouraged its transformation into book form. Others will recognize my debts to their expertise and help as well: Malcolm Bell, Simon Goldhill, François Lissarrague, and Robin Osborne all generously supplied me with copies of published and unpublished work, and Sarah Morris's response to an article derived from one of this book's chapters did much to alert me to issues that I had previously neglected. Many thanks are also due to my colleagues at Columbia and Barnard, who have shared their ideas and scholarship and have more generally provided an ideal atmosphere in which to work. Alan Cameron, James Coulter, Helene Foley, Natalie Kampen, and Karen Van Dyck are among those who have (wittingly or not) contributed to my thinking, and Roger Bagnall has been, since my arrival at Columbia, a chairman without compare. For invaluable help in gathering illustrations, thanks to Herica Valladares and Marie Mauzy

Other debts are of a more personal kind. My husband, Andrew Feldherr, who announced that he was so tired of this project that even had I proposed to dedicate the book to him, he would have declined the offer, has nonetheless been central to this, as to all my enterprises. To his forbearance, his uncanny way of knowing where I was heading long before I got there, and his willingness to find me books in the most recondite of places, the deepest, most heartfelt thanks. Nor would this list be complete without mention of the individual whose advent in the middle of the endeavor upset every schedule and hope for rapid completion: to my beloved daughter Rebecca, a thank-you for having lastingly and wonderfully alerted me to the gap between images and reality.

Finally, a few words about transliteration and translation. I have for the most part used Latinized versions of Greek names, particularly where the characters, sites, and authors cited are very well-established and familiar to readers. For less common individuals and place names, I have tended to preserve a spelling truer to their Greek form. The result is something that falls far short of standards of consistency, and may at times seem arbitrary. Names of authors and titles of texts are abbreviated in accordance with the list in *The Oxford Classical Dictionary*, 3d ed. (1996), pp. xxix–liv. My citation of long passages of Greek in the original has been reserved for places where the individual words of the text matter particularly for my argument; in other instances I have given only an English translation with the important Greek words and phrases included in transliterated version in parentheses. Unless otherwise noted, all translations are my own.

NOTE TO THE PAPERBACK EDITION

I welcome the opportunity to correct several passages in the original edition where I built on arguments developed by Richard Neer with too minimal citation. My discussion on pages 19–22, 27–29, and 48 draws on Professor Neer's arguments in Neer 1995 and in "Ekphrasis and Its Discontents. The Case of the Berlin Foundy Cup," a paper read at the 1999 College Art Association meeting at a panel on which we both appeared.

List of Abbreviations

ABV	J. D. Beazley, *Attic Black-Figure Vase-Painters* (Oxford, 1956).
ARV[2]	J. D. Beazley, *Attic Red-Figure Vase-Painters*, 2d ed. (Oxford, 1963).
CEG	P. A. Hansen, *Carmina epigraphica Graeca*, vol. 1, *Saec. VIII–V a Chr. n.* (Berlin, 1983).
DK	H. Diels and W. Kranz, eds., *Die Fragmente der Vorsokratiker*, 12th ed. (Berlin, 1966–67).
Ebert	J. Ebert, ed., *Griechische Epigramme auf Sieger an gymnischen und hippischen Agonen, Abhandlungen der sächsischen Akademie der Wissenschaften zu Leipzig*, Phil.-hist. Kl. Band 63, Heft 2 (Berlin, 1972).
FGE	D. L. Page, ed., *Further Greek Epigrams* (Cambridge, 1981).
FGrH	F. Jacoby, ed., *Die Fragmente der griechischen Historiker*, 2d ed. (Leiden, 1954–69).
GVI	W. Peek, ed., *Griechische Vers-Inschriften*, vol. 1, *Grab-Epigramme* (Berlin, 1955).
KA	R. Kassel and C. Austin, eds., *Poetae comici Graeci*, 2 vols. (Berlin, 1983, 1991).
LIMC	*Lexicon iconographicum mythologiae classicae* (Zurich, 1981–).
LP	E. Lobel and D. L. Page, eds., *Poetarum Lesbiorum fragmenta* (Oxford, 1955).
LSAM	F. Sokolowski, ed., *Lois sacrées de l'Asie Mineure* (Paris, 1955).
LSCG	F. Sokolowski, ed., *Lois sacrées des cités grecques* (Paris, 1969).
Michel	C. Michel, ed., *Recueil d'inscriptions grecques* (Brussels, 1900–1927).
N[2]	A. Nauck, ed., *Tragicorum Graecorum fragmenta*, 2d ed. (Hildesheim, 1964).
Overbeck	J. A. Overbeck, ed., *Die antiken Schriftquellen zur Geschichte der bildenden Künste bei den Griechen* (Hildesheim, 1868).
Paroem. Gr.	E. L. von Leutsch and F. G. Schneidewin, eds., *Corpus Paroemiographorum Graecorum* (Hildesheim, 1958).

PGM   K. Preisendanz [and A. Henrichs], eds., *Papyri Graecae magicae: Die griechischen Zauberpapyri*, 2d ed. (Stuttgart, 1973–74).

PMG   D. L. Page, ed., *Poetae melici Graeci* (Oxford, 1962).

Radt   S. Radt, ed., *Tragicorum Graecorum fragmenta*, vol. 4, *Sophocles* (Göttingen, 1977); vol. 3, *Aeschylus* (Göttingen, 1985).

SEG   J.J.E. Hondius, ed., *Supplementum epigraphicum Graecum* (Leiden, 1923–).

SLG   D. L. Page, ed., *Supplementum lyricis Graecis* (Oxford, 1974).

Trendall   A. D. Trendall, *The Red-Figured Vases of Lucania, Campania, and Sicily* (Oxford, 1967).

Images in Mind

CHAPTER ONE

Replacement and Replication

A MINIATURE love story frames the discovery that a certain Boutades, a Sikyonian potter at Corinth, once made: he manufactured the first portrait image on behalf of his daughter, "who was in love with a young man; and she, when he was going abroad, drew in outline on the wall the shadow of his face thrown by a lamp. Her father, having pressed clay onto this, made a relief that he hardened by exposing it to fire along with the rest of his pottery" (Pliny *HN* 35.151).

Although doubtless fictional, the anecdote poses perhaps the most critical question that an ancient image asked of its viewers: should they perceive the manufactured object as a replacement for the missing original, or could it do no more than reproduce the model's external appearance? Read one way, the terracotta functions as a substitute for the departing lover, and so belongs together with the many statues in Greek myth and history that serve as re-presentations of the absent and the dead, standing in for the lost party and maintaining communication between those separated by time and space. The efficacy of these kinds of images, I suggest, depends on a particular construction of the bond between the subject and the figurine, a bond that need not rest on any visible mimetic likeness, but on a notion of substitution, equivalence, or sympathy. In Pliny's tale, the beloved and his image do not so much resemble one another as exist in a relation of metonymy, both formal and more loosely defined; here the face of the youth stands proxy for his entire person, but any portion of his person, any object associated with or belonging to him, could do as well.[1] The part assumed by the shadow in the episode confirms that contiguity, not similarity, plays the leading role; not an exact visible replica of the body, the *umbra* none-

---

[1] Here I borrow from the categories explored particularly in Jakobson 1987a: 95–114. As he argues, all linguistic operations are determined by two models, one based on similarity (the metaphoric way), the other on contiguity (the metonymic way). He then briefly re-evokes these terms in his discussion of statues (1987b: 318–67). Brillante (1988: 21) also applies these terms to his discussion of Greek images but focuses only on the metonymic bond. For someone deeply rooted in such metonymic modes of thought, the figurative representation can literally supplant the original; in the case of aphasics affected with "selection deficiency" (an inability to perform acts of linguistic selection and substitution), discussed by Jakobson (1987a: 102), the presentation of a picture of an object actually causes the suppression of its name.

theless forms an intimate, though separable, element of the subject's identity.[2]

But within Pliny's story lies a second, and potentially less positive, account of the nature and function of images. The tale belongs to an exploration of the origins of *similitudines*, and Pliny caps the anecdote with a discussion of the properly historical Lysistratos of Sikyon (brother of Lysippos), who distinguished himself by creating more accurate and less idealizing representations of his models than his predecessors (35.153). An emphasis on exact imitation transforms the role of the plaque and grounds its consoling powers in its capacity to furnish a portrait likeness, a "photograph," which reminds the maiden of the distant youth. Where contiguity and metonymy determined the link between the original and the representation that worked as a replacement device, now similarity and metaphor supply the necessary adhesives. The terracotta mimics the beloved, and the closer the visible resemblance, the more successful the antidote to Boutades' daughter's grief.

United in this episode, the two facets of the image show how their coexistence within a single object need not preclude a deep antinomy. If the representation can summon up the beloved through contiguity, then the shadow's role in generating the terracotta does nothing to impair its efficacy. According to the many uses to which a man's shadow may be put, it not only forms a part of himself, but also can serve as one of the most decisive expressions of his vitality:[3] very much in the manner of the image, it, too, supplies a substitute or replacement for a missing party, and holds out to lovers a means of assuaging their longing for an absent object of desire.[4] But if the figurine claims to offer a mirror likeness of its living subject, then Boutades' choice to work after the *umbra* introduces an unwanted breach between the original and the copy.[5] The portrait now stands as a flawed imitation, an image of an image, a *faux-semblant* at two removes from the reality it claims to depict. Sharpening the distinctions between statues as metonymic and metaphoric accounts is the second defect the representation harbors. Boutades' daughter captures no more than the outlines of the lover (*lineis circumscripsit*), and the potter fills the mold he makes with an interior of clay. The portrait image based on resemblance fails to house the inner essence of the sub-

---

[2] On ancient views of the shadow as contiguous with but distinct from the individual, see Bettini 1992: 53–58.

[3] Ibid.: 53–54.

[4] Ibid.: 56–57; see particularly Ar. *Nub.* 973–76. Brillante (1988: 26 and n. 6) observes the same function for footprints or other traces.

[5] The term *umbra* is probably a translation from the Greek *skia* (Schweitzer [1932] 1963 includes the passage among those that he believes Pliny took over from Xenocrates). On the parallel ambiguity of the term *skia* in the Greek tradition, see Rouveret 1989: 20.

ject, just as a shadow traces only the contours of the body. A variant on the story introduces yet another reason for the vacuity of the final *typus*: even as Boutades' daughter takes the likeness, her beloved sleeps, his vital spirit absent from the body.[6]

Greek philosophers and rhetoricians of the late classical and post-classical period would develop terms for the two modes of viewing that this "first" portrait image puts into play. Where the depiction is perceived as linked to its source by virtue of an intrinsic property, where it shares with the signified an essential and enduring quality, it provides an *eikōn*, a stepping stone pointing to the original that gives the viewer access to a hidden or absent reality. To the realm of *eidōla*, imperfect, even deceptive versions of the truth, belong figures that depend on a purely visible resemblance, that limit themselves to external contours.[7] But for the statues that populate the archaic and early classical sources, these polarizations fail to capture the scenarios that the texts describe. Whether authors cite real-world images familiar to their audiences or imagine fabulous creations that come from the hands of divine and legendary artisans, the figures they envision cohabit or oscillate between the "eiconic" and "eidolic" realms. The image's relation to the original turns out to combine both metonymy and metaphor, and the manufactured work proves so handy a vehicle for poets, philosophers, and dramatists to work with precisely because it hosts the multiple and shifting positions that all representations — phantoms, words, an actor on the stage among them — occupy vis-à-vis the originals for which they stand in. That contemporary statue-makers fashion sculptures that stimulate, address, and respond to the issues posed in the texts will be the additional suggestion that this chapter makes.

REPLACING THE ABSENT

The Statue as Double

Archaeological evidence that long predates written accounts demonstrates the role of the statue as a replacement figurine that doubles for the dead.[8] In a grave at Midea (modern Dendra) excavators discovered

---

[6] Athenagoras *Leg.* 17.2.

[7] Saïd (1987: 310) suggests that the difference is already present in the morphology of the two words; both are formed on the same root *wei, but only the *eidōlon* signals its origin in the sphere of the visible (it derives from the root *weid, which expresses the idea of seeing). Saïd and Vernant (1990b) agree on the distinction between *eikones* and *eidōla* in Platonic and later thought; their debate turns about the question of whether this distinction was already present in archaic notions of figurative and imagistic representations.

[8] For this, Picard 1933; see, too, the long list of examples in Schweitzer [1940] 1963: 121–29.

a Bronze Age burial chamber inhabited by two statue menhirs occupying the place of a missing corpse. A seventh-century grave in Thera, also without a human body, contained a pair of stone images interred together with the customary grave goods,[9] and a fifth-century "pot-burial" unearthed in Italian Lokri yielded a clay bust of a woman, again an apparent substitute for the dead's absent body.[10] From the literary sources of the fifth century come several examples of characters of myth and history buried in effigy when their corpses could not be found. Herodotus records the Spartan custom of preparing an *eidōlon* of a king who had died abroad in battle (and whose body presumably went missing) and of bringing the statue home for burial with due honors (6.58.3). Euripides' *Helen* has a similar stratagem to propose when she asks permission to conduct funeral rites for the supposedly drowned Menelaus according to the customs of her native land.[11] When a puzzled Theoklymenos asks the widow how she aims to bury a mere *skia* (*Hel.* 1240), Helen replies that she will fashion a cenotaph from the garments that would normally cover the corpse (1243). Perhaps the same logic of substitution lies behind the tale preserved in later sources of the death of Alkmene: first Hermes caused her body mysteriously to disappear, and then he placed a block of stone in the chest where the corpse previously lay.[12]

The impetus for making a substitute for the missing person and performing his or her symbolic (re)interment may have two sources: first, the belief that the *psuchē* of the dead cannot find its rest in Hades until the body has received appropriate burial (as Patroklos explains in *Iliad* 23.70–74); and second, the need to appease an unquiet soul, angry at the circumstances of its death and its deprivation of the customary honors and rites it could properly expect (the sentiment to which Ores-

---

[9] Kurtz and Boardman 1971: 247–59; Faraone 1992: 82–83. These statues, several discussions suggest, provide the earliest known Greek examples of *kolossoi*, images whose particularized function was to re-present and stand in for an absent or dead individual (see Benveniste 1932; Picard 1933; Roux 1960; Vernant 1983). This interpretation has been disputed (Roux 1960; Ducat 1976), since several *kolossoi* cited in the sources carry no such associations. I believe (with Ducat 1976) that the practice was more generalized, and that there is no need to restrict this power only to those images described as *kolossoi*. Certainly in many instances *kolossoi* do play a marked "replacement" or doubling role, but so, as we shall see, do many other images that the sources describe as *agalmata*, *eikones*, or even *eidōla*.

[10] Kurtz and Boardman 1971: 259, fig. 56.

[11] As Benveniste (1932: 122) notes, the practice of making replicas seems to cluster in Doric areas of Greece.

[12] Ant. Lib. 33 (citing Pherecydes); Paus. 9.16.7. In a different scenario, Diodorus Siculus describes how, after the death of Hephaistion, lieutenant and friend of Alexander, each one of the generals offered figurines of gold and of ivory of the dead that were to be placed alongside the body (17.115.1). Cf. Hdt. 2.130.2.

tes and Electra appeal when they attempt to rouse the ghost of Aga-memnon in Aeschylus's *Choephori*). The Spartan general Pausanias joins this group of the wrathful dead. After he perished from starvation in the temple of Athena Chalchioikos, the Delphic oracle ordered the Spartans to escape from the pollution provoked by his end by reburying the general's body at the very spot where he died, and by "giving back two *sōmata* to the Goddess in payment for one." The city responded by dedicating two bronze statues to Athena "as a replacement for Pausanias" (Thuc. 1.134–35). Later, less sober accounts of the same event suggest that the images played a cardinal role in appeasing the anger of the general: both Plutarch and the anonymous author of the *Letters of Themistocles* introduce them as a device for exorcising the ghost of Pausanias that was haunting the temple entrance and terrifying people away.[13]

As the examples of Pausanias and others illustrate, the creation of a doubling image can correct the disturbance that certain forms of death generate. But the dead are not the sole constituents served by these re-placement figures; such objects may also grant communities permanent access to the powers that certain individuals host in both life and death. In Herodotus's account of the fate of Kleobis and Biton, the two exem-plary sons no sooner lay down to sleep in a temple after performing their heroic service to their mother and the goddess Hera than they "never rose more." No mention of the bodies of the youths, nor of their burial or grave site, follows; instead, the narrator rounds off his tale by noting that "the Argives made statues of them and dedicated them at Delphi, as of two men who were best of all" (1.31.5). On a second occasion, Herodotus encounters an individual whose uncanny appear-ances, disappearances, and death-that-is-no-death again conclude with the raising of a statue: Aristeas, or his corpse, twice vanishes from sight, and returns a third time in the form of a *phasma* that orders that an image be set up on the shamanlike man's behalf (4.14–15).[14] In both narratives, the signal feats that the characters perform during their lives indicate their possession of a talismanic force that sets them outside the limits that men regularly observe. In each instance, too, Herodotus in-vests the statue that takes the place of the mysteriously missing body (and some form of translation is what the different stories seem to im-ply[15]) with a quasi-sacred status,[16] suggestive of its capacity to actualize

---

[13] For these, see pp. 10–11 and note 25 below.
[14] Here, as so often, we find the conjunction of statue and ghost (a point to which I shall return on several occasions).
[15] In later stories, the notion of mysterious translation and replacement by a statue be-comes something of a leitmotif. For two examples, Ant. Lib. 13 and 40.
[16] Aristeas's image is set up (and the verb *hidrutai* at 4.15.4 is that regularly used for raising images of gods) at the recommendation not just of Aristeas, but also of the Delphic oracle, and it stands alongside an *agalma* of Apollo within a sacred space demarcated by

the individuals' power at the site and to make it continuously accessible to those who have erected the monument.

The motifs punctuating Herodotus's two tales find an echo and clarification in a context where images still more clearly function as replacement figurines designed to preserve the talismanic properties that their originals host. Miraculous disappearances, revenants, unlikely deaths, and outstanding feats of strength are all the stuff of the legends surrounding a series of athletic victors, most clustering in the early fifth century, who were elevated to the rank of cult heroes,[17] and in each instance the tale makes plain the intimate, near-symbiotic bond between the athlete and his image. Theagenes of Thasos, Olympic victor in 480 and 476, was honored with a bronze statue standing in the agora of his native city. Flogged by an enemy after the athlete's death, the statue toppled down on its assailant and, on being convicted of homicide, was thrown into the sea. Famine fell on the Thasians until, on the advice of the Delphic oracle, they recovered the statue, restored it, and worshiped Theagenes with divine honors (Paus. 6.11.6–9). The statue of one Euthykles, a Lokrian victor, suffered mutilation after its subject had been charged with betraying the interests of his city. Once again, blight and famine fell on the community, and the Lokrians were instructed by the Delphic oracle to honor the dead athlete and to offer sacrifices to his statue equivalent to those paid to the image of Zeus (Callim. fr. 85 [*dieg.* II 5] Pfeiffer). The tales of Astylos of Kroton, double victor at Olympia in 488, and of Oibotas of Dyme, the first Achaean victor at Olympia and winner of the running race in 756, confirm the very close identification between the victor and his image that these other scenarios presuppose. The anger the Krotonians felt when Astylos had himself proclaimed Syracusan (supposedly to gratify the dynast Hieron) after his further victories in 484 and 480 prompted the destruction of the athlete's statue together with the transformation of his house into a prison (Paus. 6.13.1). Oibotas, furious at being deprived of a proper *geras* for his achievement, condemned the Achaeans to defeat in all subsequent Olympic games. Only with the elevation of a statue to the athlete some three centuries after the event did the Achaeans end their long exclusion from the winners' rolls; thereafter, Pausanias reports

---

bay trees. However, note that in this story, as in the tale of Kleobis and Biton, the author uses two different terms for statues of men and gods: the mother of the Argive youths prays to the *agalma* of Hera, while the images of her sons are called *eikones*; in the second instance, Aristeas receives an *andrias* beside the *agalma* of Apollo.

[17] Kurke (1993: 154) persuasively argues that Herodotus presents Kleobis and Biton (called *aethlophoroi* at 1.31.2, and participants in their own kind of race) according to this athletic victor model. For these stories of athletes, Fontenrose 1968; S. Lattimore 1987; Kurke 1993. For the temporal concentration of these tales, Bohringer 1979.

(7.17.14), all would make sacrifices at the tomb of Oibotas before competing at Olympia, and victors would wreathe his image standing in the
Altis.

To punish or honor an individual by means of the treatment dealt out
to his statue assumes the object's capacity to represent, in symbolic
fashion, the absent original. Nowhere does this substitution work more
powerfully than in the case of the lead, clay, and wax "voodoo" images
already deployed in the curse rituals practiced in fifth-century Athens
and other parts of Greece.[18] By binding and/or mutilating the effigy, and
then placing it in a box to be buried in a grave or another site, the
aggressor hoped to contain or restrain his actual victim's vital faculties.
One such figure excavated from a fifth-century Athenian grave has its
hands twisted behind its back, while the arms of a small lead statuette
of a man found in a tomb from the Kerameikos of the early fourth
century are similarly pinioned behind its back.[19] In other instances heads
have been wrenched to one side or completely turned about, and feet
twisted or bound together. The distortions do not so much seek to inflict this specific form of suffering on the victim (any more than the
often crudely shaped dolls involve attempts to copy the appearance of
those against whom they are deployed) as to immobilize his powers of
action, speech, and thought, and so to render him impotent in those
judicial, erotic, commercial, and agonistic spheres where the figurines
chiefly operate.

A symbolic substitution or contiguity again determines the role of
images in oath rituals in archaic and classical times. An inscription from
Kyrene in Libya records how seventh-century colonists leaving for Af-
rica from their home city of Thera would fashion images (*kolossoi*)
from wax and throw them into the fire while pronouncing the prescribed formula: "May he who does not abide by this agreement, but
transgresses it, melt away and dissolve like the images, himself, his seed,
and his property" (*SEG* 9.3).[20] The efficacy of the ritual depends on the
statuettes' capacity to re-present the oath-takers, and not merely to
symbolize but rather to prefigure the perjurer's eventual fate.[21] In a par-

---

[18] Faraone (1991b: 189–90) suggests two archaic bronze figurines from Tegea may already have served this end. For detailed discussion of the phenomenon, see also Faraone
1991a; Graf 1997: 134–69.

[19] For these and other examples, Faraone 1991b: 190–91.

[20] For text, bibliography, and discussion of dating, Meiggs and Lewis 1969: 5–9, no. 5, ll.
44–49. For analysis, Gernet 1981: 170–71. For another instance of melting a figurine,
Graf 1997: 165.

[21] As Louis Gernet (1981: 171) comments of the rite, "If the threat is not merely postponed, or if something is at once accomplished by the fire, it is because the contracting
party himself is immediately brought under obligation through his 'double.'"

allel, although more mild and retroactive, form of self-consecration, Athenian archons who have committed perjury must dedicate at Delphi statues of gold, of equal height or weight to their own body (Arist. [*Ath. Pol.*] 55.5; Plut. *Solon* 25.3; cf. Pl. *Phdr.* 235d–e). Rather than give over their persons to the god, the officials offer substitutes, "stand-ins" for the guilty parts of themselves.[22]

In one final scenario, the statue's capacity to substitute for its model allows it to counteract the powers of a different, but no less potent, kind of double. A second law from Kyrene, first discovered in the city's Roman baths and preserved in abridged form by a fourth-century re-dactor, records the practice of erecting *kolossoi* as a means of ridding a householder of an unwanted *hikesios epaktos*, or visitant sent by spells, come to haunt his home.[23] The third provision reads:

> But if he does not know his name [he shall address him], "O *anthrōpos*, whether you are a man or a woman," and having made male and female *kolossoi* from either wood or earth he shall entertain them and set beside them a portion of everything. When you have done the customary things, take the *kolossoi* and [their] portions and deposit them in an uncultivated glen. (*SEG* 9.72.117–21)

By first appeasing and then removing the images that double for the *hikesios*, the individual effectively drives the phantom from his home. Later Greek sources confirm the use of statues in such ghost-banning rituals, most notably at Orchomenos, where the phantom of the dead Aktaion was wreaking havoc on the land. Following the injunctions of the Delphic oracle, the townspeople fashioned an *eikōn* not of Aktaion but of the ghost (*eidōlon*), and bound this to the rock where the reve-nant would regularly appear (Paus. 9.38.5). Pausanias's story not only signals the "fixative" powers of the image,[24] which succeeds in trapping and holding the ghost, but suggests the deeper affinities between these two doubling manifestations: in a clear instance of a magical use of like to combat like, the *eidōlon* finds its match in the *eikōn*, which operates according to the same laws of contiguity. This antagonistic combination of image and ghost makes additional sense of the two bronze statues erected by the Spartans after Pausanias's death. Not only designed to appease the general, they could additionally expel the phantom that haunted exactly the spot in the temple where the victim had died. In-deed, the later sources make the ghost-repelling role of the images quite plain: as Plutarch explains in his *Lectures on Homer*, the Spartans sum-

---

[22] See Vernant 1990a: 77.

[23] Here I follow the interpretation and translation suggested by Faraone (1992: 81–82) and Parker (1983: 348).

[24] For more on this, see chapter 3.

moned Thessalian *psychagōgoi* to rid themselves of the ghost, and the anonymous author of the *Letters of Themistocles* states still more explicitly that a revenant of Pausanias was exorcised "by means of bronze statues" (5.15).[25]

Relations between the Model and Replacement Figurine

In his description of Pausanias's end, Thucydides constructs the connection between the general and the images set up on his behalf in particular fashion: the Spartans dedicate the two bronze figures to Athena "in place of" or "in return for" Pausanias (*hōs anti Pausaniou*, 1.134.4). This turn of phrase, indicating that the statues not only stand in for the dead but also compensate both him and the goddess for a life taken away, returns in many other literary and epigraphic sources that affirm the meaning behind the expression; where statues act as replacement figurines, the emphasis often falls on their equivalence in function and/ or value to the original, and on the restitutive or recompensary powers that this bond can put into play. As Jean-Pierre Vernant explains, the object's capacity to instantiate not so much the physical appearance of its model as his properties and worth allows the image to assume a role within a larger and more extensive dynamic of exchange:

> Without resembling him, the equivalent is capable of presenting someone, of taking his place in the game of social exchanges. It does so not by virtue of similarity with the external aspect of the person (as in a portrait), but through a sharing in "value," a concordance in the matter of qualities tied to prestige.[26]

Many of the conventions and schemata that archaic and early classical statue-makers employ follow from an object's designated role: displaying the value, status, and social connections surrounding the individual for whom it stands in, the image allows its subject and/or commissioner to negotiate and display his relations with his fellow men and with the gods.

Inscriptions on grave monuments regularly include the term *anti* to indicate that the marker not only functions as a *sēma*, a metonymic sign

---

[25] Plut. fr. 126 in schol. Eur. *Alc.* 1128; and Plut. *Mor.* 560e–f. On these texts, see Fontenrose 1978: 129–31; Faraone 1992: 83. On the parallels between the two accounts of Pausanias's end, Burkert 1963: 48–49, esp. n. 67.

[26] Vernant 1990a: 75. ("Sans lui ressembler, l'équivalent est susceptible de représenter quelqu'un, de prendre sa place dans le jeu des échanges sociaux. Il le fait, non par vertu de similitude avec l'aspect extérieur de la personne (comme dans un portrait), mais par une communauté de 'valeur,' une concordance dans l'ordre des qualités liées au prestige.") As Kris and Kurz ([1934] 1979: 77) have argued, a disregard for verisimilitude goes hand-in-hand with the role of the image as replacement figurine: "The 'stronger' the belief in the magic function of the image, in the identity of picture and depicted, the less important is the nature of that image."

that announces the continued presence of the deceased in the world of the living,[27] but in some way replaces the cardinal properties that have been removed, and so variously compensates the dead, the individual mourner, and the community for the loss.[28] But the written message often does no more than spell out the symbolic content of the image itself, which issues its own directives for the pronouncement of certain descriptive terms and acts in the manner of a visual formula. In a particularly close coincidence between a verbal epithet and fashioned form, the father of one Kleoboulos erects a *kouros* on his son's behalf, "to stand in place of/in return for his virtue and moderation" (*ant' aretes ede saophrosunes*, CEG 41).[29] As discussions of *kouroi* regularly point out, the marble youths' physical forms supply unmistakable declarations of the very properties the description privileges, visibly displaying through their flawless physiques, upright bearing, and general air of disengagement the typically aristocratic values of *aretē* and *sophrosunē*. The generic qualities of the *kouros* further promote its ability to dictate the terms in which it should be viewed: the tenacity of the schema, the conservatism of its formal development, and the absence of any overly personalizing features all allow the statue to deliver the same culturally determined message wherever it is raised.

But a generalized assertion of aristocratic excellence does not exhaust the meaning embedded in the appearance of the *kouroi* that proliferated in sixth-century Greece. Their defining physical characteristics also bear a striking resemblance to the attributes that Homer had assigned to the heroic young men who fought in the front ranks of the Achaean and Trojan forces, also young, beautiful, and long of hair;[30] and legs and thighs, the locus of a warrior's speed and battle strength, receive equal prominence in both the plastic images and the poet's songs. An epitaph on a sixth-century monument to an Athenian named Kroisos (fig. 1) reiterates the visual coincidence between the epic hero and latter-day youth in verbal terms, using hexameter phrases proper to Homeric diction to lament the dead as it commemorates his service as a fighter in the vanguard where the legendary warrior also took his place: "Show pity beside the marker of dead Kroisos, whom raging Ares once destroyed in the front rank of battle" (CEG 27).[31]

[27] For this, see Sourvinou-Inwood 1995: 141.

[28] Cf. Vernant 1990a: 79–82; Ducat 1976: 243.

[29] For other examples of the image as a return for some particular virtue, see CEG 139 and 167.

[30] D'Onofrio 1982: 163–65; Vernant 1982. See, too, my discussion of the figures on pp. 212–16.

[31] Stewart (1997: 66) points out how the terms of the epitaph deliberately evoke the world of the epic hero.

To acknowledge the dead's proximity to the heroes of a bygone age is also to grant him a particular place and status in the community at large. Those who risk their lives for their polis or country by standing in the vanguard, as Sarpedon's remarks at *Iliad* 12.310–28 already make plain, and Tyrtaeus 9.23–42 affirms, are owed benefactions and honors both while they live and after their death, a conspicuous tomb among them. Not merely a statement of the martial valor of the dead, the statue presents itself as a prize justly awarded him, a recompense for his special merits and for the part that he has played in endeavors on his city's behalf.[32] Both the location of many *kouroi* vis-à-vis their tombs, and the accompanying inscriptions, which employ the standard expressions found on other votive objects (*katatithēmi* and *epitithēmi*), demonstrate their additional function as *gerata*, offerings of particular privilege that reflect the subject's social persona and remunerate him in both symbolic and tangible terms for effort expended.[33] Such self-declared gifts offer visible assertions of the continuing relationship of reciprocity between the dead, his family, and the larger community to which he belonged.

While men display their excellence in battle, marriage represents a woman's proper sphere of activity and her *telos*. The image that refigures and compensates the dead maiden or wife attempts to restore what has been taken away and to preserve the social relations that defined her in life. Most simply, an inscription from a mid-fifth-century grave stele found on Amorgos reads, "I lie here a Parian stone *anti gunaikos*" (*CEG* 153), while in more complex fashion the *korē* raised for Phrasikleia, carved in the latter half of the sixth century by Aristion of Paros, calls attention to what has been lost in death:

σῆμα Φρασικλείας. κόρε κεκλέσομαι αἰεί,
ἀντὶ γάμο παρὰ θεὸν τοῦτο λαχõσ' ὄνομα. (*CEG* 24)[34]

[This is/I am] the *sēma* of Phrasikleia. I shall forever be called maiden (*korē*), since in place of marriage this name is what the gods have allotted me.

Deprived of the possibility of wedlock, the girl receives by way of recompense the *geras* of perpetual maidenhood, which the statue and its

[32] If, as Stewart (ibid.: 68–70) argues for the Attic *kouroi*, the image owes its popularity to its ability to promote the standing of an aristocracy feeling the volatility and insecurity of its own position, then these declarations of the service the elite can render the community seem particularly well-pitched.

[33] Detailed by d'Onofrio 1982: 148–50, 162. However, note the objections that Sourvinou-Inwood (1995: 144) raises, and her reminder of the differences between the grave monument and offerings to the gods.

[34] Cf. *Anth. Pal.* 7.649 for a later echo.

iconography visibly assert:[35] itself modeled as a virgin or *korē*, the figure also holds a lotus at its breast by way of symbol of its continued and eternally unplucked state. Like the words of the inscription, the rosettes below each breast, and the additional lotuses, alternately half-open and closed, that wreathe the maiden's crown signal a blossoming into womanhood even as they affirm that this *floraison* has yet to occur. Together the different elements cohere in making the metonymic representation a visualization of the maiden in her social role,[36] preserving her at the very threshold of the marriage to which she could once have aspired.

Like the *kouros*, too, the image of Phrasikleia offers the viewer an enduring statement of the status and economic worth of the dead, and of the transfer of wealth that the bestowal of her person on a husband would have involved. The *korē's* elaborate crown, her rich jewelry, and the belted peplos that she wears (featuring a meander winding around the neck and down the sleeves, and skillfully cut rosettes over the remainder of the fabric) all attest to the material resources of her family,[37] and her carefully bound and styled hair matches the overall elegance of the figure. The maiden's very stance demonstrates her adherence to conventions determining the behavior of a marriageable girl from the social elite: the statue gathers its skirts as it steps in a gesture that Sappho reproaches a country girl for not knowing how to perform (fr. 57 LP).

Where the funerary monument seeks to compensate the dead, the votive image aims to return something in kind to the gods who have granted, or are encouraged to grant, a desired good, and more generally promotes continuing relations of reciprocity between the divine and human parties to the exchange. The object has two chief stratagems for achieving its several ends: its visual and verbal demonstration that it is commensurate in value to what has been, or will be, received, and its visible reenactment of the original donation, which perpetually reminds the god of the favor given and might additionally persuade the recipient to behave in kind. For a votive image which stands proxy for the benefaction itself and so declares the dedicator solvent vis-à-vis the gods, ps.-Aristotle cites the statue of one Diphilos set up by his son on the Acropolis and records the inscription carved on the piece: "Anthemion, the son of Diphilos, has dedicated this statue to the gods, when from the status of *thēs* he had been raised to the status of a knight (*thētikou*

---

[35] For more on this aspect of the image, p. 238.
[36] Sourvinou-Inwood 1995: 251; according to her argument, the *korē* as funerary monument is only raised on behalf of unmarried girls.
[37] Svenbro (1988: 17–18) even suggests that the dead maiden belonged to the Alkmeonid family.

anti telous hippad' ameipsamenos)" (Arist. [*Ath. Pol.*] 7.4).[38] The image, portraying the individual accompanied by his horse, confirms the change in social and economic standing and presents to the gods by way of thanks an object that displays exactly the rank they have given to the donor. Anthemion, of course, enjoys an additional benefit from the design he has selected; the statue also announces his status to mortal visitors to the sacred site and follows the examples of other offerings that still more patently boast the social standing of the donor.[39]

Other images announce themselves equivalent to some aspect of the gift bestowed, again restoring parity between the partners to the transaction. As votive object, the *korē*, exhibited in its fine clothing and rich ornaments, supplies a fitting return for economic benefits, and the accompanying inscription frequently reiterates its visual fulfillment of this role. So a potter named Nearchos dedicates a *korē* "as a tithe of his works to Athena" (*CEG* 193), and a fisherman celebrates an exceptionally good venture by setting up "this *korē* as a tithe of the catch that the ruler of the sea with the golden trident gave him" (*CEG* 266; cf. 205).[40] The small bronze statuette dedicated by one Mantiklos around 700 also offers the god a portion of the donor's wealth, but does so not only to satisfy an earlier vow (as the term "tithe" probably implies),[41] but also in the hope of stimulating an answering, and commensurate, gift: "Mantiklos dedicated me to the far-shooting Lord of the Silver Bow, a tithe. You, Phoibos, give some pleasing favor in return" (*CEG* 326).

The terms of Mantiklos's petition are carefully chosen: asking for a "pleasing return (*chariϜettan amoib[an]*)," the figurine signals its participation in the bonds of *charis* and *chreos* that join parties to a gift exchange (cf. *CEG* 371). Other dedications similarly invite the gods to appreciate the gift's beauty and worth in order to affirm their role as vehicles or catalysts for the two-way transaction. An image destined for Artemis on Paros and presented by Demokudes and Telestodike at the

---

[38] Obviously ps.-Aristotle has got something wrong here; the statue must be commemorating Anthemion, not his father. For this, see Vernant 1990a: 79–80.

[39] So a sixth-century inscription found in the flutings of an Ionic column from the Acropolis uses the epic *euchesthai* to make its vaunt: "Alkimachos dedicated me, this pleasing gift, as a vow to the daughter of Zeus; he boasts that he is the son of a noble father, Chairion" (*CEG* 195). For this, see Depew 1997: 237.

[40] That the fashioned *korē* is particularly suited to take on the part of object given in exchange Osborne (1994a: 92) suggests: real-world girls ripe for marriage are objects that regularly circulate among men, constructing and maintaining social and economic relations between the different parties.

[41] As noted by Depew 1997: 240.

end of the sixth century uses standard archaic votive diction when it describes itself as an *agalma*, an object that through its high quality and craftsmanship inspires delight in its viewer and should prompt the goddess's own reciprocal gift of *charis* (CEG 414); and a contemporary *boustrophēdon* inscription from Boeotia styles its gift a "beautiful thing of delight (*kalon agalma*) for Far-Darting Apollo," and then goes on to make its request for *aretē* and wealth (CEG 334). Just as the prayer formula regularly establishes the speaker's credentials before framing its wishes, so the image, which supplies a visible manifestation of these credentials, proclaims its fitness to petition the god.

The visual schemes adopted by many archaic and early classical votives still more immediately announce and realize these relations of give and take. Alongside the common ex-votos that take the simple form of a replica or depiction of the sacrificial animal or food brought to the god, more elaborate representations appear, showing the worshiper bringing these gifts.[42] Sometime around 560, one Rhonbos set up on the Athenian Acropolis an approximately life-sized marble statue featuring an individual (Rhonbos himself?) devoutly bearing his sacrificial calf to the sanctuary, and the larger-than-life ram-bearer from Thasos (c. 600) seems engaged in the same act of devotion. Whether the donor really had offered up such a animal or had only commissioned a statue depicting such a deed, the image lastingly reenacts the moment of dedication and invites both immortal and mortal viewer to appreciate the petitioner's status, wealth, and privileged relation to the god. In like fashion, many *korai* dedicated on the Athenian Acropolis carry offerings of crowns, fruits, flowers, rabbits, or birds; often holding the objects in their outwardly extended hands (and perhaps these hands would originally have pointed toward the altar),[43] the maidens perform a visually focalizing gesture that patently declares the act of giving. An inscription from an early archaic statue group from Samos made by one Geneleos (fig. 2) affirms that in many instances the gift-bearing *korai* were more precisely designed to stand in for their absent donors: identifying one such *korē* and her function, the extant lines read, "I am . . . oche, who has also dedicated it to Hera."[44]

By leaving an enduring simulacrum of his or her votive-bearing person in the sacred space, the petitioner guaranteed that the god would witness the offering on his visits to the sanctuary and, seeing and accepting the gift, enter into the desired relationship with the giver. The votive reliefs that first appeared around the end of the seventh century

[42] For these, Van Straten 1995 and Depew 1997: 247–52.
[43] For this suggestion, Depew 1997: 249.
[44] Richter 1968: 49–50, nos. 67 and 68, figs. 217–24.

and came to serve as more affordable alternatives to the expensive, frequently large-scale images contribute a fresh element to the scheme: by including a depiction of the god in the act of accepting the offering, they not only perpetuate the original moment of donation, but also signal the gift's successful receipt.[45] Whether set up to thank the deity for answering an earlier prayer or to lend tangible presence to a newly framed petition, the relief shows that contact between mortals and immortals has been established, and that the god, by virtue of attending the ritual, and even on occasion receiving the object the mortal holds out, is now obligated to respond. Perhaps the scenes depicted on the plaques possess one further dimension: parallel to the prayer whose midsection or *argumentum* aims to cajole and even compel the deity to grant the request, representations of the gods in the moment when they willingly receive the proffered gift and listen to the *euchē* accompanying the gesture seek to persuade and manipulate the divine viewer into adopting precisely this stance.[46]

For one final instance of a coincidence between a statue's visual configuration and its assumption of the role, social status, and divine and human relations its subject possesses, I return to the victory images cited earlier. Chiefly commemorative in intent, the statues raised in the Altis, the sacred precinct of Zeus at Olympia, seem also to have had a votive function: as many commentators note, Pausanias's use of the term *anathēmata* to describe the images sits oddly with his statement that they were among the honors bestowed on the athletes rather than dedications to Zeus (5.21.1, 5.25.1), and the bases of early victor monuments found at Olympia regularly employ the standard votive formula *anethēke* to evoke how the objects were set up.[47] Since, as Pindaric odes endlessly assert, the athlete owes his win as much to divine favor as to his own efforts, the deity requires a thank-offering for answering the contestant's spoken or unspoken prayers.[48] The earliest preserved epigram from an Olympic victory monument dating to the first half of the sixth century suggests the precise nature of the return that is owed: declaring itself "equal in height and thickness to the victor" (CEG 394), the life-sized image substitutes for the person of the athlete who haz-

---

[45] Depew 1997: 250–52.

[46] For the "persuasive" power of representations, see pp. 105–6.

[47] So the statue base of Tellon, victor in 472, and the inscription of Agiadas, victor in 488. For these, and discussion of the issue, S. Lattimore 1987: esp. 248 and 252, with full bibliography in his n. 24.

[48] Note that the inscriptions do not style the images thank-offerings for actual vows, but athletes regularly made sacrifices before competing and may well have accompanied them with a vow. Pindar may incorporate this element of the occasion in his repeated claims to have made a *euchē*—that has since been answered—on the victor's behalf.

arded his person in the competition, and whose triumphant emergence from the *agōn* stands testament to the tutelary presence of the god presiding over the event.

Whether set up at the site of the competition and or in the victor's native town, such a monument also tangibly embodied a different relationship of reciprocity: in its function as *geras*, the victory image gave return for the athlete's effort and financial outlay not just on his own but on his city's behalf, and supplied a marker of the community's gratitude for (and pride in) an achievement whose glory enhanced its own local and national standing.[49] Because the *chreos* that the city owed its native son appears embedded in the statue, the artifact becomes an obvious lightning rod when the two-way flow of goods and services suffers dislocation. In several of the tales surrounding heroized athletes, citizens angry at an athlete's failure to act as public benefactor vent their wrath on his image, sometimes mutilating the object, sometimes destroying it or expelling it from the community. The Lokrian Euthykles, whose statue was defaced, stood accused of receiving bribes to betray his city, while the Krotonian Astylos, whose statue was pulled down, had deprived his fellow citizens of their due portion of glory when he had himself proclaimed Syracusan instead of from his native town. The flogging dealt out to the image of Theagenes of Thasos, which was subsequently thrown into the sea, may have been a mark of the political divisions within the city, and of the athlete's participation in the pro-Athenian faction during his lifetime.[50] Only a renegotiation of the roles of both parties within the relationship through the person of the replacement image restores the broken equilibrium and guarantees that the reciprocal benefactions will resume their flow.

To look upon the victory monument was instantly to apprehend how the image embodied not just the athlete's achievement, but also this network of relations of *charis* and *chreos* binding him and his fellow citizens. Manifesting the physical excellence and beauty (external or internal) that are the *sine qua non* of triumph in the games,[51] the statue also regularly wears either the victor's fillet, bestowed on him immediately after the win, or the crown that he received in the concluding ceremonies; additional emphasis falls on the ribbon or wreath when the sculptor imagines his subject with his hand raised to touch the ornament, as does the Motya charioteer (fig. 3) or the copy of the lost

---

[49] The eagerness of citizens to raise victory monuments in the Altis at Olympia even long after the demise of the athlete himself suggests that the images were promoters of a city's standing, and one among several symbolic instruments used in bids for civic prestige; see discussion of the issue in chapter 5.

[50] For this, Bohringer 1979: 8–11.

[51] For a more detailed account of these dimensions, see chapter 4.

Diadoumenos of Polykleitos (fig. 4). The focus on one or other of these two literally "crowning" moments closely coheres with the function that victory images were designed to fill. If the bestowal of the ribbon or wreath signaled the individual's acquisition of the quasi-talismanic force that legends and anecdotes assign to him,[52] then the reenactment of the event in plastic form visibly declares the image invested with the same status and powers, and draws attention to its capacity to re-present the original as a source of beneficial power that can foster the community's well-being.

The terms found in some of the inscriptions included on the statue bases suggest a second message issued by the visual design. Following what seems to be standard diction in the classical and postclassical pe-riod, an epigram dated to the first half of the fifth century directs the viewer to look at the Olympic victor Theognetos, "who crowned the city of good fathers" (Ebert 35 = *Anth. Pal.* 13.15). The formula has a literal as well as metaphoric significance, alluding to the common prac-tice whereby the victor would, on his return home, dedicate his prize at the shrine of a local god or hero,[53] and so symbolically share the glory he had acquired with the city at large. The image's appearance, with its hand raised to touch the marker of the win, would denote its subject's readiness to make the viewer participant in his *kudos* and to allow him to reap his share of the benefits accrued. The honor the citizen has granted the athlete in permitting the setting up of an image on his behalf has been duly answered by a reciprocal act of *charis* on that statue's part.

REPLICATION AND ITS LIMITS

"Seeing In"

The victory statue does not rely on iconography alone to transport the viewer back to the original crowning ceremony and its aftermath; just as the messages included on votive objects reiterate the prayers spoken on the occasion when the donor presented his gift, so the inscriptions accompanying the images closely match the words that the sacred her-ald delivered as the winner stood to claim his prize, and recreate the audible as well as visual milieu belonging to the bygone event. Together the several elements combine to make the subject of the monument present in the viewer's own space (or, more properly, the viewer present in the athlete's), eliding and even annulling the distance between the inanimate object and a living reality. But the act of "presentification," which many of these replacement images seem so effectively to perform,

---

[52] As argued in Kurke 1993.
[53] For this practice, ibid.: 140 and n. 35.

does not exclude their possession of a second dimension: the inscriptions that designate the votive, funerary, and honorific statues *agalmata*, or cite the name of the artist and mention the occasion of their setting up, recall their character as material and aesthetic objects, the products of the craftsman's shaping hand and a source of pleasurable viewing for mortal and divine audiences.

The double response that these artifacts invite repeats itself still more prominently in a second group of images that exist outside the ritual, ceremonial, and magical contexts drawn on so far, and whose impact, the sources suggest, depends not least on their capacity exactly to transcribe a visible reality, to act as accurate imitations of the appearances of the things they portray. First conceived in the fantasies that epic poets weave, such skillfully modeled objects possess an almost miraculous verisimilitude and semblance of life. But unlike the *eidōla* critiqued by later philosophers, these representations do not set out to mask their "factural" nature, nor do they seek to dupe their audiences by persuading them of the reality of the pictured scene; instead, they combine their ability to call an absent body or event most vividly to mind with an emphatic declaration of their own materiality and *poiēsis*, the process of manufacture that imposes itself on the spectator and actually enhances the pleasure he experiences from the work.[54] In the terms developed by modern critics, the viewer is prompted to see the object *in* the image, rather than the image *as* the object it represents; far from mistaking the replication for reality, he apprehends both the material and representational aspects of the account.[55]

The cunningly fashioned brooch that the disguised Odysseus cites in his conversation with Penelope wins the viewers' applause:

χλαῖναν πορφυρέην οὔλην ἔχε δῖος Ὀδυσσεύς,
διπλῆν· αὐτάρ οἱ περόνη χρυσοῖο τέτυκτο
αὐλοῖσιν διδύμοισι· πάροιθε δὲ δαίδαλον ἦεν·
ἐν προτέροισι πόδεσσι κύων ἔχε ποικίλον ἐλλόν,
ἀσπαίροντα λάων· τὸ δὲ θαυμάζεσκον ἅπαντες,
ὡς οἱ χρύσεοι ἐόντες ὁ μὲν λάε νεβρὸν ἀπάγχων,
αὐτὰρ ὁ ἐκφυγέειν μεμαὼς ἤσπαιρε πόδεσσι. (*Od.* 19.225–31)

Godlike Odysseus wore a purple cloak of wool, double thick; but on it was fashioned a pin of gold with double clasps, with a *daidalon* in front: a hound was holding in its forepaws a dappled fawn, preying on it while it struggled.

---

[54] For this response in reference to painting, see the arguments in Neer 1995.
[55] The distinction between "seeing in" and "seeing as" was first formalized in Wollheim 1980: 205–29. For its application to ancient art, Neer 1995: 124 and Stewart 1997: 43–44.

All were marveling at it, how though they were gold, the one preyed on the fawn throttling it, but the other struggled with its feet as it tried to flee.

Combined in the single piece, several kinds of image "magic" are at work. For the poet's listeners, there is no mistaking the doubling (or "eiconic," to use the later term) power of the brooch, which so neatly foreshadows Odysseus's attack on the helpless suitors in the home and anticipates his address to his dogged heart after his conversation with Penelope is done. But what impresses the internal audience, whom the speaker includes in his narrative, is the seeming animation of the animals.[56] Dog and fawn engage in a continuing struggle, each moving and reacting to the other's motions.

In his description of the viewers' response, the beggar pinpoints the source of their enjoyment more minutely: juxtaposed with and punctuating the account of the "life" that the figures in the brooch seemingly possess, the object's artistry (its character as *daidalon*) and its materiality ("how though they were gold") emphatically appear. The "dappled" quality of the fawn spans the two dimensions: most immediately referring to the appearance of the animal's variegated or spotted hide, it also calls attention to the quality of *poikilia*, the element of adornment and embellishment that all fine works of art should display. It is the meeting of these two facets that prompts the wonder that the audience experiences: it marvels at how a prominent and self-assertive *technē* can coexist alongside, and in no way dilute, an act of presentification, a creation of *phusis* from inanimate matter.

More famously than the ornament that the beggar cites, the shield of Achilles also astonishes, terrifies, and charms viewers with its brilliance and the vivacity of its scenes. The singer describes the forged individuals who populate its surface as living men, who dance, sing, quarrel, and exist in real time and space. Heaping on detail after detail, and replicating the events portrayed in minute form, the artist makes the fabricated figures real presences, participants in the audience's contemporary world. But once again the description does nothing to occlude the manufactured quality of the object; instead, the poet chooses to privilege Hephaistos's artistry by imagining the god in the act of forging and decorating the shield, and throughout his account he underscores the paradox of representations that straddle the divisions between art and life, now talking of the images as though they were alive, now calling attention to the craftsmanship involved. One of the most astonishing features of the design is the depiction of the half-mown field, the cut part distinguished ("the earth darkened behind") from the area still to

---

[56] Cf. Vernant 1996: 391–92.

be reaped so that the harvesting appears to occur before our very eyes. But a reminder of the *technē* on which the marvel depends follows immediately as the poet signals the act of representation: the black earth is "*like to* ground that has been ploughed, *for all that* it was gold; such was the wonder of the forging" (*Il.* 18.548–49; emphasis added).[57] In a more riddling conjunction of reality and artistry, the poet makes the metal selected for the visualizations sometimes jibe with and sometimes closely approximate the material that might be used for the real-world object: golden talents are naturally figured in gold (507), vines stand out through poles of silver (563), and Hephaistos sets about his field ditch a fence of tin (565).[58]

In a similar manner, although with a slightly different balance between the "factural" and representational, the author of the ps.-Hesiodic *Scutum* would display the shield of Heracles as a *thauma*-inducing work (140, 224, 318) and, more obviously than the Homeric poet for whom Hephaistos's work is still in genesis, portray the finished surface as though the audience confronted a living scene. Again movement, voice, and sound punctuate the account as the audience follows the flight of Perseus (222) and hears the sharp cries of the women on the walls (243), the marriage song (274), the gnash of Fate's teeth (160); blood drips from the dead boars lying in the midst of their seemingly living companions, who move forward, their manes bristling, as they advance on the pack of lions drawn up against them (170–74). But once again, the poet simultaneously distances the viewer from the images, repeatedly recalling the technical aspect of the product with references to the gold, silver, tin, adamant, and other metals used in its creation, and scattering the terms *hōs* and *ikelos* throughout the description to signal the representation involved. In a particularly striking instance of the split-level response the artifact provokes, the noise that issues from the patently material surface depends on the (apparent) motion of the figures that it displays: as the Gorgons run in pursuit of Perseus "on the pale adamant, the shield rang sharp and clear with a loud clanging" (231–33).

Crossing the Limits

In the representations cited so far, the poet carefully balances the images' wonderful similitude with the no less astonishing element of

---

[57] Elsewhere the illusion is allowed to continue undisturbed, as when we witness the two lions gulping the black blood of the ox, or the dancers dancing. Other places where the poet recalls the audience to a proper sense of the manufactured nature of the shield include 539 and 574.

[58] Cf. 522, 598.

craftsmanship that they hold out for show. But the Homeric and Hesiodic songs are populated by another, more riddling group of artifacts, which, even as they retain their patently manufactured character, confound the two dimensions simultaneously exhibited by the brooch and shields and prohibit the kind of "seeing in" that these objects invite. In this second instance, artistic technique does not so much coexist alongside the real presences that seemingly inhabit the images as recreate or even generate life, thereby naturalizing its art and achieving a meld between *phusis* and *technē* so seamless that the viewer has no means of determining where the divisions between them might fall. From this confusion, a series of enigmas follows, concerning both the status of the representation vis-à-vis its model and the positive or negative charge that such "recreations" carry. While the act of *poiēsis* may be neutral in and of itself, the *chrēsis* or use that determines the product's design and application often involves a deliberate treachery or deceit.[59]

On a number of occasions, the Homeric gods go about fabricating figures or *eidōla* so identical to their originals that the viewer must succumb to what remain no more than illusions. When Diomedes threatens Aineas's life in *Iliad* 5, Apollo swiftly intervenes to save his protégé; removing the Trojan from harm, he fashions (*teuxe*) an *eidōlon* that is like to (*ikelos*) Aineas, wearing armor such as his (445–50) and substituting for the hero on the field of battle. In similar manner, the *eidōlon* of Iphthime modeled by Athena in *Odyssey* 4 replicates the original in her *demas* (*demas d' ēikto gunaiki*, 796) and enjoys the powers of speech and motion that should characterize the living; only the contents of her message, and her sudden disappearance when her words are done (839), alert Penelope to the visitor's true status.[60] Although they stand in for the absent, these phantoms differ from other notional and real replacement figurines on several scores: now their efficacy depends on their perfectly imitating the visible appearance of the characters for whom they act as proxy, and on their replicating the properties that seemingly indicate life. The surface resemblance linking the *eidōlon* to its prototype finds an analogue in the account that the poet supplies of how Athena disguises herself as Deiphobos to give Hector false hope in his combat with Achilles: now the goddess appears "like to" (*eikuia*) the Trojan, having taken on his *demas* and *phōnē* (*Il.* 22.227). The bond of similitude remains the same, whether it joins a crafted object to its original or an individual to the persona whose appearance he or she

---

[59] On the importance of *chrēsis* as opposed to *poiēsis*, Vernant 1983: 260–61.
[60] Note the contrast between the evanescence of the apparition and the solid character of the *stathmos* by which she stands (838–39).

assumes. This continuity highlights the paradox at the heart of the Homeric *eidōla*: the element of manufacture in no way dilutes their "liveliness," but rather signals the manner in which any person or thing can undergo a process of "being made like" before appearing in a certain guise before an audience's eyes.

A more detailed account of the seamless match between *technē* and *phusis*, and of the way in which both surface attributes and internal qualities can be generated from without, belongs to Hesiod's two narratives of Pandora's fabrication. When the gods turn to vivifying the object they have fashioned and adorned in the manner of a vessel, they continue to employ the same techniques (and the poet many of the same expressions, particularly the verb *tithēmi*) that they used for the still-inanimate surface; and while some of the quickening properties are placed inside Pandora's cavity, others, and most critically the life force that is *charis*, are applied to the figure's exterior precisely in the manner of the more tangible ornaments.[61] Nor does Hesiod mark any break between the terms used for the inanimate creatures decorating the crown that Pandora wears in the *Theogony* account — *daidala* also emanating *charis*, wondrous to see and "like to living beings with voice" (581–84) — and the fully vivified woman herself. Life, it seems, can also be a matter of manufacture, of qualities that the craftsman adds from without.

As the gods go about their work, Pandora not only becomes an animated object, but also acquires an autonomy that the Homeric *eidōla* lack. The independent nature of the object molded by the gods appears already in Zeus's blueprint for the design when, at lines 62–63 of the *Works and Days*, he orders Hephaistos to fabricate a figure and to make it "like to (*eiskein*) the immortal goddesses in its face, the lovely fair form of a maiden." The structure of the phrase contains the enigma as Zeus begins by directing Hephaistos to take a goddess for his paradigm, but then concludes by describing a very different product: Hephaistos will create no replica divinity, but a being without precedent, the archetypal lovely fair form of the first mortal maiden.[62] As Zeus continues to deliver his instructions, the initial correspondence between Pandora and the divine model becomes ever more remote. She will ex-

---

[61] Saintillan (1996: 320) defines *charis* as "l'ensemble des valeurs que doit réunir en elle la vie pour pouvoir être dite la plus vivante" ("the totality of attributes which life must unite in itself in order to be considered the most lively"). For more on Pandora's ornamentation, see chapter 4.

[62] See West 1978: ad loc. for commentary on the syntax of the phrase. As Loraux (1993: 82 and n. 60) points out, the *parthenos* is actually an object that only comes into being with Pandora's own genesis; when we look for an original behind the "copy," we draw a blank.

hibit the external markers of godhood—radiance, rich clothing, dazzling ornaments—but her thievish and canine disposition (67) suggests a closer affinity with the world of beasts. When the several deities gather to build the image, the shadowy divine counterpart moves still further from the scene. If the lavish adornments recall the gleaming appearance of divinities, Hephaistos sets out to fashion the figure "like (*ikelon*) to a modest maiden" (71), the same phrase that is used in the shorter version of events at *Theogony* 572.

Even before the gods vivify their figurine, the fashioned maiden poses the question of similitude. Although a replacement insofar as Zeus conceives her as a return for the fire that has been withdrawn (*anti puros*, *Theog.* 570) and invests her with some of the same properties as the missing element, Pandora also stands as a novel creation; constituting a new category that has no original independent of herself, she cannot be classified as a replica or a simulacrum. Expressions such as *ikelos* and *eiskein* used in the account may cover a variety of relations between their two terms, including not only equivalence and similarity but also difference and autonomy.[63] As Daniel Saintillan and Jean-Pierre Vernant have argued, the fact of Pandora's likeness or *mimēsis* does not define her as a faux-semblant, a secondary copy of an absent archetype, but looks more fundamentally to her place within the novel condition that her coming instaurates. Henceforth, they suggest, all mortals belong to a realm of resemblance rather than that of the immediate now made exclusive to the divine sphere: "Venir au jour, se donner à voir, *c'est toujours pour [vivant mortel] revêtir une 'semblance'*; et cette semblance devra être en l'occurrence *la sienne propre*."[64] Pandora's manufactured quality, in addition to framing her as substitute for the article Zeus has withdrawn, looks to her participation in this post-Mekone world; as several episodes in the Homeric songs indicate, the individual who

---

[63] See Loraux (1993: 82), who remarks of *ikelos*, "The word does not always establish a link of resemblance between two objects, or a relationship of conformity between an image and its model. Instead, at times, it indicates a curious, undoubtedly pre-Platonic kind of *mimēsis*, composed of identity and participation." In *Iliad* 5.450, *ikelos* appeared in connection with the *eidōlon* of Aineas that Apollo forged, like to the hero in appearance, but quite independent of the original seated safely beyond the battlefield. And at *Od.* 13.156–57 Zeus suggests that Poseidon satisfy his desire to punish the Phaeacians for having ferried Odysseus home and terminate the city's sea power by "making their ship into a rock like (*ikelos*) a swift ship near the land." Poseidon's subsequent petrifaction of the vessel follows Zeus's advice to the letter: the stone is both like to and different from the former ship, retaining its visible form, but stripped of the capacity for motion that gives the object its defining property.

[64] Saintillan 1996: 343, italics in the original. ("To come into the light, to show oneself for view *is always for [a living mortal] to put on an 'appearance'*; and this appearance should be under the circumstances *one's very own*.") Cf. Vernant 1996.

(re)assumes an identity withdrawn or diminished does so when the gods, behaving explicitly in the manner of craftsmen fashioning works of art, endow him with the properties necessary to restore him to a likeness to himself.[65]

In all these scenarios, art appears invested with the capacity to naturalize itself, using its technical resources to recreate and promote what gives an animate creature his or her claim to life. Because the act of craftsmanship serves as the source of the liveliness that the figures possess, these images block the split response that other works of art permit and deny the viewer the chance to practice the "seeing in" earlier described: to observe the radiance and charm applied to Pandora's fashioned body, or to hear the words that the gods have placed inside her in the manner of her external ornaments, is simultaneously to acknowledge the fact of her vivified presence. Nor is the mode of viewing that Pandora and the *eidōla* impose presented as benign. The Achaeans on the battlefield are gulled into directing their blows at the phantom Aineas, while Hesiod explicitly identifies Pandora as a *dolos* and snare (*Theog.* 589, *Op.* 83), designed as a response to Prometheus's earlier trick at Mekone, and a *kalon kakon* (*Theog.* 585) that answers the deceitful sacrificial bundle wittingly chosen by Zeus. In this instance, Hesiod has moved smoothly from one form of deception to another, aligning what begins as an artistic ruse with a different kind of sleight of hand: the treacherous character of the image comes to depend not on the fact of illusory imitation (Pandora is, after all, quite explicitly styled the first mortal *parthenos*), but on the object's capacity to host a split between a surface appearance and inner reality, to assume an exterior that belies what exists below. The disjuncture that modeled goods allow is the problem to which the classical sources will return.

DEVELOPMENTS IN LATE ARCHAIC AND CLASSICAL STATUARY

Pandora, the shields of Achilles and Heracles, the ornamental brooch of Odysseus, and the crafted *eidōla* dispatched by the gods have no existence beyond the imaginary worlds that the poets and myth-makers construct. But in exploring an artifact's relation to a visible or living reality and determining how closely an image might replicate the properties of sentient things without exceeding its inanimate status, the Homeric and Hesiodic songs anticipate the experiments that sculptors of the late archaic and early classical period would undertake. Heirs to the traditions that the epic sources describe, the historical statue-makers create representations whose imitation of living bodies comes tempered

[65] For these instances, Vernant 1996: 384–86.

by overt assertions of their material nature, and whose persuasive exhibition of *phusis* shows itself the outcome of the artists' *technē*. Contemporary with these developments are other innovations that preserve and enhance an image's continued role as replacement and substitute;[66] honing the object's capacity visually to display the cardinal qualities of the original, to imagine him in his larger social dimension, sculptors now use the body of the statue as a screen that externalizes the physical, ethical, and moral processes that go on within. Nor do these two sets of technical advances operate independent of one another: the image that offers the viewer an impression of a living body may still more convincingly assume the place of the original behind the account, while the statue's display of its subject's physiology, disposition, and experience provides fresh proof of the skill of the artist and his mastery of the medium in which he works.

Verisimilitude

Standard treatments of developments in statue-making (taking their cue, in part, from later Roman accounts of the history of Greek art) present late sixth-century and early fifth-century artists as though they were engaged in a single-minded quest for realism and verisimilitude, striving to make their images ever more anatomically correct and "true" to the visual experience that is assumed as the starting point for any act of representation. But a different story might explain the innovations of the period. Much like the poets of the late archaic and early classical ages, the artist leaves his *sphragis* on the image that he carves, using his skill not so much to persuade the viewer of the reality of what he sees as to create an *agalma*, an object whose virtuosity and pleasing appearance delight and dazzle its audience.[67]

When Odysseus first introduces the daidalic brooch, he describes how the hound tries to bury its teeth into the struggling or panting (*aspaironta*) hare (*Od.* 19.229). The detail grants the representation one of the cardinal properties that should properly distinguish the living beast or man from the inanimate piece of metal or stone: *empnoos*, he breathes. As Guy Métraux has shown, the question of respiration, and the connections between breathing and the operations of the *psuchē*, were very much on the minds of fifth-century physicians and philosophers, and the Hippocratic corpus includes one text wholly given over

[66] Contra Bruneau (1975: 461), who differentiates between archaic art, which "creates," and classical art, which simply reproduces.
[67] For this parallel between artists—although specifically painters—and poets, see Neer 1995.

to discussion of the topic (*On Breaths*).[68] Métraux's reading of four early fifth-century images, the Omphalos Apollo (extant only in a copy), the girl from Paros, and the Riace bronzes (fig. 5), goes on to observe how the maker of each piece suggested the fact of respiration within his figure, whether by including an open mouth, blood veins visible on the surface of the body (closely connected with the soul in early accounts), a swelling abdomen, or the iliac-inguinal line. The development, perhaps the outcome of exchanges between doctors and artists at the time, satisfies several goals; at a single strike, the sculptor heightens the statue's verisimilitude, suggests the presence of a soul or other animating force within,[69] and effectively realizes those art-as-life conceits that long predate the innovation. As the later Hellenistic epigrams would delight in pointing out in their evocations of some of the famed (lost) works of fifth-century statue-makers, these are "breathing images" indeed.[70]

But for all the anatomical realism that these developments promote and their contribution to the "vivacity" of the figure, are the artists really seeking to replicate the visible human body? In several instances, the decision to include certain veins comes at the price of anatomical accuracy and forces the images into postures that prove mechanically improbable or impossible. So the Riace bronzes (see fig. 5) twist their elbows in a manner no living body could achieve, holding their upper arms and elbows in an exaggeratedly supine position so as to display the cephalic veins, while the lower arm and hand are in the prone position, offering a view of the cubital veins.[71] What the statues showcase is not so much the living human form (other parts of the images' anatomy are quite free from the veins they should properly include) as the virtuosity of the statue-maker, who has chosen to demonstrate his ability to achieve a detailed and accurate description in this particular area.

Much like the veins, the iliac-inguinal line also departs from strict reality and direct observation. Changed in appearance from a straight

[68] Métraux 1995: esp. 57–58.
[69] For this, see chapter 2.
[70] In their celebrations of the fifth-century sculptor Myron's famed heifer and his statue of the runner Ladas, later poets repeatedly describe the images as *empnooi* and endow them with *pneuma*. But note how the pleasure of the works lies in the riddling union between this breathing body and the unmistakable fact of the inanimate bronze or stone: "Just as you were in life, Ladas, flying along on your windswept course, so did Myron fashion you in bronze, stamping your whole body with the expectation of the Olympian crown. . . . He is full of hope, and on his lips appears the breath that comes from the hollow flanks. Soon the bronze will leap forth to gain the crown, and the base will not hold it. O art swifter than *pneuma*" (*Anth. Plan.* 16.54, 54a).
[71] As detailed in Métraux 1995: 51–54.

line to a curving furrow,[72] the feature does not so much mirror its referent as draw attention to itself as a dividing mark, an element of patterning akin to the muscles, sinews, and abdominids that both statue-makers and contemporary painters delight in portraying. A glance back to the *kouroi* of the early sixth century suggests that the desire to achieve a pleasing pattern determines this "improvement" on reality. As the so-called Sounion group illustrates, statue-makers had long favored a series of V-shaped forms to structure their representations, making the scheme most emphatic at the groin.[73] Overall the construction of the abdomen and its juncture less resembles the actual appearance of this portion of the living body than it does the design of contemporary breastplates, which share the same shape and features; if the viewer registers the affinity, then he will further perceive the image as the product of an artisanal venture, a manufactured object akin to another highly worked artifact that follows, even as it regularizes, the human form.

No less than respiration, motion also defines the animate body, and to live and to walk can be one and the same.[74] Again Métraux aligns medical and philosophic views on the nature and source of human movement with innovations in early classical sculpture, and most particularly with the development of the contrapposto stance, which might have drawn on current ideas of universal rotation and asymmetry in the human body.[75] But the suggestion that the statue is on the point of stepping out can do more than offer a lesson in human anatomy and foster the realism of the piece; more critically perhaps, it also supplies the artist with a second means of recapturing the teasing combinations first presented in epic song. Just as the descriptions of the shields of Achilles and Heracles privilege the miracle of motion above all else, repeatedly juxtaposing the materiality of the object, forged in silver, gold, and other static metals, with the dynamism its figures seemingly exhibit and their passage through space,[76] so, too, statue-makers from the early fifth century on are able to unite in their single figures both motion and monumentality. The Tyrannicides of Kritios and Nesiotes (fig. 6),

---

[72] Ibid.: 46 for discussion.

[73] Stewart 1990: 112.

[74] For this, see the much more detailed discussion in chapter 3.

[75] Métraux 1995: 72–84.

[76] So, too, other creations of Hephaistos are remarkable for their mobility, whether the tripods that "wheel of their own motion" (*Il.* 18.376) or the golden automata who "stir nimbly" about the forge (*Il.* 18.421). The topos reappears in the interminable Hellenistic and imperial epigrams composed on the heifer that Myron sculpts, ever on the point of quitting its base and going off in search of the living herd to which it once belonged.

erected in 477/76,[77] appear to advance on the spectator, Harmodios with his arm raised to deliver the killing blow; but the modeling of the bodies, and most particularly the architectonic design of the torso, which forms a regular gridlike pattern of horizontals and verticals, prevent the viewer from ignoring the static quality of the images and forgetting the distinction between bronze and flesh.[78]

Less than two decades later, Myron would produce an image that still more patently engages in movement, but movement visibly frozen in its course. According to the extant testimonia and copies, the statue-maker presented his Diskobolos at the moment when the athlete stood poised between a backswing and a foreswing, twisting at the waist in preparation for the throw.[79] Again the image does nothing to obscure the artifice involved; as any viewer familiar with the sport would know, the pose is Myron's own conceit and corresponds to no actual position that a discus-thrower would adopt. A similar paradox informs Polykleitos's celebrated Doryphoros of c. 440 (fig. 7), a work whose impact, the several copies suggest,[80] seems to have depended on its union of naturalism and a schematization patent to the viewer. The figure, which accurately reflects how the human body behaves in motion, also adopts a posture that exactly corresponds neither to walking nor to resting, and again presents an entirely artificial, artistic construct. Not merely a didactic exercise serving to illustrate biomechanical movement (as several recent readings propose),[81] the Doryphoros also shows how an image can harmoniously combine properties such as movement and rest, tension and relaxation, in a manner that no living body can achieve.

One further *adunaton* that epic poets like to emphasize is the image's capacity for speech and sound. The *knōdala* on Pandora's crown are "like to living beings with voice" (*Theog.* 584), and the scenes depicted on the shields of Achilles and Heracles are filled with the noise, talk, music, and song that issue from the objects and individuals included in the visual field; so, too, Hephaistos equips the vivified automata that populate his foundry with *audē* (*Il.* 18.419). The images created by late

---

[77] The group is extant only in Roman marble copies, but its general accuracy is assumed on the basis of an ancient plaster cast of Aristogeiton's head from the workshop of a copyist at Baiae.

[78] A design that Stewart (1990: 135) calls "highly contrived." See, too, his discussion in Stewart 1997: 70–75. As Lucian would comment some six hundred years later, these bodies are "compact, sinewy, hard, and precisely divided into parts by lines" (*Rhetorum praeceptor* 9)

[79] The Diskobolos is the only work of Myron identified beyond doubt in the copies.

[80] On the merits of the different Roman copies of the work, and justification for using them for reconstructions of the original, see Hallett 1995.

[81] Métraux 1995; more detailed still, Leftwich 1987.

archaic and early classical statue-makers flirt with the possibility of overcoming the silence that inanimate objects must necessarily observe, and that appears, from archaic poetry on, as a defining property of the stone in which many of them work.[82] The open mouths that Métraux finds distinctive to early fifth-century images promote the illusion[83] and appear on a number of both free-standing and architectural images from the first quarter of the century. On the metope at Temple E at Selinunte (c. 470–450), Zeus addresses Hera with his mouth clearly open, and the scheme invites the viewer to hear the words that the god delivers in *Iliad* 14 when, having fallen victim to his wife's seductive wiles, he declares his overpowering desire to take her to his bed; so, too, Oinomaos on the east pediment of the Temple of Zeus at Olympia (c. 470–457) opens his mouth in order to instruct Pelops in the conditions of the fatal contest (fig. 8). A well-known narrative context may also frame the two "speaking" Riace bronzes of c. 460 (see fig. 5), who, according to some reconstructions, represent Agamemnon and Menelaus determining which warrior should meet the challenge issued by Hector. The first of the pair, a commanding figure who stands with his body braced and his now-lost shield and spear held at the ready, turns his head toward an interlocutor as though on the point of delivering an address,[84] and the figure's visibly swelling abdomen and sharply modeled ribs complete the impression, as he seems to take in breath prior to delivering his piece. The second of the two also has his mouth open as if to speak, although the wide-open eyes and the slight inclination of the head suggest words of a different tenor.[85]

Divorced from such rich and familiar settings, an image can still belong to the class of speaking, or in some instances singing, objects, and nowhere more than when it serves to reenact an earlier performance. In a recent discussion of a nude youth in the late archaic style who assumes a contrapposto stance with his mouth open and arm outstretched, Malcolm Bell cites a group described by Pausanias (5.25.2–5) and matches it with the extant piece:[86] according to the periegete, the

---

[82] For this, see the discussion in chapter 3.

[83] Pliny (*HN* 35.58) notes that the fifth-century painter Polygnotos of Thasos first introduced the practice of "showing the mouth wide open," something that contributes to the representation's loss of its "primitive *rigor*."

[84] Stewart (1990: 148) observes that the diadem and wreath the figure wears proclaim him a king and suggests Agamemnon as a possible subject.

[85] Harrison (1985: 51) suggests that we imagine the now-missing teeth as covered with silver, "in order to make it clear that the figure is a speaker," and speculates that the image shows Menelaus sadly proposing that he fight Hector when no other Achaean volunteers to meet the Trojan challenge.

[86] For this, see Bell 1996.

Messenians set up a commemorative monument on behalf of a chorus of thirty-five boys who, together with their trainer and flautist, had competed at a festival at Rhegion and had been shipwrecked during their voyage home. Here the open mouth not only identifies the figure as *choreutēs*, but also invites the audience to experience a reenactment of the original performance. But even as the monument does much to negate the powers of death and return to the youth the role he enjoyed in life, it acknowledges the fact of his absence and draws attention to its own commemorative character: the words and music that emanate from the singer's mouth are those that the living viewer audibly or imaginatively supplies, and the muteness of the stone corresponds to that which characterizes the dead.

Trends in Statue-Making: The "Eiconic" Function

The objects I have cited so far, whether statues of a now-dead choral contestant, an epic hero, an athlete, or civic benefactors raised to hero status, have a variety of functions to perform. Not only displays of technical virtuosity and sources of pleasurable viewing, many continue to act as replacement figurines that promote contacts between the living and the absent or dead and maintain their role as visible statements of the enduring relations of reciprocity linking the subject of the monument to those who witness it. But the artistic vogues and technical innovations of the period invite audiences to construe this "eiconic" connection between an image and its original in novel and modified ways: the sculptor's new concern with displaying the *ēthos* or *psuchē* of his model, with using the surface of the body to reveal the subject's behavior, attitudes, and emotions, can turn the statue into a compelling presentation of the "core" nature and qualities of the absent individual. This development also coheres with the position that many of the images now occupy: deployed within the public spaces of the fifth-century polis and the panhellenic shrines, statues erected expressly for viewing by individuals coming to define themselves as "citizens" and even as "Greeks" aim to represent those properties of its subject deemed instructive and beneficial to the city or country at large, and to serve as visual disseminators of a communal culture that can inspire emulation on an audience's part.[87] The generic, even idealized nature of so many of the images of the age may stem from the artist's desire to satisfy his double aim:[88] in stripping away surface quirks and idiosyncrasies, the

[87] For a reading of fifth-century Athenian monuments in these terms, Castriota 1992.

[88] I use the term "idealized" despite many recent attacks on the notion of idealization. Andrew Stewart observes, "In archaic and classical Greek art and thought (Plato ex-

statue-maker both produces a revelation of the enduring or underlying disposition of his subject, and allows the viewer instantly to apprehend the category to which the individual belongs and the modes of conduct that his physical bearing asserts.[89]

Although the text postdates the developments described, an episode in Xenophon's *Memorabilia* offers the most detailed introduction to the work of art in the classical age as both an externalization of the inner and a move from the individualized to the generic, idealized, and concomitantly "civic" account. In his discussions with the painter Parrhasios and the fictive sculptor Kleiton,[90] Socrates takes up the question of what precisely the artist should aim to portray: is he confined to the surface appearance of an object, or can he penetrate to the interior of what he depicts and show that to his audience? At the start of his exchange with Parrhasios, Socrates opens with the modest proposition that painting is a "representation of things seen" (*eikasia tōn horōmenōn*, 3.10.1). Colors are the chief medium for the *mimēsis* of the visible: "You painters with your colors represent (*apeikazontes*) and reproduce (*ekmimeisthe*) figures high and low, in light and shadow, hard and soft, rough and smooth, young and old" (3.10.1). But then Socrates advances one stage further, taking, as Agnès Rouveret observes,[91] the first step toward the invisible: the role of the painter is to reproduce *ta kala eidē*, the beautiful forms, which he does not copy from a single individual, but draws from any number of different bodies (3.10.2). Now the portrait does not aim at the depiction of a particular subject, but supplies a more comprehensive, generic account based on an amalgam of models.[92] Socrates' next remark widens the breach between

---

cluded), it seems that the ideal is to be understood as a concrete presentation of notions as to what constitutes the 'typical,' 'general' and so 'exemplary' human form, an 'everyman' free of individual peculiarities and quirks" (1990: 79). Others (particularly Childs) reject idealization because it pulls away from the "vital, descriptive, and eminently real" quality of images in the high classic style (Childs 1988: 13) and suggests a turning back from the increasingly lifelike figures. But as this and the previous section seek to demonstrate, these images are anything but typical or "real," and involve departures from both standards that would have been apparent to viewers.

[89] On this "leveling" process, Castriota 1992: 12.

[90] Identified by some as Polykleitos, whose name Kleiton recalls, although the identification is far from secure.

[91] Rouveret 1989: 15; see, too, the discussion in Zeitlin 1994: 192–93.

[92] Sörbom (1966: 88) suggests that here we have moved from visible things to a mental picture: "When the artist makes his work, he has a notion or a mental image which he tries to visualize; the work of art is similar to its models, but adjusted to the mental image." But this is to attribute to Xenophon ideas that would become current only in later periods. The notion of the painting or statue as a combination of different bodies, because no single person can possess perfect beauty in every feature of his body, appears on several other occasions. Besides the well-known anecdote preserved by Cicero that describes

the image and visible phenomena still further, and suggests that this very creation of an idealized body also prompts a step from surface appearance to inner properties. The fair forms that the painter imitates, he explains, do not display an external beauty, but moral or ethical qualities, and the task of the artist is to reproduce this "character of the soul" (*tēs psuchēs ēthos*, 3.10.3).[93] The proposition moves Parrhasios to object: "How could one imitate that which has neither shape nor color, nor any of the qualities you mentioned just now, and is not even visible?" But, as Socrates' reply makes plain, these properties do take external form, manifesting themselves in a man's pose and demeanor: *ēthos*, whether "noble or dignified, or base and servile . . . shows in a man's face as well as his posture, both standing and moving about" (3.10.5).[94]

Socrates' dialogue with Kleiton, the maker of statues of athletes, follows a somewhat different course, but repeats the passage from visible properties to the unseen. Again the philosopher begins by limiting the sculptor's work to the mere *mimēsis* of external forms: "Isn't it by copying the form of living beings that you make your statues look alive?" (3.10.7). But Socrates' subsequent question grants the craftsman more extensive powers: "And does not the representation (*apomimeisthai*) of the *pathē* of the bodies involved in some action also furnish the viewer some pleasure?" (3.10.8).[95] This move beyond the external appearance to the affections within permits Socrates to reach a conclusion that echoes in more modest fashion his statement to Parrhasios: "The statuemaker ought to make the outward form like to the workings (*erga*) of the soul" (3.10.8). In place of the *ēthos* of the subject, now his *pathē*

Zeuxis about to embark on his portrait of Helen and asking the Krotonians to "turn over . . . the most beautiful of these virgins while I paint the picture I have promised you, so that truth may be transferred from the living example to the mute image" (*Inv. rhet.* 2.1.1–3), there is the earlier testimonial of Arist. *Pol.* 1281b10: "Great men are distinguished from ordinary men in the same way as beautiful people from plain ones, or as an artfully painted object from a real one, namely in that which is dispersed has been gathered into one."

[93] The formula is itself a somewhat riddling one. As C. Gill (1990: 6–7) argues, *ēthos* in the classical period does not correspond to modern notions of character, with all its connotations of interiority; instead it can denote an individual's visible attributes, as distinct from his *phusis*, and suggest behaviors and attitudes that can be clearly seen. Socrates' expression describes a kind of halfway house between what lies within and without.

[94] Cf. the much later echo of the conceit in Achilles Tatius 6.6: "I do not think it right to say that the *noos* is totally invisible. It manifests itself with precision, as in a mirror, in the face."

[95] Note the emphasis on the pleasure and persuasive effects of viewing the works, signaled here and in the use of the term *psuchagōgei* (3.10.6) earlier in the exchange.

and the *erga* of his soul are the proper objects of the craftsman's representative powers.[96]

Socrates' conversations not only neatly pinpoint two central developments in fifth-century sculpture, both the vogue for conveying the *pathē* and *ēthos* of the subject through body and physiognomy and the depiction of the individual model as a paradigmatic, generic, or idealized account, but also recall the broader context in which the images that he cites must be read. Xenophon introduces the discussion as part of his demonstration of Socrates' "usefulness" not only to those who practiced the arts and crafts, but to anyone engaged in "striving toward noble ends" (3.1.1).[97] In serving this constituency, the philosopher promotes the well-being of the larger polis in which the craftsmen ply their trades; paintings and statues make manifest the very qualities that good citizens should exhibit (dignity, freedom, and discipline, in Socrates' account), and shun those (meanness, slavishness, and vulgarity among them) that their audience would do well to reject. The turn toward the inward thus combines an ethical with a civic dimension, and Aristotle would go on to spell out what is implicit in Xenophon's text. Endorsing the belief that paintings could influence the spectator in positive ways, he advises the young to go look at the works of painters and sculptors whom he dubs *ēthikōs*, whose creations best manifest human character, since exposure to these is beneficial to the polis (*Pol.* 1340a33–35, 37–40).[98] For both philosophers, the critical element is not what the image does for its subject (the glory that the athlete derives from the representation wins no mention from Socrates), but what it does for the (citizen) viewer.[99]

Not surprisingly, the individual who features most prominently in Aristotle's discussion is Polygnotos (c. 470), the artist whom others also name as the innovator in giving figures their new expressive capacities.[100] But if painters led the way, then statue-makers were not far behind: Pliny singles out the bronze statue of a lame man — probably the hero Philoktetes — made by Polygnotos's contemporary, Pythagoras of Rhegion, that apparently exhibited such pathos that spectators would actually experience the pain of the sore (*HN* 34.59). Among extant works, the images decorating the Temple of Zeus at Olympia confirm that

[96] Both Rouveret (1989: 14–15) and Stewart (1990: 83) note the rather more modest claims made for sculpture as opposed to painting, and each suggests different reasons for the gradations.

[97] For a reminder of the broader, civic agenda underlying the exchange, see Goldhill 1998: 109 and passim.

[98] For discussion of this and other comparable passages, see Castriota 1992: 9–11.

[99] As noted in Goldhill 1998: 112.

[100] His *Ilioupersis* and *Nekyia* supply much-cited examples of the novel trend.

other sculptors working in the early classical period were also experimenting with strongly characterized physiognomies and developing a "body language" designed to convey the emotions of their subjects. The treatment of Heracles on several of the temple's metopes not only registers the progressive aging of the hero, but also displays the changes wrought by the *pathē* that he experienced in the course of his labors, and his own emotional reactions to the tasks imposed on him.[101] The figure seems to acquire fresh moral and intellectual stature after each successive triumph, the fatigue visible in west metope 1 yielding to the upright and commanding figure in west metope 3, and to the display of controlled strength in his encounter with the bull in west metope 4.

On the temple's east pediment, the frieze representing the chariot race between Oinomaos and Pelops (fig. 8) again uses stance and gesture as well as facial expression to declare the distinctive personalities of the contestants in the event. The countenance and posture of Oinomaos, shown hand-on-hip in a pose of self-assertion that should more properly belong to the gods in the composition,[102] manifest the overbearing pride that will result in his downfall, while the quieter and more contemplative bearing of Pelops, with his head slightly inclined, displays the proper modesty combined with a readiness for action that, as Pindar's telling of the myth in his near-contemporary first *Olympian* makes plain, are the prerequisites for this victory. Aware of the disaster about to claim the royal house, and of the ruse, otherwise unexpressed, through which Pelops will gain his prize, the father of Melampous sits on Oinomaos's side, his face lined with apprehension, gesticulating in concern; together his motion and physiognomy remind the viewer of the outcome of the narrative whose early stages he sees before him.

But if these innovations give to the figures a quite novel degree of characterization and expressiveness, they also serve the larger end toward which the temple's decorations tend. Not just accounts of particular mythical "personalities" and the contrasts between them, the images offer snapshot visualizations of those ethical and political concerns whose articulation gives the building its broader programmatic coherence.[103] Together with the Centauromachy featured on the west pediment, the metopes and east pediment explore the nature of competition

---

[101] See Stewart 1990: 145 for this. Pollitt (1972: 50), understanding *ēthos* in its modern rather than fifth-century meaning, observes that here the "sculptors seem intent on conveying to us both what kind of man the hero basically is (*ēthos*) and also what he has had to endure (*pathos*)." See, too, Pollitt 1985: 102.

[102] Tersini 1987: 148.

[103] For detailed accounts, Stewart 1983 and Tersini 1987. Osborne (1994a: 60–61) challenges the now-standard notion that the decorative scheme reflects the recent conflict with Persia.

(a theme eminently suited to the site, and to a building financed from the spoils won by the Eleans in their war with the neighboring Pisans)[104] and display the different properties that victory and defeat have called into play: *dikē*, *sophrosunē*, and rightful submission to the will of the gods on the one hand; hubris, want of self-control, disregard of the gods, and violations of the boundaries and institutions that they uphold on the other. The message presents itself most emphatically in the figure of Apollo, shown in the very center of the Centauromachy with his right arm extended to the corner of the pediment and his hand pointing in an economical gesture of command. Emblematic of the good order and justice that Oinomaos, the Centaurs, and the bestial and human *hubristai* whom Heracles defeats all threaten to violate, the god's smooth and youthful countenance, his perfect body, frontal stance, and unmoving, quietly assertive pose set him in sharp opposition to the aggressors flanking him on either side; their contorted limbs and torsos, violent gestures, and heavily bearded, lined, and grimacing faces betray the violence, exertion, and frenzied effort from which divinity remains aloof.

The paradigmatic quality of images, and the artists' use of new modes of characterization to engage the viewer in publicly oriented ways, appear even more strikingly in representations of historical individuals. While a few extant figures may attempt to furnish recognizable accounts of a particular man or woman,[105] works commemorating real-world figures commissioned by the polis and placed in its communal spaces are not so much portrait likenesses, depictions of a body and personality unique to the single subject, as they are generic or idealized representations, which assimilate the specific to the broader type, and the mortal to the heroic.[106] In Jerome Pollitt's handy phrase, these are "role portraits" designed to convey what the viewer's society "appreciated as permanent values."[107] So the Tyrannicides (see fig. 6), transformed into civic heroes par excellence, present two body types and two distinct personalities, the better to exemplify the several contrasting *ar-*

---

[104] See Osborne 1994a: 57–62 for this emphasis.

[105] As argued by Stieber 1994.

[106] Among the numerous treatments of this issue, I have drawn on Schweitzer [1940] 1963, Sörbom 1966, Gauer 1968, Breckenridge 1968, Richter 1984, Pollitt 1986, Stewart 1990, Zanker 1995. As both the ancient sources and modern discussions note, through the late archaic and classical period, Greek society, and the Athenian democracy in particular, felt considerable reticence about making portrait likenesses of living (and dead) individuals, an act that smacked of hubris and carried with it the possible implication of heroization or apotheosis. For more on this, see chapter 5.

[107] Pollitt 1986: 59–60. For a new statement of this notion, see Zanker 1995.

etai that devotion to freedom's cause calls into play.[108] While Aristogeiton, holding his sword low and using his cloak in the manner of a shield, conveys a measured restraint and readiness to take the defensive role, Harmodios, who rashly exposes his whole body as he raises his weapon, demonstrates the courage and bold impetuosity that the attempted coup also demanded. Posture, countenance, and appearance additionally equate the two tyrannicides with the heroes of myth, shown in precisely these positions on Attic vases from shortly after 510.

Other fifth-century "portraits" also evoke the enduring physical and moral virtues associated with the generic category to which the subject belongs, and privilege what one discussion of the works has termed each individual's "Beispielhaftigkeit," or exemplarity.[109] Sometime around 460, a statue-maker produced a life-size image of Homer, of which only copies of the head now remain.[110] Perhaps commissioned as a dedication for a public sanctuary,[111] the depiction of the blind old man tempers its several touches of realism and characterization (among them the deep-sunken eyes, the furrows, wrinkles, sagging flesh, and sharply protruding cheekbones) with a more encompassing display of beauty, nobility, and above all *sophia*, which transcend its indications of advancing age. The closed eyes and furrowed brow speak of the insight that comes with the loss of physical vision, and perhaps, too, as Paul Zanker suggests, of the feats of memory that the epic poet achieves and that form part of his claim to wisdom.[112] As a declaration of the transfiguring qualities of superior mental and poetic activity, the image invests its subject with an *ēthos* calculated to inspire the same veneration that his compositions still enjoyed.

Though few would question the exalted position occupied by Homer and his works,[113] the Ionian poet Anakreon, commemorated in an image probably raised during Perikles' tenure of power (and perhaps even dedicated by the statesman or one of his circle), might pose difficulties for an artist accustomed to creating civically exemplary figures. But much as an epinician poet can transform his subject into an individual deserving of his fellow citizens' praise by casting his activities in a certain light, so the statue-maker disassociates Anakreon from the extravagant and decadent way of life with which he had been linked (and which

[108] Stewart 1990: 136. See, too, Ridgway 1981: 179.
[109] Gauer 1968: 119. Note, too, the remarks of Belting (1994: 99) on the choice between a "memorial image" and an "ideal image."
[110] For discussion of the reliability of the copies, Zanker 1995: 14–16.
[111] Ibid.: 20.
[112] Ibid.: 17.
[113] Although, as Zanker (ibid.: 20) notes, Homer's status did not go unchallenged at the time.

democratic Athens ruled out of style) and offers the viewer an account that visibly incarnates the social ideal prized by the elite (and those wishing to join their ranks) in the contemporary polis. Imagined as a participant in the aristocratic symposium, he exhibits through his upright stance, composed and impassive face, and barely moving posture the self-restraint and control that the drinking party puts to the test.[114] The poet's handsome and even youthful physique, in contrast to the venerably aged Homer, would speak particularly to the latter-day *kaloikagathoi* who pursued the very activities in which Anakreon is shown engaged: those softer pleasures of music and song, of relaxation in drink and dance, in no way render a body unfit for athletics and warfare.

To portray an individual as an ideal citizen and member of the polis, and on occasion to suggest his affinity with members of the exalted, heroic realm, was not only to serve the interests of those paying for, and playing audience to, the work. In paring away inessential, contingent details and looking to the deeper beauty and nobility that earns a man commemoration in the public sphere, statue-makers seem also engaged in an attempt to penetrate beyond the visible appearance of things, and to reveal what lies concealed within the body. Among fifth-century statue-makers, Polykleitos remains most closely associated with this pursuit of the essential character (*phusis*) of a subject.[115] Active from 460 to 410, and lauded by subsequent commentators for his mastery of *to kallos*, the artist devised a system for representing a body type at once ideally beautiful, paradigmatic, and "real," and free from individual variations or idiosyncrasies. In one of the only two extant citations from the treatise Polykleitos composed, he remarks that "*to eu* comes about by minute calculation [or 'little by little'] through many numbers" (Philo Mechanicus 4.1.49, 20).[116] Galen, commenting on the remark of the Stoic philosopher Chrysippus, gives a more complete sense of the thesis presented in the work:

> Beauty, [Chrysippus] feels, resides not in the *summetria* of the elements (i.e., of the body) but in the proper proportion of the parts, such as for example that of the finger to the finger, and of all these to the hands and the wrist, and of these to the forearm, of the forearm to the whole arm, and of everything to everything else, just as is written in the Canon of Polykleitos. For having taught us in his treatise all the *summetriae* of the body, Polykleitos supported his treatise with a work, having made a statue of a man according to the

[114] Ibid.: 24–31.
[115] Here I use *phusis* in the several fifth-century meanings of the term, at once the physical reality of the human body, the essential and less perceptible bodily constitution, and the individual's internal character and growth. On this, see Childs 1988: 12–13.
[116] On *to eu*, see Pollitt 1974: 20 and n. 6.

tenets of his treatise, and having called the statue itself, like the treatise, the Canon. So then, all philosophers and doctors accept that beauty resides in the due proportion of the parts of the body. (*De placitis Hippocratis et Platonis* 448 Kühn)

Other ancient sources confirm and round out Galen's gloss:[117] the Canon seems to have aimed at the mean, and it most probably took the form of a series of ratios, which set all parts of the body in proportional relations to each other and to the whole.[118]

In devising a set of numerical relations corresponding to the human form, Polykleitos wittingly or unwittingly aligned his enterprise with other contemporary attempts to discern the regular and harmonious structure thought to lie beneath each manifestation of an object in the physical world. Some suggest that his concern with *summetria* harks back to Pythagoras, the bronze-caster from Samos and Rhegion active in the Peloponnese earlier in the fifth century; it was this artist, Diogenes Laertius reports, who was "the first to aim at compositional *rhuthmos* and *summetria*" (8.47). The name that the sculptor shares with the more famous Pythagoras, another refugee from Samos several decades before, prompts speculation that the younger man might have incorporated the numerical theorizing of his namesake into the design of images whose *summetria* would involve "the novel application of a universal principle of some sort, perhaps the Pythagorean decad, to the proportioning of the parts of the body."[119] References to the Canon in later sources offer evidence for more direct exchanges between Pythagorean teachings and Polykleitos's system: the resemblance between Philo Mechanicus's citation of Polykleitos and the discussion of Pythagoras's number theory in Aristotle's *Metaphysics*, and the importance of commensurate numerical relationships in both the artistic and philosophical schemes, exhibit the link.[120] The unusual term *to eu* used in the original treatise may also be a Pythagorean expression,[121] and the design of the Doryphoros can even be read as a visible manifestation of several of the polarities in the table of opposites the philosopher devised.[122]

---

[117] Most pertinently Galen *De temperamentis* 1.566 (Kühn); Plut. *Mor.* 45c–d. See, too, the additional passages cited in Leftwich 1987: appendix to chap. 1.

[118] So Stewart 1978: 126.

[119] Stewart 1990: 139.

[120] For detailed discussion of the scholarship, see Leftwich 1987: chap. 1.

[121] Pollitt 1974: 20; Leftwich 1987: 32–41.

[122] Leftwich 1987: esp. 315. Precisely this "Pythagorean series" underlies Vitruvius's account of sculptors' canons ("Moreover they collected from the members of the human body the proportionate dimensions that appear necessary in all building operations: the finger [inch], the palm, the foot, the cubit. These they distributed into the perfect number, which the Greeks call *teleon*, for the ancients determined as perfect the number that is

Affinities between the activities of Polykleitos and those of the contemporary Pythagorean Eurytos attest to the common ground shared by theoreticians and artists. While Polykleitos was most probably employing the Pythagorean arithmetic mean for the mathematical progression that determined the *summetria* between the statue's different parts,[123] Eurytos is said to have been making geometric designs with colored pebbles to discover what number corresponded to what thing, and perhaps also to demonstrate the numerical proportions linking one part of the body and the next.[124] There is no determining priority here: Eurytos could have drawn on Polykleitos's conception of mathematical ratios for his diagrams of men, horses, and other species,[125] each aiming to capture the "essential number" of its subject, or some acquaintance with Pythagorean thought might have prompted the sculptor to begin thinking about the structure of his images in terms of the *summetria* and harmony between their several parts. What links both enterprises is the similar attempt to use numbers as a means of making visible a reality obscured by variations in individual examples of the type, and to display the underlying configuration of phenomena. Numbers and proportions for the Pythagoreans, and perhaps for Polykleitos, too, are the tools through which we can represent the essence of things,[126] the "causes of substances (*tōn ousiōn*) and of Being (*tou einai*)" (Arist. *Metaph.* 1092b8). While Polykleitos was not engaged in some kind of anachronistic quest for a Platonic *eidos* or idealized form, he was nonetheless seeking to represent a *phusis* that rested not just on empirical observation, but on a more absolute theoretical formulation.[127]

---

called ten," 3.1.5), and the notions of Chrysippus cited by Galen closely correspond to the views of the Pythagoreans Alkmaion and Philolaos. For discussion of these overlaps, see Raven 1951; Stewart 1978; Pollitt 1985: 98; Leftwich 1987.

[123] Of three terms, a, b, c, the third exceeds the second by the same amount as the second exceeds the first: $a + c = 2b$ (2, 3, 4). See Stewart 1978 for a detailed discussion of this point.

[124] For this, see Raven 1951: 148–49; Pollitt 1985: 98.

[125] So Raven (1951: 151), who argues that Eurytos was influenced by Polykleitos via his teacher Philolaos.

[126] In Aristotle's summary of Pythagorean beliefs, since "numbers are the ultimate things in the whole physical universe . . . they assumed the elements of numbers to be the elements of everything, and the whole universe to be a proportion (*harmonia*) or number" (*Metaph.* 986a1–4). Note the use of the term *harmonia* in Plutarch's reference to the Polykleitian Canon at *Mor.* 45c–d.

[127] Leftwich 1987: 363. That beauty was Polykleitos's explicit goal, and the quality that Galen assigns to the numerically harmonious arrangement of the statue's parts, does not preclude his participation in this more theoretical quest. As Raven (1951: 150) argues, "The step from 'beauty' to 'essence' was but a short one," and the invisible harmonies and systems of relations that the statue held up for show were themselves the source of what commentators term *ta kallista* or *to eu*.

The other chief influence regularly cited for the statue-maker comes from the medical rather than the philosophical sphere.[128] The terms used in the Canon and the principles of motion the image incorporates correspond closely to the vocabulary and teachings found in the Hippocratic texts, and echo the medical writers' concern with the concepts of extension and flexion when they discuss the different postures the bodily members must assume to achieve some action or hold a pose. But particularly relevant for my purpose is the common preoccupation with the relations between the surface of the body and its regular underlying anatomy. The Hippocratic doctor, who would rarely have the opportunity to perform dissections, was bound to rely on observing external symptoms and signs to discern the body's inner constitution, prompting the author of *Ancient Medicine* to remark, "It is necessary to learn these things from without from what is visible" (22.18). So, too, the statue-maker's "exact imitation of the way that the body in motion is effected," cited by Socrates as a source of the pleasure (*terpsis*) that a work supplies (Xen. *Mem.* 3.10.7–8), allows the viewer to discern the relation between the action of the muscles and other internal structures and the movements that result. In this Polykleitos shows himself the "imitator of *phusis*" hailed by later texts, a *phusis* that pertains to the inner rather than outer dynamics of the body.

For a fifth-century Greek audience, the symmetry and regularity exhibited by the Doryphoros might do more than declare the harmonious design and good order of the figure's physical constitution. Because a man's visible appearance — his posture, his gait, the movement of his arms and head, his hair style and dress — exists in such intimate connection with his inner being, aesthetics become an indicator of moral worth and determinant of public standing; any falling off points to imperfections in disposition and character, in the individual's *ēthos* and *psuchē* as well as his *phusis*.[129] The same synthesis of the physical and ethical would reappear in Socrates' remarks in Xenophon's *Memorabilia* 3.10.5. There the philosopher expresses the view that the task of the artist is to exhibit moral qualities that can be "reflected in the face and the attitudes of the body," and concludes that works of art are pleasing when physiognomy and posture display an *ēthos* of goodness rather than the "ugly, depraved, and hateful."

The vocabulary used by later texts in their references to the Canon acknowledges the presence of this more properly ethical dimension. Citing Varro, Pliny notes that the sculptor's works were "squarish" (*quad-*

---

[128] For detailed treatment, see Leftwich 1987: chap. 3.
[129] Zanker 1995: 49. Very pertinent here is Bourdieu's concept of *hexis*, for which see Bourdieu 1990: 69–70.

rata, HN 34.65), a translation of the Greek term *tetragōnos*, which the Roman author would have borrowed from his Greek source (most probably the third-century Sikyonian sculptor and "art historian" Xenocrates). While most commentators suggest that here Varro has in mind the blocklike and square impression that Polykleitos's images would have conveyed when set alongside the more fluid and gracile figures modeled by Lysippos,[130] the expression may carry a more positive sense.[131] As Simonides' use of *tetragōnos* in his ode to Skopas already shows, the flawlessness in both body and mind (*chersin te kai posi kai noōi*, fr. 542.2 *PMG*) that the statue exhibits is bound up with the distinctive configuration of the work, its foursquare modeling (542.3). The choice of the term *tetragōnos* indicates Simonides' glance beyond mere physical shape and stance, and his concern with the more abstract, ethical properties the song goes on the explore. Once again Pythagorean teachings reinforce the positive evaluation implicit in the phrase; here *tetragōnos* appears on the "good" side of the table of opposites cited by Aristotle (*Metaph.* 986a22), and the number four stands for justice (the very quality that Simonides' song recommends to its addressee).[132] Through its visible appearance, the Doryphoros thus "bodies forth" the good regulation and balance of its soul.

While the Doryphoros displays its maker's artistic principles through the human figure, holding out for show its synthesis of aesthetic and ethical properties, it, like so much fifth-century monumental sculpture, belongs within the broader civic milieu. Although we know nothing of where the original statue stood, nor of the public function that it assumed, the qualities made visible through its design find an echo in the political discourse of the period. The early fifth-century philosopher Alkmaion of Kroton had argued that the human body maintains its health through an *isonomia* between its contesting powers (moist and dry, hot and cold), but gets sick if one of them achieves *monarchia*. *Isonomia* had simultaneously become something of a political catchphrase; when Herodotus's Samian scribe Maiandrios attempts to replace a tyrannical

---

[130] See Pollitt 1974: 267.

[131] Contra Pollitt (ibid.: 266), who observes the overlap but denies that the metaphoric meaning of "having a character which is morally perfect" has any connection with the term's usage in the visual arts. Note, too, Ferri 1960 (critiqued by Pollitt 1974: 267–68) for an analysis of a series of passages in which *tetragōnos* refers not to squareness or blockiness but rather to "having four elements in harmony."

[132] Campbell (1982: ad loc.) sees a Pythagorean usage here, since for the Pythagoreans the square was the image of divine being (Proclus on Euclid *Elementa* 48g) and the symbol for justice. Aristotle later notes of the metaphor that both the good man and the square are complete (*Rh.* 1411b26, *Eth. Nic.* 110b20). For other equations between four and virtue, Pind. *Nem.* 3.74–75; Aesch. *Sept.* 160.

regime with a proto-democracy, he declares that all citizens will hence-forth enjoy *isonomia* (3.142.3; cf. 3.80.6), and the same term figures in the Athenian drinking song celebrating the deed of Harmodios and Aristogeiton (13 *PMG*). More than just an equality before the law, it describes the particular balance that must be maintained between indi-vidual elements of the bodylike polis so as to preserve collective politi-cal health. What makes the Doryphoros's statement of an equality and proportion among its different parts all the more compelling is the ac-tivity that the figure performs: equipped with a spear, he presents him-self in his public role as citizen-warrior who fights on his city's behalf, and who stands as one element within the larger ordered entity that the united hoplite line builds. Confronting the viewer with an idealized im-age of his own body and role within the state, the statue offers a para-digm of both physical and civic excellence, of a self-regulation that en-ables a man to fulfill his part in a public enterprise.

WORKS OF ART IN FIFTH-CENTURY TEXTS

Artistic apatē

Though Polykleitos's manual has been lost, other fifth-century sources that feature images still survive, and echo and reflect on the develop-ments that contemporary sculpture holds up for show. Affirming that statues require an audience to practice that "seeing in" earlier de-scribed, the texts also observe the troublesome quality of the works' combination of verisimilitude and *technē*: the viewers populating the accounts no longer experience the unmitigated wonderment and plea-sure registered by their counterparts in epic song but, responding with a more complex mixture of delight, suspicion, and even hostility, find a twofold mode of looking more difficult to sustain. Particularly problem-atic, the sources suggest, is the image's confusion of its eiconic and ei-dolic roles. Endowed with a heightened realism and the capacity to in-stantiate the thoughts and sentiments existing within a person, the statue now exhibits a metonymic dimension dependent not so much on its context and conventionalized appearance as on its possession of a liveliness and a visible similarity to the missing subject. Not surprisingly, the medium that finds in sculpture a particularly rich source of conceits is one that also works in the realm of representations and the conjuring up of absent persons. For the dramatists of fifth-century Athens, the statue that seemingly replicates, and even substitutes for, a living reality can supply a model for the several responses that figures onstage sim-ilarly generate.

Earliest among fifth-century explorations of fashioned artifacts is the much-cited fragment from Aeschylus's satyr play *Theoroi* or *Isthmiastai* (*P. Oxy.* 2162, fr. 78a 6–21 Radt), where the dramatist has his chorus members approach the Temple of Poseidon while thanking someone for giving them what seem to be their own portable portrait images.[133]

 ἄθρησον εἰ .[. .] . . [ ]
 εἴδωλον εἶναι τοῦτ' ἐμῇ μορφῇ πλέον
 τὸ Δαιδάλου μ[ί]μημα· φωνῆς δεῖ μόνον.
 ταδ[. .]. ει..
 ορα .[.].(.)ο.[ ]
10 χωρει μάλα

 εὐκταῖα κόσμον ταῦτ[α] τῷ θεῷ φέρω
 καλλίγραπτον εὐχάν
 τῇ μητρὶ τἠμῇ πράγματ' ἂν παρασχέθοι·
 ἰδοῦσα γάρ νιν ἂν σαφῶς
15 τρέποιτ' ἂν †ἀξιάζοιτό† θ' ὡς
  δοκοῦσ' ἔμ' εἶναι, τὸν ἐξ-
  έθρεψεν· οὕτως ἐμφερὴς ὅδ' ἐστίν.
 εἶα δὴ σκοπεῖτε δῶμα ποντίου σεισίχθο[νος
 κἀπιπασσάλευ' ἕκαστος τῆς κ[α]λῆς μορφῆς[
20 ἄγγελον, κήρυκ' [ἄ]γαυδον, ἐμπόρων κωλύτορ[α,
 .[.]. ἐπισχήσει κελεύθου τοὺς ξένο[υς] φ [

> Look hard and tell me if . . . this image full of my form, this imitation of Daidalos, lacks only a voice. . . . I bring these as a well-won ornament to the god, a beautifully designed votive. It would challenge my own mother! For seeing it she would surely turn [with a wail], thinking it was me, whom she raised. So similar this is [to me]. Come now, consider the house of the god of the sea, the earth-shaker, and each one of you nail up a messenger of his handsome self, a herald unheard, a restrainer of travelers who might hold back strangers from the road.

While noting that true realism, understood as a direct copying of nature, is not a phenomenon in early classical art, Göran Sörbom, and Christopher Hallett after him, read the satyrs' words and their allusion to Daidalos's powers as evidence that the Greeks of the period "experienced the art of their day, if not exactly as described, at least as extremely vivid and amazingly full of life," and connect the fragment to the development of increasingly vivified expressions, postures, and gestures in the statuary of the time.[134] In similar fashion, although prefer-

---

[133] For a recent discussion and review of earlier interpretations of the nature of the objects (antefixes or *protomoi* according to some readings, theatrical masks, statuettes, or votives according to others), see Stieber 1994: 86 and n. 4.

[134] Sörbom 1966: 41–53; Hallett 1986: 76–78, from whom I cite.

ring to associate the representations with trends in the late archaic art familiar to Aeschylus from his youth, Mary Stieber argues that the works are vaunted for their striking realism on a double count, both for their remarkable likeness to the satyrs and for the lifelikeness that frightens off unwanted strangers.[135]

But the naturalistic or lifelike quality of the artifacts does not seem the fragment's sole, or even chief, concern: what the speakers dwell on is not so much the artist's skill in exactly replicating nature as his ability to create a semblance of life, and to persuade his viewers to suspend disbelief even as they remain alive to his extraordinary technical feat. The early mention of Daidalos—whether he is the creator of the work, or the *eidōlon* is an imitation of an artifact made by him—gives the cue; already in Homeric song, the hero's name, and the adjectives and nouns cognate with it, belong to objects whose marvelous artistry permits them to straddle (although not actually to cross) the boundaries between the manufactured and the living, and momentarily to elide the two categories. Daidalos enters Greek song in his own person in the context of the *thauma*-inspiring shield of Achilles (*Il.* 18.591–92), and the brooch described by Odysseus to Penelope qualifies as a *daidalon* (*Od.* 19.227) as the poet succinctly signals its status as a work of art simulating life even before giving details of the design.[136] Both in Aeschylus's satyr play and in other dramas of the age, the proliferating allusions to the legendary craftsman[137] declare no naive confusion of the copy with the model, but a recognition that a virtuoso *technē* promotes rather than detracts from the "naturalness" of the piece.

Following this trajectory, the fragments' subsequent lines repeatedly juxtapose terms crediting the images with life with others that underscore their nature as works of artifice. An *eidōlon* may be a fabricated object (such as the phantom images that the gods in the *Iliad* construct) or an actual visitant from another realm; and that the image is "filled with" the satyrs' form suggests the vivifying activity that divine craftsmen can perform as they fill the hollow vessel or mold with quickening properties.[138] But the expression *mimēma* (7), the reminder that the arti-

---

[135] Stieber 1994: 92.

[136] Though the adjectival form of the artist's name can mean no more than "elaborately" or "cunningly wrought," it also frequently appears in conjunction with the more fabulous, half-animated artifacts that the epic poets include. S. P. Morris (1992: 226), summing up her investigation of the various forms and uses of the term, concludes, "Epic conventions praising artifacts in poetry invoke the role of legendary, divine or exotic craftsmanship and the *daidal*-qualities, whose effect is the animation in objects, the illusion of life."

[137] For a list of these references and discussion, see ibid.: chap. 8.

[138] For more on this, see chapter 2.

fact remains incapable of speech (7), and the term *kalligrapton* (12), announcing the skilled workmanship that has gone into the image's production, all confine the object to the realm of mere representation. While a satyr's mother would behave as though confronted with a living person, her reaction is styled erroneous (*dokousa*, 16), and the closing evocation of the messenger and herald without voice introduces two quintessential speakers only to strip them of their defining property and to return the representations to the inanimate category where objects that can be pegged up to temples properly reside.

The satyrs' astonishment at the capacity of art to mimic life might hold up a deliberately skewed mirror to an Athenian's more sober response to contemporary works of representation. As naive latecomers to inventions often long since familiar to men (including the javelin featured in this particular drama),[139] the chorus's wonderment exaggerates the sensations that the more canny audience experiences, and the beasts' attempt to practice the kind of "seeing in" that artistic artifacts demand offers a much cruder version of the mode of spectatorship natural to the sophisticate. In much the same fashion, an encounter with another work ascribed to Daidalos requires the intervention of a more seasoned individual to explicate its powers, and to set an elderly and too gullible viewer straight. In Euripides' satyr play *Eurystheus*, a speaker hastens to reassure an old man apparently startled by the vivified look of an image, and once again redirects the piece back to the category of inanimate objects: "All the statues of Daidalos seem (*dokei*) to move and see, so clever (*sophos*) is that man" (fr. 372 N[2]).[140]

But the satyrs may also be commenting on their audience's behavior in more immediate fashion, and their own efforts to determine the relations between the *technē* and semblance of *phusis* inhabiting the image resemble those in which the theatergoers are simultaneously engaged. The best way to make sense of portable, satyric-faced images endowed with a high degree of likeness to their bearers is to understand them as identical to the theatrical masks that the chorus members wear.[141] This account lends additional significance to the proposal to donate the objects to the god: in a twist on the regular practice of dedicating masks after a victorious performance in the theater, the satyrs, here acting as athletes and devotees of Poseidon rather than of their regular patron Dionysus, will present their masks to the deity who presides over the

---

[139] As noted by Stieber (1994: 91).

[140] The term *sophos* is used of Daidalos again in Pl. *Euthphr.* 11d and may carry a somewhat pejorative cast, placing the craftsman together with other fabricants of verbal and visual illusions.

[141] For discussion of this point, Stieber 1994: 86 n. 4.

different kind of *agōn* in which they compete. Now the satyrs' striking preoccupation with voice makes good sense: worn by the chorus member, the open-mouthed mask serves not only as indicator of his identity as satyr — and recall how once an actor put on his mask, he effectively became one with the individual portrayed — but also as transmitter of his words, furnishing a "talking head" whose words and lifelike appearance combine to persuade the audience of the reality of what he sees. But detached from its bearer, and consequently stripped of voice, the mask's realism and verisimilitude are insufficient to make the satyr present: instead, the image stands exposed as no more than a secondary account, and chorus and audience alike can recognize the illusionism associated with artifacts fashioned by Daidalos in contemporary sources. The satyrs' own emphasis on the act of looking (the passage not only positions the speakers as observers of the masks, and includes the opening injunction *athrēson*, but goes on to imagine the satyrs' mothers as spectators, too) complicates the issue of *mimēsis* still further: the singers assume two roles, that of actors in the drama being played out onstage, and that of viewers whose own careful scrutiny of theatrical masks now parallels the audience's own.[142]

But this does not exhaust the splits and doublings that the episode contrives. Even as the Foundry Painter's famous cup of the 480's juxtaposes the bellow-worker's face with the two similar disembodied heads hanging from the wall above in order to call into question the "liveliness" of the one and the representational status of the others, so, too, by confronting his audience with detached masks of satyrs side-by-side with masked satyrs, Aeschylus blurs the boundaries between seemingly different realms. Are the apparently living, moving, speaking satyrs any more "real" and any less mimetic than the objects to whose manufactured quality they alert the audience, and does the fact that they speak while the open-mouthed and all-but-talking artifacts are silent give them a more compelling verisimilitude? Indeed, the satyrs might seem to protest too much: their repeated assertions of the muteness that the works of artistry must observe (and that their very appeal to Daidalos, known for his power to "envoice" his creations, undermines) begin to sound like vain attempts to persuade the audience of their own superior "reality."

By way of capstone to the confusion, the episode flags the masks' votive function, and their consequent role as objects capable of preserving the very liveliness that normally belongs only to the animate. The donor who presents an image to the god, whether the offering displays his own person or supplies some surrogate of the same, leaves in the

---

[142] Cf. Zeitlin 1994: 138–39.

sacred space a substitute or stand-in for his missing self, and a figure
that can lastingly reiterate his wishes and his thanks before the divinity.
In placing works so reminiscent of their appearance and their role
within this votive setting, the satyrs have summoned up the eiconic facet
that artistic representations inevitably possess and have closed the gap
between the image and the absent reality in ways that craftsmen inde-
pendently cannot: the masks nailed up on the temple wall are no less
declarations of the satyrs' presence than the masked actors assuming the
creatures' (mythical) personas on the stage. No wonder perplexity follows as the satyrs struggle to determine the source of the object's eiconic
powers, and to establish the limits that bound its mimetic aspects.

The precise status of works of art and the paradoxes that their several
roles can generate return in an episode from Aeschylus's *Agamemnon*
where the playwright underscores the uncomfortable emotional response that may be sparked by the artist's combination of naturalism
and *technē*. In the first stasimon of the drama, the chorus sings of conditions in Menelaus's palace and, evoking the statues or *kolossoi* standing there, remarks that "the *charis* of well-formed (*eumorphōn*) statues
is hateful to the husband" (416–17). Commenting on the lines, Eduard
Fraenkel plausibly suggests that Aeschylus was prompting his audience
to visualize statues "like those of the Attic *korai*,"[143] and a more recent
reading, which imagines *korai* as actual portrait images of particular
maidens, corroborates his view and argues that the playwright here
looks back to artistic developments in his youth.[144] But even if we assume a striking likeness between the *kolossoi* and Helen, the spotlight
falls less on the realism of the works of art than on their paradoxical
status, their capacity to oscillate between two antithetical realms. If the
term *eumorphoi* declares the skilled craftsmanship that has gone into
the creation of the artifacts, then the emotions that they generate depend on their ability to bring the living Helen most vividly and potently
to mind, to seem actual re-presentations and doubles of the queen. In
similar fashion, the quality of *charis* that the images possess carries, as
in the case of Hesiod's Pandora, a twofold meaning here: the radiant
emanation from within that gives an inanimate vessel its status as a
living being, it also functions as the attribute that all finely fashioned
objects possess, and that is applied by the craftsman from without. The
hostility experienced by Menelaus follows exactly on from the images'
combination of metonymy and metaphor. Seeing the *kolossoi as* Helen,
he feels longing for the missing object of desire; but understanding the
technical, mimetic nature of the works, and the "factural" rather than

---

[143] Fraenkel 1962: ad loc.
[144] Stieber 1994: 104–14.

living quality of their *charis*, he recalls the gap between a statue and reality, and suffers fresh pain on that account.

What these two very different passages suggest is that Aeschylus and his audiences did not apprehend images as simple transcriptions of reality; instead, their impact (like that of the other products of the "mimetic" arts) was thought to depend on their ability to engage a viewer through the manifest technical skill of their makers and the persuasive effects that artists could devise.[145] But already apparent in the dramas is an almost antagonistic relationship between the artist and his public, and the possibility that skillfully crafted works can both make a dupe of the looker and expose him to the unpleasant sensations that a reminder of the artificial nature of the "reality" portrayed might generate. According to near-contemporary sources, the solution could lie in complicity between the craftsman and his public, where the former practices an *apatē* — a term signaling art's ability to trick the eye and ear — to which his audience willingly and consciously succumbs. An anecdote preserved by Plutarch has Simonides remark that the Thessalians were too stupid to be deceived by him (*Mor.* 15d), and Gorgias suggests that the dramatist who fails to exercise his illusion-building skills necessarily fails in his task: "Tragedy deceives by myths and the display of various passions;[146] and whereas the tragic poet who deceives is more just than he who does not, the deceived is also wiser than the one who is not deceived" (B23 DK).[147] But both the mask-bearing satyrs and Menelaus reveal the special pleading that such statements might involve: are the theatergoers that much wiser than their counterparts onstage, and are they not party (even as they sit and watch the representational dramas unfolding before them) to the same confusions and disappointments?

---

[145] Cf. De Angeli 1988. On the parallel emphasis on *technē* in the verbal arts, Rosenmeyer 1955: 236.

[146] These two devices coincide closely with innovations in early fifth-century statuary, with its introduction of narrative and use of emotive expressions and gestures.

[147] An anecdote, which must have been composed long after the event, but which may capture something of fifth-century responses to the *trompe l'oeil* in which the artist dealt and the viewer delighted, features a contest between two leading statue-makers of the age. The Byzantine author Tzetzes describes how the Athenians commissioned both Pheidias and his pupil Alkamenes to build statues of Athena, designed to be placed high on a column. Pheidias, whom the text introduces as accomplished in the art of optics and a geometrician to boot, created an image whose appearance caused such outrage when the piece was first exhibited that he barely escaped a stoning. Alkamenes, lacking his master's skill in the requisite areas (*atechnōs . . . kai optikēs kai geōmetrias*), gave his image the correct, actual dimensions and seemed set to win the prize. But as soon as the two statues were placed upon their columns, all could see the superiority of Pheidias's work (8.353). The story might have been designed by way of illustration for a passage from Plato's *Sophist*, which presents makers of colossal images engaged in achieving precisely these calculated visual effects. On this see pp. 64–65.

The Inner Person

If individuals within dramas respond to works of art in ways that seem to accord with contemporary images' combination of naturalism and *technē*, then what of the statue-maker's other enterprise, his attempt to externalize moral and ethical attributes and attitudes? The visual vocabulary that artists were developing in order to imprint the *pathē*, *ēthos*, and *erga* of the soul on the faces and bodies of their works also finds its echo on the Attic stage, where speakers liken themselves and others to paintings and sculptures at moments when they seek to express dimensions of feeling, experience, or personality that might otherwise go unremarked. While the works of art cited in the texts lack the paradigmatic and didactic elements that belong to real-world statues, they match them on a different count, giving to the person momentarily transformed into an image the heightened persuasive power and emotive appeal that are the preconditions for engagement and emulation on the viewer's part. But the very response that these objects inspire may also throw up a fresh paradox and reminder of the common ground that artists and playwrights occupy: can a self-declared work of representation display a hidden reality, or must the manufactured quality of what is exhibited, and the *apatē* that has gone into its creation, diminish the truth-telling power of the image?

Twice in the course of pleading with Agamemnon to grant her vengeance against Polymestor, Euripides' Hecuba turns to the artistic idiom. When the Greek leader first beholds the body of the unknown Trojan—who turns out to be Hecuba's murdered son Polydoros—the queen has her back turned and Agamemnon cannot see her face. But once she has resolved to supplicate him, she asks not only that he look at her, but that he perceive her in a particular way: "Pity me, behold me, and like a painter standing at a distance, gaze at me in my sufferings" (*Hec.* 807–8). The remark suggests a double transformation: in casting Agamemnon in the role of artist, Hecuba also imagines herself being seen, whether in the manner of a figure already painted or of one about to become the subject of a representation and so an object of the painter's careful scrutiny. The opening term of the phrase indicates the goal of the projected metamorphosis: by virtue of being observed as a work of art by a skilled spectator, one who knows how to adopt the correct viewing distance, Hecuba aims to inspire a more acute awareness of her sufferings, and hence a more sympathetic response than her own living person and words can provoke.[148]

[148] See Zeitlin 1994: 142. Cf. the greater accuracy of perception that Polystratus gains by virtue of looking at an *eikōn* from a distance in Lucian's *Pro eikonibus* 12, with discussion in the epilogue.

But the distance separating the artist from the painting can produce a different result. For Hecuba to equate herself with a painted image that elicits pity from a skilled and attentive viewer is not only to engage the audience in the verities of her suffering; it must also underscore the act of self-figuration and "objectivization" that she performs.[149] In exchanging her living status for that of an image (and we might imagine the actor striking a particularly piteous *schēma* here, perhaps one borrowed from the painter's repertoire), she necessarily recalls the larger business of mimesis that frames the episode, and implicitly declares her own character and identity as a representation expressly designed to inspire compassion in an actual audience of theatrical connoisseurs. Even as Euripides reminds the viewer of the artist's power to create images so visually expressive of emotion that they move us as real individuals do, he has commented ironically on the mechanics of the scene, offering up one representation aping another, and a figure who bases her emotive and truth-telling powers on those which these secondary accounts possess.

Moving to the crescendo of her entreaty, the queen then introduces another visual object:

εἴ μοι γένοιτο φθόγγος ἐν βραχίοσιν
καὶ χερσὶ καὶ κόμαισι καὶ ποδῶν βάσει
ἢ Δαιδάλου τέχναισιν ἢ θεῶν τινος,
ὡς πάνθ᾽ ἁμαρτῇ σῶν ἔχοιντο γουνάτων
κλαίοντ᾽, ἐπισκήπτοντα παντοίους λόγους.   (Eur. *Hec.* 836–40)

If only there might be a voice in my arms and my hands and my hair and my footsteps either through the arts of Daidalos or one of the gods, that all together they might clasp your knees, and launch words at you of every kind.

The reference to the *technē* of Daidalos and the gods makes clear the type of artifact the queen has in mind: a statue, whether one literally endowed with speech, like the figures that Hephaistos creates, or one whose features and other body parts possess such visual fluency that they *seem* to deliver their spoken message to the audience (this more the province of the illusion-working Daidalos and of the contemporary artists who emulate his example). More emphatically than in the previous instance, the turn to a work of art signals the limitations of the verbal medium, which normally allows individuals to experience empathy with the sufferings and joys of others and serves as the transmitter of emo-

---

[149] I take the phrase from Zeitlin (1994: 142). See, too, Frontisi-Ducroux 1995: 30–31 for other instances in which characters imagine an external representation of the self—sometimes in the form of the *prosōpon* that is the "face" presented to the outside world.

tion from within to without; now the body must become the chief issuer of the spoken text, and through its own powers of visual articulation win conviction and sympathy in a way that the speaking voice alone cannot.[150] In pronouncing her lines, Hecuba momentarily demonstrates to the audience exactly the image that she has in mind, assuming the suppliant's pose and turning herself into that very "eloquent" artifact that her words have evoked.

The pathos-filled display achieves its end: Agamemnon yields to the queen's appeal, acknowledging the pity that he feels (850–51) and granting her the means to achieve her sought-after revenge. But again the terms in which Hecuba describes her self-generated image make clear that the sensations that she arouses in her chosen viewer depend on the *technē* of the statue-maker (in this instance Hecuba herself), and on a skilled manipulation of the matter in which she works, the body parts that, as Socrates would later comment, are the chief means for conveying emotions and experience. For all their expression of inward sensations and suffering, Hecuba's limbs, hands, hair, and the rest have all been modeled from without.[151]

But appeals to images also come free of these suggestions of the conscious deployment of artistic skill; on other occasions they more simply emphasize the verity that the representation puts on display and affirm its superior powers of revelation. According to Theseus's false perception of his son in Euripides' *Hippolytus*, the purity and beauty of the youth's physiognomy and visible person offer a misleading, counterfeited account that hides and belies the depravity within.[152] In a vain attempt to meet the charge, Hippolytus voices his desire to fashion a counterrepresentation, something like a portrait able to exhibit his inner nature and to display its coherence with the surface to the outside viewer. Using a phrase that admits two possible readings, he declares

---

[150] Cf. Aesch. *Ag.* 240–42, where Iphigenia, "striking as in a painting," also uses her body and visual faculties in the place of words.

[151] Here, too, the language simultaneously implicates and distances the theater-viewers from the action on the stage: though their response to the "statue" they see before them should follow Agamemnon's, they are also reminded of the continuities between bodies in drama and in art, representations that both adopt stylized and conventional poses designed to elicit feeling on the spectator's part.

[152] A theme signaled right at the start of the encounter when Theseus refers to the enduring problem of distinguishing appearance from the true account: there should be a *tekmērion saphes* that might allow a man to recognize the false friend from the true (*Hipp.* 925–26). The dramatist more broadly fills his play with references to the counterfeit nature of phenomena, to the existence of a surface and an interior that inevitably mismatch. Woman herself is a counterfeit coin (616), and the writing tablet's double folds (864–65; cf. 985), like the *skenē*'s two-leafed doors, tease protagonists and audience with their ability both to conceal and reveal a reality hidden from view.

that he wishes to conjure up a spokesman to testify on his behalf, "a witness such as I am myself" or "a witness to what manner of man I am" (*hoios eim' egō*, 1022). That the hero intends both shades of meaning here, and has something akin to Hecuba's self-representation in mind, his second hopeless longing affirms. Just as the queen imagined herself in the likeness of a painting that another might look upon and feel compassion toward, so Hippolytus seeks to make division of himself, creating a viewer and a viewed that move their audience to tears: "Would that I were able to stand opposite and look at myself so that I could weep for myself at the woes I suffer" (1078–79). No painting or statue here, what the youth has in mind seems most like a reflection in a mirror, a device that allows the viewer to assume a double identity "as a subject seeing and as an object being seen."[153] While Hecuba transforms herself into a work of art in order to rouse the sympathies of her interlocutor, Hipploytus's evocation of a mirror image spells out his more profound isolation and inability to touch his father: both subject and object, and mourner and mourned, he alone can respond to the spectacle he creates.

Replica or Original?

The split that Hippolytus knows is impossible to achieve, another character actually experiences. In Euripides' *Helen*, the dramatist imagines a situation where the protagonist finds herself afflicted with a double, a fashioned *eidōlon* so indistinguishable from its prototype that the boundaries between image and reality become hopelessly blurred. That artistic representations and the problems they raise stand at the heart of the play is declared from the start by the vocabulary used of the double. For all its phantasmal nature, its vacuous constitution of cloud, there is no mistaking the status of the *eidōlon* as a tangible, three-dimensional work of art. It qualifies as an *agalma* (1219) and *mimēma* (875), a thing modeled by the *technai* of Hera (33–34, 583, 930). But the chief proof of the phantom's statuelike nature comes from another, surprising source: intimating either that Helen has been "contaminated" by the properties of the manufactured double or, more tellingly, that the copy takes its cue from the imagistic and plastic character of the living protagonist, Euripides visualizes the queen herself as a work of artistry. No sooner does Teuker enter the stage than he addresses Helen as an *eikō phonion* (73), a likeness or statue of what he considers her real self,[154]

---

[153] Zeitlin 1996: 266; as she observes, Artemis will later fill this role of viewer, but will singularly fail to weep for Hippolytus's sufferings.

[154] Note, too, *hidrusato* at 46, the technical term for the setting up of a cult image, and 77,

and a conceit on which Helen picks up when she later wishes that she could "have been erased, like a painted *agalma*, and have got an uglier form instead of the beauty I have now" (262–63).[155] Artifice, in both senses of the term, has gone into the making of Helen, too, her own body generated by the shape-making skill of her father Zeus (19–20).

These and other moments that prompt the audience to view Helen herself in terms proper to the *eidōlon* cohere with Euripides' suggestion that the double might supply no less accurate a guide to the queen's true nature than the living character whom we witness onstage. The drama no sooner establishes the sharp distinction between Helen and the *eidōlon*, the truth and innocence of one, the fictive and guilty nature of the other, than it proceeds to elide the differences between the two. Beyond their common depiction as modeled artifacts, Euripides endows both Helen and her image with bodies (67, 588, and 160–61) that exercise beguiling powers, and attributes similar sentiments to both (608–11); he even concludes the action by having Helen reperform the very deeds imputed to her double, a departure from her would-be-husband and an escape on board ship with a "stranger" who abducts her from her home, a flight (and eventual ascent to divine realms) that echoes the *eidōlon*'s earlier journey and translation back into the air (1516). The phantom's disappearance halfway through the play does not so much remove these confusions as confirm that the crafted object displays the more enduring, as well as the visible, attributes of the original: as the protagonists engineer their escape, the audience witnesses Helen's full resumption of the powers to seduce and deceive that epic had first assigned to her, and that Euripides had seemingly relocated to the *eidōlon*.[156] Now she appears a spinner of illusions as powerful as those gen-

---

where Teuker repeats the term *eikōn*. The same crossovers mark the figure of Theonoe, originally called Eido (a name obviously suggestive of the *eidōlon*) and described as an *aglaisma* (11).

[155] Although commentators divide on whether the term should be rendered "painting" or "statue" (see Xanthakis-Karamanos 1980: 82–83), a statue must be meant. The formula presupposes a painted figure in the round, whose surface appearance could be changed while the underlying person remained the same. In a play on the customary conceit, Euripides has inverted the natural equation between moral beauty and beauty of form, the *kala eidē* later evoked by Xenophon's Socrates; because of all the evil associated with Helen's loveliness and the consequent assumption that her beauteous appearance must necessarily conceal a moral wickedness within, only an ugly *eidos* can accurately transmit the true merit and virtue of her character.

[156] So the manufacture of the cenotaph (an artifact that counterfeits the truth) and the production of a lying but persuasive story (whose verbal plays and double entendres make it seem the real account to the easily duped lover Theoklymenos) transform this *kainē Helenē* back into the craftswoman, poetess, and creator of potentially fictive stories who appeared in the *Iliad* and *Odyssey*. For more on this, pp. 290–91.

erated by the phantom and proves as successful in deceiving her Egyptian audience as was the phantasmagoric double in tricking its Greek and Trojan viewers.

Invested with this status and equipped with all the persuasive, beguiling, and deceptive powers that images possess, Helen inspires in those who witness her a response analogous to that elicited by works of art. As the encounters first with Teuker and then with Menelaus illustrate, viewers of the queen repeatedly try to test and verify what their senses report to them, and to resolve the question of where the distinction between reality and what they believe to be no more than an imitation or replica lies. For Teuker, the individual whom he meets on Egyptian soil comes to resemble Helen only in body or external appearance, not in inner constitution; this *mimēma* does not reproduce the queen's own very different *phrenas* (160); so, too, Menelaus, after wondering whether the figure he encounters is a ghost dispatched from the nether realms (569–70), chooses to reject what his eyes witness (580–81), and once again would limit the apparent equivalence to the *demas* alone (559).

After the disappearance of the crafted copy, the problem of Helen's relation to the *eidōlon*—is she a mere imitation, or one and the same?—turns into the more critical question of the coherence between the queen's outer and inner person and the capacity of the one to hide or reveal the other. In order successfully to dupe Theoklymenos, Helen transforms her surface appearance, working like an artist on the matter of her body and adopting the guise of a widow mourning her lost husband (note Theoklymenos's fear lest she mar her skin with tears, 1419). While those privy to the plot can practice the kind of "seeing in" that proved impossible as long as the *eidōlon* was still at large, perceiving Helen and the fictive character at a single glance and enjoying the skill that the fashioner has exercised in crafting her account, the Egyptian prince and his followers fall victim to the artistic ruse and accept the representation for reality. If Menelaus was proved wrong in distrusting the evidence of his eyes, then Theoklymenos's failure to observe the same caution costs him his bride-to-be. Works of art, it seems, are sometimes what they appear, accurate portrayals of the individuals whom they depict, and sometimes beguiling and misleading accounts, designed to catch out unwary viewers.

LATE CLASSICAL IMAGES AND THE PLATONIC ACCOUNT

Trends in Later Classical Statue-Making

Several of the issues that images allow playwrights to probe gain an increasing topicality through the course of the fifth century, and nowhere more than in the city where the dramas were performed. Questions concerning the relations of representations to the things they supposedly describe cluster in the debates of the sophists who taught in Athens in the century's second half, and in his treatise *On Nature* (B3 DK) Gorgias famously suggests that speech cannot reproduce sensible reality, and that every *logos* must involve some falsification of the thing to which it refers; insofar as it claims faithfully to reproduce phenomena, it qualifies as no more than deception or *apatē*. Even as sophists vaunt the powers of verbal representations to create their own realities and demonstrate their persuasive impact, dramatists and historians mount a counterattack, warning audiences of the dupery that they may suffer from the products of a speaker's *technē*. To read Thucydides' record of the Mytilenean debate is to hear several of the themes pegged to works of art now broadcast in the context of political rhetoric: an audience's willingness to be the dupe of a speech delivered with a self-assertive skill; the suspicion that awareness of the deceit that the clever speaker may practice can generate toward both the orator and his creations; the possibility that the artfully arranged discourse may nonetheless contain the truth.[157]

While most late fifth-century texts make only glancing use of statues to illuminate these problems, the Platonic dialogues turn frequently to sculpture for their illustration, explication, and eventual resolution. But before looking at how the texts handle the motif, I want briefly to set Plato's discussion against the background of innovations in statue-making just prior to or contemporary with the philosopher's lifetime, pinpointing those which seem to touch most closely on his account.[158] My suggestion will be that new ways of manipulating the spectator's visual, kinesthetic, and sensual response, and of presenting the image as an actual transcription of its subject rather than a self-proclaimed material, monumentalized, and schematized version of the same, demand a still more exacting definition of the relations between a statue and its model; so, too, the sculptor's production of an object that engages the viewer to a novel degree, inviting him to participate in and react to the story that the figure tells, gives new urgency to the question of an image's beguiling property, and to that of its ethical charge.[159]

---

[157] See particularly 3.38.4–7, 40.3, 43.2–3.

[158] Many discussions, including those of Schuhl (1952: 3–7) and Rouveret (1989: 34), simply assume that Plato is responding to contemporary images, and many have suggested a particular connection between Pliny's account of the innovations attributed to Euphranor, Lysippos, and others, and the Eleatic Stranger's remarks at *Soph.* 235e–236a. But Keuls (1978: 112) rightly rejects the association with Lysippos on chronological grounds.

[159] For comprehensive accounts, Robertson 1975; Ridgway 1981; Stewart 1990.

Accounts of developments in the late fifth century highlight the several dazzling optical effects that artists sought increasingly to produce, and nowhere more than in their treatment of drapery. On the much-cited parapet built around the bastion of the small Ionic temple dedicated to Athena Nike in Athens (c. 420–400), a procession of Victories brings offerings to the goddess, the maidens clad in diaphanous garments (fig. 9).[160] Through the use of the running drill, the artists achieve a contrast between the smooth surfaces where the drapery presses up against the body, delineating the forms beneath, and the deep furrows extending beyond the body itself, setting up calligraphic patterns of swirling lines and light and shade. The wide, flat folds with undercut edges used for some of the garments give them an apparent filminess and transparency, while the so-called Master C chisels his drapery into myriad scintillating facets, "like the surface of a diamond."[161] Paionios's Nike of c. 420 (fig. 10) appears similarly clad, with her dress now clinging to her naked form, now streaming off in the gusts of air, and the figures on the pediments and akroteria of the Temple of Asklepios at Epidauros (c. 380–370) feature the same "ribbon drapery," their garments carved with swirling folds that crisscross and surround the bodies. The overall effect is to prompt the viewer to focus on the surface of the image, and to be caught up in its complex visual dynamics.

A second result of this innovation is the heightened sense of fluidity and motion it imparts even to figures in inactive poses. The drapery that curves and sweeps about the body, playing in ripples across it or cascading down the limbs, forms part of a general taste for pronounced and exaggerated *rhuthmoi*, which replace the balanced, "quieter" poses found in the fifth century's middle decades. A Diomedes of c. 420, tentatively attributed to Kresilas and known through fragments, coins, and several copies, challenges the model that the Doryphoros proposed.[162] Here there is no question of equipose or a motion merely latent; instead, the hero seems to propel his body forward, his free leg, left hip, and shoulder set further to the side and front, and his supporting leg and hip jutting out. Several monuments from the turn of the century display figures engaged in equally violent and emphatic movements: on the frieze from the Temple of Apollo at Bassai, constructed at the fifth century's very close, the fighters lunge forward, their muscles and veins contracted; and a youth on the east pediment of the Temple of Asklepios at Epidauros hurls himself out of the left-hand corner, extending

[160] For more detailed discussion, see pp. 241–42.
[161] Stewart 1990: 166.
[162] Ibid.: 168.

his right leg while bending the left tightly up against his stomach.[163] No less dynamic is the centrally placed Nike on the temple's west akroterion, who twists her body, seemingly cut free from all support, in space. Her design anticipates later fourth-century images characterized by the same dynamism. Most famously, Skopas's Maenad of c. 360, known only through a worn and fragmentary Dresden statuette and through Callistratus's textual account (*Statuarum descriptiones* 2.1–4), registers the divine madness that possesses her as her body spirals upward through the left leg and right arm, while her head turns sharply the other way.[164]

While these poses prompt the viewer to see the figures as though in the act of moving (and Paionios's Nike, when observed from below, would appear to be landing on her pillar), unquiet contours and experiments in three-dimensionality additionally foster the illusion of bodies occupying and traveling through real space.[165] If a Roman copy of the Diskobolos provides an accurate account of the original of c. 400, then the athlete breaks out of his confines as he advances his right leg, extends his right arm, and turns his head to the side; posed on the diagonal, the image invites the spectator to move around it and view it from its several different angles as though it were a living form.[166] The same concern reappears in the monuments of the time: on the pediments of the temple at Epidauros showing the Amazonomachy before Troy and the Ilioupersis, the artists give their figures an apparent depth through the use of three-quarter poses and bodies portrayed in twisting motion. Once again the viewer is made to engage with the image, to follow its movement with his own, and to believe in the reality of the action it performs.

With the departure from the architectural framework and palpable sense of order that high classical images conveyed, and the replacement of their harmonious and schematized patterns with other more seemingly (if not really) unregulated effects, the statue acquires a new proximity to the appearance of real-world bodies and a still more emphatic physical presence. Promoting this sense of immediacy, and prompting the viewer to respond as he would to the living subject, is the sculptor's treatment of physiognomy. Gone from many images of the early fourth

---

[163] Ridgway 1981: 31–32, 94–96.

[164] Robertson 1975: 455.

[165] Stewart (1990: 176) suggests that these innovations should be seen in conjunction with contemporary advances in solid geometry, which were taught in the Sikyonian painting school from c. 370.

[166] Contrast Myron's earlier account, which, as Childs (1988: 11) comments, shows the body of the athlete "compressed into a narrow band parallel to the viewing plane . . . the statue acts more as a relief that as a statue in the round."

century are the impassive, expressionless faces characteristic of figures from earlier decades, and in their place the carved countenances exhibit the full gamut of emotions. The Amazon on the west pediment of the Temple of Asklepios at Epidauros displays a calm and passion-free face only because death has claimed her, while all about her the still-living individuals betray the physical strain and mental suffering that their combat demands.

If these emotive bodies and faces were not enough to engage the audience, then the sculptor's treatment of his particular medium might do the trick. Although the work of Praxiteles largely postdates Plato's lifetime, the artist's ability to use the marble in which he worked to suggest the radiance and translucence of flesh, and to convey its soft and tender quality through his modeling,[167] may already have been visible in his early pieces; in a Pouring Satyr of c. 370, evoked in multiple copies and Pausanias's account (1.20.1), the sculptor introduces in place of the bearded, coarse-featured creature of early representations a smooth-bodied, graceful youth, whose pliant and satiny flesh seems to belie the resistance of the stone used for his creation. Exactly the age to play the part of *erōmenos* and cast in the patently Ganymede role, he is designed to entice the viewer and to make the apparent abolition of the distance between marble and flesh part of the pleasure that contemplating the work can afford.

Other technical devices in the sculptor's repertoire allow him to manipulate the audience response. The maker of the Diomedes cited earlier modifies the proportions sanctioned by Polykleitos and anticipates Lysippos in giving his figure a smaller head, slimmer torso, and longer legs; the inevitable result is that the hero appears taller than he really is. Pliny describes Euphranor, a painter and sculptor whose acme is dated to the 360's, as the creator of "colossal statues, marble works, and reliefs" (*HN* 35.128) and presents him as another innovator who experimented with the dimensions of the human body.[168] While praising the artist for his ability to achieve "good proportions," he notes that "he was too slight in his structure of the whole body and too large in his heads and joints" (129). The comment may refer to Euphranor's attempts to achieve a new *summetria*, one designed to slim down the body while preserving the heads and limbs at their original size, so as to achieve a more supple-looking figure than the Polykleitan Canon could

---

[167] For discussion, Stewart 1990: 176 and 1997: 201–2.

[168] Rouveret (1989: 34) suggests some link between his activities and the issue of the illusionism practiced by makers of monumental pieces described in Plato's *Sophist* 235e–236a (usually dated to the 350's). For more on this, see the concluding portions of this chapter.

yield.[169] On the basis of the "art histories" produced by the Greek and Roman sources of imperial times and evidence drawn from (copies of) the statues that fourth-century sculptors produced, it seems that their makers did not so much abandon the idea of a set of mathematical relations capable of expressing the perfect human figure as modify those relations so as to make them convey the appearance of bodies in space, their apparent rather than real and measurable proportions. Where the system of Polykleitos, the later commentators suggest, left nothing to chance or to optical illusion, but lay rooted in unchanging and verifiable mathematical principles, the *eurhuthmia* achieved by his successors re-lied on *opsis* rather than *alētheia*, and transmitted a seeming rather than an actual harmony.[170]

If artists of the late fifth and fourth centuries modeled figures de-signed to reflect the aesthetic standards of their viewers, they were no less capable of flaunting contemporary notions of the Body Beautiful. In the realm of portraiture, standard discussions cite a new regard for indi-viduality and a willingness to represent the personal and idiosyncratic.[171] Frequently mentioned in this regard is Demetrios from the Attic deme of Alopeke, whose works would prompt Quintilian to comment that he was "fonder of similitude than of beauty" (*similitudinis quam pulchri-tudinis amantior*, *Inst.* 12.10.9).[172] Although none of his pieces survive (four bases with his signature and dated to the first half of the fourth century are all that remain), he is credited with having produced a bronze image of a Corinthian general named Pellichos, and Lucian would delight in describing the protruding belly, bulging veins, and un-

---

[169] Stewart 1990: 179; Schuhl 1952: 6.

[170] Pollitt (1974: 29) proposes that we understand the *eurhuthmia* sought by the new artists in the light of the remark by "Damianus" (cited in note 179) and suggests that his comment implies that "there is a real, measurable *eurhuthmia* and a *eurhuthmia* that one sees or feels, and an artist could strive for one or the other." For a rather different reading, see Childs (1988: 12), who suggests that "illusionism" actually forms part of Lysippos's vision of *phusis* or reality.

[171] This trend should not be overemphasized. Much more common than these still rare experiments in the atypical, idiosyncratic, and "realistic" (for which see Breckenridge 1968: 99; Stewart 1990: 173) are the idealized accounts of politicians, soldiers, and thinkers that the city-states would erect in ever greater numbers. As Zanker (1995) shows, in fourth-century Athens, where the reticence about setting up honorific images commem-orating real-world individuals both living and dead was increasingly overcome, the "good citizen" model seems to have been used to embrace a broad range of subjects, and trans-formed the personalities on which it went to work (Konon, Miltiades, Aeschylus, Sopho-cles, and Euripides among them) into repetitive and benign exemplars of civic virtue.

[172] In regard to the term *pulchritudo*, Pollitt (1974: 426) suggests that like *kallos*, the term was used to contrast the properties of Greek art in the classical period with the trend toward realism (*homoiotēs–similitudo*) in Hellenistic art. On Quintilian's remark, see, too, Rouveret 1989: 444–45.

kempt hair that the work held up for display (*Philops.* 18). Still extant, a bronze head of an old man recovered from a shipwreck of c. 400 involves just such a departure from the earlier mode; with its hooked nose, wispy hair, scraggly beard, and sharply lined forehead, it presents an individual in all his (unattractive) physical immediacy and uses the physiognomic features to suggest the personality of the man. According to the scheme that Pliny later traced out, this evolution in portraiture involved a shift from the beautification of the subject to a more accurate mimesis, and he would credit Lysistratos of Sikyon, the brother of Lysippos, with contributing to the change: having developed "the method of correcting a casting produced by wax poured into the plastic mold . . . he introduced the practice of making likenesses, for before him they took pains to make portraits as beautiful as possible" (*HN* 35.153).[173] If Pliny is drawing on a Greek source here (and Xenocrates, himself from Sikyon, offers the most probable candidate), then the tendency toward realism or *similitudo* as opposed to *pulchritudo* that both he and Quintilian note may be more than a topos of later Roman criticism, and may have a historical foundation.

Appropriately enough, it is a representation of Socrates that suggests the questions that this seemingly more "realistic" mode of copying can generate. In a depiction of the philosopher made some ten to twenty years after his death and known through Roman copies in Naples and Munich, the artist invites the viewer to ponder the (mis)match between the surface and the inner man. Borrowing, although in modified and softened fashion, the common comparison of Socrates to Silenus, the representation gives its subject the flat face, broad, short nose, balding head, ears set high and back, and full lips characteristic of the satyr type, and offers a startling departure from contemporary standards of physical beauty. But as Paul Zanker's discussion suggests,[174] the unsightliness of the account may not so much tend toward an accurate portrayal of its subject as be essential to its meaning; for those versed in Socratic teachings, it recalls not only the disjuncture between Socrates' ungainly surface and his almost divine depth,[175] but also the broader gap between reality and representation that the philosopher's own words repeatedly emphasize.

While nothing directly links these developments in sculpture to the topics debated in Plato's dialogues, the arguments voiced by his characters do offer responses to the issues that the late fifth- and early fourth-century works raise, and propose ways of escaping some of the traps

---

[173] Pollitt (1974: 433) questions whether the anecdote should be believed.
[174] Zanker 1995: 38–39.
[175] For Alcibiades' use of an *eikōn* to express this, see pp. 88–89.

that artists can spring. Even as the statue-makers bring the truth value of the older, idealized images into question and seek to fashion figures whose apparent verisimilitude and seductive forms beguile their audience into accepting the surface account, Plato meets the challenge by restoring the union between truth and beauty, and by transferring that union to a supramundane realm. By locating *to kallos* firmly beyond what our distorting senses convey and confirming its relations with the unimpeachable realities that belong to mathematics and measurement, he returns to a point of view more closely akin to that of Polykleitos and his school. In answer to the artist's claims that he can offer a portrait indistinguishable from its subject and can transcribe reality, Plato bids his reader take a closer look and recognize the element of difference that inevitably accompanies an image's similitude, preventing a relation of identity between the two; the metaphoric bond that links a copy to a model invariably proves inferior to a metonymic one, and the artist who does no more than transpose a visible likeness is revealed as a trader in illusions, not verities.

Reality and Representation

For the Eleatic Stranger of Plato's *Sophist*, works of art challenge our ability to distinguish not only reality from beguiling representations, but also mere belief and fictive report from the true account. False beliefs are the particular stock-in-trade of that elusive and polymorphic individual whom the dialogue aims to define, the sophist seemingly able to evade every category devised to pin him down. Some way into the conversation, the Stranger tries to track his quarry by using an analogy between the sophist and the artist, and by introducing visual artifacts by way of comparison for the less tangible verbal illusions in which his opponent deals. What individual, the Stranger first asks, boasts that he knows how to fashion and do all things by a single *technē* (233d)? After identifying the painter as the author of this claim, the Stranger goes on to caution against believing in the truth of what the artist displays: "Suppose that by being expert at drawing he produces things that have the same names as real things. Then we know that when he shows his drawings from far away, he will be able to deceive the less intelligent sort of children into thinking that he can actually produce anything he wants to" (234b). The equation between the visual and verbal realms becomes more explicit still: "Well, then, won't we expect that there is another kind of expertise, this time concerning words, and someone can use it to trick young people when they stand even further away from the truth about things? Wouldn't he do it by bewitching their ears, and by showing them spoken images (*eidōla legomena*) of everything, so as to make them believe that the words are true and the speaker knows more than anyone else?" (234c). But the illusion does not persist. With the advent of age and the onset of experience, the sophist's originally credulous listeners are able to come close up to real things, "and are forced by their experiences to touch up palpably against them." These close encounters successfully cure young men of their taste for sophistry and destroy the power that the speeches earlier held. "Won't most of them inevitably change beliefs they earlier had, which made larger things appear smaller and easy things appear hard? And won't the facts they have encountered in the course of their actions completely overturn all the appearances (*phantasmata*) that had come to them in the form of words?" (234d).

Up to this point the Eleatic Stranger's critique concerns *eidōla*, whether in the realm of art or language, that deliberately deceive their audience. Making the larger appear small is tantamount to creating a false belief by compelling the viewer or listener to accept illusion for reality. The underlying paradigm draws on visual objects (so far paintings) because, like the artist, the sophist is primarily concerned with sense perception, and his words involve accommodating the object to the perspective of his audience.[176] But the Stranger does not leave things there. Instead, he proposes taking a closer look at this so-called *eidōlopoiikē technē* (235b) and, by using the powers of diairesis, dividing it up into its two component parts. To the first of these the speaker assigns the name *eikastikē technē*, the art of making likenesses or *eikones*:[177] "That is the one whenever someone produces an imitation by keeping to the proportions of length, breadth, and depth of his model, and also by keeping to the appropriate colors in each of its parts" (235d–e).[178] When Theaetetus wonders whether this point-by-point replication is not the goal that all artists set themselves, the Stranger reminds him of those who "sculpt or draw *megala erga*. If they reproduced the true proportions of their beautiful subjects, you see, the upper parts would appear smaller than they ought, and the lower parts would appear larger, because of our seeing the upper parts from farther away and the lower parts from closer" (235e–236a). The result is that the craftsmen opt for the proportions that seem beautiful, and substitute for a genuine *summetria* one calculated to produce an appearance of beauty

---

[176] As noted by Rosen (1983: 171).

[177] Vernant (1991: 179) observes of the term *eikōn* here that it "has a technical sense in the fourth century and designates the representational image in its materiality (e.g., a statue)."

[178] An account similar to those in *Cra.* 434a and *Laws* 668d–e.

in the eye of the beholder.[179] The only issue remaining is what to call "something that appears to be like a beautiful thing, but only because it is seen from a viewpoint that is not beautiful, and would seem unlike the thing it claims to be like if you came to be able to see such large things adequately" (236b).[180] The participants in the exchange agree that this particular enterprise should be styled a *phantastikē technē* since it involves the creation of a *phantasma*, illusionary appearance (236c).

But this portion of the dialogue does more than equate the powers of painters and sculptors with those of the sophist and confirm their parallel abilities to engage in the fabrication of illusions that only ape the truth. It additionally allows Plato to address a far more fundamental question, one that will dominate the remainder of the dialogue. The reason behind the division of *eidōla* into *eikones*, which are genuinely like what they are copies of, and *phantasmata*, which are not, becomes evident in the Stranger's summation at 236d–e.

> Really, my young friend, we are engaged in a very difficult investigation. This appearing, and this seeming but not being, and this saying things but not true things — all these issues are full of confusion, just as they always have been previously and are now. It's extremely hard, Theaetetus, to say what form of speech we should use to say that there really is such a thing as false saying or believing, and moreover to declare this without being caught in a verbal conflict.

The picture or statue that appears to be what it is not, and the statement that says something that is not true, are plagued with the same difficulty: how can we represent, or talk about, that which is not with-

---

[179] As Keuls (1978: 111–12) points out, nothing of such colossal pieces survives; nonetheless, she argues that monuments from the second half of the fifth century, particularly the sculpted portions of the Parthenon, do incorporate such visual adjustments. For an earlier discussion, see Schuhl 1952: 29–30, 74–77; note, too, Gombrich 1961: 191–93. Diodorus of Siculus may have the same practices in mind when, probably drawing from the third-century Hecataeus of Abdera, he observes that Egyptian statue-makers differ from those in Greece in choosing not to endow their images with the proportions that the eye conveys to us: "For with them the symmetrical proportions are not fixed according to the appearance that they present to the artist's eye, as is done among the Greeks" (1.98.5–9). Cf. Vitruvius 3.5.9 and the fragment, discussed in Pollitt 1974: 134, attached to the manuscripts of Damianus (*Optica*, ed. Schöne, pp. 28ff.) in the sixteenth century, and sometimes attributed to the late Hellenistic (?) Heron of Alexander, sometimes to Gremios (whose date is also uncertain, but who seems to have been a contemporary of Posidonius; see Schuhl 1952: 74–77). This describes how architects alter the *rhuthmoi* or forms in their buildings through devices that the author styles *alexēmata* ("defenses") against "the deceit of sight."

[180] On this beautiful vantage point, see pp. 74–75.

out incurring the charge of having depicted, or referred to, nothing at all? "This form of speech of ours supposes the hazardous assumption that that which is not is." The very confusion in which fifth-century sophists took delight, and which constituted the very excellence of their rhetorical *tours de force*, creates an impossible situation from the perspective of the philosopher wedded to the separability of appearance from truth. The speakers must cut through the seeming impasse, and the statue that proves the existence of false belief will emerge as a stepping stone toward the development of clear distinctions that prevent the willing and unwilling surrender to illusion.

Likeness and Difference

I left the Eleatic Stranger at the point where he faced the challenge of dissolving the equation between false stating and "stating that which is not." He will undertake the enterprise in two steps, first arguing that "that which is not" is an intelligible, non-self-contradictory notion, and then building on this foundation to demonstrate how we might go about stating "that which is not." It is the first part of the argument that concerns me here, since it again draws on the *eidōla* and *eikones* that have featured in the debate, and calls into play a quality that archaic as well as classical sources consistently assign to sculpted images: statues belong simultaneously to two realms, offering a site where similitude and difference coincide; the likeness that the image involves always means similar in some respects, and not in others.[181]

The stratagem pursued by the Stranger requires the demonstration that "that which is not" and "that which is" are not necessarily contraries, and that being and nonbeing do not stand to one another in a relation of mutual exclusiveness (257b, 258a–b). In the example "change is not rest," change involves both likeness and difference (256a–b):

> We have to agree, and that wholeheartedly, that change is the same and not the same. When we say it's the same and not the same, we aren't speaking in the same way. When we say it's the same, that's because it shares in the same in relation to itself. But when we say it's not the same, that's because of its association with the different. Because of its association with the different, change is distanced from the same, and so becomes not it but different. So that it might rightly be said that it's not the same.

According to this argument, a thing "is" by virtue of partaking or being; and that same thing "is not" by being different from, and so "not

[181] See Mitchell 1986: 33.

being," something else.[182] Likeness and difference, being and not-being can coexist because of the Stranger's deployment of "not"; the term does not signal the contrary of the word that follows it, but indicates difference from it (255e–257e).

The *eidōla* and *eikones* already introduced by the Stranger can be read as a preamble to or anticipation of this argument; earlier he defined these representations as phenomena that simultaneously involved likeness and difference, and that participated at once in being and non-being. The critical moment occurs at 239d when, after a discussion of whether we can talk about that which in no way is, and the Stranger's demonstration that we do assign properties to that which is not, the copy-making sophist pops up once again and challenges his accusers to make good their charge that he traffics in false beliefs or *eidōla*; how would they define these *eidōla* in which they say he deals without imputing being to them, and so acknowledging that they exist? Theaetetus takes up the challenge (240a–c):[183]

ΘΕΑΙ: Τί δῆτα, ὦ ξένε, εἴδωλον ἂν φαῖμεν εἶναι πλήν γε τὸ πρὸς τἀληθινὸν ἀφωμοιωμένον ἕτερον τοιοῦτον;
ΞΕ: Ἕτερον δὲ λέγεις τοιοῦτον ἀληθινόν, ἢ ἐπὶ τίνι τὸ τοιοῦτον εἶπες;
ΘΕΑΙ: Οὐδαμῶς ἀληθινόν γε, ἀλλ᾽ ἐοικὸς μέν.
ΞΕ: Ἆρα τὸ ἀληθινὸν ὄντως ὂν λέγων;
ΘΕΑΙ: Οὕτως.
ΞΕ: Τί δέ; τὸ μὴ ἀληθινὸν ἆρ᾽ ἐναντίον ἀληθοῦς;
ΘΕΑΙ: Τί μήν;
ΞΕ: Οὐκ ὄντως [οὐκ] ὂν ἄρα λέγεις τὸ ἐοικός, εἴπερ αὐτό γε μὴ ἀληθινὸν ἐρεῖς.
ΘΕΑΙ: Ἀλλ᾽ ἔστι γε μήν πως.
ΞΕ: Οὔκουν ἀληθῶς γε, φής.
ΘΕΑΙ: Οὐ γὰρ οὖν· πλήν γ᾽ εἰκὼν ὄντως.
ΞΕ: Οὐκ ὂν ἄρα [οὐκ] ὄντως ἔστιν ὄντως ἣν λέγομεν εἰκόνα;

Th.: What in the world would we say an *eidōlon* is, stranger, except another such that is made like the true thing?
St.: Do you mean by another such thing a true thing? What do you mean by this such?
Th.: Not that it is true by any means, but that it resembles the true thing.
St.: Meaning by true, really being?
Th.: Exactly.
St.: And by the not true, meaning the opposite of the true?

[182] Here I draw on the paraphrase of the argument in White 1993: xxi.
[183] For particularly helpful discussions of the exchange, Rosen 1983: 191ff.; Vernant 1991: 166–68.

Тн.: Of course.

Sт.: So you are saying that that which is like is not really that which is, if you speak of it as not true.

Тн.: But it is, in a way.

Sт.: But not truly, you mean.

Тн.: Except that it really is a likeness.

Sт.: So it's not really what is, but it really is what we call a likeness:.

In this quasi-definition, *alēthinon*, "true," in the sense of "genuine," refers to the original. The image, "another such," lacks this truth or genuineness. Despite the Stranger's play on the riddling relation between true and really being, and between *on* and *einai*, Theaetetus does not allow himself to be caught in these verbal traps. For all its lack of truth, an image, he asserts, is not nothing at all: *qua* image it has an ontological status and truly is an image. A shift in vocabulary signals his affirmation of the reality of the phenomenon described as he substitutes the term *eikōn* for the *eidōlon* used at the start of his attempted definition.[184] Its being is "truly" to be an image, and to be an image is to be and not to be the original, in the same respect. The conclusion that the Stranger draws from the exchange anticipates what he will declare again at 241d, that "that which is not" must be woven together with "that which is." The image "is" insofar as it is a likeness, but it "is not" insofar as it has no other "existence" than being similar to the model; according to this account, it participates in both likeness and difference, being and nonbeing.

The debate initiated by the Stranger draws on the terms *eidōla* or *eikones* for a host of different phenomena, applying them to such disparate objects as verbal arguments, images reflected in mirrors and bodies of water, and outsized artifacts fashioned by painters and sculptors (239d–e). So while it would be wrong to see anything more than a passing glance toward statues here, a second dialogue appeals to the sculpted image in more exclusive fashion and affirms the object's handiness for exploring issues of likeness and difference, and the paradoxical combination of the two. Socrates introduces the *eikōn* in the *Cratylus* when he, like the Stranger in the *Sophist*, finds himself caught up in a discussion concerning the possibility of false statements. At this point in the argument, Cratylus has refused to admit that we can misstate; a man who has expressed a notion that most people would call incorrect has simply made a noise and nothing more (430a). Socrates counters his assertion by forcing Cratylus to admit that a name and a nominee are two different things, and by demonstrating that we could put the wrong

---

[184] As noted by Rosen (1983: 191); see Saïd 1987 for a detailed exploration of the difference between the two terms.

name to something (as when Cratylus is called Hermogenes) just as we could allot someone the wrong picture (430e–431a). Cratylus tries to reinforce his weakened position by claiming that the picture analogy does not work for names; if you add, subtract, or otherwise misplace one letter, you have not merely miswritten the name, you simply have not written it at all (431e–432a). Socrates concedes that the proposition would be correct if numbers were at stake: when we add or subtract something to the number ten, it necessarily stops being ten, and becomes another number in its place. But different laws prevail in the matter of "anything that is qualitative or represented by an image" (*tou de poiou tinos kai sumpasēs eikonos*). And as in the *Sophist*, the speaker goes on to give a definition of that *eikōn* which depends on its simultaneous possession of likeness and difference: to qualify as an image, the copy "must not by any means reproduce all the qualities of that which it images" (*oude to parapan deēi panta apodounai hoion estin hōi eikazei ei mellei eikōn einai*, 432b).

As yet Socrates has not specified precisely what kind of *eikōn* he has in mind. But he immediately goes on to back up his assertion by citing an artistic representation, and what eventually must emerge, I think, as a figure in the round.

ἆρ᾽ ἂν δύο πράγματα εἴη τοιάδε, οἷον Κρατύλος καὶ Κρατύλου εἰκών, εἴ τις θεῶν μὴ μόνον τὸ σὸν χρῶμα καὶ σχῆμα ἀπεικάσειεν ὥσπερ οἱ ζωγράφοι, ἀλλὰ καὶ τὰ ἐντὸς πάντα τοιαῦτα ποιήσειεν οἷάπερ τὰ σά, καὶ μαλακότητας καὶ θερμότητας τὰς αὐτὰς ἀποδοίη, καὶ κίνησιν καὶ ψυχὴν καὶ φρόνησιν οἷάπερ ἡ παρὰ σοὶ ἐνθείη αὐτοῖς, καὶ ἑνὶ λόγῳ πάντα ἅπερ σὺ ἔχεις, τοιαῦτα ἕτερα καταστήσειεν πλησίον σου; πότερον Κρατύλος ἂν καὶ εἰκὼν Κρατύλου τότ᾽ εἴη τὸ τοιοῦτον, ἢ δύο Κρατύλοι; (432b–c)

If there were two things, such as Cratylus and an *eikōn* of Cratylus, if someone of the gods not only were to make it with regard to your color and shape, just as painters do, but also were to make all the internal qualities like yours, and were to grant the same gentleness and warmth, and were to place inside the movement and *psuchē* and thought such as you have, and in a word everything that you possess, and were to stand this other thing close to you, would there then be Cratylus and an *eikōn* of Cratylus, or two Cratyluses?

Cratylus's admission that we would seem to confront two of himself allows his interlocutor to carry his point, that an image identical to its model no longer counts as an image at all: "You see that it is necessary to seek some other [principle of] correctness of images . . . and that it's not necessary, if you should take something away or add something, for it no longer to be an *eikōn*" (432c). A closer look at the object devised by Socrates to illustrate his claim reveals a necessary shift in paradigm midway through the account. The *eikōn* of Cratylus begins firmly in the realm of painting, as the speaker first endows the representation with the two cardinal properties of pictures, color and shape, and explicitly evokes mortal *zōgraphoi* as analogues for his divine craftsmen. But when the story turns to the replication of the internal properties of Cratylus, *ta entos*, then Socrates must look to a different scenario. Just as Hephaistos animates his automata by endowing them with motion, thought, and soul, and inserts the quickening elements of speech and mind into Pandora,[185] so the gods of Socrates' conceit gradually bring the statue image to life, filling the internal cavity with the requisite vivifying qualities[186] and producing an autonomous being independent of the original.

In passing from the painting to the statue, the speaker declares his willingness to engage with the most serious challenge to the position he has staked out. While Socrates is careful to name only the gods as the creators of images that so exactly reproduce both the external and internal properties of an individual that they become live doubles rather than fashioned objects, his audience might think of the statues produced by fifth- and fourth-century artists, of their ability to convey the impression of a living figure moving in time and space, whose *ēthos* and soul seem visible on the surface of the body. If the simulacrum is to be restricted to its proper sphere and prevented from generating false visualizations, statements, and beliefs, then the philosopher must define the precise area in which the works of artists and statue-makers stand distinct from their archetypes. The solution proposed in both dialogues is to underscore the blend of likeness and difference that lies at the heart of the image. The Stranger of the *Sophist* establishes a set of conditions that an *eikōn* must satisfy to qualify for the name: if thing A is to be an *eikōn* of thing X, then it must be similar to X; it must not be of the same sort as X; and it can have no other "existence" than being similar to X.[187] In the *Cratylus* the definition is a looser but related one: every image, to be an image, must fail to resemble the original in some respects. As Socrates concludes at 432d, "Don't you see how far images are from having the same properties as the things of which they are images?"

---

[185] Note the same verb *entithēmi* used both by Plato and by Hesiod at *Op.* 67 and 79–80.
[186] For more on filling the interior of a statue, see chapter 2.
[187] As Sörbom (1966: 154) paraphrases the last of these conditions, "If we took away all similarities to men from a sculpture representing a man it would cease to exist except as an amorphous piece of stone." Note, too, Gosling 1973: 211–12.

Names and Things

The *eikōn* in the *Cratylus* also has its place within a broader argument, and it touches on Plato's more central concern throughout the text: the question of nomination, and the relationship of names to the phenomena they describe. In using a statue to illuminate the problem, Socrates places himself, whether deliberately or not, within a long tradition that links images and names in a variety of ways. In Hesiod's Pandora narrative, Hermes assigns a title to the now completed and animated artifact: "And he named this woman Pandora" (*WD* 80–81). But when the god goes on to explain his choice, he supplies a surprising etymology (81–82), inverting an active to a passive construction and altering the meaning of a term as it is found in conjunction with other deities.[188] In Hermes' formulation, Pandora signifies not the giver, but either the one to whom the gods have given all gifts or, in an ambiguity already noted in the scholia, and wholly in character with Hermes as master of enigmatic speech, the one given as a gift. Whichever reading we prefer, the emphasis has shifted from the woman as a bestower to one who receives, and who is vessel for the attributes she hosts. This name, which seems to mean one thing but turns out to mean something else, neatly accords with the character of its bearer. The title "Pandora" can no more be dismissed as a false representation than the manufactured figure itself; rather, it expresses a new order in which giving comes only on condition of something being given, and in which both appearance and inner properties are acquired from without.

A different paradox, but one that also bears very directly on the links between names and their carriers, turns about the figures of the protagonist and her manufactured double in Euripides' *Helen*. Perplexed by the words of the old woman at the door, who has identified the resident of the palace as the daughter of Zeus, of the family of Tyndareos, and native to Sparta, Menelaus tries to resolve the puzzle of the apparent existence of two Helens by attributing exclusive properties to the name that an individual person or place carries (490–93). But he soon gives up the attempt and admits that single names may describe multiple nominata: "I do not know what to make of it. There are many things, as is likely, in all the world having the same name, city to city and woman to woman" (496–99). But for Helen, the problem cannot be so simply dismissed, particularly when the two instances of her name carry antithetical versions of her conduct. Instead, she seeks constantly to separate herself from the obloquy that clings to her *onoma*, and discovers

---

[188] When used of Anesidora, the fertility goddess iconographically cognate with Pandora, the title means "giver of gifts." On this, see West 1978: ad 81; and Faraone 1992: 102.

that freedom from the misrepresentation adhering to "Helen" can only come with a divorce from the actions assigned to the cloud double (e.g., 66, 198, 250, 927–32, 1100). In a final act of exoneration at the ending of the drama, the Dioskouroi will actually invest her name with a new significance (1674–75).[189]

The revelatory quality of names and the question of their exclusive bond with the phenomena to which they belong are precisely the matters that Socrates sets out to test. Probing Cratylus's point of view and seeking a secure basis for the connection between names and things, he begins by making his interlocutor agree that name and named are separate elements, and that the former is an imitation of the latter (430a–b). But as Socrates has already established, mimeticism in names involves more than mere imitation of the outer aspect of a nominandum. By contrast with *mimēsis* in music and art, which replicates only the sound or figure and color of the original,[190] the imitation informing names must reproduce not just externals, but the essence or *ousia* of a thing (423c–e).[191] The divine *nomothetēs*, Socrates explained, does this by fixing his eyes on the form name as his guide and fashioning the word accordingly (389d). The two Cratyluses argument, which most obviously forces Cratylus to admit that likenesses are by their very nature imperfect, and so to reject a belief in mimetic names, exposes the problem implicit in this earlier distinction. The gods who model the *eikōn* of Cratylus effectively imitate not just his visible, contingent qualities, but his internal properties as well, producing a perfect image equivalent to the perfect name. But, as the illustration makes clear, this replica inevitably generates a hopeless confusion when two Cratyluses stand in the place of one genuine subject and a mere image of the man. Now the second reason for Socrates' move from the graphic to the plastic arts stands clear: to clarify his contention, he needs an example that allows for more than the simple reproduction of surface appearance, and that admits, precisely in the manner of the names in which Cratylus believes, the replication of the inner essence of its subject.

The paradox that the two Cratyluses argument exposes then lays the ground for Socrates' own very different account of the *mimēsis* that determines names, one that casts them neither as identical to their nominata, nor as second-rate copies. In his refutation of what Timothy Bax-

---

[189] Cf. the etymological plays at Aesch. *Ag.* 681–90.
[190] In the example offered by Baxter (1992: 166), "baa-baa" is not a sheep's proper name.
[191] The argument returns, somewhat altered, at 434a, where Cratylus is forced to agree that likeness must be the basis for the representation of names by things. Socrates then returns to the analogy of pictorial representations, describing first the *mimēsis* that graphic arts involve, and then that which exists in naming. Through the colors that nature has placed at its disposal, painting can imitate the *chrōmata* found in natural objects.

ter styles the "infallibalist" view[192] — where any change in the picture or image that is the name means that the nominatum has changed, or that one has said nothing at all — he asserts that names may be more or less correct as long as they reveal the *tupos* or outline of the thing signified (432e).[193] This redefinition allows names to possess varying degrees of similarity to their nominata, while retaining some general relationship to the object they describe. Perhaps the expression that Socrates chooses to formulate his notion glances back to the paradigmatic statue of Cratylus: now the *eikōn* has been emptied of its interior and only exists as the hollow mold or schematic tracing. Far from transposing the *ousia* or *ta entos*, the name gives no more than a general impression, shape, or casement.

The statue provides a stumbling block for Cratylus's argument for reasons similar to those that made it so handy in the demonstration of the properties of likeness and difference characteristic of the *eidōla* and *eikones* in which the sophist dealt. The link between names and things, like that between images and originals, depends on the ability of the signifier to supply a visible and/or audible display of the subject of the representation. Ideally a name provides a *dēlōma* (423b), an illustration of the *ousia* of the nominatum, while a statue visualizes the inner *phusis* and ethical disposition of the individual as well as his external qualities. But in both instances the relationship between the model and its replica can only go so far, and names and *eikones* both must include some element of difference from the objects they depict; otherwise they would cease to be copies and would become doubles instead. Better a name that gives only a partial representation of a phenomenon than two Cratyluses who cannot be told apart.

If the introduction of the *eikōn* allows Socrates to advance the argument on these several fronts, it also takes him back to a more particular problem posed at the very start of the debate. There the speakers began by examining proper names for their applicability to the people so described. Hermogenes provided the test case: should Hermogenes be called Hermogenes, a name that suggests a family connection with Hermes, when he has had such poor luck where money is concerned (384c)? Socrates returns to the matter again at 429c, where he and Cratylus define more exactly the area where names and individuals should ideally correspond. Now Cratylus declares that the name Hermogenes fails as a picture of Hermogenes' nature, and so cannot rightly be his name; since the name a person carries must be a perfect representation

---

[192] Baxter 1992: 166.
[193] *Tupos* itself is a term that may include many different sets of relations between the original and the copy. For its range of meanings, see Pollitt 1974: 272–93.

or "portrait likeness" of its subject, appropriate to him and no one else, only someone with the appropriate *phusis* should be called Hermogenes.[194] But the two Cratyluses argument reveals the problems inherent in this proposition: the *eikōn* that exactly reproduces the internal nature of the original would rightly qualify for the same name, and, in place of a Hermogenes wrongly named, Socrates has now raised the equally alarming specter of two Cratyluses correctly named. Euripides' *Helen* had already explored the consequences of that.

Beyond the Senses

The problems that Plato attaches to the statue, whether it appears under the name of an *eikōn* or an *eidōlon*, resist easy solution and call Socrates' and his interlocutors' best powers of dialectic into play. Alongside its disorienting combination of likeness and difference, and its potential to exhibit internal essence as well as surface appearance, the object poses a further threat: the sculptor's use of artifice determines the statue's very ability to create an appearance of the truth. Earlier I noted how the Eleatic Stranger of the *Sophist* charges the makers of *megala erga* (painters and sculptors both) with abandoning the genuine beauty that resides in the correct replication of proportion, and with preferring a seeming beauty more calculated to delight and persuade their viewers' eyes. The two subcategories into which the speaker then separates the "*eidōla*-making *technē*" expose the dangers these *phantasmata* hold out. Because they correct a natural defect in human perception, they possess a verisimilitude, a seeming "truth" that surpasses that of the *eikones* placed in the other camp. As for the honest artist who produces images that preserve the genuine proportions of things, he now finds himself in the unenviable position of confronting his audience with copies that do not appear like the original (given the laws of perception) and so look not only less beautiful, but also less "true."[195]

There is only one way out of the seeming impasse that Plato has deliberately contrived. In response to those who would assert that our perception of the beautiful necessarily involves the distortions imposed by our sense of sight, the Stranger has introduced the notion that beauty

---

[194] When Socrates goes on to raise the hypothetical case of mistaken identity, Cratylus claims that the person addressing him wrongly would be merely uttering hot air (430a). The picture example explores the problem of false statement further as Socrates draws a partial analogy between presenting a picture to someone and saying this is your picture, and presenting a name and saying this is your name. On this, see Baxter 1992: 35, with the relevant bibliography.

[195] For discussion, Rosen 1983: 172.

resides in an entirely different place.[196] When he asks Theaetetus what name should be given to these seemingly fair representations, the *phantasmata*, he notes that their beauty depends on their being seen "from a viewpoint that is not beautiful" (*Soph.* 236b). This troublesome vantage point determines our misapprehension of the truth value of the sculpted artifacts: were we able to see large things properly, they would no longer seem like the objects that they claim to be. The same must hold true for the *eikones* produced by the more scrupulous craftsman; viewed without the deformations introduced by the eye, they would be accounted more, and not less, like the models they reproduced, and would consequently possess all the beauty that their inferior kin seem to monopolize. It is not that beauty and truth inevitably diverge, or that more accurate *mimēsis* necessarily generates works both less lovely and apparently less "real," but that our visual powers prove unable to assess the veracity of what we see. Without explicitly alluding to the Forms at this point in the dialogue, the Stranger's reference to a "beautiful vantage point" presupposes a mode of viewing that operates independent of the organs of sense.

Plato returns on many other occasions to the problem of the misconstruction of reality that our sense of sight imposes, and offers an antidote to its distorting powers. At *Resp.* 602c–d Socrates observes that the process of viewing and listening to *mimēmata* depends on a faculty or *dunamis* of the soul. When we look at phenomena, we may either perceive them and believe what our senses report (as do the residents of the cave confronted with "men passing along the wall carrying all sorts of vessels and statues and figures of animals made of wood and stone and various materials" at *Resp.* 514c), or we may measure them and acquire a firmer and more "correct" knowledge about what we see. Only the arts of "measuring and numbering and weighing" are sufficient to counteract the various tricks that the eyes otherwise play upon the unwary viewer.[197] In the *Philebus*, Socrates establishes a direct link between the results of this measurement and numbering and our apprehension not only of the true but also of the beautiful, and joins this apprehension to the delight we take in things. In his attempt to distinguish between apparent and true pleasures, he notes that among the latter he would classify "those related to colors . . . or to shapes" (51b–c), and then goes on to clarify what he has in mind:

---

[196] Cf. Rouveret 1989: 30.
[197] See Sörbom 1966: 140–41 for discussion. Note the scene in Aristophanes' *Frogs* where mathematical tools and the arts of weighing and measuring are used for the assessment of literary artifacts, as though these supply a more accurate means of evaluation.

> By beauty of shape I don't in this instance mean what most people would understand by it—I am not thinking of animals or certain pictures, but, as the thesis goes, a straight line or a circle and resultant planes and solids produced on a lathe or with ruler and square. . . . On my view these things are not, as other things are, beautiful in a relative way (*pros to kala*),[198] but are always beautiful in themselves.[199]

Plato's location of beauty not in the enhancement or idealization of the visible form, but in the geometric proportions that measurement alone reveals, determines the aesthetic preferences shared by different speakers in the dialogues. Repeatedly individuals approve only those visual artifacts informed by a true understanding of the relations between the parts of the object, of the *summetria* that dictates the arrangement of its elements. In his discussion of how works of art should be judged, the Athenian Stranger of the *Laws* sets out a series of conditions (668d–e). The competent critic should make an assessment based on whether the piece "preserves the proper dimensions and positions that each of the bodily parts possesses, and has caught their number and the proper order in which one is placed next to another, and their colors and shapes as well—or whether all these things are fashioned in a confused manner." His prescriptions not only hark back to the emphasis on correct relations and proportions found in Polykleitos's Canon, but more immediately recall the terms used by the Eleatic Stranger when describing the art of likeness-making: this occurs "whenever someone produces an imitation by keeping to the proportions of length, breadth, and depth of his model, and also by keeping to the appropriate colors in each of its parts" (*Soph.* 235d–e).[200]

These several references to "good" works of art, to a form of representation that involves no deliberate or unwitting distortion of the original, opens up the possibility that some pieces might avoid the stigma that Socrates ascribes to artistic *mimēsis* elsewhere.[201] If the painter or

---

[198] See Gosling 1975: ad loc., on the translation of the expression.

[199] True beauty (as well as *aretē*), a later portion of the dialogue concludes, should be sought on the grounds of measurement and *summetria* (64e). Cf. *Phlb.* 51c–d and *Resp.* 510b.

[200] The larger point of the argument in the *Laws* is to show that the person who does not know the subject matter cannot possibly know whether the artistic representation is accurate or not; only by virtue of a thorough acquaintance with the subject can he assess whether the mimetic presentation is correct. However, it is striking that this knowledge does not help the judge in gauging whether the representation is *kalos* (668e–669a); for this he must additionally have moral discrimination.

[201] Most notoriously in *Resp.* 596–98; cf. 601b. For discussions of the thesis that Plato's philosophy could accommodate works of art that do reflect the Forms, M. W. Bundy 1927; Sörbom 1966: 133–38; Pollitt 1974: 47; Vernant 1991: 169 n. 6.

sculptor could preserve all the correct dimensions, measurements, and colors of the original, then might his products not be thought to model themselves after the unchanging, everlasting Forms and so to visualize the genuine phenomena that lie beyond the sensible world? A passage in the *Timaeus* (28a–b) explicitly portrays the demiurge working in the manner of an artist, fixing his eyes on "that which is always the same" so as to fashion his cosmos according to this eternal and unchanging paradigm. But the artist of this tale is no mere copyist: he does not reproduce the appearance of an essence that by definition has no visible, tangible shape, but transposes the deeper attributes that only the intellect can apprehend.[202] Neither the activity of this divine demiurge nor the Eleatic Stranger's distinction between the two forms of mimeticism[203] contradicts the more general assertion of the *Republic* where the painter's bed of 598b–c, whether it exactly reproduces the proportions of the craftsman's bed or whether it is intended to create an illusory account, never rises above its status as an imitation of the visible bed that the carpenter fashions. It can imitate neither the idea nor the essence of the original.[204]

In addressing artistic representations as no more than aesthetic objects frequently marked by *apatē*, Plato has deliberately robbed images of half of their significance: granting no place to their powers of replacement and substitution, he denies the metonymic link between the statue and its subject, and treats any "reality" that the work projects as a mere illusion, liable to disappear on closer inspection. Divorced from the contexts, whether funerary, votive, cultic, honorary, magical, or the rest, that still framed most images,[205] the artifacts imagined in his texts aim to do no more than to replicate (imperfectly) the visible world. But where the philosopher does stand very much heir to the tradition extending from archaic to classical times is in the types of question that he uses both painted and plastic images to puzzle out, and in his recognition of the threats that they pose to the strict divisions that he would

---

[202] The demiurge is comparable not to the artist of the *Republic*'s account, but more to the carpenter who fabricates his bed with his "eyes fixed on the *idea*" of his work (596b).

[203] Note that the Stranger goes on to offer at 240a–b a generalized negative definition of all *eidōla*, whether *eikones* or *phantasmata*.

[204] Cf. Vernant 1991: 169.

[205] In a passing reference to cult statues in the *Laws*, the Athenian Stranger signals the inanimate character that belongs even to divine idols and gives them a distinctly oblique connection to the reality that dwells elsewhere ("Some of the gods whom we honor we see clearly, but of others we set up statues as images, and we believe that when we worship them, lifeless [*apsuchous*] though they be, the living gods feel great goodwill toward us and gratitude," 931a).

maintain: challenging attempts to differentiate between the seeming and the real, the original and the secondary account, works of art force both Socrates and other participants in the dialogues to confront the capacity of manufactured objects to generate a new or different reality that still retains some intimate relation to the archetype.

That Plato's discussions echo much earlier concerns, a glance back to the Pandora image fashioned in the Hesiodic texts affirms. Already present in the poet's account in the *Theogony* are the two facets of the statue, its eiconic and eidolic sides, and its power to bring into being something quite different from what existed before. In his introduction to the episode, Hesiod glosses Zeus's intention in ordering up the figure — "He fashioned an evil for man in place of (*anti*) fire" (570) — and rounds out the scene of manufacture with a repetition of the same construction, this time characterizing Pandora as a *kalon kakon* fabricated "in place of a good" (585). But even as the poet presents the new-made gift as a substitute or replacement figure, one that implicitly stands in metonymic relation to the fire now withdrawn (cf. WD 705, 586–89), he signals its role as an imperfect replica, one that aims to replicate an antecedent model: the modeled clay should be "like to a modest maiden" (572). If, as noted earlier, that archetype is one that only Pandora's own advent can initiate, it is not because Hesiod's logic has failed him here. Instead, he has alerted his audience to the paradox that neither he nor later sources can fully resolve, that of objects able, by virtue of their powers simultaneously to imitate and replace, to assume a life and autonomy of their own.

CHAPTER TWO

Inside and Out

IN A FAMILIAR fragment, Heraclitus ridicules those who "pray to *agalmata* as if they were chattering with houses, not recognizing what gods or even heroes are like" (B5 DK). The depiction of an individual talking with a house exactly pinpoints the matter at issue: was there someone inside, a sentient presence within the inanimate object? Heraclitus's remark sharply indicates a negative response; using his characteristic term for correct philosophical insight, *gignōskō*,[1] the speaker accuses devotees of mistaking the true nature of gods and heroes, of misdirecting their prayers and gossiping with mere empty shells. But for all his critical tone, the philosopher has succinctly expressed the way in which Greeks of his and other ages commonly imagined the relationship between the god (or hero) and his visual representation, and has acknowledged the concept underpinning the efficacy ascribed to images venerated in cult: the statue acts as a vessel, a potential or actual container for the numinous power that could take up residence inside. This belief, I propose, informed modes of portraying and displaying the immortals in plastic form, and shaped the character of the ritual practices surrounding idols.

From this notion of the image as a two-leveled vessel, a second question follows naturally on: What precise links might exist between the container and the contained? Does the surface of the statue stand in tension with the imperceptible contents within, or can it actually exhibit the indwelling force through its visible appearance? Again, the schemas that statue-makers use to figure divinity explore these several possibilities in turn and, evolving over the course of the archaic and classical ages, match other contemporary efforts to define the nature of the gods and to determine how men might conceptualize and interact with their largely unseen presences.

But in the hands of poets, dramatists, and philosophers, the riddling relations between form and content characteristic of so many cult idols frequently provide a point of entry into a much more earthbound question. Whether they appear in the course of an anecdote, myth, simile, or metaphor, statues repeatedly articulate the problem of how closely façade and interior, surface and depths cohere. Not just the nature of the

[1] As noted by Kahn (1979: 266).

gods, but that of fellow men and women can be at issue here. Like the composite image, the human body exists as a vessel, receiver and emitter both, which comes equipped with external surfaces and internal spaces. From the archaic period on, texts appeal to statues by way of signaling the potential split between an individual's appearance, form, and activity and the thoughts, feelings, drives, and desires that reside within; correctly construing the proximity or divergence between inside and out, as Heraclitus's remark already suggests, proves the cardinal challenge that we, both as worshipers of the gods and as participants in human relations, must regularly confront.

REPRESENTING DIVINITY

The Aniconic Image: Container and Concealer

Fundamental to the Greek view of divinity is the reluctance of gods and goddesses to show themselves directly to the eyes of men. Only immortals may look upon one another face-to-face, while those denied access to celestial realms are restricted to more oblique and mediated encounters with the gods.[2] Olympians adopt all manner of incognitos for their appearances before Homeric heroes, sometimes cloaking themselves in a fog, sometimes assuming the likeness of a mortal familiar to the character whom they visit, sometimes transforming themselves into the birds that descend effortlessly from their lofty perches.[3] Odysseus, one of the few heroes who succeeds in making his tutelary goddess reveal herself, knows that he stands as exception to the common rule: "It is difficult for a mortal encountering you to recognize you, goddess," he remarks to Athena, "for you are able to liken yourself to everything" (*Od.* 13.312–13). The poets of the *Homeric Hymns* attribute much the same behavior to the divine subjects of their songs, introducing Dionysus in the guise of a beautiful young man, and describing how Aphrodite takes on the *megethos* and *eidos* of a maiden for her seduction of Anchises, and only resumes her awesome divine demeanor after the consummation of the affair.[4] The blindness, paralysis, or unconsciousness that seizes those to whom the gods do display themselves (even fleetingly) in full majesty provides one rationale for disguise: such is the brilliance and power of divinities that mortals are incapable of sustaining their

[2] Vernant 1991: 43–45, 142. Numerous myths — those of Teiresias and Aktaion to name but two — detail the often fatal consequences of direct encounters.
[3] For a detailed account, see Rose 1956.
[4] *Hymn. Hom. Bacch.* 3, *Hymn. Hom. Ven.* 82. Cf. *Hymn. Hom. Cer.* 275–80. I return to these passages later in the chapter.

gaze[5] and must immediately turn away in reverence and fear if they are to escape the consequences of the encounter.[6] Concealment and containment thus form two dimensions of the single enterprise: in assuming a form or body not his or her own, the god simultaneously masks and contains an untenable force.

The aniconic images so common in Greek cult practice of the archaic and classical periods may supply the tangible counterparts to the visitations imagined in epic song; now the idols' patently unnaturalistic appearance serves as another of the many façades or "fronts" that deities could assume for their encounters with mortals, and match the disguises that the gods of myth and epic take on both to shield men from too-direct exposure and simultaneously to test their ability to discern the identity of the visitant inside the borrowed bodies and clothes. Cult, as I argue later, requires statues that make accessible the immortal presence without directly reproducing it, and the aniconic or semi-iconic idols not only suit the gods' own preferred mode of action, but answer to that need. Examples of these curiously shaped representations are legion.[7] Apollo Karneios adopts the form of a pyramid, and the common Apollo Aguios appears as a conical pillar erected before the doors of houses (fig. 11).[8] Pausanias encounters a Zeus Meilichios in the likeness of a pyramid together with a columnar Artemis (2.9.6), and individuals might worship Hermes through the medium of a heap of stones, or as an upright, barely anthropomorphized herm. Dionysus, the god most notorious for his taste for metamorphosis and distracting disguise, would attend the rituals celebrated on his behalf in the likeness of a phallos, a pillar, a tree trunk, a mask, or a mask-and-pillar image.[9]

For all the assertions of the sources of the Hellenistic and imperial periods, neither the crude animism nor the minimal craftsmanship of

[5] E.g., *Hymn. Hom. Ven.* 182; *Hymn. Hom. Cer.* 275–78. For much more on the consequences of face-to-face encounters with the gods, see chapter 3. A fundamental paradox exists within the practice of divine disguise; their inability to confront the gods directly notwithstanding, mortals must suffer for their failure to penetrate beneath the surface covering.

[6] Cf. this same, still more strongly expressed prohibition in the Judaic tradition: at Exodus 33.26, when Moses asks to see God's face, God answers, "You cannot see My face, for man may not see Me and live."

[7] Among the many discussions of the aniconic, I have drawn particularly on Gordon 1979, Donohue 1988, Freedberg 1989. Note, too, the material collected in Clerc 1915: chap. 1.

[8] In Megalopolis, Pausanias notes, he appears instead as a rectangle (8.32.9). For other examples of aniconic representations, see Paus. 1.44.2, 3.19.1–2, 7.22.4; cf. Plut. *Mor.* 478a.

[9] For recent accounts of these, see Frontisi-Ducroux 1991; and Sissa and Detienne 1989: 253–64.

bygone ages can explain away these aniconic representations.[10] Communities maintained the cults addressed to their planks, pillars, and stones long after they had developed the skills necessary to depict the gods in fully lifelike fashion, and would house the ancient idols (sometimes called *xoana* in the later authors) alongside properly anthropomorphic renderings of the gods.[11] Nor does the argument that religious conservatism alone guaranteed these images their status and lasting worship hold much weight. The Greeks continued to develop new aniconic forms through the classical period and beyond.[12] Herms and the mask-and-pillar images used in the worship of Dionysus appear in Athens only in the sixth and fifth centuries, and are actual innovations rather than outdated formulas that happen to linger on.[13] From Tegea come stelae that span the fourth to the second century B.C.; some of these columns topped by small pyramid caps carry dedicatory inscriptions, but others bear only the nominative form of the divinity's name, supporting Pausanias's statement that this kind of monument was called by the name of the god whom it represented (7.22.4).[14]

A series of aetiological myths told in postclassical sources, but describing archaic images long venerated in their communities and sometimes preserved in the numismatic evidence of much earlier times, frames several of these aniconic or semi-iconic objects, alerting audiences to the precise significance of the god's mode of self-manifestation. Featuring the discovery or sudden advent of a representation of unfamiliar and unlikely shape, these stories all turn about the divergence between a misleading external appearance and a divine presence within. Callimachus and Pausanias tell parallel tales about curious artifacts that

---

[10] This point is argued at great length in Donohue 1988, and I reproduce some of the examples from her analysis.

[11] For examples of this practice, Stewart 1990: 44 and 137; Romano 1980: 87–89; and discussion later in this chapter; see, too, Paus. 2.19.3.

[12] The sources of the Hellenistic period are the first to record the presence of *baituloi*, animated stones with supernatural powers of prophecy. Arnobius records how in A.D. 204 a small black meteorite venerated as the Great Mother arrived in Rome; the stone was encased in silver and set in the mouth (or face) of an existing image of Cybele: "We all see it today put in the image instead of a face, rough hewn, giving the figure a countenance that is by no means expressed with imitation" (*Adv. nat.* 7.49; cf. Herodian 1.2.1; Appian 7.56). See, too, Damascius (fr. 203 [Zitzen]), who describes the objects as fallen meteors capable of moving, speaking, and predicting the future.

[13] On the origins of the herm, Osborne 1985: 47–51; Frontisi-Ducroux 1991: 213–16; Parker 1996: 80–83. According to Frontisi-Ducroux's reading (222, 224), it was precisely the intimate involvement of Hermes and Dionysus in the daily lives of men that determined the creation of patently nonhuman forms, visible reminders of the gap that remained between gods and mortals for all their familiar intercourse.

[14] Donohue 1988: 224. The ambiguity between an offering to the god and the statue of the god is frequent, and exists within the term *agalma* itself.

emerge from the depths of the sea.[15] In a fragment preserved in the *Diegesis* (fr. 197 [*dieg.* vii and viii] Pfeiffer), the poet describes some fishermen of Ainos who haul up in their nets a block of wood. When they try to split it for firewood, the object refuses to burn, and when they throw their catch back into the waters, it reappears in their nets a second time. The image turns out to be that of Hermes Perpheraios, fashioned by Epeios, the reputed maker of the no less talismanic Trojan horse.[16] Belatedly the Aineans recognize the divine character of the block and set it up in a shrine.[17] Precisely the same motifs structure Pausanias's story of the disembodied head that some Methymnean fishermen retrieve from the sea. Its anomalous appearance suggests "a touch of the divine, but it was outlandish, and unlike the normal features of Greek gods" (10.19.3). The cautious community consults with the Delphic oracle, which immediately identifies the object as the god Dionysus Phallen[18] and directs the Methymneans to institute prayers and sacrifices on the new divinity's behalf.

When Pausanias characterizes the riddling head, he describes it with the adjective *xenēn*, the term that recurs in his account of how a second outlandish statue of Dionysus found its destined home. Many years before the advent of the (image of the) god, the people of Patras received an oracle informing them that a "strange (*xenos*) king would come to the land, bringing with him a strange (*xenikos*) divinity" (7.19.6). When the Greek hero Eurypylos arrives carrying a chest containing an *agalma* of Dionysus hidden inside, the prescient community recognizes the newcomer for the individual announced in oracular form: "Seeing a king whom they had never seen before, they also suspected that there was some god inside the chest" (7.19.9). The box featured here takes on the role played by the aniconic appearance of the images already cited, and still more patently articulates the notion of the deity concealed within an external casing that gives only the most oblique hints of its cargo.[19]

But there is an additional twist to this particular story as Pausanias

---

[15] On the close relationship between *agalmata* (more broadly defined as talismanic objects) and the sea, see Gernet 1981: 80, 91.

[16] Another object whose external appearance belied its internal reality.

[17] Romano (1980: 155–57) suggests that some still-extant coins from Ainos include depictions of the god; so, too, Freedberg 1989: 34, fig. 13, which reproduces a fourth-century drachma with an enthroned cult image of Hermes Perpheraios.

[18] See Frontisi-Ducroux 1991: 193–201 for discussion of the epithet and its variants.

[19] In a second displacement or distancing device practiced by the tale, the question of identification has been transferred from the god to the ambassador who brings him; by solving the puzzle the stranger poses, the people may simultaneously guess the divine character of his baggage and institute the requisite cult on behalf of the hidden Dionysus Aisymnetes.

relates it. No sooner had Eurypylos first opened the chest (which fell to him as part of his spoils from the Trojan War) and spotted its contents than he instantly lost his wits (while continuing to enjoy the occasional moments of lucidity that would permit him to complete his allotted mission).[20] In this incident, which invests the statue with all the powers belonging to the divine original, the chest holding the *agalma* again fills the function that the aniconic artifact assumes, providing a means of blocking and mitigating the full force the god deploys when he manifests himself to mortals. The people of Patras, having deduced the presence of the divinity within the image-in-the-box, do not risk a second exposure; instead, the chest remains enclosed within a temple, and the priest only carries it outside on one night of the god's annual festival (7.20.1).

It comes as no surprise to discover statues of Dionysus attracting these tales. He is the epiphanic god who repeatedly comes as an unknown *xenos* from abroad, and who tests the hospitality of the communities who receive him;[21] he is also notorious for his readiness to conceal himself beneath an unfamiliar guise, whether he presents himself as the youth of the *Homeric Hymn*, the Lydian Stranger of the *Bacchae*, or in theriomorphic form as bull, lion, or snake.[22] By masking their divine essence beneath an outlandish or enigmatic appearance, the cult images of the god merely recapitulate the nature of their original and, like Dionysus in his own visitations, challenge viewers to see what lies below their surface. A scholion to Aristophanes offers one final version of this scenario,[23] describing how the divinity first came to Athens in the form of a statue carried from Eleutherai by an otherwise unknown individual called Pegasos. When the Athenians cold-shoulder the new god and fail to institute a cult on his behalf, he afflicts the male population with a genital disease. While the commentator gives no reason for the city's neglect, a fragment of Euripides' *Antiope* (203 N²) might provide the missing piece. The Eleutherians, a speaker in the drama reveals, worship Dionysus in the form of an aniconic pillar, an ivy-draped *stulos*; and if this was the image brought to Athens, then the city would join the many other communities and individuals who resisted the new deity, deceived by his unfamiliar and outlandish external appearance.

For all the aniconic images described so far, the patent asymmetry

---

[20] The theme of statues capable of maddening their viewers is a frequent one; cf. Paus. 3.16.7–11; *FGrH* 2 F 28. For much more extensive treatment, see chapter 3.

[21] Most obviously in Euripides' *Bacchae*, where the term *xenos* returns repeatedly (233, 247, 353, 441, 453, 642, 1059, 1077). For treatments of the theme of Dionysus as the disguised and epiphanic god, see Massenzio 1969; Henrichs 1993.

[22] Eur. *Bacch*. 1017–19, with note in Dodds 1960: ad loc.

[23] Schol. ad Ar. *Ach*. 243a (cf. Paus. 1.2.5 and 1.38.8); discussion in Parker 1996: 93–94.

between the god and his statue articulates the notion of concealment and indwelling, and demands some act of literal "insight" on the celebrant's part. But a second rationale may inform representations of gods in these curious shapes and guises, one that depends not on unlikeness or a merely convention-based bond, but on an affinity between a particular divinity and the statue-vessel, and the consequently metonymic relationship between the two: aniconic images can promote contacts between men and gods not by resembling the immortals, but by being directly associated with one facet or characteristic of the divinity whom they represent. As Greek poetry and myth illustrate, gods do not restrict themselves to their homes on Mount Olympus or underground, but additionally occupy natural sites, the rivers, rocks, trees, meadows, and groves where men may seek them out. Idols and other objects of veneration reproduce or preserve these natural settings, and visibly demonstrate that to worship the tree, rock, or stone is to gain access to the live force inside.[24] So in Laconia, Pausanias encounters an Artemis Soteria in the form of a myrtle (3.22.12), the plant whose antaphrodisiac qualities echo the goddess's own virginal nature, and several statues, still extant or reproduced on coins or vases, imagine gods and goddesses barely differentiated from the tree trunk used for the modeling, or portray the figures in the act of emerging from the wooden casement: an archaic statuette of Artemis from Ephesos has a trunk growing from the top of its head,[25] while the cult titles carried by Dionysus, Endendros and Dendrites, find matching expression in fifth-century mask-and-pillar images of the god, composed of a trunklike column encircled by ivy leaves and topped with an anthropomorphized mask.[26] A red-figure krater from c. 470 (ARV^2 569, 40) depicts a Dionysus in this mask-and-pillar form and shows the god's head as it emerges from the leafy column that envelopes and hides the remainder of the body.[27] The arrangement exactly captures the sense of a divinity whose own propensity for bursting out of any vessel that seeks to contain him "explains" the generative powers of vegetation, the burgeoning of the vines and fruits that exist beneath his sway.[28]

---

[24] As Romano (1980: 5) notes, fully aniconic images were probably not housed in temples, but remained in outdoor shrines. Only gods who manifested themselves in more humanized form required the protection of an enclosed dwelling.

[25] Meuli 1975: 1051 and plate 48 (together with many other examples); also Freedberg 1989: 73.

[26] On these titles, see Frontisi-Ducroux 1991: 37 and passim; note, too, Maximus of Tyre, who describes how peasants "honor Dionysus, fixing in their garden a wild trunk as a rustic *agalma*" (8.1). Zeus also carries the title *endendros* (Hsch. s.v.).

[27] For a similar depiction, ARV^2 672, 14.

[28] For Dionysus as a force that spills out of any container, Eur. *Bacch.* 107–8, 113–14.

If the sacred aura belonging to a particular location, or mere wonder at the fecundity of nature, lay behind the perceived affinity between a god and a tree, rock, or other site, then an aetiological myth might embroider the association and spell out the fact of habitation: the divinity had been in direct contact with the place, and had even on some occasion dwelt inside. The third-century historian Xanthos the Lydian employs this logic in explicating the very ancient worship of Hermes in the form of a mound of stones. When the god stood trial for his slaying of Argos before his fellow Olympians, the divine jurors cast their voting pebbles at him so that a heap grew at his feet (*FGrH* 765 F 29); effectively concealing the god beneath the cairn they formed (and the lapidation would itself have symbolized a form of punitive burial), the stones retain the trace of the divinity, and so supply a prime means of access to the god himself.[29]

The more congenial the residence, these and other tales suggest, the better the chance of direct contact with the god within, and of an answer to a celebrant's petitions and prayers. But equally efficacious are idols that attract the deity through a different kind of affinity, echoing his indwelling and hidden nature through the fact of their own concealment within the natural objects that numinous powers regularly frequent. An inscription from Magnesia records the discovery of a little image of Dionysus within a plane tree that had fallen to the ground,[30] and local lore explains that Artemis Ortheia also bears the cult title Lygodesma ("willow-bound") because the image was found "in a thicket of willows, and the encircling willow made the image stand upright" (Paus. 3.16.11).[31] Pliny includes a variation on the topos, noting

---

[29] According to a much later story, Eleuthera of Myra actually lived in a cypress tree; when two evil men once wanted to chop down the sacred habitat, the goddess (curiously manifesting herself in the form of her cult image) chased them away from her chosen home. For this, Meuli 1975: 1057–58. The notion of the god's immanence within the object may likewise underpin Pausanias's account of two Corinthian representations of Dionysus crafted from a particular tree. After the dismemberment of Pentheus, he reports, the Pythian priestess commanded the Corinthians to discover the tree that Pentheus climbed in order to spy on the Maenads, and "to worship it equally with the god" (2.2.7). The injunction makes sense if we assume that the wood originally served as a vessel for Dionysiac power, and that the god present in the unworked stock continued to occupy the space when the wood was crafted into the shape of a cult idol.

[30] For the inscription, Michel no. 856.

[31] A figure depicted on Spartan tetradrachms and dated to the late third century B.C. (for which see Romano 1980: 119) may correspond to the statue that the sources describe: a vegetable ornament worn by the goddess on her lower skirt could refer to the *lygos* bush originally encircling her. The myth preserved by Athenaeus (15.672, with Romano 1980: 250ff.) supplies an *aition* for the application of the same epithet to Samian Hera: here the willow branches surrounding the *agalma* of the goddess serve to prevent a second flight after the statue's mysterious disappearance from its temple. But a much simpler affinity

that at the quarries of Paros "there is an extraordinary tradition that once, when the stone breakers split a single block with their wedges, a likeness of Silenus was found inside" (*HN* 36.14).

The installation of images within temples and shrines may have sought to recapitulate the notions expressed in these myths. Just as numinous powers choose to hide themselves, or only to allow a rare glimpse of their epiphanic presences, so the idols that housed the god should properly do the same, conveying something of the divinity's own mode of oblique self-representation and the fleeting quality of his self-display. If the information relayed by Pausanias furnishes an accurate guide to older practices (and the caveat is a large one), then many of the most venerated images were at best only partially exposed. In the temple of Athena Polias, the visitor cannot see the figure of Hermes behind its covering of myrtle boughs (1.27.1) and discovers that a mass of laurel leaves and ivy similarly obscures the lower part of an image of Dionysus Acratophoros, leaving only the face visible to the worshiper (8.39.6).[32] Pausanias has difficulty describing other statues he comes upon because of the many garments surrounding them, hiding the divinities' bodies from view,[33] and in this instance earlier epigraphic evidence can bear him out. By the second quarter of the fourth century, the image of Artemis at Brauron wore no fewer than five garments, and a contemporary record from Samos details the thirteen chitons belonging to Hera.[34] While these clothes were first and foremost votive offerings, they may also be regarded as coverings for the deity, acting much in the manner of the enveloping cloak that so muffles Dionysus in representations on several Lenaea vases that only his head emerges from the opening at the neck.[35] Conveying a sense both of the god's concealment and of his enclosure, they also replicate his only partial or transient self-manifestations; as those who are witness to divine epiphanies know, no sooner are the gods apparent than they are gone from sight.

Over and above the foliage and garments used to envelop or screen the divine image, the very design and furnishings of the temple or shrine, or the restrictions surrounding access to the sacred spot, fostered

---

joining these two divinities with the *lygos* bush may underpin the elaborate anecdotes that the different communities develop; the close association between *lygos* and chastity explains why Artemis, the tutelary goddess of unmarried girls, and Hera, responsible for prenuptial rites on the island of Samos, should dwell within the branches of the willow.

[32] For a very suggestive discussion of the split between the body and the head, Frontisi-Ducroux 1991: 190 and passim. I return to this theme in chapter 3.

[33] E.g., 1.43.5, 2.11.3, 2.11.6.

[34] Cited in Romano 1980: 90–91.

[35] E.g., *ARV*² 569, 40; *ARV*² 672, 14.

these notions of a presence hidden and contained.[36] On some occasions the figure might stand behind a curtain,[37] or within an inner room where designated members of the community alone could penetrate. In a sanctuary of Aphrodite at Sikyon, a female verger was the sole individual able to enter the space where the goddess resided: "All others," notes Pausanias, "are accustomed to view the goddess from the entrance and to pray from there" (2.10.4; cf. 2.35.11). Such was the sanctity or power of the goddess Sosipolis at Olympia that the single woman permitted entrance to the inner part of the temple was bound to cover her head and face in a white veil (Paus. 6.20.3). Pausanias mistimes his visits to the shrines of Eurynome near Phigaleia and of Artemis at Hyampolis in Phokis, and arrives on days when they are shut; he enjoys better luck when visiting the *hieron* of the Mother Dindymene near Thebes, and because he arrives on the one day of the year when access is permitted, he can see the statue of the goddess.[38] These examples could be multiplied: through the course of his travels, Pausanias encounters veiled images, statues in boxes, idols concealed within a sealed-off part of a temple, and representations of divinities that reside in the homes of individual priests or priestesses, where they alone enjoy unimpeded access.[39]

For a literary conceit that cites an image uniting many of the issues explored so far — the asymmetry between the façade a god assumes and the divine essence concealed inside, the statue as a container with something within, the capacity of the image to suggest an epiphany in the making — there is the representation included by Plato in one of his dialogues. When the drunken Alcibiades breaks in on Agathon's dinner party and proceeds to deliver his encomion to Socrates, he begins by declaring that he intends to portray his subject *di' eikonōn*, through the "images" that will turn out to be figures of speech and statues both (*Symp.* 215a).[40] The speaker then goes on to liken the philosopher to the Silenus figurines that sit in the shops of carvers of herms, which may be

---

[36] In dealing with the larger question of access to temples and sanctuaries, caution is needed, and Corbett 1970 remains an excellent and careful guide. As he demonstrates, most temples permitted access, although sometimes a preliminary sacrifice (as at Delphi) was required. Nor is the issue purely one of access to the image of the deity; similar restrictions existed even when the temple did not contain a statue.

[37] E.g., Hera of Samos, as described by Romano 1980: 257. Belting (1994: 80–81, 186, and 299) describes the frequent use of curtains and other covering devices for icons that offer many suggestive parallels. Cf. Halbertal and Margalit 1992: 48, on the use of the curtain in the Jewish Temple.

[38] For the shrine of Eurynome, Paus. 8.41.4–6; for Artemis, 10.35.7; for the Mother, 9.25.3.

[39] E.g., 2.13.7, 3.14.4, 3.15.11, 4.33.2; see Corbett 1970: 151.

[40] For more detailed discussion of the incident, see Steiner 1996, and pp. 132–33 below.

opened up to reveal divine *agalmata* inside. When Alcibiades returns to the simile later in his speech, he refines the analogy further. Socrates' outer appearance, or *schēma*, replicates the ungainly appearance of the carved Silenus, but when Alcibiades once opened him up and looked at what lay inside, then he caught sight of images that were "divine, golden, supremely fair and wondrous" (216e). In the absence of any extant statues that match Alcibiades' account (although some fifth-century terracotta figurines do include quite complex internal mechanisms),[41] it may be that the speaker has imagined the design for the purposes of his address. But whether real or fanciful, the idol within the *eikōn* belongs very much in the tradition of cult images and exactly captures the experience of the worshiper (or in this instance, the would-be lover) confronted with the representation of divinity. Just as the loftiest gods conceal themselves within statue-vessels that can be crude and uncouth, so, too, Socrates has taken on an external, fashioned covering that radically belies the nature of the inner person, that warns against assuming homology between visible appearance and the reality within; and like the momentary glimpse of the cult image that a celebrant might achieve, so, too, it seems that Alcibiades enjoyed only a fleeting vision of the divinity shielded by the grotesque surface, but remained ever marked by what he saw.

Iconic Images: Closing the Gap

The Greeks of the archaic and classical ages did not encounter gods only in these oblique and fleeting guises. Also standing in temples, shrines, and sanctuaries, as well as in individual households, were more properly iconic images of divinities, which granted the immortals anthropomorphized bodies and faces. From sentiments already voiced in the sources of the sixth and fifth centuries (and preserved, naturally enough, in the polemics of the later Church fathers) come suggestions that the act of fashioning gods in human form was not an unconsidered or unproblematic one: should men really imagine that the immortals, conceived as perfect, unchanging, and everlasting, were endowed with mutable and perishable mortal bodies?[42] Xenophanes stands early witness to the debate, remarking that divinity is *megistos*, and like to men in neither his *demas* nor his *noēma* (B23 DK). While men suppose that "like themselves, the gods have clothing, language, and a body" (B14 DK), pictorial and plastic images of the same assume a false identification between mortals and the divine: "If oxen, horses, and lions had

---

[41] On these, see Lissarrague 1990a: 55.
[42] Vernant 1991: 27–33 provides an essential discussion of this question.

hands with which to draw and make works like men, horses would represent the gods in the likeness of a horse, oxen in that of an ox, and each one would make for them a body like the one he himself possessed" (B15 DK). In the second half of the fifth century, Protagoras notoriously issued an even more radical challenge to men's ability correctly to configure the gods: "Concerning the gods I am not in a position to know either that [or how] they are or that [or how] they are not, or what they are like in appearance (*idean*); for there are many things that are preventing knowledge, the obscurity of the matter and the brevity of human life" (B4 DK).[43] Although later antiquity would cite the statement as evidence of Protagoras's atheism, the words more properly seem to counsel an agnostic attitude: given the bounded scope of their knowledge, mortals simply cannot fathom the nature or appearance of the divine.

What these remarks suggest is that an image that models an immortal after the human shape courts both error and a want of decorum: it not only risks misrepresenting its subject, but also can diminish the status of the god by bringing him too close to the lowly mortal form.[44] Jean-Pierre Vernant describes the challenge that the cult statue, and its maker, must take up:

> In its attempt to construct a bridge, as it were, that will reach toward the divine, the idol must also at the same time and in the same figure mark its distance from that domain in relation to the human world. It has to stress the incommensurability between the sacred power and everything that reveals it to the eyes of mortals in what can only be an inadequate and incomplete way. In the context of religious thought, every form of figuration must introduce an inevitable tension: the idea is to establish real contact with the world beyond, to actualize it, to make it present, and thereby to participate intimately in the divine; yet by the same move, it must also emphasize what is inaccessible and mysterious in divinity, its alien quality, its otherness.[45]

Faced with these potentially conflicting demands, late archaic and classical sculptors seem to have responded by depicting their gods with bodies that simultaneously declared their proximity to men and reminded the viewer of the breach between a familiar surface appearance and an ineffable, invisible reality that could be neither directly "imaged" nor reproduced.

[43] For the variant reading, see Cic. *Nat.D.* 1.63, and discussion in Kerferd 1981: 165–67.
[44] Hallett's important treatment of the issue (1986) resumes the problem in somewhat different terms: "By strengthening the illusion of life in their figures [Greek sculptors] inevitably brought them closer to the living world, and sacrificed some of the timeless monumentality of the archaic style, some of its mysterious and supernatural power" (79).
[45] Vernant 1991: 153.

Among several possible stratagems, statue-makers commissioned to refurbish and recreate deities already extant in aniconic form might choose to preserve something of the strange and otherworldly character of the earlier account. Citing Aethlios of Samos's description (c. fifth century) of the Samian Hera, Clement of Alexandria indicates that the planklike character of the original still remained visible: the image was "a wooden beam at first, but afterwards, when Prokles ruled, it was made statuelike [or humanized] (*andriantoieides*) in form" (*Protr.* 4.40).[46] In his study of Athena Polias, J. H. Kroll attributes the alterations made to the original aniconic olive wood core to the sixth-century sculptor Enodios, proposing that it was he who added the face, arms, and feet that gave the goddess a recognizably human appearance.[47] But the ancient sources' failure to supply an account of what this very well-attested image actually looked like suggests that it continued to preserve its primitive appearance; too crude to qualify in the eyes of writers as a work of art, there may have been "practically nothing to describe."[48] In both instances, the talismanic and apotropaic powers ascribed to the statues (the Athena Polias, venerated since remote antiquity, supposedly fell from heaven, and the Samian Hera was credited with a series of miraculous doings) may have forestalled any more radical stylistic changes. In similar fashion, the sculptor Onatas turned his back on the technical innovations of his age and fashioned a Black Demeter of Phigaleia around 470 in the same unnaturalistic guise that the original image, destroyed in a fire, had apparently possessed. To do anything else would have been to risk disaster: when the Phigaleians earlier neglected to have a replacement made, famine promptly fell on their land (Paus. 8.42.3–8).

If preservation and replication were two means of maintaining the properly sacred aura that a cult image should possess, then, according to some accounts, archaizing supplied a third.[49] A statue that incorpo-

[46] Pausanias (7.42.3) says that Prokles took Samos at the end of the heroic age, but Callimachus attributes the changes to the possibly sixth-century sculptor Smilis; for discussion, Romano 1980: 252–55.
[47] Similarly, at some stage in their sanctuary's history, a priestess of Hileria and Phoebe replaced the old faces of the cult images with ones that Pausanias describes as "modern in workmanship" (3.16.1); during the 320's the Athenians fashioned a magnificent face together with other embellishments for what was an apparently primitive image of Dione at Dodona (Hyperides *Pro Euxenippo* 24–25).
[48] So Shapiro 1989: 25. Tertullian (*Apol.* 16.6) compares the Polias to the shaft of a cross, an unshaped pole (*rudis palus*), and an uncut log.
[49] Although all agree on the survival of archaic forms into the late fifth and fourth centuries, there is little consensus on the motives for the preservation of these traits. For a review of the different positions, see Willers 1975. Ridgway (1993: 445) draws a careful distinction between archaizing and archaistic works; in the first instance, the work retains

rated or borrowed in modified fashion preclassical forms, whether the rigidity, frontality, and archaic dress that characterize many terracotta idols down to the third quarter of the fifth century, or details such as the arch of snail curls found in the so-called Ephesos Type of herm created after 450, may reflect a deliberate attempt to invest the object with the requisite hieratic quality.[50] Most frequently cited in this regard (although art historians continue to debate the dating of the works and the reasons for the apparently archaizing traits) are two images produced by Alkamenes, a sculptor assigned to the mid-fifth century but still active around 403. He is named the maker both of the triple-bodied Hekate Epipyrgidia, on the Acropolis, and of the Hermes Propylaios, also in Athens.[51] The Hermes, known through two inscribed copies from Pergamon and Ephesos, displays a formalized beard and hairstyle in the archaic style attached to a classically modeled head; the whole was then grafted onto a block of stone complete with phallos. In Brunilde Ridgway's reading, the conventions of the Hermaic pillar prompted Alkamenes' stylistic choice, since a fully classical head would have appeared too dissonant when joined to the more traditionally conceived body of the god.[52] And to deprive the statue of its ithyphallic blocklike form would be to strip it of its powers as guardian of the gate, and so to negate the primary function of the object. The three-bodied Hekate no less obviously rejects all attempts at naturalistic representation, and even the more minor details of the statue include unmistakable archaic touches—the strong axial pleat marking the skirt, the catenaries over the legs, the curve at the edge of the apoptygma in the otherwise classical-style peplos.[53] Again the archaizing traits give the figure of this hoary and primitive goddess an otherworldly and mysterious air, and so preserve her apotropaic quality intact.[54]

Representations that deliberately deny the gods fully human bodies or endow them with curious or outmoded appearances not only signal that divinity does not look like you and me, but may also visibly declare the metonymic rather than similarity-based relations linking the immortal to his image. Following the axiom that the divine remains unknowable

---

some of the familiar traits of the archaic style; in the second "Archaic traits predominate, and only a few anachronistic elements betray the sculptor's knowledge of later styles"; but see Harrison (1965: 50), who points out the limitations to the distinction. I use the term "archaizing" more loosely here to describe both trends identified by Ridgway.

[50] Contra Havelock 1965.

[51] Paus. 2.29.2. See discussion in Stewart 1990: 267, and the very detailed treatment in Willers 1975.

[52] Ridgway 1993: 459–60.

[53] Ibid.: 460. See, too, Harrison 1965: 53.

[54] So Stewart 1990: 165.

and unseeable, the statue-makers have chosen not to depict their subjects in their living forms, but to present them only in one of the most
frequent "fronts" that they adopt for encounters with mortal viewers,
that of a self-declared idol. So for the Peplos *korē* (fig. 21), whose
"late" style sits curiously with the old-fashioned garment that the
maiden wears, Ridgway proposes that the artist intends us to see not
just a depiction of a goddess, but of an image, something like the *kolossoi* and *xoana* familiar from earlier times.[55] The rigidity of the figure,
combined with its hieratic costume, would counteract the modern plas-
ticities present in the statue and announce that this was no mimetic
account, but an image that merely evoked the deity. Although standing
outside a strictly ritual context, the statues included as part of architectural sculpture in the second half of the fifth century and early fourth
observe the same conventions.[56] At least two such works are depicted in
the Parthenon metopes, two in the Argive Heraion, and one in the frieze
from the Temple of Apollo at Bassai, where the Lapith women seek
refuge at the idol's feet (fig. 28); so, too, in the early fourth-century
Temple of Asklepios at Epidauros, a hand, presumably that of Cassandra, clutches at a small representation of Athena. In each instance
the artist has used an archaic style to carve the statue and has clearly
differentiated it from the other figures he portrays: in contrast to the
movement and activity that surround them, the idols are generally frontal and rigid and often are clothed in simple drapery with regular folds.
While the narrative context framing several of these scenes motivates
the presence of a statue, the juxtaposition of two modes of representation, one mimetic, the other more metonymic, might call to mind distinctions between men and gods; the former can be reproduced in all
their visibility and liveliness, but gods manifest themselves only in this
mediated form.

As these last instances suggest, sculptural representations of the immortals, not only in the form of images that received ritual worship, but
even as figures within the larger decorative schemes used to adorn temples, sanctuaries, and other public buildings, need not entirely renounce
that element of divine difference so critical to the impact of the works.
Even where the same concern for anatomical accuracy, for portraying a
figure acting according to current understanding of how the human
body behaved, characterizes depictions of deities and makes them styl-
istically indistinguishable from accounts of heroes and men,[57] artists

[55] Ridgway 1993: 148; cf. Stewart 1990: 123.
[56] For these, see Havelock 1965: 333–34.
[57] This continuity explains why most discussions of the period make no division between
images of gods and other kinds of works and, allowing the sacred dimensions of the
former to fade from view, treat them purely as aesthetic objects rather than as figures in

nonetheless remind viewers that godly agents observe laws unique to themselves. Where the carved bodies of men frequently engage in violent physical activity, or appear in the moment of rest immediately preceding or following the motion itself,[58] for divinities even the most strenuous of deeds remains easy, and a single effortless gesture brings about a decisive change. The deities included in the pediments of the Temple of Zeus at Olympia convey their wishes and commands by a turn of the head, or a motion of the arm or hand, and nothing is allowed to disturb their erect and frontal stance.[59] Although the Artemision bronze of c. 450 (fig. 12), identified by some as Poseidon and by others, more convincingly, as Zeus,[60] imagines the god at the very instant when he hurls his weapon and endows the figure with the muscles, articulated joints, and blood veins that belong to the mortal human body, the deity performs his action as though it exacts neither strain nor pain; barely leaning forward into the throw, he keeps his body, neck, and head upright. Also reserved for divinity is the dispassionate, distant expression and unwavering gaze that the same Artemision god displays; returning in other representations of immortals, it sounds only one of the several emotional notes that the neutral classical expression can achieve,[61] and counterbalances the god's engagement in mortal affairs and proximity to men with its declaration of remoteness and impassiveness. These distinctions combine to recall the unique status of those represented, and perhaps allow the images to preserve their potentially operative quality in whatever setting they appear; depending on the mentality with which the viewer approaches them, even gods included as part of architectural schemes may possess all the power and dynamism of the immortals themselves.[62]

---

the viewer's religious sensibility. According to the (unstated) assumption shaping these accounts, the statue no longer serves first and foremost as a means of achieving contact with or "presentifying" the divine, but exists quite simply as a work of representation, of mimesis. Whether this reading accurately describes the mode of viewing practiced by a fifth-century audience or, more probably, reflects the art historian's own concerns remains an open question; as some of the evidence I treat suggests, distinctions between representations of men and those of gods did persist, and depictions of the divine continued to possess a sacred dimension that could, on occasion, be called into play.

[58] Ridgway 1970: 10.

[59] See the discussion in chapter 1.

[60] Wünsche 1979.

[61] On these variations, Hallett 1986: 80.

[62] Or so the events of Euripides' *Ion* suggest. When confronted with an image of Athena included on the façade of Apollo's temple at Delphi, the chorus recognizes her as Pallas Athena, "my goddess" (211), equating her with the city goddess venerated in cult. As Zeitlin's reading of the play proposes (1994: esp. 150–51), the singling out of Athena at this early stage paves the way for the event that occurs at the drama's close. Now Athena

To read these images against accounts of divinities in the Attic trage-
dies of the age is to witness a common effort to determine just how
closely gods may come to men without suffering a loss of potency, sanctity, and status. Although gods can and do assume visible and anthropomorphized form in the plays, they never become indistinguishable in
appearance (or in placement on the stage) from their mortal counterparts;[63] although they may display the passions that move men, the love,
pain, and anger that they entertain should be tempered, and never result
in their loss of power;[64] and while mortal life remains filled with pain
and strenuous exertion, for the immortals everything is easy, and they
perform their actions without visible effort or strain.[65] Against those in
contemporary society who might debate the very existence and reality
of the gods,[66] the tragedians and artists reply most emphatically that
they are present in our midst, but stand eternally outside the laws that
govern human behavior. And to charge immortals with modes of activity that seem to undermine their transcendence and perfection may ultimately be to mistake the nature of the divine itself.[67]

Divine Epiphanies

Despite the unwillingness of gods to show themselves in unmediated
form, divine epiphanies do occur, and the epic sources and *Homeric*

---

enters once again, but this time in all the magnificence of a divine epiphany. It is as though
we had witnessed the progressive "animation" of the element in the decorative program,
and the evolution of a work of representation into the living figure of the same.

[63] So the emphasis on the strange quality of Dionysus's face in Euripides' *Bacchae* (438–
39) and Athena's radiant face in his *Ion* (1550). For more on this topos, see chapter 3.

[64] See Eur. *Bacch.* 1348; Artemis, quitting Hippolytus at Eur. *Hipp.* 1339, acknowledges
that she feels some pain on her protégé's behalf, but then goes on to assert the different
laws that govern divine conduct.

[65] As the chorus in Aeschylus's *Suppliants* declares, "All the work of divinity is effortless.
Without even moving from his holy seat right there he completely accomplishes his will"
(100–103). Dionysus's palace miracles in Euripides' *Bacchae* and Artemis's easy departure
from Hippolytus (note the contrast between the "long allegiance" and the adverb *rhadiōs*
at Eur. *Hipp.* 1440–41) are but two among a host of examples.

[66] Most notoriously, Protagoras B4 DK; see, too, Eur. fr. 286 N^2. The denial of the gods'
existence is parodied in Ar. *Eq.* 30–34, *Thesm.* 448–52. For discussion of the agnostic
and skeptical currents in fifth-century Athens, see Parker 1996: 199–217; Yunis 1988;
Mikalson 1983; Kerferd 1981: 163–72. While older discussions tend to speak of the
religious "crisis" that overwhelmed Athens in its closing decades and cite Thucydides'
comment concerning the abandonment of all "fear of gods" and piety as a result of the
devastation of the plague (2.53.4), more recent evaluations demonstrate that civic religion
and cult retained all their vigor, and may even have enjoyed a resurgence at the century's
end.

[67] So Eur. *Heracl.* 1340–46, with discussion in Yunis 1988: 155–66; also Eur. fr. 292.7 N^2.

Hymns include frequent descriptions of these moments of self-revelation.[68] Using the songs by way of guide, I propose that these episodes anticipate (and perhaps even generate) a different set of techniques and conventions used by artists for their depictions of deities and imagine another means of achieving the requisite blend of likeness and difference vis-à-vis the mortal paradigm. Perhaps, too, in replicating the properties assigned to the epiphanic immortals in the early texts, sculptors aim to supply viewers with experiences akin to those that the heroes of myth enjoyed, allowing the celebrant to imagine the god present before him, revealing him- or herself in full majesty. But, as sources and practices contemporary with the images illustrate, this very fact of exposure can also change the nature and function of the representation and complicate relations between the viewer and the viewed. Once artists seek to make the gods appear before a mortal worshiper and to allow face-to-face contemplation, audiences respond in ways quite different from before.

For detailed depictions of divine epiphany, there are the matching accounts of Demeter and Aphrodite in their respective *Homeric Hymns*; each protagonist first modifies her external shape for her descent to earth, then, after a partial revelation, casts off the disguise so as to display herself in all her godliness. Demeter begins by assuming the likeness (*enalinkios, Hymn. Hom. Cer.* 101) of an old woman, veiling her head and shrouding herself in an all-enveloping cloak (182–83). But despite her precautions, the goddess's true nature still betrays itself: no sooner does she arrive at Metaneira's home than, standing at the threshold,[69] "her head reached the roof and she filled the doorway with a divine radiance" (188–89);[70] confronted with the spectacle, Metaneira feels that mixture of awe, reverence, and most particularly fear (190) that mortals regularly experience on coming face-to-face with divinity. But the goddess, who promptly seats herself and veils her face, disarms her host's initial suspicions and postpones a full self-disclosure until provoked by Metaneira's desire to take back her child. After Demophoon is snatched from his divine nurse, Demeter reclaims her proper *megethos* and *eidos*, "thrusting off" old age (275–76) as though it were a surface covering, even a second skin she were sloughing off. And then the divine presence declares itself in full force: "Beauty breathed about her and a lovely fragrance was spread from her sweet-smelling robes,

[68] See the very comprehensive treatment in Richardson 1974: 208ff. and 252ff.
[69] The position, as other examples will show, is an important one; emergence from a temple or a sudden appearance at a doorway are regular elements in divine epiphanies.
[70] For the link between supernatural stature and beauty, Richardson 1974: 252. Note, too, Maimonides' remark in his *Guide to the Perplexed*: the masses believe that "God would not exist if He did not have a body with a face . . . except that it is larger and brighter" (1.1).

and from the goddess's immortal skin a light beamed far out, while golden hair flowed over her shoulders,[71] so that the strong house was filled with radiance as with blazing light" (276–80).

For Aphrodite, a descent to mortal spheres poses a different challenge. She must retain enough of her irresistible beauty and allure to effect her seduction of Anchises, but she must avoid warning off the object of her desire with too-clear demonstrations of her lofty provenance. Already the goddess's preparations at Paphos include several elements that suggest an epiphany in the making: after performing her toilette, Aphrodite emerges from the closed doors of her temple anointed with oil and radiant in her golden ornaments (*Hymn. Hom. Ven.* 59–65). Fresh details are added at the moment of her meeting with Anchises, teasing both the mortal hero and the audience with anticipations of the complete self-exposure still to come. Now, through Anchises' wonder-struck eyes,[72] the poet alerts his listeners to the goddess's extraordinary *eidos* and *megethos* (85) even as he modifies certain of the ingredients required for an actual epiphany scene: the radiance that should properly emanate from the divine form here comes only from the maiden's "glistening garments," and particularly from the golden robe that "shone brighter than the blaze of fire" (85–86). Finally, once the affair has been consummated and Anchises has been roused from sleep, Aphrodite quits her disguise. Much in the manner of Demeter at the threshold of Metaneira's home, she stands upright in the shelter, and "her head touched the well-fashioned roof-beam; and from her cheeks shone out immortal beauty, such as belongs to fair-crowned Kythereia" (173–75).[73]

These examples could be multiplied from other Homeric songs and hymns. Apollo declares himself to his worshipers at Delphi in a blaze of flame and brilliant light (*Hymn. Hom. Ap.* 442, 444), Athena's presence (or, strictly, that of her lamp) makes Odysseus's house seem as though it were on fire, alerting witnesses to the scene to her imminence (*Od.* 19.33–40), and radiance regularly comes from the god's body, especially from his head and face (Hes. fr. 43(a).73f.; *Il.* 5.7; *Od.* 18.354–55).[74] When Athena prepares Odysseus for his own "epiphanic" self-

---

[71] An early fifth-century stele from Eleusis shows a seated Demeter with her hair flowing down over her shoulders; for this, Richardson 1974: 254.

[72] As Smith (1981: 45) points out, at this stage Anchises feels wonder (*thauma*, 84), but not yet the *tarbos* or awe that he will experience at 182.

[73] The beauty that Aphrodite displays in such superlative form has a different quality from her earlier allure: through the use of the predicative genitive in the description, the poet marks it out as no product of the external garments, cosmetics, or jewelry that the goddess wears, but as unimpeachably hers. So Smith 1981: 123 and n. 71.

[74] Cf. Eur. *Bacch.* 1083, and other examples cited in Richardson 1974: 208.

revelation to Telemachus (who will instantly mistake him for a divinity
and react in the conventional fashion, with awe and fear), she naturally
invests him with the increased stature and youthfulness typical of the
gods (*Od.* 16.174).[75]

The epic poets extend these selfsame properties to immortals represented in plastic form. When he includes several gods on the shield he
designs for Achilles, Hephaistos takes pains to distinguish them from
the men in the scenes, marking them out through their augmented
beauty, stature, and radiance. Ares and Athena leading the troops on
one of the rings are both outsized, worked in gold (the metal of the
Olympians in all accounts), and dressed in golden clothing: "They were
beautiful and large in their armor, being divinities, and both conspicuous from afar; but the people were on a smaller scale" (*Il.* 18.518–19).
These same attributes return when the Homeric poet, looking to the
work of the artisan, describes how mortals are invested with a godlike
physique prior to their own epiphanic appearances. Even before Odysseus reaches Ithaca, and there undergoes his disguise and momentary
metamorphosis into supernatural form for his reunion with his son,
Athena has intervened to modify his appearance and transformed him
into the likeness of a god. In Book 6 of the song, she beautifies the
travel-stained hero washed up on the Phaeacian shore:

> τὸν μὲν Ἀθηναίη θῆκεν, Διὸς ἐκγεγαυῖα,
> μείζονά τ' εἰσιδέειν καὶ πάσσονα, κὰδ δὲ κάρητος
> οὔλας ἧκε κόμας, ὑακινθίνῳ ἄνθει ὁμοίας.
> ὡς δ' ὅτε τις χρυσὸν περιχεύεται ἀργύρῳ ἀνὴρ
> ἴδρις, ὃν Ἥφαιστος δέδαεν καὶ Παλλὰς Ἀθήνη
> τέχνην παντοίην, χαρίεντα δὲ ἔργα τελείει,
> ὡς ἄρα τῷ κατέχευε χάριν κεφαλῇ τε καὶ ὤμοις. (*Od.* 6.229–35)

> Athena, born of Zeus, made him taller to look upon, and thicker, and
> down from his head she arranged the curling locks like to hyacinth
> petals. And as when a skilled man pours gold on silver, he whom
> Hephaistos and Pallas Athena have taught in every skill, and who com-
> pletes grace-filled works, so Athena poured grace on his head and shoul-
> ders.[76]

The goddess's improvements recall the divine epiphanies in double fashion; Odysseus becomes larger than life and, through the overlay of

---

[75] Like Demeter, Odysseus has been "in disguise" following his assumption of the outward
appearance of a ragged beggar in Book 13.

[76] In similar fashion grace was poured on the Pandora image (Hesiod *Op.* 65). See, too,
S. P. Morris (1992: 229), who compares Athena's action here to that of a statue-maker. I
return to this, and to the episode that I next treat, in chapter 4.

gleaming gold on silver, shines with the radiance usually restricted to the immortals. Nor is the analogy lost on the witnesses to the scene: when the newly fashioned Odysseus approaches Nausikaa, he looks to her "like the gods who possess the broad sky" (6.243). Later in the poem, Penelope is treated to the same refurbishment that her like-minded husband has undergone. By way of preparing the queen for her appearance before the suitors, Athena not only makes her protégée "taller and greater to behold," but additionally endows her with the luminosity that belongs to "new-sawn ivory" (18.196), as though the queen were a carved artifact. Included in the episode are also several hints that its protagonist is being transformed into something more than human: Athena gives Penelope "immortal gifts," and freshens her countenance with the very ambrosia that Aphrodite uses (191–94; cf. 8.364–65); her appearance before the suitors a few lines on will have all the power of the love goddess's own self-manifestation in Demodokos's earlier song, as she lay displayed before the other divinities in Hephaistos's bed (8.339–42).

In their conceits, the poets anticipate and match the strategies adopted by statue-makers when they come to fashion images that are supremely beautiful, larger-than-life, and shining with an otherworldly radiance. Although, like the gods imagined by Homer and the authors of the *Homeric Hymns*, these plastic deities possess recognizably human bodies, the artists so exaggerate their corporeal perfections that they temper the impression of affinity that the representations might otherwise create.[77] The proportions of a statue provide an instant key to its nature and powers, and to build a colossal figure, as Greek sculptors did from the end of the seventh or early sixth century on, was both to set it outside the human realm and to express the notion that its power could not be contained within normal bounds.[78] Among early images of vast dimensions are some of the *kouroi* that most likely serve as evocations of Apollo himself (see fig. 17),[79] and two representations of the god, both dated to the first half of the sixth century, adopt the scheme:

[77] Vernant 1991: 31.

[78] So Gordon (1979: 14), in his extremely illuminating account: "Statues of gods permitted the Greeks to register this aspect of the 'otherness' of the gods by playing precisely on this issue of size." The author's discussion also observes the variety of techniques designed to visualize the gleaming and brightness that distinguish the Olympians.

[79] Stewart 1986: 64; cf. Spivey 1996: 109–10. While *kouroi* were equally commonly used as representations of human beings and of heroized men, the attributes of some of the images clearly signal their identification with Apollo. So the Piraeus statue comes complete with what looks like the remains of a bow and *phialē*, and *kouroi*-like Apollos on coins and vases, several copied after cult statues, possess other such defining attributes. On the *kouros* as Apollo, Diod. Sic. 1.98.5–9; cf. ARV^2 1010, 4. For applications of the *kouros* type, Richter 1970: 1–2.

the Naxians dedicated an Apollo measuring 8.5 meters, complete with bronze bow and arrow, on Delos; a second image of the god, this time at Amyklai, exceeded all mortal proportions, standing, in Pausanias's estimation, at about thirty cubits or fourteen meters (3.19.2).[80] The trend continues through to the late fifth century, and Strabo's latter-day impression of Pheidias's Olympian Zeus registers the shock that the out-sized dimensions of the statue must have provoked. The image was "so big that, although the temple was very large, the artist seems to have failed to hit the right proportions; for although the god is represented as seated, he almost touches the peak of the roof, and so gives the impression that if he stood up, he would unroof the temple" (8.3.30).[81] The account exactly matches the topos repeated in the *Homeric Hymns*, where divinities at the moment of their epiphanies reach to the roof, and dwarf whatever man-built dwelling houses them.

If the dimensions of an image were not enough to remind the viewer of the incommensurate nature of what he witnessed, then the combined richness and radiance particular to statues of the gods would quite literally dazzle him. Gold, silver, and ivory, together with bronze, marble, and iron, all possess the sheen thought to characterize the immortals, and by the end of the sixth century, these costlier, richer media have largely displaced the wood, clay, and limestone that sculptors previously employed.[82] According to the historian Theopompos, the Spartans wanted to gild the face of Apollo at Amyklai, but could not find gold enough in Greece and had to purchase the material from Croesus in Lydia (Ath. 6.232a); in similar manner, the Delian Apollo may also have been covered in plates of hammered gold.[83] This vogue for conspicuous display reaches its acme with chryselephantine images, already produced in the archaic period, but the particular forte of Pheidias and his pupils;[84] they provide the consummate example of the sparkle and preciousness sought by craftsmen and celebrants alike, reproducing in tangible fashion that brilliance that adheres to divinity and that confuses

[80] For discussion, Romano 1980: 99–101. The colossal head discovered at Olympia in 1878 is frequently identified as a surviving fragment of the archaic cult statue of Hera seen by Pausanias (5.17.1). For the counterview, Romano 1980: 137–40, with bibliography.
[81] Cf. Paus. 10.37.1 for an Artemis image "taller than the tallest woman." In Herodotus's tale of Peisistratos's attempt to take the city of Athens, the would-be tyrant arrives in the city accompanied by a girl of exceptional size (and beauty) who poses as (an image of?) the goddess Athena (1.60.4–5).
[82] Stewart 1990: 36.
[83] Romano 1980: 170.
[84] The only indisputably archaic chryselephantine image recorded in the sources is Kanachos of Sikyon's Aphrodite (Paus. 2.10.4–5); that of Artemis Laphria (Paus. 7.18.8–13) probably dates to the early fifth century.

and blinds mortals foolhardy enough to look on the immortals face to face. To cite perhaps the most familiar example, the Athena Parthenos, standing with her base some 11.54 meters high, displayed an ivory face, arms, and feet, while over a ton of beaten gold covered the rest of the image. Pausanias provides another glimpse of such a work in progress when he reports of the unfinished Zeus at Megara begun by Theokosmas (c. 430): "The face is of ivory and gold, but the rest is of clay and gypsum. . . . Behind the temple lie some half-wrought blocks of wood: Theokosmas intended to adorn them with ivory and gold to complete the image" (1.40.4).

From Pheidias's workshop at Olympia come other clues to how fifth-century artists endowed their divinities with the requisite luminosity. A series of terracotta molds preserving excerpts from the drapery of a vast female figure (presumably a goddess) were used for "slumping" the Phoenician glass found in the same deposit. The glass, later inserted into the gold, may have been thinly painted or gilded so as to replicate the sheen that the divine garments featured in epiphanies so frequently possess.[85] The finishing process would contribute additional brilliance to the statue: the use of precious stones for the eyes and of objects inlaid with enamel, glass, silver, and gold for the attributes, the gilding of the hair, and the adornment with vestments and jewels must have turned the images into an ever-shifting play of sparkling light.[86] So the eyes of the Parthenos gleamed with costly stones, while the golden pendants that hung from her ears, the golden Nike in her hand, and the shield with its reliefs possibly done in silver gilt would have made the radiance quite literally dazzling. Nor did this final adornment mark the end of the attentions that such images received: statues were regularly polished and rubbed with perfumed oils, perhaps matching the emanation of fragrance that forms so regular a part of divine epiphanies.[87]

To complete the impression, the gleaming, costly, and fragrant image could be displayed in a manner calculated to reproduce the sensations experienced by a witness to an actual visitation. Within the Parthenon where Pheidias's Athena was housed, everything was arranged to en-

---

[85] For this, Stewart 1990: 40.

[86] On this finish, see ibid. The ornaments of Athena Polias are listed in a temple inventory as "a diadem that the goddess wears, the earrings that the goddess wears, a band that the goddess wears on her neck, five necklaces, a gold owl, a gold aegis, a gold *gorgoneion*, and a gold *phialē* that she holds in her hand" (quoted in Kroll 1982: 68). Note, too, the second-century description of an image of Leto from the Delian inventories: her linen dress carried "a golden decoration with three studs missing, four gold bosses some of which carry precious stones . . . on the shoulders, gold brooches, and also a purple band embroidered in gold and a golden girdle" (*IDélos* 1428, ii, 53–58).

[87] Richardson 1974: 252.

hance the goddess's luminosity, from the two big light-giving windows on either side of the great door to the large water basin cut into the floor before the image; designed chiefly to prevent the wooden core from drying out, the pool would additionally have supplied an indirect source of light, reflecting in its surface the gold and ivory, and being reflected back in the polished materials in turn. Just as Demeter and Aphrodite emerge from closed doors or stand filling a threshold for their radiant epiphanies, so Pheidias's image would have appeared to the visitor through the great east door of the temple, left wide open on the occasion of major festivals, but partly closed at all other times.

That a peerless beauty belonged to these statues, as it did to the immortals when they showed themselves to men, needs little demonstration. Outsized stature and physical perfection always form a close pair in contemporary accounts,[88] and the youthful appearance that the gods regularly display is a *sine qua non* of the Greek definition of the beautiful. If majesty would have been the chief impression that the viewer of the Athena Parthenos received, then a second depiction of the goddess by Pheidias, his no longer extant Athena Lemnia, seems to have delighted postclassical audiences with its extraordinary loveliness, winning the nickname *morphē* for its beauty. Both Pausanias (1.8.2) and Lucian (*Eikones* 6) single out its perfections for special mention,[89] and the latter borrows the "facial contours, sides, and shapely nose" as well as the lips and neck for his *eikōn* of that quintessence of female perfection, Panthea.[90]

The aesthetic pleasures granted by these images would seem nicely calculated to enhance the religious awe that depictions of the divine should properly inspire.[91] But, according to later testimony at least, some fifth-century viewers may have found representations produced by contemporary sculptors wanting in precisely this hieratic quality and would have perceived a tension between their sacred status and the delight that skilled craftsmanship regularly affords. So Porphyry cites Aeschylus on the contrast between recent and traditional modes of portraying the gods: "The old, though simply made, are held to be divine; the new excite admiration for their outstanding workmanship, but give less of an impression of divinity" (*Abst.* 2.18; Aesch. T114 Radt).[92] Affirma-

---

[88] Examples in ibid. Note, too, Hdt. 1.60.4–5.

[89] So, too, Himerios *Or.* 68.4.

[90] See the epilogue for his account.

[91] As Cormack (1997: 23) remarks in his discussion of icons in the Orthodox tradition, "Art objects . . . both help viewers participate in the contemplation of the 'sacred' and appeal to their aesthetic sensibilities. In other words, one of the processes involved in the operation of 'religious art' is the sense of beauty."

[92] Cited by Hallett (1986: 79) and Stieber (1994: 97–98) as genuine, but dismissed by

tions of the particular sanctity or more numinous status belonging to
the cruder, less naturalistic account come from the preservation of the
so-called *xoana* alongside the gods displayed in their grandiose and
fully anthropomorphized forms. Two statues of Artemis appear in the
temple inventories from Brauron, one an archaic *xoanon* made of
wood, and perhaps believed to be the talismanic object carried off by
Orestes from Tauris (Paus. 1.23.7), the other a fifth-century representation of the goddess in marble. At the Argive Heraion, an outsized chryselephantine *agalma* of Hera supplemented but did not depose the ancient seated *xoanon* rescued from a fire of 428.[93] While the dazzling
appearance of the goddess in her new manifestation might delight the
viewer, the older idol, in Pausanias's account (2.17.4), comes complete
with the detailed genealogy, history, and hieratic design guaranteed to
endow it with the requisite sacred character.

The absence of religious practices surrounding the newer images and
the *xoanon*'s enduring role in ritual activity are further proof that the
two modes of depiction occupied separate niches. In Athens the large
gold and ivory Dionysus by Alkamenes, the pupil of Pheidias, failed to
attract anything comparable to the rites surrounding the ancient statue
from Eleutherai, which remained in the older building on the site. So,
too, the image of Athena Polias, now housed in the sanctuary on the
northern slope of the Acropolis, continued to supply the focus of cult
worship even after Pheidias's Parthenos claimed the chief temple of the
site. Nothing better expresses the different roles that these two Athena
statues play than the perhaps deliberate discontinuity between the Parthenos and the episodes depicted on the temple frieze framing the image. Featured in the decoration's central scene, placed over the very
entrance to the temple at the east, are preparations for the event that
formed the high point of the Panathenaic festival, the presentation of
the newly woven peplos to Athena Polias. But the viewer, whose progress around the building would have made him imaginatively participate in the procession leading up to this solemn moment,[94] never completes the ritual act depicted in genesis. Instead he finds himself
confronted not with the object of his worship and recipient of the city's

---

Donohue (1988: 136). The much later response of Pausanias reveals not only his an-
tiquarian tastes, but something of the same sense of diminution and loss: describing a
xoanon attributed to Daidalos, he observes that "all the works of this artist, although
outlandish to look at, are nonetheless distinguished by a quality of the divine within
(*entheon*)" (2.4.5).
[93] Romano 1980: 3, for these and other examples. The very status and fame of a shrine
often depended on its possession of a statue that could be claimed to be very primitive and
to possess multiple connections with Greece's heroic and mythical past.
[94] On this, Osborne (1987), who also notes the disjuncture.

gift, but with the great chryselephantine image, which he can do no more than contemplate, and which demands no gesture other than that of being seen. From agent in a communal religious event, he has become a passive and lone perceiver.[95]

Modern commentators account for distinctions between the treatment directed at these two types of statue by classifying one group as "votive," the other as "cult" images. But such strict categories would probably have been lost on the ancient viewer,[96] and they reflect nothing of how the design and character of the images themselves might have determined the very different responses that they elicited. By showing the god in all his or her majesty, the new-style portrayal seemingly externalizes the divine essence that the *xoanon* contains and conceals; but because gods do not reveal themselves to mortals at the viewer's wish and will, nor with any constancy, the idol can be no more than an artistic representation, stripped of the vessel-like quality that the older accounts retain. So, too, the awed spectatorship prompted by the depiction could focus attention not so much on divine perfection and majesty (as an actual epiphany does) as on the *technē* of the object's maker, whose skill is evident in the production of so grandiose an image. That sculptors were not reticent about declaring their shaping role, Pheidias's design for the Parthenos makes plain; including in its decorative schemes the birth of Athena, an event that was itself a technological feat, and the creation of Pandora by a divine artisan, it clamorously calls attention to the act of craftsmanship, and in so doing reminds the viewer of its own status as a work of art created by a mortal's hands.[97] The objections voiced in the *Book of Wisdom* and echoed by iconoclasts of later times seem amply justified here: these are no more than "graven images," dead things formed by human labor.[98]

---

[95] For a general statement of this shift, Vernant 1991: 158–59. Note, too, the very different roles the images play in promoting the well-being of Athens. Where the Parthenos could contribute to the city's financial resources in times of need (Thuc. 2.13.3–5), the Polias had earlier been held so essential to its salvation that in 480, when the people were abandoning the city on the eve of the Persian invasion, they took the talismanic *agalma* with them (Plut. *Them.* 10.4)

[96] The terminology found in the postclassical sources reflects the confusion; in Strabo's account at 8.3.30, Pheidias's Zeus constitutes the largest votive offering at Olympia, but Dio Chrysostom, delivering his twelfth oration at Olympia in A.D. 97, calls Pheidias's work the first cult image of Zeus at the site (54).

[97] The iconography of the Parthenos proves distracting on a further count: by asserting the wealth of the city that has erected the image and by presenting, through its iconography and the scenes on its shield, sandals, and below its feet, a snapshot declaration of Athens's own self-fashioned identity, it directs the viewer's attention as much to himself as citizen of the polis as to the divinity portrayed.

[98] For this topos, see note 188 below, and Camille 1989: 27–49. By contrast, the origins

CULT ACTIVITIES

Cult images should ideally offer one among several privileged habitations for the god, or so the special efficacy ascribed to prayers performed in front of the representations in archaic and classical sources suggests.[99] While the Athena image supplicated by the Trojan women in *Iliad* 6 indicates its refusal to grant the petitioners' requests, and the *agalmata* to whom the Theban chorus in Aeschylus's *Seven against Thebes* direct their impassioned pleas remain unmoving and unmoved, statues more frequently prove responsive and lend the desired aid. Herodotus describes how the wife of the Spartan king Ariston was so ugly as a baby that her nurse would carry her daily to the shrine of Helen and pray to the image there that her charge's looks might be improved; the child grew in time into a great beauty (6.61). So, too, the mother of Kleobis and Biton finds the request she directs to a statue of Hera swiftly answered (1.31.4), and in Euripides' *Andromache*, Neoptolemos prays before the statue of Apollo in his temple, asking for the forgiveness that he seeks, and that will be granted, from the god (1117). But prayer is only one of a large number of ritual activities addressed to images, and it belongs with the much larger set of gestures designed to call the numinous presence into play, to harness the force credited to the idol. These actions, I suggest, offer fresh evidence for the conception of the statue as vessel: assuming the god resident within the habitation that the image supplies, they aim to make divinity emerge and act on behalf of those performing the rite.

The efficacy of these rituals depends on a second and no less critical notion shaping Greek attitudes toward cult images through the classical period and beyond.[100] As recent work argues, the idols were not so much "representational" as "persuasive" objects, whose external ap-

---

of aniconic artifacts remain unknown, or are ascribed to the gods themselves. So Pausanias reports (and dismisses) the common view that the image of Athena Polias fell from heaven (1.26.6; the same conceit was applied to *baituloi*; see, too, West 1966: ad 498–500), and several sources tell a variety of extravagant tales detailing how the Palladion, first constructed by Athena and wrapped in her aegis, was thrown by Zeus together with Ate into the land of Troy (Apollod. *Bibl.* 3.12.3 and *Epit.* 5.10; Clem. Al. *Protr.* 4.42–43; schol. ad Aristides 1.187.20. For the miraculous doings attributed to the image, see Strabo 6.1.14). For other examples, Romano 1980: 352–54.

[99] As observed by Corbett (1970: 151).

[100] Contemporary with many of the practices I document are the divergent views expressed in the literary sources that variously confirm or question the point of such ritual attentions (e.g., Aesch. *Sept.* 216–17; Eur. *Tro.* 1060–80, *Hipp.* 73–87; see, too, note 66 above). But for all the skepticism that characters in drama and elsewhere express, images seem to have suffered scant loss in status, and continued to inspire the same veneration and ritual activities that they had traditionally elicited.

pearance and deployment were thought directly to influence the conduct of the divinities portrayed. By visualizing the subject in a certain guise, and by manipulating the statue in particular fashion, the devotee persuades, encourages, or even constrains the god to behave in analogous manner.[101] Thus a community depicts a figure of Apollo with the attributes of peace so as to guarantee that when the god attends its rites, he will do so in his benign and tranquil aspect,[102] and the incarceration or burial of an image imposes a like immobility and/or passivity on a dangerous divinity who might otherwise inflict harm. Both mimetic and compelling in intent,[103] the rites addressed to the surface of the image, and, on occasion, to its internal space, also act out the desired scenario—the god's emergence from his vessel and demonstration of his power—and in so doing encourage or even force that action to occur.

External Manipulation

Among the different gestures that visualize and so realize the anticipated rousing of a beneficent or apotropaic force are the several forms of exposure that many of the cult images venerated in Greek city-states undergo, and that punctuate the idols' more regular residence within a temple or shrine. Just as the display of a talismanic robe,[104] fleece, or lock of hair[105] both enacts and prompts the release of whatever benign or malignant influence the object hosts, so taking out a statue that is normally enclosed describes the god's self-manifestation even as it invites or persuades the divinity to follow suit. Images of tutelary gods worshiped in Greek cities were anything but static, and, unlike the unwieldy "votive" images whose very size and weight prohibited all mobility, many were carried about in annual processions designed to allow the deity to visit the various chief sites in his or her constituency and reclaim them as his own. The prefestival procession featuring Dionysus

---

[101] For the most lucid explication of this notion, see Faraone 1992: 117–20.

[102] A well-known instance is the Delian Apollo, who carries not only the bow but also the Graces.

[103] Cf. Vernant 1991: 155–56.

[104] When the Trojan women go to supplicate the image of Athena for protection from the attacking Greeks, Hecuba brings with her a piece of clothing by way of offering and inducement for the goddess. Following Hector's instructions, she makes a careful and considered choice: entering the *thalamos* where the royal treasures are stored, the queen takes a gloriously embroidered robe that shines magically like a star and "that lay undermost of all" (*Il.* 6.288–95). The nethermost location of the object is more than a gratuitous detail added by the poet: its very efficacy depends not only on the luxuriousness that can charm the gods, but on the powers it has husbanded through the marked lack of prior exposure (a point brought out in Gernet 1981: 100–101).

[105] For this, Apollod. *Bibl.* 2.7.3 (cf. Paus. 8.47.5).

Eleutherios marked the starting point of the City Dionysia at Athens each year. In a route carefully selected to include many of the key civic spots, the journey visibly reenacted the original advent of the *xoanon* to the city and guaranteed, through the various acts of hospitality that it and other preliminary rites involved,[106] that the god's influence would be a favorable one. So, too, the gold-clad statue of Artemis of Ephesos would, on feast days, process in grand style down to the sea, visit the land owned by the city, and preside over the festival performances at the theater. The very name of Hermes Perpheraios declares the fact of his regular "carrying around," and the phallic simulacrum of Dionysus venerated on Delos was placed in a wagon and paraded through the streets on the occasion of the god's annual festival in the month of Galaxion.[107] Not surprisingly, this progress of the "god," an occasion on which the idol moving from place to place would seem an almost live presence,[108] coincides with the displays of power upon which postclassical sources like to dwell. The protagonist of Apuleius's novel must wait until the annual appearance of the image of Isis, borne in such majesty through the streets, for his metamorphosis back into human form (*Met.* 11.8–13).

No less dramatic were the occasional journeys performed by the so-called Artemis Soteria at Pellene, an image that belongs in the category of those dangerous statues which inflict blindness, madness, or sterility on their viewers.[109] For this reason, Plutarch reports, the Pellenians say that the image

> usually stands untouched, and when a priestess happens at any time to re-
> move it and carry it out from the temple, nobody looks at it, but all turn their
> faces from it; for not only is the sight terrible and harmful to mankind, but it
> even makes the trees past which it has been carried become barren and cast
> their fruit. (*Arat.* 32.2; cf. Paus. 7.27.3)

But the same hazardous powers that prescribed the statue's concealment might also be directed against an outside aggressor, and the goddess exercises her influence on the community's behalf. Plutarch goes on to explain that Artemis's epithet refers to the moment when the priestess carried the image out of its temple to confront an Aetolian army threatening the city: "By turning it in the faces of the Aetolians, [she] robbed them of their senses and took away their reason."

---

[106] For the preplay rituals as acts of *xenismos*, and the statue's route, see Sourvinou-Inwood 1994.

[107] Kötting 1950 and Romano 1980: 9 for these and other examples.

[108] For the dramatization of the image's power through the fact of its participation in a procession, Belting 1994: 47–48.

[109] For more on this episode, see chapter 3.

Nothing better expresses this notion of a persuasive-cum-mimetic confinement and release than the chained images venerated in Greek cities, and although most of the evidence dates from postclassical times, the practice most likely reaches back to a much earlier age.[110] Homer includes the curious tale of how the sons of Aloeus placed Ares in chains in a bronze cauldron (*Il.* 5.385–91), and Christopher Faraone would connect this unlikely story of divine incarceration to an inscription from the first century B.C., and to later literary accounts, which tell of bound effigies of this particular god; behind the rite lies the desire to check Ares' activity as inimical plague-bringer, a character he assumes in Boeotia where many of the tales cluster.[111] Though binding a god prevents him from exercising his malignant powers, it can also block a benign influence that otherwise keeps a community sound. In Aristophanes' *Peace*, Ares turns the tables and visits the same chaining and confinement that he suffers on other occasions upon another divine victim. Not only has he concealed Athens's tutelary goddess Peace underground, hidden from view beneath the stones that her antagonist has piled on top, but, according to the priest who threatens to disrupt the closing ceremony, the divinity has additionally been placed in chains; the intruder claims to know of an oracle declaring, "It was not yet ordained that the bonds of Peace should be loosed" (1073). The use of an outsized image to take the role of the goddess throughout the drama elides the distinction between Peace and her representation and assumes the symbiosis between the two.

If removing a statue from its sanctuary, unfettering it, or moving it about makes the divine influence operative in the community, persuading the god to demonstrate his power even as the idol is displayed, then, as Aristophanes' drama also suggests, the concealment of a representation normally open to view marks the period when that force goes into abeyance, and the occasion may rank as a dangerous or unlucky one. The Athenians considered the moment when members of the Praxiergidai removed the adornments of Athena Polias, veiled the statue, and performed secret rites as among the most inauspicious days of the year, and several sources report Alcibiades' unfortunate choice of this date for his return from exile. As Plutarch comments, the people regarded the advent as ill-omened, for "the goddess did not appear to receive Alcibiades in a well-disposed or propitious fashion, but rather to veil herself from him and repel him" (*Alc.* 34.1).[112] Other activities surrounding the event reflect the temporary suspension of the beneficent

[110] For more detailed treatment of binding, see chapter 3.
[111] Faraone 1992: 74–78. I return to this episode in chapter 3.
[112] Cf. Xen. *Hell.* 1.4.12 and discussion in Parker 1983: 26.

powers usually ascribed to the image: an inscription from the second quarter of the fifth century describes how for the entire month of Thargelion, when the Praxiergidai went about their task, the archon sealed the temples and surrendered the keys to the women, and Pollux similarly records that *ta hiera* were roped off for the duration of the rite.[113]

The name given to this annual ritual, the Plynteria, signals that it was also the occasion for Athena's robes to be removed and cleaned; the two girls responsible for the act, variously called the *loutrides* or the *plyntrides*,[114] would return the newly washed garments to the goddess, and the reclothed statue could then be restored to view. Other communities also regularly disrobed and rerobed their cult idols as part of the yearly religious round. Sixteen Elean women performed the annual task of weaving a new peplos for Hera, and the adornment of the goddess in her fresh garment must naturally have involved the removal of the old;[115] so, too, at Amyklai, Apollo received a new chiton on the second day of the Hyakinthia.[116] By presenting fresh clothing, the participants in the rite naturally sought to please the gods notorious for their love of finery, and to satisfy the very pragmatic demands of an annual spring-cleaning. But the periodic and ritualized character of the gestures, and the prescriptions surrounding the manufacture of the dress, suggest that they carry an additional dimension, and that they perhaps offer microcosmic versions of the larger rituals of display and withdrawal surrounding the statues. While garments may, as I earlier proposed, contain and conceal the indwelling god, robes and ornaments intimately associated with a specific divinity can also share in the numinous character of the idol. To strip the god of these attributes signals the diminution of the power emanating from it, and to reclothe the image declares the restoration of that influence in new or refurbished form.

If dressing idols in fresh finery enhances the powers the statue contains, then it forms a piece with other practices that also tend toward such "regenerative" ends: through ritual gestures regularly performed, the celebrant not only makes the habitation attractive to the deity and/or elicits the numinous force already resident within, but also guarantees that this force remains operative and suffers no attrition or loss of efficacy. The bathing and purification of the statue, which frequently accompany the removal of the god's or goddess's adornments, belong

---

[113] *IG* I³ 7.20–22; Pollux 8.141.

[114] Phot. and Hsch. s.v. *loutrides*.

[115] Romano 1980: 132.

[116] For these and other occasions on which statues were clothed, see Frischer 1982: 114 n. 78; also Romano 1980. It is striking that chryselephantine and gold images seem not to have received clothing.

within this category. Robert Parker conjectures that the term *loutrides* used of those responsible for cleansing Athena Polias suggests the washing not just of the garments but of the image itself,[117] and once a year the Samians carried their cult statue of Hera down to the sea and most probably bathed it there.[118] In a comparable yearly rite, the Ephesians mounted a procession that conducted the idol of Artemis to the seashore, accompanied by a salt bearer, a wild-celery bearer, a singer, a cloth bearer, and a so-called *kosmos* bearer. Down by the water, the statue would receive its yearly bath prior to its readornment with the cloth and other items carried by the celebrants.[119]

One discussion of statue bathing cautions against applying a single reading to a practice that appears a polysemous one:[120] the baths given to the image of Hera at Plataea and Samos display a prenuptial character, symbolically renewing the goddess's virginal status, while Callimachus's fifth *Hymn* suggests that "Pallas's bath" in Argos "is simply taken for bathing's sake."[121] But the aetiologies that lie behind several of these rituals also suggest a common strand: just as in Euripides' *Iphigenia Taurica* the heroine proposes carrying the *bretas* of Artemis down to the sea to cleanse it from the miasma spread by the polluting presence of Orestes (1199),[122] so bathing more generally represents an attempt to give renewed power to an image whose numinous quality has suffered depletion or impairment.[123] According to the tale that Athenaeus preserves from Menodotos of Samos,[124] usually dated to the third century, some Ephesian pirates attempt to make off with the *bretas* of Samian Hera, and only abandon the image on the shore when their boat mysteriously refuses to put out to sea. When the members of the Samian search party discover the missing object, they assume that the goddess ran away of her own volition and bind the fugitive with branches to preempt a second flight. Since binding is the choice, and perhaps the only way of suspending divine powers,[125] the Samians' ac-

---

[117] Parker 1983: 26–27; as he notes, the verb *louō* is normally used of washing a person rather than clothing.

[118] For this, see Romano 1980: 252. Since an inventory dated to 346/45 catalogues, among other garments, the thirteen chitons, two *chitōniskoi*, two shoulder wraps, and three veils that belonged in the goddess's wardrobe, the purification may also have involved unclothing and reclothing the statue.

[119] Romano 1980: 242.

[120] Parker 1983: 27–28.

[121] Ibid.: 28.

[122] For parallel purifications, see *LSCG* 154 B 24f.; *LSAM* 79.14f.; *FGrH* 532 D.

[123] This suggestion was also made by Bonner (1950: 16–17).

[124] Ath. 672a–e; other sources include Callim. fr. 101 Pfeiffer; Paus. 7.4.4.

[125] See Delcourt 1957: esp. chaps. 1 and 4; and the more recent treatment by Faraone (1992: 74–93).

tion effectively deprives the goddess-cum-image of her power. But there is no need to render this benign (although alarmingly peripatetic) divinity inoperative; instead, Admete, the individual responsible for the original dedication of the image, unfastens the *bretas*, purifies it by bathing, and sets it back on its pedestal. The annual Samian festival of the Tonia commemorated the event in the yearly procession that included the goddess's washing down by the sea. The same sequence of a binding followed by a bath reappears in the legend accompanying the image of Artemis Phakelitis. After Orestes brought the statue to Sicily wrapped in a bundle of sticks, he washed and dedicated the goddess before establishing her in her new home.[126]

If washing may be read as a gesture aimed at the renewal and revivification of the power in the image, then other acts of cleansing and refurbishment may serve similarly restorative ends. From early on Eleusis assigned a special individual to the task of cleaning its images,[127] and Pausanias's account of the care given to Pheidias's Zeus at Olympia notes that "the descendants of Pheidias, called Cleansers (*Phaidrutai*), have received the privilege of cleaning the image of Zeus from the dirt that settles on it, and they sacrifice to the Worker Goddess before they begin polishing the image" (5.14.5). The description of the task as a *geras* reserved for a select few, together with the sacrifice the Phaidrutai perform before embarking on their work, points to the highly ritualized character of the act, and suggests that this particular "votive" object had acquired the sacred aura possessed by earlier images elsewhere.

In addition to being cleansed and polished,[128] Pheidias's Zeus also receives a regular dose of olive oil: "There exists in front of the image a raised rim of Parian marble, to keep in the olive oil that is poured out. For olive oil is beneficial to the image at Olympia, and it is olive oil that keeps the ivory from being harmed by the marshiness of the Altis" (Paus. 5.11.10). The same technical imperatives may determine the application of unguents to other cult statues: each year the image of Apollo on Delos was cleansed with a weak acid solution prior to being

---

[126] For the tale in the ancient sources, Hyg. *Fab*. 261; Probus proem. in Verg. *Ecl*. 3.2, p. 326 Thilo, citing Cato *Orat*. 3; discussion of the statue in Meuli 1975: 1050. A differently structured account explains the origins of the Athenian Plynteria. Athenian lore declared that the festival commemorated the moment when the women of the city first washed their clothes after a year of mourning for the death of Kekrops's daughter Aglauros (Phot. *Bibl*. s.v. *Kallynteria*; Hsch. s.v. *Plynteria*). If the cleansing does not directly refer to the restoration of the goddess's powers following a period of abeyance, the festival nonetheless marks a point of renewal and revival after prolonged mourning. For discussion, Parker 1983: 28.

[127] See ibid.: 27.

[128] Havelock (1995: 16) discusses the practice of polishing and buffing marble images.

rubbed with oil, waxed, and perfumed,[129] and a third-century epigram (*Anth. Pal.* 9.144) describes a *xoanon* of Aphrodite as *liparon*, perhaps shining with the oil used in the preservation of wooden statues.[130] But for all the practicality of these measures, they also cohere with the very ancient custom of anointing talismanic objects in an effort to maintain the force they hold and to preserve their vitality.[131] When fulfilling his kingly functions, Nestor takes his seat on a stone always glistening with oil (*Od.* 3. 405–8), and the Ainaeans smear a stone venerated as sacred with the fat of sacrificial victims (Plut. *Mor.* 294c); in his travels Pausanias comes across a smallish stone at Delphi, designated as the object that Kronos once swallowed believing that it was the infant Zeus: "Over it each day they pour olive oil, and at each feast they place on it unworked wool" (10.24.6).[132] That anointing and oiling images was considered an act informed by belief in the animate nature of the idol, the many critics of the practice attest, and the gesture repeatedly appears as a choice example of credulous and outmoded behavior held up for ridicule: Theophrastus's superstitious man anoints stones at crossroads and venerates them (*Char.* 16.5),[133] and the Christian apologist Arnobius much later recalls that before his conversion he would worship stones "anointed and smeared with oil," and would address himself to them "as if some force was present within" (*Adv. nat.* 1.39).[134]

In one of the very rare descriptions in fifth-century sources of how an idol would be set up, a final ritual gesture appears. Rescued from the confinement that Aristophanes' Ares has devised, Peace emerges from her cave, and Trygaios prepares to (re)install what has clearly assumed the character of a cult statue. At line 923 the mortal protagonist declares it necessary to accompany the dedication of the image with an offering of pots, the *chutrai* filled with food, and a scholion to the line explains the practice: "Every time there were altars to be set up, or statues of a god, they boiled peas and gave some of the porridge as a

[129] Stewart 1990: 42. For more on oiling and statues, see Donohue (1988: 39) who cites additional bibliography and notes the parallel Punjabi practice of covering the image of the goddess Durga every day with ghee.
[130] But, as Donohue (1988: 39) observes, the description is just as likely to be figurative, alluding to the dazzling quality of the goddess.
[131] For the connection between anointing with oil and vitality, Onians 1988: 188–92, 210–11.
[132] See Cook 1940: 883, 898, 906, 912, 918; Frischer 1982: 114 n. 78; West 1966: ad 498–500.
[133] Cf. *Char.* 21.10, where the figure of the Mikrophilotimia, should he "have cause to dedicate a bronze finger or toe in the Temple of Asklepios, is sure to polish it, wreathe it, and anoint it every day."
[134] Cf. Lucian *Alex.* 30, *Dial.D.* 12; Clem. Al. *Strom.* 7.4.26.

first-fruit offering to the altar or image."[135] Other evidence bears out the scholiast's account, recording how tables designed to receive food for the gods would be placed in temples, shrines, and even private homes, and typically would be positioned before the divine images there.[136] The late eighth-century Temple of Apollo at Dreros includes a table for offerings side-by-side with the bench for the cult statues,[137] and building accounts for the fifth-century Hephaisteion at Athens provide for cult tables along with statues; on the Athenian Acropolis a large table stood in front of the image of Athena Hygeia.

These cooked offerings, often styled *trapezōmata* in later sources, supply fresh evidence for belief that the statue houses a divine force capable of responding to the attentions the object receives. Although the accounts never specify exactly how the food was thought to be consumed, the notion of feeding (images of) the gods — a curious departure from the more common assumption that the immortals differentiate themselves from men by their freedom from the incessant demands of the stomach, and their preference for purely ethereal substances — clearly underlies the practice. In accounts of the origins of the annual procession in honor of Ephesian Artemis, the sources describe how the ritual began as a result of a game played by Klymene, daughter of the king, who together with her companions had prepared a meal of salt for the goddess down by the shore; the meal was specifically prepared for the cult image, which thereafter required a yearly reenactment of the feast. Several sacred laws describe the transfer of choice portions of meat from the sacrificial animal to the tables and couches spread before cult statues, and Pausanias preserves a story of an individual punished for his failure to render the hospitality due to the Dioskouroi by way of explaining why images of the two deities are now treated to a meal placed on their tables (3.16.2–3). Particularly indicative is the "rationalizing" change that sources from the early fourth century on register: now the laws pertaining to many cults specify that the priest was to receive not only his traditional share of the offerings, but that portion assigned to the gods as well. Perhaps the too-patent evidence of the gods', or their images', failure to consume what was placed before them prompted the shift.

[135] The scholion cites Ar. *Plut.* 1197–98 (with its own explanatory comment in the scholia) and fr. 265 for closely parallel episodes. Ar. fr. 591.84–6 preserves the beginning of another similar episode. The altar, mentioned alongside the image, had always been a privileged site for contact with the divine; indeed, the primary element of a sanctuary in the archaic age was the altar rather than the cult image.

[136] For this, and the examples that follow, see D. Gill 1974.

[137] Romano 1980: 274.

Filling the Image

In the ancient Near East, in Egypt, Babylonia, Sumer, and Assyria, these same acts of washing, cleansing, clothing, anointing, and feeding belong to the elaborate ceremonies surrounding the animation and consecration of new statues of gods, of mummies, or of figures destined for magical purposes; the gestures serve to identify the image with the deity or human being whom it represents and to imbue the still-inert object fashioned by the craftsman with the life and personality of the original.[138] An extant Babylonian text directs the priest in each of the ten operations he must carry out: he begins by anointing the statue of the god with a butter-and-honey mixture, and binds strands of white, red, and blueish wool about its neck; at a later phase in the ceremony, he serves up a dish of "pease meal" to the image (a meal strikingly similar to the peas, beans, lentils, and gruel that Greek idols receive) and erects three banquet tables, on which he places dates, wine, and other substances. At five different points in the proceedings, the officiant performs a gesture called the "washing and opening" of the mouth, which aims to promote the vivification of the piece by introducing into it life and breath. In Mesopotamia, the statue fashioned by the craftsman undergoes a ritual birth and animation:[139] after lustrations, the object is carried down to the Euphrates and turned from west, the direction of death, to east. The priest whispers in the statue's ear, washes its eyes with hot water, and declares the god free. Texts and images from the period of the New Kingdom in Egypt record many of the same gestures: among his thirty-odd duties, the individual performing the rite must clothe the newly made idol in colored cloth, anoint it with unguents, and rub it with milk; using a special tool he pries open the mouth in order that life, or the *ka*, may enter the body. By the ceremony's close, the mouth, eyes, and ears of the statue are deemed invested with the faculties of a living being.[140] Nor do the attentions lavished on the images end at this point: the statues continue to be treated as living manifestations of the gods, and must be fed, clothed, and taken on journeys by the priests responsible for their maintenance and care.

Read against these Near Eastern practices, many of the gestures I have described might take on an additional dimension: do the cleansing, washing, clothing, anointing, and feeding of an image serve not only to

---

[138] My account follows that of Blackman 1924. See, too, Freedberg 1989: 82–83.

[139] The verb used of fashioning the image is the same as that used of giving birth. For a fascinating account of the analogies between birth and the production of images, see Brett-Smith 1994.

[140] For a visual representation of the ceremony on wall paintings, see Quirke and Spencer 1992: pl. 113.

rouse the force latent within a vessel already deemed sacred, but also to introduce a numinous spirit into an otherwise inanimate, inefficacious, and vacant object?[141] Certainly the question is one that first- and second-century Greek and Roman sources, and most particularly those engaged in polemics for or against the worship of images, would frequently pose. "When," asks the Christian Minucius Felix in his attack on pagan idolatry, "does the god come into being? The image is cast, hammered, or sculpted: it is not yet a god. It is soldered, put together, and erected; it is still not a god. It is adorned, consecrated, prayed to — and now, finally, it is a god once man has willed it so and dedicated it" (*Octavius* 22.5).[142] More dispassionate authors also note the change in the status of the image that acts of consecration can bring about. Dio Cassius (22 fr. 76) reports that Lucullus refused to return images borrowed for the dedication of a temple on the grounds that they had now "become sacred," and both Plutarch and Dionysius of Halicarnassus include an anecdote concerning a statue that began to speak the very moment after its consecration, as if life had entered it at the instant of the ceremony.[143] But nothing in the earlier material suggests that the activities surrounding images, whether those performed at their first installation[144] or on subsequent occasions of veneration or reconsecration, possessed a parallel significance. Worshipers addressing their prayers to the image based their appeals for succor and favor on the assumption of the god's presence,[145] but how that living presence first entered the idol is an issue rarely broached in the archaic and classical sources.

For a rare exception to this general rule, albeit one largely confined to the realm of myth and magic, the Near Eastern material proves illu-

[141] See the useful remarks in Freedberg 1989: 83–84; as he suggests, consecration may confirm the sacred status of object, or may actually introduce life into a previous inanimate vessel.

[142] See the very similar remarks in Tertullian *Apol.* 12, *De idolotria* 15, *De spect.* 13.

[143] Dion. Hal. 8.56, Plut. *Coriolanus.* 37.3.

[144] The sources say remarkably little about any rituals of installation/consecration, for which the terms *hidruō*, *anatithēmi*, *hieroō*, and *teleō* can variously be used. The scholion to Aristophanes' *Peace* cited earlier, and a similar one explaining the food offerings made to Ploutos at the end of his *Ploutos*, are among the rare accounts. Andrew Stewart in his remarks at the 1996 annual meeting of the American Philological Association suggested that statues, and the attentions paid to them, may have been borrowings from the East, and that the images were incorporated into already existing cult practices.

[145] But note a further difference between the Greek and Near Eastern beliefs: the Mesopotamian god always resides within the statue once it has been animated and put in place, and to witness the representation is to be in the presence of that god; but Greek deities continue to inhabit Mount Olympus. To reach a god, and to persuade him to respond to a request, a Greek might pray before a statue, but he just as commonly performed a sacrifice whose smoke would ascend to the upper realm where the Olympians were present to receive it.

minating. Just as the texts already cited describe priests inserting life into an image previously deemed vacant and inert by means of rites addressed both to its surface and to its internal portions (with special attention to the eyes, mouth, and ears, which serve as conduits between the two levels), so a handful of Greek sources similarly imagine the vivification of empty statues through the manipulation of their two parts: in addition to adorning, washing, cleansing, or making offerings to the exterior of the object, the individual also goes to work on the hollow space inside. This scenario looks directly to the notion of the statue that I introduced at the chapter's start; beneath the surface lies a second level, in this instance a cavity that the fabricant or celebrant literally fills.

The motif has its earliest soundings in those myths and legends that imagine the transformation of inanimate vessels into living beings (or close approximations of the same). Pandora supplies the first and paradigmatic instance. In the two versions of her creation in Hesiod, Hephaistos mixes earth and water, and fashions the woman like a potter who shapes a vessel.[146] While the poet of the *Theogony* focuses exclusively on the surface decoration, presenting Pandora as nothing more than a compilation of her clothing and adornment,[147] in the *Works and Days* he pays equal attention to the cavity inside. Now Zeus gives specifications concerning the product's two parts and details the very different properties that each will host (61–67). The acts of filling and inserting, signaled by the verb *entithēmi* and the preposition *en*, punctuate his instructions, and reappear when the gods set about their task: decorating the vessel's outside, they also deposit the requisite attributes within.

Various models lie behind the picture that Hesiod has presented. As commentators note,[148] the sequence recalls other episodes in which goddesses dress and adorn themselves with the help of their attendants prior to a seduction scene,[149] and the gods' activities also bring to mind the final stages in the preparation of cult images and the subsequent attentions addressed to them; the decoration of the figure with its rich vestments and jewels anticipates later accounts of the *kosmēsis* or adornment of statues, while the anointing, clothing, wreathing, crown-

---

[146] *Op.* 61, *Theog.* 571 (in this version only earth is used). Perhaps taking their cue from the text, visual artists follow suit and depict Pandora in the likeness of a vase whose form reduplicates that of the container on which the image is displayed. For this, see *LIMC* s.v. Pandora no. 4.

[147] For this, Loraux 1993: 81 and discussion in chapter 4.

[148] See in particular the detailed discussion by West (1978: ad loc.).

[149] So in the *Hymn. Hom. Ven.*, the Graces bathe the divinity, who then decks herself out with earrings of gold and necklaces (61–65) in preparation for her meeting with Anchises.

ing, and displaying[150] of Pandora match the prescriptions for the installation or veneration of images of divinities on the occasions of their
festivals. Indeed, this affinity between Pandora and the statue of a goddess may be precisely what Zeus and his minions have in mind as they
beguile men into accepting a gleaming gift that, in the manner of a
tutelary image, seems to promise only good.[151]

But analogues to the vivification of an image through the filling of its
cavity lie in a different area. In his Iliadic foundry, Hephaistos builds the
mechanical serving girls whom he has quickened by placing within them
noos, *phrenes*, *audē*, and *sthenos* (mind, wits, voice, and strength), and
who, like Pandora in the prototype Zeus originally intends (*Op.* 63–64),
are skilled in the works of the immortal gods (*Il.* 18.417–20). In other
accounts from both archaic and postclassical times, Hephaistos fashions a
more specialized subset of theriomorphic statues whose possession of
psuchē or other animating properties allows them to act as guardians or
phylacteries before a door or gate.[152] The gold and silver dogs in front of
Alkinoos's palace belong to this company: not only do they appear extraor-
dinarily true-to-life, but they also stand parallel to the actual guard dogs
who protect dwellings elsewhere in the song (*Od.* 7.91–94). Hephaistos
fashions another golden dog similarly characterized as *empsuchos* and
designed to serve as guardian in the *temenos* of Zeus's sanctuary at Crete.[153]
And Nicander of Kolophon names as the progenitor of the marvelously
swift Chaonian and Molossian hounds "a dog that Hephaistos, after casting it from Demonesian bronze and setting a *psuchē* in it, gave as a gift to
Zeus, and he gave it as a gift to Europa" (fr. 97 Gow and Scholfield).[154]

Fresh parallels suggest themselves for the final element that Hesiod
includes in his second version of the Pandora tale. No sooner has Epimetheus taken in his bride than she raises the lid off the jar that she
carries and allows all the evils hidden within to scatter abroad (*Op.* 94–
95). The *pithos* with its baneful contents recapitulates the character of
its bearer as the jar reveals itself as a second manufactured object
stocked with the germs of illness and affliction poised to attack the race
of men.[155] Other myths attested only in later sources feature gods and

---

[150] Hephaistos "brings out" the image he has fashioned and shows her to gods and men
(*Theog.* 586).

[151] Faraone 1992: 102.

[152] The fullest discussion is in Faraone 1987.

[153] Schol. ad Pind. *Ol.* 1.91a.

[154] Note that, like Pandora, who stands as progenitor of the *genos* of women (Hes. *Theog.*
590), this animated image also gives rise to a whole race.

[155] Its design finds parallels in Near Eastern tales featuring sealed copper kettles filled with
disease, which individuals inadvertently open and whose contents escape. For these, see
Bonner 1956.

sorcerers who again design statues that they fill now with propitious, now with dangerous drugs or *pharmaka* (a divergence that Pandora's own mixed *pithos*, where hope remains even after the harmful contents have been disseminated, anticipates): Hephaistos models a lion stocked with beneficial herbs, while the products Medea places inside a hollow statue of Artemis are designed to wreak havoc on the city that unwittingly welcomes the image.[156]

There is also evidence, although scant for the classical period, that the Greeks emulated the behavior of the divine and mythical sorcerers imagined in their myths, and that they, too, created talismanic and efficacious objects by inserting substances into the hollow interiors of vessels.[157] Athenaeus quotes one of the few rituals preserved from the much earlier texts of the Athenian expounders of the city's sacral law:

> The *sēmeia* of Zeus Ktesios should be set up in this way; take a new jar (*kadiskos*) with two ears [handles] and a lid to it, and wreathe its ears with white wool, and stretch a piece of yellow — anything you can find — from its right shoulder and its forehead, and pour ambrosia into it. Ambrosia is a mixture of pure water, olive oil, and all manner of fruits: empty these ingredients in.[158] (473b–c)

The instructions match Hesiod's narrative on several counts: again a vase or jug is anthropomorphized through its ritual adornment or *kosmēsis*, and again the interior is filled, this time with a substance that carries divine and propitious associations. The description also recalls the creation of the animated phylacteries ascribed to Hephaistos; like them, Zeus Ktesios appears to act as a guardian of property capable of preventing the theft of supplies.[159]

According to a passing reference in Aristotle, statues imagined or treated in the manner of receptacles filled with quickening and vivifying substances were familiar enough to offer matter for the comic stage. Quoting a fragment of Philippos (which Euboulos attributes to Themistios, fr. 22) to illustrate his discussion of motion as a function of the

---

[156] *P. Oxy.* 3711 col. 1 lines 14–32; Diod. Sic. 4.51.1–5; for discussion, Faraone 1992: 19–20, 100 and n. 41.

[157] It is intriguing to speculate on how the development of the so-called *cire-perdue* method, which can be documented from the middle of the sixth century on (and is clearly described in Stewart 1990: 38–39), would have played into these beliefs. According to the highly speculative account proposed in Cook 1914: 723–24, the innovation informs the myth of the image of Talos, and his destruction through his loss of the fluid filling his internal cavity.

[158] See Faraone 1992: 7, whose translation I follow, and note 30.

[159] Aesch. *Supp.* 443–45. Perhaps some trace of these notions also belongs to Aristophanes' introduction of the *dinos* or pot that the misguided Strepsiades worships in his *Nubes*, for which see pp. 129–30.

body and soul, Aristotle compares the theories of Democritus, who taught that the soul generates movement in the body, to a joke on Dai-dalos: "They say that Daidalos made his wooden statue of Aphrodite mobile (*kinoumenēn*) by pouring (*encheant*') quicksilver into it" (*De an.* 406b15–22). While Byzantine commentators on the passage take the conceit literally, supposing that Daidalos included special hollows in the image to hold the quicksilver, and aligning his device with the practice of animating divine statues by placing liquids and substances inside them, for an Athenian audience the humor of the remark would depend chiefly on the sexual innuendo of the terms:[160] the statue (appropriately that of Aphrodite) stands equivalent to the female body, a vessel that a man might also "set in motion" by filling its orifices in the act of love. But perhaps the joke also amused because it touched more nearly on current cult practices in Athens and elsewhere,[161] and because it invested a religious act with an entirely different significance.

For detailed accounts of how to animate an image by the ritual inser-tion of prescribed substances, we have to look to the sources of the postclassical age. The recipes included within the *Greek Magical Papyri* follow the same two-step process adopted for Pandora and the *ka-diskos*, instructing the practitioner of the rite first to shape the statue out of some inert material, and then to place a particular set of objects or a certain text in the interior cavity;[162] the finished product, thus viv-ified, becomes a source of omens and oracles.[163] The papyri tell of magic names inscribed on gold leaf enclosed within a statue, or of a hollow Hermes with a magical substance inside, consecrated by a garland and the sacrifice of a cock. These are the precise practices adopted by the theurgists of the imperial age; exercising their "telestic" art, they, too, would manipulate statues in order to endow them with life and move-ment in the hope of obtaining oracular messages.[164] A letter of Psellos supplies the most explicit and detailed account, as the author describes how the theurgist fills the interior of an *agalma* with such animals, plants, stones, roots, seals, and texts as are deemed "in sympathy" with

---

[160] As noted by S. P. Morris (1992: 225).

[161] Although he rationalizes the activity, Pliny's discussion of the image of Ephesian Ar-temis reports the curious custom of pouring oil into the apertures of the statue (*HN* 16.79).

[162] These papyri are generally dated to the third or fourth century A.D. But by their very nature they are probably the result of a long period of accretion, and Nock (1972: 176–88) argues that the prototypes of the existing collection belong to some time in the first century B.C.

[163] E.g., *PGM* viii 52–65; iv 2359–73, 3125–72.

[164] The clearest account remains Dodds 1951: 291–95, with the bibliography cited there; see, too, Bonner 1956; and Freedberg 1989: 87–88, 93–95, who draws the analogy with reliquaries.

the god, while uttering certain verbal formulas also designed to invoke the god (*Epist.* 187 Sathas). The statue becomes animate, or, in Psellos's words, *empnoos*. If theurgy has been dismissed as "vulgar magic," and as the last refuge of a despairing intelligentsia,[165] then its mode of vivifying images may belong within a much more ancient tradition.[166]

VACANT OR FULL?

Ever quick to debunk, Lucian will later focus on the interiors of images and find not a numinous force but something quite other lying inside: beneath the radiant exterior of chryselephantine statues of the gods, there exists "a tangle of bars and struts and nails driven right through, and beams and wedges and pitch and clay, not to mention the legions of mice and rats that hold court there" (*Gallus* 24). Lucian's jibe stands within a broader and much older polemic reaching back to late archaic and classical times; when the Greek sources seek to discredit the power of images, they do so by turning the idol inside out and inviting the too-credulous devotee to look beneath the gleaming surface.

Nothing better declares the currency of the notion of the statue as a split-leveled and charged container than these repeated attacks that the ancient proponents of "high culture" launch against popular belief:[167] explicitly and implicitly describing images as artifacts endowed with surfaces and depths, the sources fault their audiences for their failure properly to construe the nature of what exists, or does not exist, inside. But the disjuncture between exterior and interior that idols so handily exemplify extends well beyond the religious realm and feeds into a much broader epistemic question. Repeatedly poets, historians, and philosophers use the statue as a vehicle for focusing an audience's thoughts on the divergent relationship between visible appearance and internal reality, and for reminding them that unseen forces can work within a vessel whose outer configuration yields no clue, or only oblique indications, of an indwelling presence. As the last chapter already argued, and these texts reaffirm, the composite and dual image offers an ideal means of configuring the twofold nature of phenomena, both divine and hu-

---

[165] So Dodds 1951: 288.

[166] Well beyond the scope of this study lie the rituals practiced in Byzantine times to rid statues of the demons thought to live within (see in particular Mango 1963). However, these form the logical corollary to the beliefs I have discussed: if the spirit is initially inserted into the image, then it must be similarly possible to get it out.

[167] Others have documented these attacks and have tended to treat them as precursors to the iconoclastic controversies that would mark a much later age. See particularly the material collected in Geffcken 1919 and Bevan 1940. For the sources of the imperial period, see Clerc 1915; and for additional discussion, Camille 1989: chap. 1.

man, and allows the ancient authors to probe the issue of how to discern from outward shape and form the essence concealed within.

Empty Idols

When Heraclitus ridicules those who "pray to images as if they were chattering with houses" (B5 DK), he may be echoing Xenophanes' earlier critique of the fashion for depicting the immortals in paint and stone in anthropomorphic form.[168] But while Xenophanes only charges men with having slavishly modeled divinities after their own self-image, Heraclitus offers a more wholesale and harsher condemnation of the veneration of statues: the *agalma*-worshiper engages in an act whose absurdity the analogy of conversing with houses—something no sensible individual would ever do—aims to expose.[169] The philosopher's dismissal of this patently ridiculous behavior forms a piece with the approach he adopts in disparaging a second and more particularized religious rite: "If it were not Dionysus for whom they march in procession and chant the hymns to the phallos, their action would be most shameless" (B15 DK). Again Heraclitus holds up a traditional act of worship to the harsh light of reason, and shows how a gesture acceptable in a religious context would seem quite nonsensical under any other circumstances.[170]

But whatever the target of Heraclitus's attacks, the examples he selects and the analogies he employs reckon with the image very much on its own ground. Fragments 5 and 15 both tacitly grant that the idol's power and appeal lie precisely in its ability not to replicate the god, but to suggest the presence of a divine resident within.[171] A phallos depends for its potency and fecundity on the imperceptible force that moves beneath its surface, and its visible action responds to the play of that interior impetus; it supplies so apt a symbol of Dionysus because, much in the manner of the *thyrsos*, the mixing bowl, and the mask-and-pillar or tree-trunk idols that also hold out the promise of divine epiphany, it provides a vessel for a power whose unseen workings become manifest. Much more obviously than the phallos paraded at the Lenaea, the buildings introduced by Heraclitus as parallels for the idol also preserve the notion of an indwelling presence. Houses have doors, windows, and

---

[168] Cited pp. 89–90. For Xenophanes' influence on Heraclitus, Gigon 1935.

[169] Babut 1975: 51–61.

[170] Ibid.: 40–51.

[171] Ramnoux (1959: 319) suggestively contrasts fr. 5 with fr. 78, "Human nature (*ēthos*) has no set purpose, but the divine has," and suggests that Heraclitus selects the term *ēthos* with its older meaning of "habitation" in mind. In a human house, there is nothing inside, but a divine one is filled with thoughts.

residents inside, and if no voice answers back, it must because they are nothing more than mere structures of wood or stone, empty of all sentient and responsive force. That houses might actually emit sound, and speak of the unseen occurrences behind their façades, is the *adunaton* or fantasy with which several characters in fifth-century tragedy flirt.[172]

Heraclitus's skill in deploying the ideas implicit in image worship against *agalmata* themselves may also inform his choice of the expression *ou ti ginōskōn . . . hoitines eisin* ("not recognizing . . . what they are like") to characterize the misguided individual who chatters with the empty form. As Charles Kahn notes in his comments on the philosopher's use of the term, Heraclitus selects *gignōskō* as the verb that describes cognition in a privileged sense and that refers to that "insight which men lack and which his own discourse attempts to communicate."[173] The second part of the phrase also dovetails with formulas used in other fragments, most closely resembling in structure and meaning the programmatic statement at the start of the collection where Heraclitus declares most men deaf and blind with regard to the *logos* that determines all things, and in need of an elucidator who might, by dividing up (*diaireōn*) the phenomena apparent to the senses,[174] reveal "each according to its nature, signaling how it is" (*phrazōn hokōs echei*, B1 DK). In both instances the philosopher contrasts a deeper form of understanding with the inferior awareness most men exercise: just as Heraclitus presents himself as the dissector, or even haruspex, who, by delving into phenomena, exposes truths hidden from most men's view,[175] so, too, he directs his attack against the individual who believes a divinity resident inside the statue, but singularly lacks the true "insight" necessary to understand the internal makeup of what he perceives. To take the argument one step further, here Heraclitus's own text possesses precisely the depth and revelatory power that *agalmata* are mistakenly believed to have, and guides his audience toward a just understanding of the forces that they venerate.

A remark attributed to Democritus (and ancient doxography, or the Christian apologists, ascribe to any ancient philosopher worthy of the name a statement declaring the vacancy of idols) exposes in more straightforward fashion the folly of image worship. Prizing open the artifacts to find mere emptiness within, he calls statues "*eidōla* conspicuous in their dress and adornment for the viewing (*theōriēn*), but empty

---

[172] Aesch. *Ag.* 37–38; Eur. *Hipp.* 1074–75.

[173] Kahn 1979: 104.

[174] See my discussion of the term in Steiner 1994: 21–22.

[175] E.g., Eur. *El.* 838–39. For discussion, Padel 1992: 15–16; Steiner 1994: 21–22 and n. 32.

(*kenea*) of heart" (B195 DK).[176] The terms of the remark set up a clear
dichotomy between the external features designed to produce a compelling spectacle or object of *theōria*—itself a disengaged mode of viewing,
more suited to a pleasing aesthetic spectacle or work of art than to an
operative image—and the internal vacancy that only a more acute form
of observation can intuit. But if a second evocation of the divine image
also belongs to Democritus, then the philosopher may have held a more
nuanced view, one that plays off popular belief in the charged quality of
the object, but tries to replace the crude literalism of contemporary worship with a finer notion of symbolic or oblique representation. Describing the names of the gods as *agalmata phōnēenta* (B142 DK), Democritus (or whoever it was who first articulated the sentiment)[177] seems
to entertain the popular notion of the animate statue, calling to mind an
idol that delivers the words of the deity resident inside. But according to
the gloss supplied by the Alexandrian Neoplatonist Hierocles, a speaking statue constitutes neither the full nor the true meaning of the phrase;
drawing out the succinct analogy, the commentator explains that a
name is a symbol or *eikōn* fashioned by the first name-giver, who revealed the characteristics of the gods by means of sounds, just as the
skilled sculptor exhibited these in stone.[178] Viewing the statue of a god,
and hearing or pronouncing the divine name, are activities that in parallel fashion grant us access to the otherwise imperceptible properties of
the subject of the representation.

But if Democritus's remark is to be made to accord with his views on
the convention-based nature of language so firmly stated elsewhere (B26
DK), then the access and revelation granted by the *agalmata* must remain a very partial one. Following the linguistic model the philosopher
constructs, plastic "pictures" would operate not through similarity, but
through a more oblique, metaphorical, or conventional relation to the

[176] Clerc (1915: 71) cites two doubtless spurious fragments attributed to Sophocles (*adesp.*
618 Radt) and Euripides (fr. 968 N²) that echo these views. In another attempt to demonstrate the point, the notorious fifth-century atheist Diagoras (if later Christian writers and
the scholia are to be believed) took a wooden *xoanon* of Heracles, chopped it up for
firewood, and used it "to cook his turnips" without ill effect (Clem. Al. *Protr.* 2.24; schol.
ad Ar. *Nub.* 830; Athenagoras *Leg.* 4.1).
[177] For a strongly argued refutation of the fragment's authenticity, see Hirschle 1979: 63–
65. He suggests that the *agalma–onoma* equation belongs instead to the Pythagoreans
and cites Proclus (*In Platonis Cratylum commentaria* 5.25–8.14), who names the Pythagoreans as the authors of the theory. For other discussions, see Philippson 1929; Oehler
1984.
[178] "The name of Zeus is a *sumbolon* and an *eikōn en psuchēi* of the creative nature, since
the first man who assigned names to things, through abundance of wisdom, like skilled
statue-makers, showed the power of things through names as through *eikonōn*" (*In car-
men aureum* 25, p. 105, 4ff. Köhler).

things they describe, using their visual signs in the manner of words to stand in for divine properties and attributes. Democritus's notion of men's limited ability to apprehend the realities that they seek to depict, whether through verbal or pictorial means, widens the gulf between the representation and the referent still further. Because we fashion our notions of the phenomena about us on the basis of *eidōla*, emissions sent out by streams of atoms, and because these emissions, although exact replicas of their generators, convey information concerning nothing more than the world of convention registered by the senses, we are kept firmly locked in the sphere of "obscure opinion." *gnōmē skotiē*, while reality, consisting of atoms and void, remains unseen.[179] A god's image no more reveals the essence of divinity than a statue can actually emit voice.

A brief glance forward to an author of the imperial era shows how the later sources stood heir to the approach that the fifth-century philosophers trace out. In Dio Chrysostom's imagined dialogue with Pheidias in his twelfth *Oration*, the sculptor is made to defend his decision to give his Zeus at Olympia a man's shape, and to define exactly how that shape relates to the divinity himself.[180] According to Pheidias's argument, the outward, anthropomorphic form offers a crutch for those who cannot imagine for themselves the true objects of their veneration, the divine mind and intellect guiding all things, which remain hidden from sight.

> But as for that in which this intelligence manifests itself, men having no mere inkling thereof but actual knowledge fly to it for refuge, attaching a human body to god as the container (*angeion*) of wisdom and reason in their lack of a better illustration, and in their perplexity seeking to indicate that which is invisible and unportrayable by means of something portrayable and visible, using the function of a symbol (*sumbolon*) and doing so better than certain barbarians, who are said to represent the divine by animals—using as the starting point symbols that are trivial and absurd.[181] (59)

While commentators generally focus on Dio's use of the notion of the *sumbolon* to characterize the relationship of Pheidias's work to the living god (the image stands as the perceptible object that communicates or symbolizes, but does not directly mirror the more acute *epinoia* of

---

[179] Here I follow the argument of Oehler (1984) in his attempts to reconcile Democritus's apparently inconsistent views of language.

[180] For a very detailed analysis of the oration, and its place within the wider second-century debates about the role of images, see Clerc 1915.

[181] M. W. Bundy (1927: 113–14) sees the tendency of Greek artists to anthropomorphize as part of the "realism inherent in Greek art." But as Dio's account shows, this realism could also be accommodated to a symbolic reading.

the deity dwelling in the mind of artist and viewer both), the first expression that the sculptor has selected carries an equal significance. Together *angeion* and *sumbolon* neatly link two related conceptions of the image. The first, a commonplace and even pejorative term,[182] recalls the very old tradition of god-as-vessel and suggests to the audience that the statue might supply an external container that preserves and can release what lies within. At the closing of the address, Dio even intimates that the divine power may be resident in the casing, and all but emerging from it: encouraging his audience to raise their eyes toward the work and to contemplate the divine beauty of Zeus, he declares, "In truth, he looks at us with such goodwill and solicitude that it seems to me that he almost speaks" (85). But the earlier description of the human shape as *sumbolon* deflects the possibility of an actual divine epiphany; what the sculptor presents is only one half of the two-part whole, a visible sign that does no more than point toward an invisible and all but ineffable reality residing within.[183]

Surface Appearance and Internal Nature

In describing the divergence between the representation and the god informing the account, Heraclitus, Democritus, and Dio Chrysostom all point to the more fundamental dichotomy between the external appearances of the phenomena, which men apprehend, and their inner realities, which only the philosopher (or supreme artist), and those equipped with the teachings he conveys, prove able to grasp through their intellectual powers. In the appeals that archaic and classical sources make to statues, the notion of this split features again and again, and frequently serves to express a still more radical sense of disjuncture: to introduce a manufactured image, whether as an agent, simile, metaphor, or exemplum in a tale, is not just to signal the oblique relations between inside and out and the dislocations that occur in ef-

---

[182] As noted by Russell 1992: ad loc.

[183] The relationship between the statue's two complementary parts, and the use of the container as a metonymic depiction of the contained, finds its most comprehensive account in Augustine's citation of Varro: "Those who made images of these gods in human form, says Varro, appear to have been guided by the thought that the mortal mind that is in the human body is very much like the immortal mind. For example, it is as if the vessels were set up to denote the gods, and in the temple of Liber a wine-jar were placed to denote wine, the container standing for the thing contained. Thus the image that has a human form signifies the rational soul, since it is in that sort of vessel, so to speak, that the substance is contained of which they wish to imply that the gods consist" (*De civ. D.* 7.5.2). Mitchell (1986: 72) notes that the standard way of representing the goddess Durga in Bengali ritual is with a clay pot viewed as an "icon" of the deity, "a symbol that contains the essential reality it denotes."

fecting a passage between the two levels, but also to announce the antithetical character of visible and internal properties, and the error and deception that can follow.

Standing at the head of this tradition is, of course, Hesiod's Pandora, a modeled vessel whose radiant exterior offers so sharp a contrast to the wickedness that the gods have concealed within. The division between inside and out, and men's inability to discern the genuine nature of goods hidden beneath their external packaging, forms the leitmotif of the larger tale that the statue-woman's genesis concludes. The final weapon in the battle of wits waged between Prometheus and Zeus, an engagement that turns from the start on the ability of the like-minded antagonists to devise "gifts" that present one thing to the eye and contain something very different inside, the Pandora image caps and recapitulates the earlier series of "exchanges":[184] the sacrificial bundle offered up to Zeus, its indigestible bones concealed in an attractive blanket of fat,[185] the fire that has been withdrawn and then returned hidden inside a hollow fennel stalk, and the *bios* or livelihood placed by Zeus beneath the ground. And should the audience have missed the moral of the tale and failed to realize that they should judge no divine gift by its alluring surface, Pandora comes equipped with the *pithos*, whose own contrasting shape and contents mirror its bearer's duality. While the visible form of the jar suggests an interior filled with seed, oil, or other sustaining substances beneficial to the owner, Pandora no sooner lifts the lid than she provokes the escape of the many evils (themselves invisible) that lurk inside (*WD* 100–103).

For fifth-century sources, the statue again offers itself as a means of signposting men's propensity to evaluate phenomena on the basis of their external appearance, and their inability correctly to fathom the connection between the package and its contents. The manufactured image regularly figures the individual whose outer shape, role, or accoutrements remain at odds with his inner nature, and who, like Pandora, displays a fundamental inconsistency or breach in the two dimensions of his person. This inconsistency is perhaps the defining feature of the Egyptian Amasis, whose meteoric rise from thief and *dēmotēs* to pharaoh Herodotus charts in Book 2 of his *Histories*. Amasis's entire reign stands marked by his repeated attempts to mix properties more normally kept apart as he oscillates between conventional kingly behav-

---

[184] For this reading of the story, see Vernant 1980: 183–201. As he notes (192), the series of episodes describes how good things are hidden so that they can only be obtained through the evils that envelop them, while evils are hidden under the beguiling appearance of something desirable.

[185] Note the words *doliē technē* used of Prometheus's initial contrivance (*Theog.* 540); the term *dolos* will again be used of Pandora (*Theog.* 589, *Op.* 83).

ior and conduct of quite another stamp.[186] In a career filled with outrageous acts, one best describes his uneasy relation to the sovereign power he has come to occupy. In the narrator's report,

> He had innumerable other good things, and especially a golden footbath, in which both he and his drinking companions all used to wash their feet on each occasion. This he chopped up, and he made a statue of a god from it, which he then set up in the most suitable place in the city. The Egyptians, constantly coming upon the statue, treated it with profound reverence. And Amasis, when he learned what was done by the citizens, calling the Egyptians together, made a revelation, saying that the icon had come into being from a footbath, into which the Egyptians formerly vomited and pissed and washed their feet, but at present they revered it greatly. He went on to say that his experience had been much as the footbath, for if he previously was a commoner, at present he was their king, and he ordered them to honor and respect him. (172.3–5)

For some scholars of iconoclasm, the story belongs together with the critiques of fifth-century philosophers designed to discredit the worship of images;[187] Herodotus has merely clothed a familiar Greek sentiment in Egyptian dress, articulating the same notion as Epicharmos, who comments that a piece of wood could serve equally well as a god or a prison plank (fr. 131 Kaibel), or setting in reverse the conduct of the notorious fifth-century atheist Diagoras, who supposedly took a wooden *xoanon* of Heracles, chopped it up for firewood, and used it to cook his turnips without ill effect.[188] But neither an attack on idols nor a demonstration of a sophistic notion of relativity can be the point of an episode that Amasis has devised to demonstrate and validate his newfound status. Instead, the pharaoh aims to capitalize on his subjects' readiness to determine the essential, inner nature of phenomena from their outward function and form, to assume a one-to-one correspondence between the two levels. When the object bore the shape of a foot-

---

[186] Most patently demonstrated in the parable of the bow that he tells of himself at 2.173. For more detailed discussion, see Kurke 1995: 58–61 and, in a revised form, 1999: 89–100.

[187] Geffcken 1919: 288–89.

[188] The notion of the lowly origins of images, and of their consequent want of power, appears in rather different form in the thinking of Zeno the Stoic (fr. 264), who insisted that anything made from terrestial substances or worked by human hands was simply unworthy of the gods. Cf. Horace *Satires* 1.8.1, where Priapus remarks, "Once I was a fig-tree, good-for-nothing wood, when a craftsman, after hesitating whether to make me a stool or a Priapus, decided for a god." Old Testament literature adopts precisely this line of attack in its constant battle against idolatry; so Psalm 135.15: "The idols of the nations are silver and gold, the works of men's hands"; cf. Isaiah 44. For additional examples, Bevan 1940: 17–23.

bath, the Egyptians thought it suitable for dirty water and refuse; now recast in the likeness of a cult statue, it is revered as the embodiment of a divine presence. According to the logic of the argument, Amasis's own transformation from commoner to king rightly earns the same change in response.

But for Herodotus's audience, the anecdote may invite a different reading, one that warns against the too-facile equation of appearance, function, and essence that dictates the Egyptians' response. Even before the vessel undergoes its change in status, it displays the hybrid quality that belongs to Amasis himself. While its material is gold—for the Greeks the finest of all metals, associated with the gods, symbolic of moral excellence and of true and just sovereignty[189]—its interior regularly holds dirty water and polluted substances; surface and contents are sharply at odds, the gold debased by the matter filling it. While the recasting of the pot into an idol seemingly removes the inconsistency, Amasis's declaration of the object's lowly origins and his equation of the image with himself raise the possibility that the breach persists in an altered form: the visible image no more incarnates the true god than Amasis does the genuine pharaoh, and a mere redefinition of function and form cannot produce a parallel transformation in the internal essence of a thing. More than that, the ruler's action betrays his fundamental misunderstanding of the character of kingship and godhead both. Gold is the choice substance of immortals and sovereigns precisely because it resists adulteration and change and remains, like the gods and their earthly counterparts, eternally the same, consistent through and through. To reconfigure gold and to suggest that its significance can fluctuate or be multiple, as Amasis does, is to misconstrue its unalterable nature.

Amasis's address within the story meets this objection head on: because the despot claims the power to determine signification and to select the meaning that things carry as he sees fit, the pot is an idol as long as his words (and his subjects' beliefs) make it so.[190] As the pharaoh's use of the object as metonym for his own situation makes plain, nowhere does this prerogative prove more critical than in the self-refashioning that he and so many of Herodotus's Eastern tyrants must perform, which depends on the absolute authority, linguistic and otherwise, that they possess. In the historian's tales of the barbarian rulers, the despot relies on the external insignia of power to shore up his au-

---

[189] But note Kurke (1995: esp. 50–64), who convincingly argues that when Eastern tyrants attempt to use gold to symbolize their royalty and legitimacy, Herodotus always manages to destabilize the equation. This is a point amply demonstrated by Amasis's actions.

[190] For the argument that the subjects willingly accede to the system Amasis sets up, Kurke 1999: 97–98.

thority,[191] and by virtue of aping the behavior of the true king ("sitting solemnly all day on a solemn throne," as an adviser urges Amasis to do at 2.173.2) achieves that semblance of the legitimacy he necessarily lacks. But the metamorphosis is no more than surface deep and leaves unchanged the inner person who drapes himself in the trappings of the genuine king. Like chamberpot and icon, what determines the true meaning of the individual is not the symbolic significance ascribed to him, but the more unalterable nature of what dwells inside.

Amasis does not stand alone in his creation of idols that turn out to be all surface and no internal substance, and that rely on the conventional character of words to make them what they claim to be. When the protagonist of Aristophanes' *Nubes*, the gullible Strepsiades, visits Socrates in his Phrontesterion, his new teacher instructs him to abandon his outmoded belief in the Olympian gods and to worship the Clouds, Tongue, and Dinos or whirl in their place (381). It is only toward the end of the play that the hero, freshly trained by Socrates in the scrutiny of names, suddenly perceives the consequences and significance of the change. As Pheidippides prepares to beat his father, Strepsiades urges his son to respect Zeus Patroios and to hold his blows. The appeal carries little weight for this second and much more adept convert to Socratic ways of thought: "Zeus Patroios? How old-fashioned you are. What kind of a thing is Zeus?" (1469–70). When Pheidippides goes on to deny the existence of the god whom the new-crowned king Dinos has displaced and moves to the assault, the significance of the new idol breaks in on Strepsiades; admitting the error of his ways, he proceeds to castigate a *dinos* onstage and to acknowledge his folly in having mistaken a humble earthenware vessel for a deity because Socrates deemed it so (1473–74). The hero's recognition of the nature of the seeming god puts paid to the logic-chopping linguistic games earlier in the play: now Strepsiades confronts a veritable "speaking *agalma*," an image whose name, form, and function perfectly coincide. No deity this, but exactly the pot it has been all along.

But Strepsiades' eleventh-hour recantation involves an additional twist that reiterates the uselessness of Socratic teaching and its reliance on controverting and redefining the conventional, and in this instance true, value of words. The false idol or *dinos* supplies a visual counterpart to a second object also present onstage, the herm that has protected Strepsiades' home from the first,[192] and to which the hero now turns in supplication (1478). He begs the image to forgive him his folly,

---

[191] Steiner 1994: chap. 4.

[192] As Dover (1970: ad 1473) argues, since there has been no point in the dialogue at which Strepsiades could have gone indoors to fetch the object, the *dinos* must also have been standing at Socrates' door for the length of the play.

invokes it as witness, and solicits its advice. A brief pause in the action follows as we are invited to believe that Strepsiades first listens to Hermes speaking through the statue, and then reveals the instructions he has received.[193] As Bernard Frischer notes, the rejection of one image and appeal to the other marks a pivotal moment in the drama's course: "Aristophanes formulates the return to traditional religion from Socratic impiety as a contrast between a principle which is seen to be only a pot and a stone which is really infused by divinity and which can listen and respond sympathetically to a worshipper's entreaties."[194] The juxtaposition also sharpens the irony implicit in Socrates' choice of symbol; a pot is like a divine image insofar as it, too, suggests the existence of something inside, but this vessel stands empty, its vacancy exposed by the display of the live and efficacious force animating the herm. Very much in the manner of the comedy's mastertrope for the new cognitive order that Socrates would set in place, the clouds whose surface melts away to airy nothingness, the hollow *dinos* replicates the character of the philosopher's teachings.

Socrates' very different role in Plato's dialogues would offer a corrective to Aristophanes' comic portrait; throughout the Platonic account, the philosopher shows himself acutely concerned with the contents beneath the surface and refuses to leave unprobed the external appearance or outer designation of things. In the case of the *Charmides*, a reference to a statue near the start of the text may form part of this leitmotif and point the audience toward the particular focus of what is to come. On his return from Potidaea, Socrates visits the palaestra to recount his adventures and to learn about the state of affairs back at home. Already in the opening moments the speaker introduces the possibility of a division between physical and moral or mental excellence; asking after the condition of philosophy during his absence, he wants to know whether any of the young men are proving exceptional "either with regard to beauty, or with regard to wisdom, or with regard to both" (153d). No sooner has he posed his question than Kritias looks to the door and names one of those entering, his cousin Charmides, as preeminent in loveliness. In Socrates' admiring account, the youth's advent and appearance have all the qualities of a divine epiphany: outstanding in stature (*megethos*) and beauty, he inspires *thauma*, awe, and consternation (*ekpeplēgmenoi te kai tethorubēmenoi*) in those would-be *erastai* who move entranced in his wake, and the philosopher grants that there is something truly marvelous (*huperphuōs*) about his physical perfection.

---

[193] Similar are the one-sided dialogues in Aristophanes' *Peace* 661ff. See Dover 1970: ad loc. and Kassel 1983: 6–7, for further discussion.
[194] Frischer 1982: 117.

Concluding his description, Socrates remarks that all look on the youth as on an *agalma* (154c–d).

Both Charmides' status as object of desire[195] and his physical proximity to (a representation of) a divinity motivate the choice of simile. But Plato may also select the term because Charmides' approach will prompt Socrates and his companions to examine the relationship between the young man's visible surface and the invisible contents lying beneath this most beautiful of forms. Immediately anticipating the unstated objection of his audience, Kritias assures them that Charmides does not just display a pretty face; were they to remove his clothing, they would discover so lovely a naked body that they would forget his countenance (154d). But even the body stripped of its garments cannot satisfy Socrates. Wishing to pass to a third and still more intimate level, he asks whether Charmides' soul is equally well constituted (*eu pephukōs*, 154e).[196] Kritias's response assures Socrates of the perfect concordance between appearance and inner nature: using terms that belong to both the physical and the moral spheres, he declares his cousin "wholly fair and good" in respect to his soul (154e). This is all the invitation that the philosopher needs. He will proceed to lay bare not the physique but the soul, and to pass from the *eidos* of face or form to that of the internal organ. Not that the exploration promises to be an easy task; even the briefest glimpse of the bodily loveliness beneath the garment (*ta entos tou himatiou*, 155d) so inflames Socrates that only a stern effort of self-control permits him to resume his investigations, and to resist the distracting influence that visible surfaces exercise.[197]

The play between the surface and the interior, and between the physical and spiritual levels of the individual, also informs the ostensible motive for the scrutiny that Socrates undertakes. Charmides, we learn at the dialogue's start, inexplicably suffers from headaches, an affliction that suggests to the philosopher that some moral or mental flaw belies his external perfection, and that betrays some inconsistency or disharmony in his inner person. After several introductory exchanges concern-

---

[195] For this, see chapter 4.

[196] The term *pephukōs* clearly establishes the difference between the external and internal registers as the questioner turns to the *phuē* and *psuchē* that belong to the very deepest stratum of a person's being, innate within him, the essence of the self.

[197] The erotic element introduced at the start also remains latent in the remainder of the dialogue. While Socrates will resist Charmides' physical allure, his eagerness to pass beneath the covering of cloak and body signals that his desire has been rechanneled into a different, more intellectualized form. The dialogue will also chart the same role-reversal that occurs in Alcibiades' speech in the *Symposium*: while Socrates begins as the would-be lover desiring to take possession of the youth, by the conversation's end it is Charmides who would possess Socrates.

ing the patient's character and mode of conduct, Socrates reveals the reasoning behind his mode of examination: since the health of the body depends on the health of the soul, Charmides' headaches can only be cured when the internal disturbance has received the appropriate doctoring (157a).

If this seems a large structure to build on a passing reference to an *agalma*, then the images included in the *Symposium* sound the same theme in much more explicit fashion, figuring Socrates himself as the individual who exemplifies the division between surface and depth that he normally locates in others. As Alcibiades declares at the beginning of his address to the company assembled at Agathon's party, the philosopher resembles nothing so much as a crudely fashioned Silenus *eikōn* that, when opened up, reveals the golden *agalmata* housed inside (215a–b). The representation not only parallels the dichotomous quality of Socrates, whose satyrlike physiognomy and body belie the beauty of his internal soul, but also matches his teachings, which similarly mask their wisdom, beauty, and quasi-divinity beneath an ungainly, cheap, and comic surface. For those who are foolish, or are simply unfamiliar with his mode of discourse, Socrates' arguments will seem ridiculous; but for the individual willing to penetrate the surface and discover what lies inside, the words prove to be replete with figures or *agalmata* of virtue (221d–222a).

But for the maker of the simile, the *eikōn* does much more than express the split in Socrates' constitution and language. It also, quite patently, looks to his longing to penetrate the philosopher's bodily and mental depths, to gain at one and the same moment the sexual and epistemic pleasures that his idol could provide, if only he would allow the worshiper access.[198] Together the youth's choice of terms and account of his behavior in Socrates' company speak of his attempts and lasting desire to achieve his goal: to his eye, the reluctant *erōmenos* resembles not only the Silenus *eikōn* with its hinge or crack, but also Marsyas (215b, e), the satyr whom Apollo (read Alcibiades?) had stripped of his skin. In the seduction scene that Alcibiades describes in such painful detail, the notion of infiltration sounds still more explicitly. The wooer mistakenly imagines that his verbal propositions have, like an arrow, struck their victim (219b); then, first covering Socrates with his own cloak, he proceeds to place himself beneath the single garment (219c). But as the sorry aftermath to the evening makes plain, the philosopher has remained intact, and has demonstrated the same imperviousness to amorous wiles that he does to the hunger, cold, fatigue, and other external forces evoked in the next portion of Alcibiades'

---

[198] For more on this, see chapter 4.

speech (219e–221c). Unlike the *eikōn* of his laudator's words, which includes the requisite mechanism for exposing its depths, Socrates resists all penetration from without.

Even as it reflects the speaker's thwarted eros, Alcibiades' choice of simile also holds up a mirror, albeit an inverted one, to his own physical and ethical properties. Possessing a surface beauty at odds with the flawed character of his soul, he invites the charge that Socrates levels at him in repelling his advances:

> If it happens to be true what you say about me, and there really is in me (*en emoi*) the power to make you better, then you can see in me an indescribable beauty entirely different from your fair body (*eumorphia*). But if seeing this you undertake to enter into partnership with me, and to exchange beauty for beauty, you seem to me to want more than your proper share; in return for the mere appearance of beauty, you want the thing itself, "gold in exchange for bronze." (218e–219a)

Implicit in Alcibiades' quest for Socratic gold is a second point of contrast with the *eikōn* he has fashioned. Where the image resembles the philosopher in its plenitude, Alcibiades repeatedly suggests his own inner vacancy and his consequent openness to the impact of externals. If Socrates remains impervious to the words and actions that his would-be *erastēs* directs at him, then the younger man finds himself smitten, possessed, and penetrated to his depths by the philosophic *logoi* that he hears and proves powerless to block out (215c, 215d, 217e–218a).[199] And even as he complains of the suffering that his own permeability has brought on him, he continues to seek out Socrates in an effort to achieve that sense of fullness which, he believes, the philosopher can supply.

Positioned behind the *eikones* that Alcibiades introduces loom other, more sinister figures of stone. The Socrates images seated in the herm-makers' shops (*hermoglupheiois*, 215b) offer one among the dialogue's several glancing allusions to the dark aftermath that would follow on the exuberant evening of January 416: just a little over a year later, a drunken band of revelers would mutilate the herms standing in the city, and popular opinion would charge Alcibiades with a leading role in the affair.[200] Although the youth most probably had no part in the attack, and Plato may well have known as much, it suits the text's larger design that Agathon's last guest be linked to the event, and that readers be

---

[199] For Alcibiades' "openness," see Nussbaum 1986: 192. She suggests that the youth has no clear sense of his inner person as distinct from his outer, and speaks of his soul "as something of flesh and blood like the visible body."

[200] For all the pointers toward the incident that the dialogue includes, and the connections between the Socrates *eikōn* and the herms, see Steiner 1996: 99–103.

prompted to juxtapose his words on this most lighthearted of occasions with the scandal that would so damage his political career. According to the construct Plato has devised, the assault on the herms becomes the logical outcome of Alcibiades' frustrated desire for an unyielding *eikōn* that will not allow him to penetrate its depths.

Among the many counts on which the Socrates' *eikōn* and the herm coincide, two prove most relevant to the argument I have set out. First, just as Socrates' appearance signals the mismatch between a man's surface and his depth, so the herm of fifth-century Athens patently exhibits that disjuncture between an aniconic, uncouth exterior and an efficacious, godly force that (as Strepsiades finds) dwells inside. And second, just as Socrates holds out the promise of attaining an almost divine wisdom and virtue to anyone who gains access to his internal spaces, so the herm, perhaps more than any other fifth-century image, offers the possibility of contact with the god whom it hosts. The popular hysteria sparked by the attack on the statues (Thuc. 6.27) suggests as much: fueling the panic was not just political outrage,[201] but perhaps the citizens' more visceral fear at the destruction of objects that supplied the most familiar, friendly, and accessible of vehicles for exchanges with the divine, and that seemed to bring a deity already intimately involved in their daily lives into particularly close proximity. Herms are, for fifth-century verbal and visual artists alike, the divine images that most commonly respond to the attentions they receive, that acknowledge those who make them offerings,[202] react to petitions, and give advice in times of need.

Informing the dynamism of the objects is, of course, the nature of the divinity whose presence they instantiate: Hermes is the god whose principal role is to preside over the passage between inside and out, and who repeatedly forges (or disrupts) the connection between the two levels. Lord of the pivot, the threshold, the inner-city boundary, the frontier between one space or realm and the next, he also conveys silent, internal thoughts into their external, perceptible form: speech.[203] Master, too, of enigma, riddle, and coded communication, he embodies the possibility of twofold meaning that his depiction in statue form holds up for show.

---

[201] See Osborne 1985 for the herms' association with the radical democracy and their deployment as dedications made by the *demos* and its representatives.

[202] See *LIMC* s.v. Hermes nos. 141 and 105.

[203] Padel 1992: 6–8.

CHAPTER THREE

The Quick and the Dead

WHEN HECUBA and the other Trojan women go to supplicate the image of Athena for help against the army of the Greeks, through a single motion the goddess refuses their prayers: "Pallas Athena turned her head away" (*Il.* 6.311). At no point in the episode does the poet distinguish between the deity and the statue standing in the temple; rather, he makes the single term "Athena" do duty for both. Nor can the audience tell precisely who performs the gesture of denial; is it the statue that turns its head aside, or the goddess herself, present at the site and witness to the supplication? Theophanies (the appearance of a god) and *agalmatophanies* (the appearance and doings of a numinous statue) are so hard to tell apart not only because the Greek literary and epigraphic sources regularly use the term *theos* for the god and his representation both,[1] but also because the behavior of the Olympians seems so frequently to "spill over" into that exhibited by their images: the very modes in which the gods of myth, anecdote, and literary account declare their presence and demonstrate their prerogatives determine, and are matched by, the activities ascribed to their images.

Nowhere does this overlap appear more marked than in two of the cardinal areas where gods distinguish themselves from men. In imagining the immortals' actions and epiphanies, the sources repeatedly dwell on their subjects' ability to move with supreme and uncheckable ease, and on their extraordinary countenances, not just faces suffused with radiance, but more particularly their uncanny, shining eyes, whose brilliance mortal witnesses cannot sustain.[2] The ancient authors' emphasis on these attributes finds a threefold echo in the images' domain: in the "miracle tales" clustering about the idols, where the focus so frequently falls on the objects' ability to move and see; in ritual activity, where celebrants seeking to articulate or harness the power thought to adhere to the statue direct their gestures toward the images' kinetic and visual properties; and in the appearance of the statues themselves, whose

---

[1] In fourth-century inventory accounts, both the *xoanon* of Samian Hera and Athena Polias are called *hē theos*; for this confusion, see Faraone 1992: 72 n. 87; Romano 1980: 2–3; Gordon 1979: 7–8.
[2] As I shall show, eyes and countenance are closely intertwined; for this, see, too, the discussion of Frontisi-Ducroux 1995: 20ff.

faces, eyes, and limbs may receive their sculptors', exhibitors', and worshipers' special care.

But present in the attention that these particular faculties command lies a central paradox, one to which archaic and classical audiences were very much alive: the notion of the seeing, moving, and not infrequently speaking image runs up hard against the inanimate character assigned to sculpted works in Greek sources, which present the fashioned objects as quintessentially immobile, blind, and deaf and dumb. From the contrasting depictions supplied by the texts, and even from the designs of the artifacts themselves, a fresh dimension of the image's versatility as cognitive tool becomes apparent: whether as a tangible object in the historical landscape, or as a figure of thought in literary and philosophic texts, it allows audiences to formulate and reflect on some of the chief distinctions separating the three classes of being inhabiting the tripartite cosmos: the immortal gods, living men, and the dead.

INANIMATE IMAGES AND THE DEAD

Motion, Sight, and Speech

According to an enduring set of conceits in Greek thought, statues are prime exemplars of lifelessness and the absence of sense and sensation. A host of semi-proverbial expressions declares the nullity of the image: it frequently carries the epithets *akinētos* ("unmoving"), *apathēs* ("unfeeling"), *aphōnos* ("voiceless");[3] to be silent is to be like *tois chalkois andriasi* ("bronze images");[4] to lack feeling is to be a *bretas anaisthētos* ("unperceiving statue").[5] So unresponsive is the statue that its arousal supplies a common *adunaton* to which writers may appeal.[6] When Clement of Alexandria later delivers one of his many strictures against idolatry, he bolsters his attack by gathering together these various topoi, which reach back to archaic and classical times:

> For even though there are some living creatures that do not possess all the senses, as worms and caterpillars, and all those that appear to be imperfect from the first through the conditions of their birth, such as moles and the field mouse . . . yet these are better than the *xoana* and *agalmata* that are entirely dumb. . . . There are also many kinds of living creatures, such as the oyster family, that possess neither sight, nor hearing, nor yet speech; neverthe-

---

[3] For these terms, see Kassel 1983: 1.
[4] Aeschin. fr. 37 Dittmar; cf. Xen. *Lac.* 3.5.
[5] Anaxandrides fr. 11 KA.
[6] *Paroem. Gr.* 1.347.

less they live and grow and are affected by the moon. But the *agalmata* are motionless things incapable of action and sensation. (*Protr.* 4.44–45)

To convey the fact of immobility, the Homeric songs already look to the fashioned stone. When Poseidon arrests the rapid onrush of Alkathoos, who is about to assail Idomeneus, he chains his "shining limbs," one of the chief loci of a hero's vitality, rooting him to the spot (13.435). The warrior, now able neither to flee nor to protect himself, stands "like a stele" before his opponent, who prepares to deliver the killing blow. Still more evocative is the simile describing the momentary arrest of the divine and supernaturally swift horses of Achilles, stopping stock-still in grief for Patroklos's death. They, too, assume the likeness of the grave monument, "*empedos* as stands a stele, which is set over the tomb of a dead man or woman, so they stood holding motionless the fair-wrought chariot" (17.434–36). In both instances, the poet's evocation of the unmoving pillar of stone is the more striking for the swiftness that both warrior and horses have so recently displayed.

Poets of the late archaic and classical ages inherit and embroider the epic conceit. Pindar cites the immobile *agalmata* lastingly fixed to their bases at the start of *Nemean* 5 by way both of demonstrating the peripatetic (and hence superior) nature of his traveling, *kleos*-bestowing song (1–5) and of calling his audience's attention to the particular excellence of the Aiginitan choral dancers performing the ode: no unmoving statues these, but bodies weaving elaborate figures that negate the very stillness that their words describe. Fifth-century drama returns to the statue as a foil that can cast a swift, easy, and graceful motion into sharper relief. The *kolossoi* cited by the chorus of Aeschylus's *Agamemnon* highlight the contrasting and uncanny powers of movement that the living Helen has herself just displayed in the earlier lines of its song; while she took a rapid and uncheckable departure from Argos, these blocklike images, limbless and rigid in stance, remain to vex Menelaus with reminders of the fixity the ever-peripatetic Helen so patently lacked (403–19).[7] In a very different vein, Euripides turns to the statue for his evocation of the captive Andromeda, pinioned to the rock in the likeness of an *agalma* as she waits for the advent of the monster from the sea (fr. 125 N[2]). Visualizing the motionless stance of the bound prisoner (and her erotic appeal), the *agalma* simile underscores the rapid advent of the hero, equipped with the winged sandals that the gods have given

---

[7] For much more detailed exploration of the passage and ancient evidence for the quintessentially immobile character of the *kolossos*, see Steiner 1995b. The quality of motion is one that the literary sources from Homer on repeatedly attribute to Helen; in this she presents a sharp contrast to other mortal women who, once married, are (relatively) stationary.

him,[8] and signals the parallelism between the new labor that Perseus must perform and his earlier and most famous exploit: defeating the monster and slaying the Gorgon both rid the world of creatures capable of turning their victims to immobile stone images.

Many myths of petrifaction—the transformation of men, beasts, and animate objects into monumental, and sometimes explicitly, statue form—build on the opposition between fleet-footedness and the fixity peculiar to the fashioned stone. The preternatural swiftness the victim has displayed often prompts the metamorphosis, as the punishment falls on those who have moved too fast, or with an ease that challenges divine supremacy in this domain.[9] The petrifaction of the Phaeacian ship at *Odyssey* 13.163–64 may broadly serve to seal off the world of Scheria and prevent any future intercourse with this Wonderland, but it more immediately answers the poet's account of the mysterious self-moving vessel, which travels with the speed of a wing or thought (7.36); just prior to the transformation, the motion of the ship is described by the adverb *rhimpha* (13.162), a term frequently reserved for the uncheckable passage of the gods themselves.[10] The fabulously mobile vessel that attracts Poseidon's wrath offers a miniaturized account of the Phaeacians' own defining attribute, that suprahuman swiftness and lithe character which makes them preeminent seafarers and dancers.[11] A no less punitive and divinely imposed stillness also claims the Teumessian fox and dog of Kephalos described in later sources: the rapidity of the fox who can never be caught, and of the hound who never misses its prey, is the reason for gods' decision to resolve the conundrum by turning them both into unmoving stones.[12]

Nothing better declares the defining immobility of the image than the

[8] Later poets would adopt the same conceit: see Achilles Tatius's ekphrastic evocation of Andromeda (3.7.1–2), and Ov. *Met.* 4.672–6, where the contrasting mobility of Perseus receives particular emphasis. For the play between motion and immobility, and the theme of petrifaction in the larger episode, see Barkan 1986: 52–56.

[9] For the divine monopoly on motion, see the second section of this chapter.

[10] See the remarks of Fraenkel 1962: ad 407.

[11] As the unpublished discussion of Marta Steele argues, the immobility that the Phaeacians must now maintain (reinforced by Poseidon's threat additionally to bury their city beneath a mountain at 13.152) suggests that they have brought on themselves the very condition that Odysseus most profoundly desires. From the paradigmatic wanderer and displaced individual of the song's opening lines, he seeks to achieve the fixity that the term *empedos* denotes, and that his home-rooted artifacts themselves possess.

[12] On this myth, see Forbes Irving 1992: 146 (with sources listed at 299). Note, too, that although Perseus escapes the fate that the petrifying Gorgon would inflict on him, the confrontation between the hero and the monster suggests the close relation between their parallel and antithetical powers: the two present such worthy antagonists because the Gorgon is uniquely able to strip her assailant of the quality of motion that he most superabundantly displays.

category of statues that quite literally escape the general rule. By contrast to the static figures that mortal artists sculpt, myth proposes a series of peripatetic objects modeled by divine, heroic, and daemonic artisans. In the foundry that Homer designs for Hephaistos, the automata crafted by the god are self-movers (perhaps in contrast to their maker's own more cumbersome motion): the golden *amphipoloi* attend him on his rounds, and the tripods he forges can roll themselves about at will (*Il.* 18.417–18, 375–77; cf. Arist. *Pol.* 1253b36). Legends preserved in later authors invest other magical statues fashioned by Hephaistos with the same powers of mobility and name him creator of Talos, the bronze image that walks thrice daily around the periphery of Crete, pelting with rocks anyone who threatens to approach the island.[13] Sources from the fifth century and beyond make Daidalos heir to Hephaistos's particular skill, and like to dwell on this single and most troublesome aspect of his products: unless chained in place, they up and leave the bases on which they stand. So individuals in comic dramas wonder at the disappearance of the statues that the craftsman built,[14] and Socrates claims Daidalos as his progenitor when he compares his arguments to images that stubbornly refuse to stay in place; only binding can hold them down and prevent them from escaping in the manner of the sculptor's runaway works (*Meno* 97d).[15] Other figures closely related to Hephaistos also inherit his mobilizing powers. Sons of the craftsman-god in some accounts, the daemonic and wizardlike Telchines appear as both magicians and fabricants of images.[16] Their statues could be seen walking along roads, and the craftsmen of the island of Rhodes, where the Telchines lived, drew their own skills in fashioning images that looked as though they walked (so Pind. *Ol.* 7.52) from the example of their mythical antecedents.

If poets and mythmakers are content to play off of, and at times deny, the fixed quality proper to the statue, then the magical rites practiced by

---

[13] Apollod. *Bibl.* 1.140–2 and 3.197–98; Ap. Rhod. 4.1639–93; Paus. 8.53.5. Much earlier sources refer to Talos, but in the extant fragments the focus falls on how he consumes intruders with his fiery heat; see Simon. fr. 568 *PMG* and Soph. fr. 160–61 Radt. For discussion, Delcourt 1957: 160–62 and Frontisi-Ducroux 1975: 125–34.

[14] In Kratinos's *Thracians* (fr. 75 KA), a Pan statue has mysteriously vanished, and Daidalos is named as the author of the peripatetic representation; see also Plato Comicus fr. 204 KA.

[15] For additional references to Daidalos's moving images, Overbeck 120–37. The rationalizing glosses of later commentators would translate these animated statues into examples of technical innovations in the art of image-making: the historical sculptor first devised the means of separating the legs of his pieces and making them look as though they walked. For the fallacy of the argument, see S. P. Morris 1992: chap. 9.

[16] See Diod. Sic. 5.55.1–3; Hsch. s.v. For further discussion, Deonna 1935: 233; Delcourt 1957: 168–70; Detienne and Vernant 1978: 259–60.

the Greeks make more direct appeal to the figure's inability to walk, and harness that handicap to their own ends. In a previous chapter I cited the role of images in ghost-banning rituals and suggested that the doubling figurines provided one means of putting a stop to the havoc wreaked by the unquiet souls of the dead and ghosts that roamed at large, causing private or public afflictions. Among their other properties, revenants are so very troublesome because they enjoy an uncheckable mobility and show themselves no less unexpectedly than they disappear: as those who try to hold them in their arms discover, they can be neither restrained nor pinned down, but slip away with their irrepressible motion.[17] In several ghost-repelling rites, the practitioner calls on the immobile quality of the statue to supply an antidote to the revenant's vexing power. The "exorcism" preserved in the Kyrenean sacred law directs the householder plagued by the *hikesios epaktos* or evil spirit conjured up by spells to fashion male and female *kolossoi* and, after entertaining them to a meal, to "deposit them in uncultivated ground" (*SEG* 9.72.111–21).[18] If, as has been argued, absence of motion distinguishes the *kolossos* with its rigid stance, its undifferentiated legs, and its blocklike shape,[19] then this statue type is ideally suited to combat the ghost, instantiating the immobility that the householder would impose on his unwanted visitor. By way of further guarantee, the legless image must be taken to a place distant from human habitation, where it is either planted in the earth or, according to a different reading of the text, actually buried beneath the ground.[20]

A statue employed as part of a second ghost-banning ritual still more vividly suggests the blow dealt by the static figurine against the too-mobile revenant. When Pausanias describes the measures taken by the people of Orchomenos to rid themselves of the problematic *eidōlon* of Aktaion, which was "running amok and ravaging the land," he notes the two provisions that the Delphic oracle recommended: the community should erect a bronze image of the ghost and use iron to fix the statue to the rock where the double appeared (9.38.5). Here the twofold stratagem works to counter the spirit's rapid visitations as the statue immobilizes the *eidōlon*, and the iron attachments reiterate and enforce the fact of motionlessness. The episode also recalls events at Kyrene, replacing the interment of the *kolossoi* beneath ground with the no less efficacious binding of the image.

According to the ancient sources, statues suffer a further deficiency; not only incapable of walking, they also remain deaf and dumb. Em-

---

[17] Most famously at *Il.* 23.99–101.
[18] For this, see p. 10.
[19] Roux 1960.
[20] Faraone 1992: 92 n. 66.

pedocles draws on the conceit when he traces the genesis of mankind and describes human evolution through the paradigm of the craftsman modeling a fashioned object: the ancestors of men and women were inanimate *tupoi*, hollow molds or outlines, before voice or language was added; these vacant objects possessed "neither cry nor any innate voice for men" (fr. 62 Wright).[21] So, too, the *eidōla* that the satyrs in Aeschylus's *Theoroi* contemplate seemingly possess all indices of life and only betray their manufactured status through their silence: "this imitation of Daidalos lacks only a voice."[22] The trait of voicelessness is one that statues share with the typically silent and unhearing stone so often used for their creation: Theognis cites the *lithos apthongos* by way of simile for the condition he will assume after his life is done (568–69), and the silent and unresponding Medea moves the Nurse to compare her charge to a rock that can hear nothing of the advice addressed by friends (Eur. *Med.* 28–29). Reiterating the notion that neither stones nor the artifacts fashioned from them can speak, one of the women admiring a group of remarkably lifelike sculpted figures in Herondas's fourth *Mime* would remark: "If it were not stone, the work, you will say, would speak" (32–33).

Just as the artifact's immobility served to emphasize the remarkable feats of motion another figure displayed, so, too, its silence can throw signal performances of speech and song into sharper relief. Even as Theognis in the lines stated above muses on his fate after death and his transformation into the silent monument, the present song demonstrates the singing and musical powers that he so abundantly possesses and gives to their loss a particular poignancy. The *agalmata* introduced by Pindar at the start of *Nemean* 5 offer a twofold contrast to the poet's ode: not only do they remain fastened to their bases, but they fail dismally in the chief task that a commemorative device should undertake, that of broadcasting the victor's triumph so that all can hear it. Now the poem, assuming the voice of the herald who originally proclaimed the win, declares that it will amply fulfill its brief (*diangelloisa*, 3), and goes on to supply all the requisite details of Pytheas's achievement. The contrast between the rigid, silent stone and the dance and sounding song peculiar to choral activity returns a second time toward the closing of the ode, when the singers are invited to approach the victory image of Pytheas's dead relative, Themistios, and to deliver his praises, too. As though the performers risk the stillness and muteness characteristic of the statue, the poet bids his chorus not to stiffen (*rhigei*), but to give voice (*didoi phōnan*, 50–51).[23]

---

[21] S. P. Morris 1992: 221 discusses the fragment.

[22] For this, see discussion of this fragment in chapter 1.

[23] For more detailed treatment of the relations between songs and statues in the ode, see chapter 5.

Fresh demonstrations that speech and figures of stone cannot coincide belong to myths of petrifaction where the gods exact the penalty expressly to silence a sinner.[24] Although Homer chooses not to make direct mention of Niobe's metamorphosis, his version of the tale in *Iliad* 24 obliquely recalls the heroine's fate (611; cf. 617) and makes her act of speech provoke the punishment that the gods deal out (608). In dramatizing the story, Aeschylus would also refer to the "boldness of mouth" (*thrasustomein*, fr. 154a.17 Radt) that Niobe displays, and the audience might see in the tableau of the silent protagonist that opened the play (if Euripides' parody in Aristophanes' *Frogs* is to be believed) a prefiguration of the fate that would overcome this prime practitioner of importunate speech.[25] In claiming her victims, the Gorgon not only strips them of their ability to move but renders them mute as well. Socrates plays on the notion when, in his gentle mockery of Agathon's verbal dexterity, he declares himself afraid of being left incapable of speaking when his turn comes. Likening the dramatist's rhetorical powers to those of the spellbinding Gorgias, he puns on the rival teacher's name even as he parodies his style: "And you see, the speech reminded me of Gorgias, so that I actually experienced what Homer describes: I was afraid that Agathon would end by sending the Gorgian head, marvelous at speaking in a speech, against my speech, and, by afflicting me with speechlessness, it would turn me to stone" (Pl. *Symp.* 198c).[26]

Just as the walking images manufactured by gods and legendary craftsmen pointed up the inert character that the objects should properly preserve, so, too, the same artifacts distinguish themselves from the common round through their possession of voice. Earliest among these *adunata* are the machinelike maidens populating Hephaistos's Iliadic

---

[24] For discussion, Forbes Irving 1992: 145.

[25] Several postclassical texts contrast the silence Niobe doubly observes, as mourning mother and as stone image, with her previous chattering; e.g., *Anth. Plan.* 16.134. In other sources, individuals guilty of boasting, importunate or lying chatter find themselves translated into figures of stone. Already in *Hymn. Hom. Merc.* the poet underlines the silence that the old vine-digger, witness to the theft that the infant god has performed, should observe in order to keep out of danger ("Strictly remember not to have heard what you have heard, and to keep silent," 92–93). Perhaps building on the injunction, Hellenistic authors would name the old man Battos and describe the petrifaction that he suffered as a result of his garrulous revelations. See Forbes Irving 1992: 286–87 for the sources and development of the story. Most emphatic is Ovid's use of the motif at *Met.* 2.696, where Battos promises silence: "That stone will speak of your theft before I do."

[26] The remark forms a piece with the several other moments the *Symposium* includes when Socrates assumes a likeness to images of stone, and perhaps looks forward to the transformation of his own living words into the quintessentially frozen and silent medium of the text that the reader now confronts. For this, see Steiner 1996.

foundry, whom the craftsman has equipped with *audē* (18.419). Voice and language are, of course, among the chief attributes granted Pandora in her vivification (Hes. *Op.* 61, 78), and powers of speech also belong to the daidalic *knōdala* on the woman's crown, which are "like to creatures with voice" (*Theog.* 584). A fragment from Pindar's eighth *Paean* includes an intriguing reference to golden statues displayed on the pediment of the Temple of Apollo at Delphi, which together the divine artisans Athena and Hephaistos built: these six *kēlēdones*, the lines suggest, actually sang (70–71). In other fifth-century sources, Daidalos appears as the author of speaking images. When Euripides' Hecuba imagines herself a statue made by the master craftsman, every part of the body would have powers of articulation (*Hec.* 836–40), and a scholiast on the line confirms that Daidalic images did indeed both move and speak (*kineisthai kai phthegesthai*).[27] The comic poets take the conceit one step further, presenting works fashioned by Daidalos that actually enter into conversation with their interlocutors: a fragment from an unnamed play of Plato's (fr. 204 KA) refers to a "Hermes of Daidalos" and makes the object respond to the question "Won't you speak? . . . Why are you silent?" by first affirming its possession of voice (*Hermēs egōge Daidalou phōnēn echōn*), and then going on to act as partner in the dialogue. These powers of articulation, sometimes the actual emission of sound and voice and sometimes merely a simulation of speech, would become a standard element in later inventories of the remarkable properties that characterized Daidalos's works.[28]

Third in the triad of uncanny attributes that Daidalic images display is the ability to see. Euripides combines walking and sight when a character in one of his satyr plays declares that all of Daidalos's *agalmata* "seem to move and see" (fr. 372 N[2]), and later authors endlessly report and try to rationalize the popular belief that the craftsman animated his statues by opening their eyes and granting the previously blind artifacts powers of sight.[29] Before the advent of the image-maker, sculpted figures were eyeless, or *aommatoi* (schol. ad Pl. *Meno* 97d) or had their eyes fast closed (*tois ommasi memukota*, Diod. Sic. 4.76.3; cf. Suda s.v. *Daidalou poiēmata*), but after his innovations, they seemed capable of seeing. Since the course of Greek statue-making singularly fails to dovetail with this account, and "closed eyes" never characterized a phase in its

---

[27] In support, the scholion also quotes the fragment from Euripides' *Eurystheus* (fr. 372 N[2]) cited in chapter 1, which features the moving and possibly speaking statues of Daidalos; note the variant reading *legein* (proposed by F. G. Schmidt) for the more probable *blepein* in the lines, with discussion in Kassel 1983: 5.

[28] E.g., Zen. *Proverbia* 3.7.

[29] E.g., Overbeck 70, 71, 72, 125, 133.

evolution,[30] the sources must be attempting to fit long-standing traditions featuring Daidalos's extraordinary sighted works to their more sober "art historical" schemes, and to reconcile them with the trajectory that they imposed on innovations in sculptural techniques.

Nor does the connection between statues and blindness remain restricted to Daidalos's sphere. In other fifth-century sources, poets evoke the unseeing statue by way of foil to the visual powers belonging to the subject of their verse, and references to images suggest themselves precisely when visual contact, the prelude to any act of communication or fellow feeling, fails to occur.[31] Earlier I noted how in Aeschylus's *Agamemnon* the chorus's appeal to the unmoving *kolossoi* drew attention to the unstoppable motion of the queen. But these statues diverge from the absent Helen in another, still more critical respect: because they lack *ommata* (418), they can neither stimulate nor respond to the passion that always depends on an exchange of glances between lover and beloved.[32] Once again Aeschylus's conceit depends on relations of contrast between Helen and the images standing in the palace. The inability of the blind statues to inspire love recalls Helen's power to do precisely that, and in the second stasimon of the drama the chorus will elaborate on its brief allusion here, describing the soft but deadly dart, the heart-piercing flower of love that the queen emits from her eyes (742–43).[33]

If petrifaction responds to and cancels out an individual's ability to move with excessive speed or to speak too much, so, too, it exists in close and antithetical relation to a victim's powers of sight. Seeing and being seen figure centrally in the Perseus myth, from the hero's theft of

[30] For this, Deonna 1935: 224; S. P. Morris 1992: 242. As Morris also notes, there is no evidence for the chronological coincidence of open eyes and limbs positioned as though in walking.

[31] Although Medea's Nurse compares her charge to a rock chiefly for her unwillingness to hear, the simile follows immediately from her observation that the queen "will not raise her eyes nor turn her face from the ground" (Eur. *Med.* 27–29). And when Xenophon wishes to evoke the chastity of young Spartans and their reluctance to exchange those charged looks of love, he remarks that "it would be easier to make the eyes of bronze statues turn" (*Lac.* 3.5). For a complex play on the normal equation of the nonlooker with the statue, see the tale of Anaxarete in Ovid *Met.* 14.698–761. The maiden's failure to look at her would-be lover while he is still alive, and willingness only to contemplate him when he is dead, anticipates her transformation into an image.

[32] On the grounds for assigning the eyelessness to the *kolossoi*, see Steiner 1995b: 179. Just as mobility defines Helen from the start, so, too, her appearance in *Iliad* 3 indicates the cardinal importance of her visual faculties: the Trojan elders compare her face to that of goddesses (158), using the term *ōps* (cognate with *opsomai*), which, as Frontisi-Ducroux (1995: 19–20) has demonstrated, signifies both looking and being looked at.

[33] We might contrast the impotence of Iphigenia's earlier visual (but voiceless) appeals for pity, conjured up at the moment when she is described as *prepousa hōs en graphais* ("striking as in a picture," 240–42).

the eye of the Graiai to the cap of invisibility he receives, and Perseus's success in defeating his opponent depends on his avoiding visual contact with the target of his attack, turning his head aside, and, in sources from the fifth-century on, using the shield by way of mirror. By momentarily assuming the "facelessness" that characterizes the blind, the hero has effectively anticipated and so forestalled the condition that Medusa would impose on him.[34] Other myths and conceits included in later sources feature lithification as a punishment for the voyeur whose eyes have seen what should be hidden, and the *contrappasso* underlying the penalty depends on the (unstated) assumption that stones cannot see. The faithless Battos, the aged vinekeeper witness to the infant Hermes' act of theft, is turned to stone not only for his inability to keep silent, but also for his failure to respect the order issued by the god already in the *Homeric Hymn*, that he make invisible what he had seen (92). In other tales of mortals who similarly intrude wittingly or unwittingly on the divine sphere and observe things that should remain hidden from sight, blindness and petrifaction exist as two interchangeable or sequential elements:[35] when Kalydon spots Artemis at her bath, he is instantly turned to stone, while blindness claims Apollo's son Eurymanthos for his glimpse of Aphrodite bathing after her union with Adonis.[36]

Death and the Image

The repeated conjunction of walking (upright and on the ground), talking, and seeing in accounts of animated images has an evident logic of its own. The triad of activities not only distinguishes men from other animals in Aristotle's definition,[37] but more fundamentally marks out things sentient and alive from the inanimate and the dead. I want to pursue this division, and to propose that the archaic and classical sources introduce allusions to statues as a means of signaling an individual's momentary or more lasting departure from the society of the living, and of underscoring the rupture between that character and the community to which he formerly belonged; deprived, whether through his own volition or against his will, of powers of motion, speech, and

---

[34] For this, Vernant 1991: 135–36; Steiner 1995a.

[35] See Steiner 1995a for these.

[36] Ptolemaios Hephaistion in Phot. *Bibl.* cod. 190 pp. 146–47; see, too, Forbes Irving 1992: 288–89. For the literalization of these images of petrifaction as a result of importune viewing, note Apuleius's description of a statue representing Aktaion being transformed into a hart as he spies on the goddess Artemis (*Met.* 2.4); the hero's own voyeurship here anticipates the motif of petrifaction that runs through the remainder of this portion of the tale.

[37] *Hist. an.* 1.8.491b; *Part. an.* 3.1.662a.

visual exchange, the "statuefied" character already shows his kinship with the dead.

The Greek sources equate walking and living so closely that a single term evocative of motion can do double duty. Mobility, figured as conventional movement with two feet upon the ground, distinguishes men that live, and animate beings may simply be styled "creatures that walk."[38] No wonder that death, or the Homeric "fate of death" (*moira thanatou*), declares itself in the form of the sudden arrest of motion, of a bond that ensnares, paralyzes, and holds its victim fast, freezing the shining and supple limbs that symbolize vitality already in archaic songs.[39] Once an individual has joined the realm of the deceased, he acquires a new and anomalous mode of locomotion, or stops walking altogether: the *psuchai* of the suitors who follow Hermes down to Hades flit about in the manner of bats (*Od.* 24.6–7), and iconographic representations of the soul portray it as a miniaturized replica of the individual, which no longer travels on the ground but flies from the motionless body down to Hades.[40] According to one variant reading of a gloss by Hesychius, the dead are *abantes*, those who do not walk.[41]

Deprived of the ability to move about, the dead are reimagined and re-presented in forms indicative of their new condition. The stone, stele, or funerary image that tops the grave, which is defined as fixed, unmoving, and in Homeric terms *empedos* (e.g., *Il.* 17.434), visibly declares the static character of the occupier of the grave and, as Vernant has suggested, offers a structural parallel to the *psuchē*, which, flying off from a man at the moment of his death, travels above ground; the fixity of the one and the extraordinary mobility of the other both exist in opposition to the living man who walks with his two feet upon the earth.[42] For poets and composers of epitaphs, this immobile funerary marker or monument can supply a means of figuring an individual on the point of death, or one already deceased. In the Homeric passage cited earlier, where the singer likens Alkathoos to a grave stele, the simile acts as a harbinger of the fate about to claim the Trojan warrior. The expression *atremas hestaota* ("standing fixed," *Il.* 13.438), positioned exactly midway between the tenor and vehicles of the phrase, applies

[38] E.g., *Il.* 17.447; Pind. *Ol.* 7.52; cf. Arist. *Hist. an.* 1.8.491b for man as two-footed walker.

[39] E.g., *Il.* 4.517; *Od.* 18.155–56; Pind. *Pae.* 6.81–85; with discussion in Onians 1988: esp. 327–28, 372–73. Note, too, *Hymn. Hom. Ven*, where the advent of debilitating old age declares itself in the cessation of Tithonos's motion and in his inability to move his previously supple limbs (233–34).

[40] For examples, Vermeule 1981: 9, fig. 4; 65, fig. 23.

[41] S.v. *kolossoi*; for this reading, see Roux 1960: 35–36.

[42] Vernant 1983: 313.

equally to the victim, whose "shining limbs" Poseidon has already chained, and to the stele or high-leafed tree rooted to the earth that his stance recalls.[43] So, too, Theognis imagines how he will lie (*keisomai*) eternally both like and in the form of the grave *lithos* (568), and the mid-fifth-century marble stele that announces, "Here I lie in place of the woman" (*CEG* 153), declares its own position equivalent to that of the dead for whom it stands in. In the *Agamemnon*, the term *eumorphoi* first used of the motionless *kolossoi* of Helen cited by Aeschylus's chorus returns in the very next dyad, where the singers reapply it to the corpses of the Greeks whom the Trojan soil holds fast in its unrelenting embrace (454–55); the images retrospectively seem not statues of a beautiful woman but funerary monuments and doubles for those firmly held and never-to-return warriors who died on the queen's behalf.[44]

The dead or almost dead are not alone in assuming the character of monuments and statues, and the same trope can be used for those who voluntarily declare their oneness with a beloved deceased. In his second appeal to the stele in a simile, Homer imagines his subjects in the form of mourners as well as funerary markers. Emulating the posture of the grave stone as they stand stock-still, the divine horses of Achilles hang their heads and weep in longing for their absent driver (*Il.* 17.436–39). Like the other modes of behavior that the grieving person adopts, the immobile stance announces a momentary withdrawal from the community of those who live and move, and empathy with the condition of the dead.[45] Perhaps this same confusion between grave monument and mourner informs the appearance of Niobe at the start of Aeschylus's treatment of her tale. Introducing the grief-struck heroine as she is seated on her children's tomb,[46] the playwright might invite his audience to see her as part of the commemorative marker, and a much later source makes the connection explicit when he remarks that Niobe was confused with a statue on her children's tomb (Palaephatus 8).

For the Euripides of Aristophanes' *Frogs*, the singularity of this Niobe lies not with her immobility, but with her inability or refusal to speak

---

[43] The two terms introduce a poignant opposition between the living tree, so often a symbol of generational continuity, and the sterile stone. Note, too, that *atremas* is also used of Odysseus holding his eyes as fixed or motionless as though they were "of horn or iron" (*Od.* 19.211–12).

[44] Note the idea of fixity made so emphatic in the terms *katechousin*, *echontas* and even the sound of the term *echthra* evocative of the other expressions.

[45] Longing to quit a life that no longer holds any charms for him since the loss of his wife, Admetus voices his distaste for walking on the ground (Eur. *Alc.* 869) and envisions adopting a style of life that will keep him fixed indoors.

[46] Ar. *Ran.* 911–13; Aesch. fr. 154a Radt.

(*Ran.* 913–24). Like motion, powers of articulation belong among the
defining properties of living men, and their loss characterizes the dead,
the dying, and those who would embrace the experience of the deceased.[47] Individuals suffering a loss of consciousness find their voices
growing thick inside their throats, and the only faculty that distinguishes the superannuated Tithonos from the dead is his continued possession of voice (*Hymn. Hom. Ven.* 237). When Zeus puts an end to
Castor's life, he does so by "releasing his voice" (Pind. *Nem.* 10.90).
Evocations of the condition of those destined for or already in Hades
imagine them unable to speak at all, or merely uttering inarticulate
sounds. The Homeric poet paints the souls of the suitors twittering or
squeaking in the manner of bats as they travel down to the Underworld
(*Od.* 24.7, 9), and, once resident in the gloomy depths, it seems that the
eidōla require an infusion of liquid offerings before they can answer the
questions addressed to them by a living man (*Od.* 11.88–89, 96, 98–
99).[48] Silence is the more generalized condition that prevails down in
Hades, where few if any sounds penetrate,[49] and Pindar can assign no
greater glory to his song than its power of traveling down below the
earth and continuing to sound out in the infernal realms (*Ol.* 14.21).
Indeed, one of the strange "miracles" that the epinician genre can
achieve is precisely the envoicing of the silent and nonsentient dead.
Nearing the conclusion of *Nemean* 4, the chorus imagines how the victor's dead grandfather "will gladly sing" (89–90) the praises of another
dead relative, his maternal uncle Kallikles, prompting a scholion to the
line to observe: "Euphanes will celebrate him, clearly as a dead man
celebrating a dead man, showing that in Hades, too, there are those
who admire outstanding people and that they possess the power of perception there."

In imagining Euphanes singing in his underground home, Pindar has
met the injunction earlier imposed on him, that he raise "a stele whiter
than Parian stone" on Kallikles' behalf (79–81). The efficacy of his poetic monument, and its superiority to the marble grave marker on which
the conceit draws, depend precisely on the creation of a work that not
only has still greater visible radiance than the physical artifact, but also
possesses the voice that the fashioned stone necessarily lacks (82–85).
Within the relations that the closing strophe and antistrophe set up, it is

[47] In the rationalizing accounts that Cicero (*Tusc.* 3.63) and Philemon (fr. 101) would later
offer, Niobe does not suffer a literal petrifaction, but her transformation into a lithified
object symbolizes the eternal silence that she maintains as part of her mourning for her
slaughtered children.
[48] This may be part of the common equation between death and dryness, for which see
Onians 1988: esp. chap. 6 and 254–56.
[49] Vernant 1983: 311–12.

the dead grandfather who becomes that polished and sounding stele as Pindar hands over to him, as the more trustworthy eyewitness to Kallikles' bygone deed, the task of creating the song of praise. By virtue of his sounding tribute, Euphanes not only memorializes the triumph, but also has transcended his own "monumentalized" condition in the realm of the dead.

But Pindar's epinician world stands as an exception to the common rule, and more generally poets liken individuals to monuments and images so as to emphasize the silence that they share with the dying, the dead, or a grief-struck mourner.[50] When Euripides' Admetus first announces his intention of having a statue made to set in the marital bed in place of his soon-to-be-dead spouse (*Alc.* 348–54), the conceit does no more than underscore the lifelessness about to overcome the heroine of the drama (and the extravagant nature of her spouse's grief). But if the playwright intends an echo of this image in his account of the figure of Alcestis who returns from death at the ending of the drama,[51] then Admetus's words acquire a more extended and proleptic reach. Behaving much as though she had been transformed into the inanimate artifact of her husband's musings, Alcestis preserves so curious a muteness throughout the final scene that Admetus wonders at her silence, and charges Heracles with providing an explanation (1143–46).[52]

If walking, talking, and living form so tight a composite, then seeing forms the third element in the definition of what it is to be alive. The Homeric songs already equate sight with existence above ground,[53] and the Attic tragedians endlessly echo and ornament the notion: Xerxes is declared safe because he "lives and sees the light" (Aesch. *Pers.* 299; cf. Eur. *Hel.* 341), and Iphigenia mistakenly supposes that Orestes "no longer looks on the sun, nor sees the light" (Eur. *IT* 564). The coming of death takes the form of a dimming of the eyes, or of a mist or black night that pours down and covers the victim's features.[54] The dead man

---

[50] Although textual problems prevent a certain reading here, the portrait of the disconsolate Menelaus supplied by the chorus in Aeschylus's *Agamemnon* seems to indicate the prince's own affinity to the *kolossoi* that the singers go on to cite in the lines immediately following: seated in silence in the palace, the prince assumes the character of an inanimate object, mute and deaf to all the appeals addressed to him (412–13). The matching account of the Argive women grieving for their men lost at Troy to whom the singers turn (430–36) confirms Menelaus's role as silent mourner in his home.

[51] Segal 1993: 37–50; Bassi 1989 for this suggestion.

[52] Silence is also the condition that Admetus wishes to preserve after the death of his beloved spouse as he seeks to turn his home into a place void of all music and song and to shut himself off from all social intercourse (*Alc.* 343–47).

[53] E.g., *Od.* 14.44.

[54] Among many examples, *Il.* 5.696, 13.580; Simon. 9.2 *FGE*; Eur. *Alc.* 385; additional discussion in Onians 1988: 422–25. The enveloping cloud of death can be designated

in his sightlessness becomes one with Hades, the god whose name the ancient commentators gloss as the unseeing one (A-idēs),[55] while the reciprocity informing Greek notions of vision — where seeing necessarily involves being seen — renders both the deity and his victims invisible.[56] Nothing better reveals the blindness and invisibility assigned to the dead than the Greeks' refusal to grant them a *prosōpon*, the face so closely bound up with the fact of sight because it allows its owner to see and be seen.[57] Beyond mere existence, vision also means the possibility of communal living, of entering into the social bonds that an exchange of glances so often initiates and fosters.[58] Individuals who seek to avoid relations with others, whether through grief, anger, madness, or shame, regularly lower their eyes, cover their heads, and turn their backs on their interlocutors so as to prohibit visual contact.[59] In so doing, they anticipate the isolation that will claim them after death, when all such "eye-to-eye" encounters must necessarily cease.

In several of the examples already cited, an allusion to a stone, stele, or statue conveys or reinforces the visual rupture that the dead, and those wishing to assume a deathlike state, undergo. The divine horses of Achilles likened to a grave stone hang their heads to the ground as they mourn the loss of their driver (*Il.* 17.437), and Euripides' Medea, rock-like in her refusal to respond to those about her, will not raise her eyes or lift up her *prosōpon* (*Med.* 27–28). In a fresh link back to the statue conceit used earlier, and a nod toward the third of the three handicaps that the dead and statues both suffer, Euripides takes pains to emphasize that when Alcestis returns from below, she neither sees nor is seen.[60] The heroine has her face covered in a veil and must wait until the decisive rite of the *anakaluptēria* (*Alc.* 1121) that Heracles performs for the

---

with the term *achlus*, and Theoklymenos's mantic vision allows him to view the suitors in Odysseus's hall already mantled in the death-heralding mist (*Od.* 20.351–52).

[55] Hades shares this property with his near-synonymous fellow divinity Ploutos, whom the sources regularly depict as blind. For identifications of the two gods, see Soph. fr. 273 Radt; cf. Pl. *Cra.* 403a; Timocreon 731 *PMG*; Theoc. 10.19.

[56] For the invisible dead, Aesch. *Ag.* 466; it is Hades who possesses the cap of invisibility and who comes upon his victims unawares. On the reciprocal nature of sight, Frontisi-Ducroux 1995: esp. 20.

[57] As Frontisi-Ducroux (ibid.: 36) explains, "La réciprocité grecque du voir et de l'être vu exige que le visage devienne invisible dès lors que les regards du mourant s'éteignent" ("The Greek notion of the reciprocity of seeing and being seen demands that the face become invisible as soon as the looks of the dying are extinguished").

[58] Ibid.: 22–25, with examples.

[59] E.g., Eur. *Hec.* 739, 343; *Or.* 467–69; *Hipp.* 720. Vase depictions of Achilles hearing the ambassadors sent by Agamemnon depict the hero not looking at the speakers, and shrouded in his cloak.

[60] In an earlier episode, Admetus begs his dying wife to raise her *prosōpon* and look at her children (*Alc.* 388).

recovery of her visual faculties. At the moment of unveiling, Admetus celebrates the fact of mutual seeing and being seen: following Heracles' injunction (*blepson*, 1121), he looks upon his wife (1124, 1129) and, convinced at last of the reality of what confronts his eyes, declares the renewal of reciprocal vision interrupted by Alcestis's death (1133–34).[61] But this process of revivification did not occur without its attendant risks: even as the husband had reluctantly reached out his hand to lead the revenant into his home, he averted his gaze "as though beheading the Gorgon" (1118). Still marked by her passage through Hades, the guest has an infectious quality, and might turn the one who looks at her into a second thing of stone.

Representations of the Dead

The imaginary monuments and statues devised by the archaic and classical sources do not exist uniquely in the literary domain; instead they belong in the context of real-world images raised on behalf of the dead, familiar features in the everyday landscape of the audiences for the texts. These representations display their own reflections on death, and offer sometimes matching, sometimes contrasting treatments of the silence, stillness, and lack of reciprocal vision that are the common properties of the dead and statues both. While the artifacts, together with their accompanying epitaphs, may juxtapose the faculties that the individual enjoyed while still alive with his now lamentably diminished state, both the image and the inscription no less frequently work in tandem to negate the fact of loss, seeking rather to reendow the deceased with the several powers he no longer possesses. Indeed, one of the most remarkable features of these funerary monuments, and perhaps the source of their consoling powers, is precisely their reluctance to recognize those distinctions between the living and the dead which other media are so quick to assert.

In the very conventionalized language of the epitaphs, the dead frequently figure as lying in their graves, and the term *keimai* regularly describes their condition. But far from imagining their subjects as immobile, late archaic and early classical monuments seem eager to suggest that the dead, or rather the memory of the social persona of the deceased that the marker serves to symbolize, should be perceived as engaged in the vigorous activities that he performed while still alive, and quite explicitly in walking. The selection of the *kouros* as the funerary image of choice declares as much, and Brunilde Ridgway draws

---

[61] Note the reference to the *omma* at *Alc.* 1137.

attention to the central modification that the Greeks introduced to the Egyptian model so as to enhance the images' dynamism:

> Contrary to present belief, I am convinced that the *kouroi* do not simply stand with one leg advanced: they walk. To enforce this "hieroglyph" of striding, the Greeks even removed the back support of their Egyptian prototypes, and the stone screen between the body and the advanced leg, which to their eyes froze the male figures into statuesque immobility.[62]

The better to reinforce this impression of motion, funerary *kouroi* from the later period (that belonging to Aristodikos, for example)[63] unite the walking or striding pose of the lower body with arms that are bent and held away from the sides. The same convention appears in other figures used for grave markers. Most of the standing, draped youths decorating monuments advance forward, one foot and leg placed well in front of the other,[64] and Attic grave stelae from the second half of the sixth century on regularly show figures in a walking pose (Fig. 13). So the young man on the monument from Nisyros (c. 470–460 B.C.) and the little girl on a funerary stele from Paros (c. 470–460 B.C.) assume the same characteristic stance, one foot planted before the other and the knees flexed.[65] Other carved figures on stelae still more emphatically signal motion by depicting the dead as warriors, athletes, and horsemen, engaged in the roles that occupied them while still alive.[66]

The negation of death implicit in such movement-filled poses, often reinforced by the messages inscribed on the statue bases (so Kroisos, Fig. 1, and others are imagined "fighting in the vanguard," even as the image itself strides visibly forward), might serve a comforting end, declaring that the individual still participates in the world he has left behind and retains the property peculiar to living men. But the continuity between the dead and the living that these stelae and statues promote can take a different and more troublesome form. Just as Odysseus exits

---

[62] Ridgway 1993: 31. Even where the leg and foot are less emphatically placed in front, the action indicated by the figure is still that of potential walking or striding (Fig. 13, and Sourvinou-Inwood 1995: 253). It is also striking that funerary *kouroi* (and *korai*) are indistinguishable from those found in sanctuaries, where they fulfill a votive role.

[63] Richter 1970: no. 165.

[64] For exceptions and discussion, see Sourvinou-Inwood 1995: 232.

[65] If Métraux's thesis is correct (1995: 84), then the motion of the limbs was one way of suggesting the workings of an animating force and of asserting the liveliness of the representation.

[66] Stewart 1990: 50 for these. The figures carved on bases designed for *kouroi* engage in particularly energetic activity — wrestling, playing ball, and hockey (see the so-called ballplayer bases and hockey-players base from the Themistoklean Wall, dated to c. 500). Of course, these activities also look to the social status of the dead, and their participation in the elite pastimes of their age.

hastily from the borders of Hades, alarmed lest Persephone "send up against me some gorgonish head" that would make him incapable of escape (*Od*. 11.634–35), and Admetus fears that contact with a dweller of Hades might turn him into stone (Eur. *Alc*. 1118), so, too, the individual who confronts the representation of the deceased might experience transformation into a second frozen figure; infected with the immobility that the dead and even the most naturalistic and vivid plastic accounts must jointly observe, he risks losing his own faculty of motion.[67] The funerary epitaphs signal the change that the static image visually threatens to perform; frequent in inscriptions of the late archaic and classical periods are injunctions to the viewer to stop his progress along his path and stand still (*stethi*) while he observes the monument.[68] Although the stasis does not last, and the earliest surviving grave epigram from Attica (c. 575–550, *CEG* 13) allows the reader to resume his journey once he has paid his dues,[69] the traveler's own posture apes that of the dead and of the stone or marble monument for as long as he contemplates the stele and follows its command. Perhaps there is even the sense of an exchange of properties or role reversal going on; the striding statue borrows its motion from the observer, while he himself adopts the immobile stance of the deceased.[70]

Parallel variations and inversions surround the silence that grave monuments and the dead are bound to maintain. While funerary *kouroi* keep their lips closed in their enigmatic smiles, and figures on grave stelae do not display the patently open mouths that simulate articulation in some images of the early classical period,[71] the commemorative markers have other means of playing on the conventional distribution of speech and silence, and here the relation between the image and its

---

[67] A threat that may be reinforced by the representation of an apotropaic Gorgon, sometimes standing over the grave as a statue in the round, sometimes shown on the stele in relief, as part of the monument. For the Gorgon, Ridgway 1993: 229, 236, 237.

[68] E.g., *CEG* 27, 28, 174.

[69] "Let each man, whether a citizen or foreigner coming from elsewhere, pass by only after pitying Tettichos, a good man, who perished in war and lost his fresh youthfulness. Once you have lamented this, move on to a good deed."

[70] The much later so-called Ilissos grave relief, dated to c. 330, most patently shows the exchange of properties that goes on, as the mourner becomes "infected" with the attributes of the individual for whom he grieves. The artist depicts the figure of the dead as a powerfully muscled youth, leaning against a pillar evocative of the tombstone; although he does not walk, the bent knees, crossed legs, and delicately flexed foot signal his capacity for motion should he choose to quit his seemingly temporary post. The rigidity characteristic of the dead has passed to the old man who stands contemplating the young man, his own body draped in a mantle that reaches from his head to the ground.

[71] See chapter 1 for this. Métraux (1995) finds slightly parted lips in some funerary figures, but these serve as indices of the respiration necessary for the motion that the images perform.

inscription assumes particularly intricate forms. Where the statue or carved stele itself claims a voice by virtue of the epitaph, frequently announcing itself, in the first person, the *sēma* or *mnēma* of the individual whose grave it tops, the monument's ability to transcend its own mute state makes the silence of the dead still more emphatic: in place of the once-articulate individual, a stele or statue now must speak.[72] More detailed messages mark the same distance between the speaking grave and the voiceless resident. To cite Kroisos's epitaph once again (fig. 1), the *kouros* employs its own voice on behalf of the deceased as it bids the passerby to "show pity beside the marker of dead Kroisos, whom raging Ares once destroyed in the front rank of battle" (*CEG* 27); more "egocentric" still, an Attic *korē* of the mid-sixth century focuses on its own merits and history: "[? A parent] set me up for his/her dear child, me [the marker] beautiful to behold. And Phaidimos fashioned [me]" (*CEG* 18). In these and other instances, the monument acts in the manner of the spokesman or *prostatēs* whom those barred from speaking in the fifth-century polis would later employ: stating the claims, merits, and achievements of the silenced party, it makes the case on his or her behalf.

Other monuments are more willing to renounce their leading role and to cede their voices to the dead, who address viewers in the first-person singular.[73] The stele of Mnesitheos from Euboea, dated to the first half of the fifth century, displays the words of the deceased, who opens in emphatic fashion, "I, dead, am lying here" (*ego de thanon katakeimai*, *CEG* 108). Mnesitheos then goes on to distinguish himself from his monument, describing the *mnēma* that his mother raised for him and bidding the passerby read the words inscribed there. More ambiguous is the *korē* of Phrasikleia, which seems to elide its identity with that of the dead, leaving the bystander uncertain as to whom precisely the voice belongs: "[This is/I am] the *sēma* of Phrasikleia. I shall forever be called maiden. . . ." Although no naive confusion of the statue and the maiden is intended, the effect of reading the inscription and viewing the marble girl is to grant both the dead and her *sēma* speech. From this negation of death's silence, a role reversal consistent with that earlier described follows. Whether the speaker is the monument, the dead, or the two in tandem, the syntax and form that many of these inscriptions assume compel the reader to lend his vocal powers to the otherwise silent party

[72] In some this first person is explicit, in others merely implied through the formula *tode sēma/mnēma* plus the genitive form of the name of the dead. According to Svenbro (1988: 37–42), this second class of inscriptions should be read, "I am the monument of *x*."

[73] E.g., *CEG* 80, 108, 114, 119 (where the speaker switches from the dead to the *sēma*; so, too, 159), 171.

and to slip into the persona of the marker or the grave dweller as he pronounces the lines.[74] Though not consigned to the muteness that afflicts the dead, for the duration of his reading his voice is not his own.

Just as the inscriptions and monuments may call into question the silence and immobility that should characterize representations of the dead, so, too, they can both affirm and deny the blindness of those dwelling underground and their inability to participate in "face-to-face" exchanges. The funerary *kouros* with its frontal look refuses to engage with the viewer, ignoring him as it stands, sometimes over lifesize, on its base,[75] and figures on grave stelae and reliefs often keep their eyes bent toward the ground, or refuse to respond to the glance addressed to them by the mourners depicted within the scene.[76] While indistinguishable in all other respects from the still-living family members whom the sculptor so frequently includes (a continuity that powerfully affirms the enduring character of the *oikos*), the gaze of the deceased may on occasion mark him or her out. Particularly poignant is the figure of Theano on an Athenian grave stone dated to the end of the fifth century (fig. 14); although the woman uncovers her face, she does not answer the loving look addressed to her by her husband Ktesileos, his own countenance lowered as it vainly seeks out that of his seated wife.[77] From the same period comes the grave stone of Hegeso from the Kerameikos (fig. 15), showing the deceased with her head tilted downward and her gaze drifting vacantly off into space. Seemingly unmindful of the slave girl holding out a box of jewelry before her, and seated in the *naiskos* that marks her out as dead, she exists in her own unreachable space.[78] That the figure of Death itself displays this vacancy and inability to respond is suggested by a curious set of fifth-century busts, perhaps representations of a funerary deity, that stood over graves at Kyrene: the faces of some statues have been left blank, in striking contrast to the carefully

---

[74] For this argument, Svenbro 1988: 33–52 and passim.

[75] For more on the gaze of *kouroi*, Stewart 1997: 66–67.

[76] E.g., the Attic grave stele of Aristion (Fig. 13) and of Megakles (Richter 1961: figs. 73–79).

[77] For this, see Stewart 1990: 167.

[78] Later stelae of the fourth century tend to emphasize the continued intercourse of the dead and living by showing a meeting of their eyes (Stewart 1990: 93), but the youth on the Ilissos relief cited in note 70 remains in grand visual isolation: while the figure of the mourner is shown in profile, his eyes bent toward the object of his grief, the young man adopts a frontal pose, staring out imperiously into the distance. If this frontality or *apostrophē* in vase representations signals the rupture between the character so depicted and other figures shown in profile in the same scene, as argued by Frontisi-Ducroux (1995: chap. 7), then here it might mean the same: the youth who looks outward has lastingly left the community to which he once belonged.

modeled hair, while others wear veils covering over the lightly sketched-in features.[79]

When the epitaph is factored in, the visual dynamics of the monument gain new dimensions. On occasion, although the sentiment appears more frequently in the postclassical age,[80] inscriptions contrast the present condition of the dead with the powers of vision, of seeing and being seen, they used to enjoy, and describe their former existence as one illuminated by the sun, which makes sight possible. A stele dated to c. 410, showing a seated woman embracing a child, laments a time when both were living and looking (*ommasin . . . zōntes ederkometha*) on the light of the sun (*CEG* 89), and another bemoans Kobos's departure from the light of day (*CEG* 171).[81] But even as some monuments affirm that the dead are unsighted and unseen, others suggest that it lies in the mourner's power to make good that loss. References to the act of viewing punctuate epitaphs from the late archaic and classical age: a stele base found in the Kerameikos enjoins the passerby to "halt and pity, having looked on (*idon*) the marker of Thrason" (*CEG* 28), and a late fifth-century marble base adopts the same formula, bidding its addressee to "feel pity, looking upon this *sēma* of a dead child" (*CEG* 51; cf. *CEG* 68). So, too, among the standard formulas the inscriptions adopt is the theme of an unspecified "I" who expresses feelings of sorrow while looking at the grave monument, and the grief that the reader experiences may be explicitly pinned to his contemplation of the marker.[82] The very act of spectatorship that the image commands or persuades the viewer to perform (sometimes through a reference to its own beauty, as in *CEG* 18) might do more than to prompt the requisite sensations of pity and loss; it additionally serves to restore the visual relations that death has so abruptly broken off, and gives back to the dead, or to the re-presentation of the same, the twinned powers of seeing and being seen.

DIVINE MOTION AND SIGHT

If the dead define themselves by an absence of movement, speech, and sight, and statues can offer reflections on their altered state, then the

---

[79] See Freedberg 1989: 72 and fig. 28; Frontisi-Ducroux 1995: 37, for the suggestions that we read these representations as images of a funerary deity, or of death itself. Alternately, the figures might be images of Persephone. Rather differently, an anecdote preserved by Plutarch suggests the relationship between the eyes of an image and the end of an individual's life: the death of the despot Hiero at Leuktra was apparently foretold when the eyes fell out of the statue erected on his behalf (*Mor.* 397e).

[80] For this, see R. Lattimore 1962: 161–62.

[81] See, too, *CEG* 98, 132.

[82] For this and examples, Sourvinou-Inwood 1995: 175, 176.

deities who inhabit the world's other pole exhibit at least two of these life-declaring powers to a superlative degree. Divine epiphanies prove as much: the god manifests himself from beneath a temporary disguise with motions and glances that proclaim his true identity to a mortal protagonist and dispel all doubts as to the nature of the visitation. But these faculties do not belong solely to the gods in their moments of self-revelation; they also extend to the images that stand in for divinity, and statues demonstrate their own charged nature, their talismanic qualities, through their mobility and their visual (and sometimes speaking) powers. These uncanny expressions of the divine presence, attested in anecdotes, legend, and ritual practice alike, indicate anew the potentially epiphanic quality of the representations, and their character as objects invested with a quickening force that may declare itself to the viewer. More broadly, they form part of the slippage between the deity and the cult image, and encourage the almost imperceptible work of substitution that the veneration of idols so frequently involves: transferring to the symbol some of the traits of the thing symbolized, celebrants treat the image not so much as a representation of the absent god, but as an object that has assumed his predicates, too.[83]

Gods and Their Images Both Move

The Homeric and Hesiodic poems give ample evidence of divine powers of motion and the role these play in setting gods apart from men. In evocations of Olympians and other divine creatures, the immortals' light and rapid flight forms a critical part of what defines their superiority to mortals constrained to walk, or frequently to creep (*herpein*) laboriously along the ground.[84] Gods possess sandals that are winged,[85] transform themselves into swift-flying birds,[86] and betray their divinity by an uncannily rapid departure when they quit their mortal disguise.[87] The adverbs *rheia* and *rhimpha* repeatedly describe Olympian travels, and the fleeting, easy movement of the horses that draw Poseidon's chariot over the sea to Troy (*Il.* 13.18–19, 29–30) appears the more remarkable for the cumbersome advance and retreat of the mortal heroes flanking the description on either side; so delicately does the chariot skim the waves that it remains quite dry, while Hector's own

---

[83] For a compelling statement of this process, Halbertal and Margalit 1992: 44.
[84] Hence the humor of *Hymn. Hom. Ven.* 156, where the goddess, assuming the behavior of a modest maiden, "creeps" (*herpe*) to the bed.
[85] Most obviously Hermes (see *Il.* 24.340–41), but Iris and other divine messengers, too.
[86] On some occasions the transformation is a literal one (e.g., Athena in *Od.* 3.371–72 or 22.239–40); on others the poet simply compares the movement of the god to that of the bird (e.g., *Od.* 5.51–53).
[87] E.g., *Od.* 1.319–23, 3.371–73.

chariot had its axle bloodied by the corpses it earlier ran over in its stumbling passage (11.531–37). Nor do divine creatures ever suffer weariness in their limbs, however far or fast they travel: Typhoeus is in constant motion and his feet, like those of other immortals, are *akamatoi* (Hes. *Theog.* 824). Mortal invocations of the gods more generally assume their capacity for instant motion from far-flung cult sites and from Olympus to the spot where the petitioner or suppliant stands and addresses his pleas. As Detienne and Vernant comment, one of the principal prerogatives of the god is his "power of instantaneous movement from one spot to another."[88]

To turn from evocations of the Olympians to the activities their images perform is to find fresh instances of remarkable and improbable movement. Just as the deities surpass mortals in their powers of locomotion, so, too, their representations transcend the limitations that statues normally observe and manifest their charged status by moving on or from their bases. In many instances, as in the Iliadic episode cited at the chapter's start, the motions of gods and their images prove difficult to tell apart, and the two may form an almost seamless whole. In his fragmentary song recommending that his archenemy Pittakos be stoned (626 *SLG*), Alcaeus introduces a cult image (emphasized as such by the use of the term *agalma* with the genitive at line 9 rather than the simpler designation of the object by the goddess's own name) whose initial inertia belies the live and dynamic force perhaps conceived as resident within. When the fleeing Cassandra first embraces this statue of Athena in the temple of the goddess, all the desperate movement belongs to the suppliant (8–10). Ajax's mad dash into the sacred space further underscores the immobility of the image, so still that the hero feels no fear as he lays his impious hands on the victim of his assault (16–23). But in the space of four lines, and without a marked break in the narrative flow, a sudden change occurs: no sooner has Ajax committed the sacrilege while "standing by the *agalma*" (21) than the poet replaces the idol with the "Gorgon-faced child of Zeus" (23–24) and introduces in its stead the divinity who glances terribly from her eyebrows, her face livid with anger (24–25). In the same instant we realize that Athena—goddess or statue?—has left her pedestal: with all the speed that the Olympians possess she darts (*aize*) over the seas and stirs up the storm winds that will claim the Achaean fleet (26–27). At no point has the poet spelled out the relationship between the image and the living deity; rather, he has allowed the mutation of one into the other to occur before the audience's eyes.

The confusion that Alcaeus's song creates finds its visual match in the

---

[88] Detienne and Vernant 1978: 115.

black-figure repertoire, where the artist can still more closely conflate the several stages of the narrative and show the goddess as immanent within the statue through a single synoptic figure.[89] The Athena *agalma*, as most extant early compositions depict it, appears not a static representation, but an animate and moving figure that charges at Ajax and occupies the same groundline as the other characters in the scene (fig. 16). In contrast to later red-figure accounts, where the goddess stands motionless and mounted on a base, and in some instances bears the archaizing traits that signal both the venerable and the plastic character of the object, the earlier painters invest the artifact with a triple character: at once the site where Cassandra vainly seeks refuge, it is also the talismanic object that Ajax violates, and the goddess herself who will punish the hero for his sacrilegious act.[90]

If later sixth- and fifth-century artists prefer to return the Palladion to its strictly inanimate status, poets and historians continue to blur the lines between the actions of gods and their representations, and suggest that at least the credulous among their audience believed that moving images were concrete signs of the divine presence. The image of Artemis tended by Iphigenia supposedly turns away *automaton*, using the gesture to mark its awareness of the pollution visited on the shrine and to protect itself from witnessing the same (Eur. *IT* 1165–67); and when the Athenians try to carry off the talismanic images of Damia and Auxesia from Aigina, the objects signal their resistance by falling to their knees and refusing to be removed from their place of residence (Hdt. 5.86.3).[91]

Nor do these incidents figure only in popular anecdote and the playwrights' imaginations. As the previous chapter documented, the ritual occasions when idols would be taken out of their shrines and escorted

---

[89] For detailed discussion of the scene in both black- and red-figure vase painting, see Connelly 1993 and B. Cohen 1993.

[90] So Connelly 1993: 101. Contrast Polygnotos's volute krater (Malibu, J. Paul Getty Museum 77.NA.198), which shows a frontal statue of Athena accompanied by the living goddess, who stands at the statue's side.

[91] The baroque imaginations of postclassical authors multiply references to statues moving of their own accord, and autokinesis figures prominently among the activities performed by images credited with oracular and other powers. See, for example, Plut. *Cam.* 6.3; Strabo 6.1.14 (cf. Verg. *Aen.* 2.172–75), Ath. 672c–d (citing the third-century Menodotos); Lucian *Syr. D.* 10. The material collected in the appendix to Donohue 1988 also supplies a riche cache of examples. It is striking how many of these stories gravitate to images styled *xoana* (also frequently associated with Daidalos), supporting the suggestion of Frontisi-Ducroux (1975: 105, 111) that mobility is a critical theme in legends pertaining to this kind of figure. We might think of the *xoanon* as opposite in nature to the *kolossos*: while the one is defined by its immobility, the other is repeatedly involved with motion.

in procession through the city streets might seem to realize the conceit of the moving image,[92] and Herodotus reports how the Athenians, before the battle of Salamis, sent a ship to Aigina "to fetch the Aiakidai" (8.64) in order that the heroes might lend their aid. If, as commentators suggest, the ambassadors actually went in quest of images of the sons of Aiakos, then the objects' advent would visualize the coming of the tutelary heroes themselves. So, too, individuals might be granted a vision of divinity when that immortal appeared in the shape of his or her cult image, and when that object seemed to approach the witness of its own volition: Pindar was granted one such epiphanic moment when he saw "the stone statue of the Mother of the Gods nearing on foot" (literally "with her feet"),[93] and the widely diffused votive pictures or reliefs showing two feet may on occasion bear witness to the miraculous advent not of the deity, but of his representation in plastic form.

Inhibiting Divine Motion

According to the sources of the postclassical age, fear of an image's departure from a site might prompt answering actions on the part of men. In their accounts of the events preceding Alexander's attack on Tyre, Diodorus Siculus, Plutarch, and Quintus Curtius Rufus all mention Apollo's threat to abandon the city, and the people's attempt to prevent his flight by binding or nailing a *xoanon* of the god to its base, using cords or chains of gold.[94] Pausanias's explanation for the fettered image of the war god Enyalios that he witnesses in Sparta follows the logic informing these other tales:

> The belief of the Lacedaemonians about this statue is the same as that of the Athenians about their wingless Victory: they believe that Enyalios, bound as he is in fetters, will never escape and go away, while the Athenians think that Victory, having no wings, will always remain in place. (3.15.7)

But the popular view that Pausanias preserves may be a latter-day misconstruction of the original impetus behind Enyalios's binding. As Christopher Faraone has argued, the chains placed about statues of divinities may originally have been designed not to hinder the gods' departure, but rather to "control directly the potentially dangerous activities of powerful deities of an arbitrary and often malicious disposition."[95] I want to follow his suggestion and to propose that the bonds

---

[92] In postclassical times at least, it was customary to carry about the god's statue and to read from its motions the answers to divine questions; for this, Macrob. *Sat.* 1.23.13.

[93] For this, see Versnel 1987b: 46.

[94] Diod. Sic. 17.41.7–8; Plut. *Alex.* 24.5–8; Quintus Curtius Rufus 4.3.21–22.

[95] Faraone 1992: 137.

and chains used for images supply fresh evidence for the transfer of kinetic properties from the gods to their representations, and for the broader continuity between divinities and their idols in Greek thought. Just as the statue shares in the deity's own powers of extraordinary motion, so, too, that motion can be restrained only by stratagems that work against the gods themselves. Incapacitating the statue disarms its subject precisely because the idol re-presents or houses the divinity and exists in a "persuasive" relationship to the numinous power on which its efficacy depends.

The uncheckable movements that characterize gods in their visitations to mortals also mark their dealings with one another and make the clashes occurring in the early stages of divine history so violent and hard-fought. In the theomachies vividly depicted by Hesiod, a god can repel attack only by paralyzing his aggressor, by checking his mobility through one of several modes. It is Kronos who first sets the mighty-limbed Hundred-Handers in chains because he envies their strength (*Theog.* 617–20; cf. 152) and makes them dwell far beneath the ground.[96] That this binding plus burial effectively paralyzes the three brothers, Zeus's later countermeasures suggest: he undoes the creatures' bonds (652), brings them back up to the light (626), and feeds them nectar and ambrosia, which revive their *thumos* and renew the powers made dormant by their long incarceration (640–41). The subsequent fate of the Titans mirrors that of their many-armed antagonists: once defeated, the rebels are set deep beneath the earth and bound in chains (717–18). Amid the fearsome powers belonging to Typhoeus, the poet cites his untiring feet (824), and only the answering motion of Zeus, beneath whose limbs the earth groans out as the king rises up to meet the attack (842–43), defeats the awesome threat. On this occasion the challenger finds himself not only buried beneath the earth, but actually deprived of limbs; blasted by the thunderbolt, he is nothing more than a maimed torso as he falls (858).[97] A final and more subtle challenger must be hobbled and placed in chains before Zeus's new regime achieves its final stability. The "painful bonds" that confine Prometheus (522, cf. 616) and, in Aeschylus's later account, the shackles that cripple his feet (*PV* 76) are the penalty the Titan pays for his attempt to outwit Zeus.[98]

[96] Kronos himself will be bound by Zeus (Hes. *Op.* 173b; cf. Pind. *Pyth.* 4.289ff.), while Poseidon, Apollo, and Hera all threaten Zeus with binding in turn (*Il.* 1.399–401). For these episodes, see Delcourt 1957: 69–70.

[97] In later sources Typhoeus suffers not only incarceration beneath a mountainous mass, but binding as well; for this, Pind. *Pyth.* 1.27–28; Apollod. *Bibl.* 1.6.3.

[98] See Griffith 1983: ad loc. for the pinioning in Aeschylus's play. Gernet (1981: 242) has linked the posture of the bound Titan in literary and pictorial accounts to that adopted by victims of the particularly cruel penalty called *apotumpanismos*, where the condemned

These motion-inhibiting devices reappear beyond the divine battle-field, and in more domestic settings allow gods to block a rival or pun-ish a miscreant. Hephaistos notoriously entraps Ares, swiftest of all the gods, with the invisible web he constructs over his marriage bed (*Od.* 8.296–98), and punishes Hera by immobilizing her on a magic throne equipped with chains.[99] Immortals lull one another to limb-loosening (*lusimelēs*) sleep,[100] using *pharmaka* and other means to reduce their victims to immobility and to paralyze them for as long as the charm endures. So Hera enlists the aid of Hupnos when she would keep Zeus in his passion-induced coma, and Orphic myth describes how Kronos falls asleep after having bitten into the "food of trickery that Zeus made him taste by luring him with honey, with head nodding on heavy neck, fettered in the bonds of *hupnos* which can tame all creatures" (Orph. fr. 148, 149; Porphyry *Cave of Nymphs* 16).[101] A no less effective paralysis seizes those who threaten to disrupt immortal harmony with discord and strife; after the divine perjurer drinks from the waters of the Styx, he lies "spiritless and voiceless on a strewn bed; and a wretched *kōma* covers him" (Hes. *Theog.* 797–98).

In their efforts to prohibit, contain, or redirect the mobility that gods so abundantly possess, men apply the same or closely analogous mea-sures to the images standing in their midst. Again, no clear distinctions can be drawn between the statue and the god;[102] popular belief may credit the image with the ability to move and act, and regard binding, hobbling, and incarceration as so many ways of restricting and fore-stalling its interventions in human affairs; or the stratagems may be applied to the figurine in an effort to persuade or even coerce the deity

---

man pinioned to a column would assume a position symbolic of virtual death and the annulment of all his faculties.

[99] Pind. fr. 283 Snell-Maehler; Pl. *Resp.* 378d. See, too, *P. Oxy.* 670, with discussion in Merkelbach 1973. For extended treatment of Hephaistos as binder, Delcourt 1957: esp. chap. 1.

[100] The formula is that of *Od.* 20.57, and Alkman fr. 3.61 *PMG*.

[101] See Detienne and Vernant 1978: 116. Plutarch affirms this version of events, describing how the deposed god is relegated to the island where he sleeps, guarded by Briareus or confined in a deep cavern: "This is the sleep that Zeus contrived for him in order to chain him up" (*Mor.* 420a, 941e–f). On another occasion, Plutarch explains that, according to Phrygian belief, Kronos sleeps the winter away among the Phrygians, whereas in the springtime Bacchic dances rouse him once again; the alternation between sleep and wak-efulness evidently parallels binding and release, as the author also notes that, according to the Paphlagonians, in winter the god is bound, and in the spring he is freed from chains (*Mor.* 378e). The tradition of the slumbering Kronos reappears in later times as he is moved ever further west — into never-never land — eventually appearing on the utopian island of Britannia, asleep or in chains; on this, see Versnel 1987a: 126.

[102] So *Il.* 5.385–91 seems to describe an incident when two heroes, the Aloadae, bind not a statue, but Ares himself; for discussion of this, Faraone 1992: 74–75.

represented by the statue to respect the wishes of his devotees. A variety of motives may prompt communities and individuals to place restraints on the images they erect, but one common thread runs through the different instances of the practice: all suppose the link between a divinity's movement and his display of his powers and assume that to limit or direct one is to control the other.

Gods whose prerogatives lie in particularly dangerous domains are prime candidates for the chains and other restrictive devices that men apply to their statues, both in myth and in actual practice. Ares, the bound Enyalios whom Pausanias cites, not only fosters warfare, but also figures commonly as plague-bringer; incarcerating and fettering his image are two possible means of checking his terrifying advance and of preventing the diffusion of the sickness and war that he unleashes.[103] Chaos of a very different kind follows from Aphrodite's interventions in human affairs, and Pausanias duly encounters a venerable chained *xoanon* of the goddess (with the perhaps euphemistic title Morpho) inhabiting a temple in Sparta:

> Morpho is a surname of Aphrodite; she is seated, wearing a veil, with fetters on her feet. Men say that Tyndareos put the fetters on her, meaning to symbolize by these bonds the faithfulness of women to their husbands. The other explanation, that Tyndareos punished the goddess with fetters because he thought that through her agency his daughters had come to shame, is one that I cannot accept for a moment. (3.15.11)

The story rejected by Pausanias as mere nonsense may reveal the impetus that informs the binding of this and other images: as instigator of love (the role in which Tyndareos casts the goddess here), Aphrodite's passage among mortals leaves havoc in its wake, and nowhere more than when it incites women, most notoriously Helen and Clytemnestra, to exercise the mobility required by adultery and illicit affairs. Both seated and fettered, the goddess finds herself deprived of her capacity for motion, and her baneful influence receives a consequent check.[104]

In an effort to activate the beneficial and apotropaic facets that even these most dangerous of divinities possess, communities might also al-

---

[103] In addition to *Il.* 5.385–91, note *Anth. Pal.* 9.805; see, too, Faraone 1991b: 167–72 for other examples. This penalty makes all the better sense in the light of the Homeric Demodokos's claim that Ares "is the swiftest of the gods who dwell in Mount Olympus" (*Od.* 8.331), and hence most particularly in need of the restraints that Hephaistos fabricates to punish an offense of a purely domestic kind.

[104] The story is a particularly suggestive one given the intimate relations between Aphrodite and Helen (the second acting almost as proxy for the first in the bed of Paris, as her words to Aphrodite in *Il.* 3.408–9 suggest). Note, too, that in this instance, the representation is seated.

low regularly chained images periods of release. Some hint of this cyclical activity already belongs to the tale that Homer tells of the Aloadae and their dealings with Ares: the detail that the god remains imprisoned for only thirteen months (*Il.* 5.387) prompts several commentators to suppose the myth linked to a ceremony native to Boeotia, which featured the annual binding and release of an image of the god.[105] In view of the varied capacities that Ares exercises, not just bringer of war and plague but also representative of the martial excellence a community desires, and an extremely effective apotropaion in the face of attack by others, the limited but regularized period of exposure makes good sense. The mere display of the statue reassures the celebrants of the continued presence of a power that they may deploy when need arises.[106]

The sequence returns in the tales and rituals surrounding the figure of Kronos, and once again an archaic source offers an early pointer toward a practice documented only for much later times. A passage from Hesiod's *Theogony*, although believed interpolated by some, indicates that Kronos shared in the incarceration imposed on his allies, the Titans (851; cf. 718).[107] Ritual activity from postclassical times coheres with (or even takes its cue from) the mythical account. Roman sources record that the feet of the statue of Saturn were shackled or wrapped in woolen bandages, while also noting that these were removed on the occasion of the annual Saturnalia.[108] A fragment of Apollodorus of Athens referring to bound images of Kronos, and dated to the second century B.C., suggests that the practice may even have originated in Greece and spread to Rome from there.[109]

That Kronos should be a prime candidate for these complementary gestures again accords very well with the dual character that he carries already in archaic and classical sources, and with his familiar capacity to usher in both chaos and delight. As H. Versnel's rich discussion documents,[110] Kronos is the figure to whom myth ascribes the heinous deed of castrating his father, who presides over an era marked by acts of egregious cruelty and the absence of all ethical standards, and whose rites supposedly involve all sorts of bloody offerings.[111] But other texts

---

[105] Burkert 1985: 169; Faraone 1991b: 172.

[106] For discussion of this point, Faraone 1992: 138–39.

[107] See Versnel 1987a: 124; Detienne and Vernant 1978: 68–72 for the textual problems here. Note that Kronos's own binding responds to his powers of binding others; for this, see *Theog.* 501–2 and the Orphic sources cited by Delcourt (1957: 21–22).

[108] Macrob. *Sat.* 1.8.5; Min. Fel. 22.5; Stat. *Silv.* 1.6.4; Arnobius 4.25.

[109] *FGrH* 224 F 118. The statement may refer to a Roman custom familiar to the Greek writer, but Versnel (1987a: 131) argues for an authentic Greek origin. As he notes, the figures of both Kronos and Saturn in chains become a topos in later magical papyri.

[110] Versnel 1987a.

[111] Cannibalism supposedly enters his reign, and infanticide, human sacrifices, and bloody offerings all feature in the rites connected with the god. For these, ibid.: 124 and 129.

offer a radically different scenario: a golden age of agricultural abundance, of peace, harmony, and vegetarianism prevailed while Kronos was king. In Old Comedy he is the god of Cockaigne, and in fifth- and fourth-century philosophy the ideal ruler of a realm of peace.[112] The same structural oppositions appear in the festivals celebrated on Kronos's behalf, with their distinctive mixture of license, misrule, and lawlessness blended in with feasting, liberation, abundance, and the momentary abolition or reversal of social hierarchies. Thus Kronos "is primeval chaos in person, in its dual aspect of freedom as a joy and freedom as a threat."[113] The fetters that normally inhibit the god's influence guarantee that for much of the year the status quo can remain in place, while the paradoxical character of the celebration that accompanies Kronos's release visibly demonstrates both the delights and the dangers following an abandonment of conventional norms.

If chaining checks potentially inimical activity, whether that of the god or that of the image itself, then hobbling supplies a second and related way of preventing the disruption that a divinity's advent or presence can provoke. This is the method proposed by the protagonist of Aristophanes' *Peace* when he wishes to arrest the onset of Kudoimos, or Battle Din, a henchman of Ares: addressing the audience, Trygaios cries out, "And if anyone happens to have been initiated at Samothrace, now is a good time to pray that [Kudoimos's] feet be twisted back (*apostraphēnai*) as he advances" (277–79). The action that Trygaios recommends not only refers to a form of restraint or torture performed on living individuals,[114] but also looks to a convention used for visual representations of potentially dangerous divinities; a scholion to the line glosses the expression with the verb *diastraphēnai*, which figures a second time in Pausanias's description of the depiction of Sleep and Death on the sixth-century chest of Kypselos, where the two figures have their feet "completely twisted about" (5.18.1).[115] Once again, the character of the divinities invites precisely this mode of restraint; from archaic poetry on, the twin brothers appear equipped with the wings and light bodies that enhance their swift passage and guarantee that their victims can neither apprehend nor arrest their coming.[116]

[112] Ritual practices also reveal the god's more gentle facets: some texts expressly indicate his preference for bloodless offerings, for bread in the place of meat (so Versnel, ibid.: 129).

[113] Ibid.: 143.

[114] Ar. *Eq.* 263, *Lys.* 455; *Od.* 22.173, 189–90; Soph. *OT* 1154.

[115] For this, see Delcourt 1957: 55–56, 131; also Faraone (1992: 134), who suggests an actual ritual of apotropaic foot-twisting at Samothrace. The term used by Pausanias has been connected to the same distortion found in "voodoo dolls," for which see Faraone 1991b.

[116] Vermeule 1981: 147ff.

Of all the immortals, Hephaistos is the one whom myth and iconography most commonly imagine as lame, and who seems singularly
deprived of the easy mobility that defines his fellow members in the
pantheon.[117] But rather than reading the handicap as the price exacted
from the god for his artisanal and magical powers, as some have done,[118]
we might see it as a preemptive strike against the dangerous mobility he
would otherwise display. As Detienne and Vernant argue, visual and
verbal depictions of Hephaistos with his feet curiously configured
(sometimes the left foot points forward while the right is bent back,
sometimes the feet are placed heel to heel, each facing in a different
direction, and sometimes the god has his head turned so as to face forward as his feet face backward) should not be confused with representations of the god as club-footed and lame. Instead of highlighting his
deformity, these visualizations suggest quite the contrary, endowing Hephaistos with the ability to move in two different directions simultaneously, and to enjoy a versatile and multiform manner of locomotion.[119] This power in turn demands the measures that other artists and
poets include in their accounts: both the Corinthian and Laconian
black-figure vases portraying the god with one foot twisted completely
about and comic depictions of the lame craftsman in archaic song serve
as persuasive representations, designed to cripple and so to disarm the
deity, who can move in alarmingly swift and uncheckable fashion.[120]
    Detienne and Vernant further propose that the god's ability to travel
in two directions at a single moment follows naturally from his role as
blacksmith and metal-worker: laboring with the ever-shifting fires,
winds, and minerals that are the elements of his craft, the artisan must
match and surpass their own unpredictable and rapid movements.[121]
The intimate association between Hephaistos and fire, the element in
which he chiefly works and which on many occasions he symbolizes,
makes control over the god's motions imperative and inspires the different ways in which art and myth depict his epiphanies.[122] By imagining

[117] His encounter with Ares in Demodokos's song in *Od.* 8 of course turns on the contrast
between the "swiftest of the gods" and the lame craftsmen; see particularly 8.330–32 for
Hephaistos's skill as antidote for his handicap.

[118] For discussion, Delcourt 1957: 110ff. Note particularly 126–27, where the author distinguishes between the "infirmity" and the "deformity" of the god; the first she understands as the ransom exacted for his magician's powers, the latter as a symbol of his
forces and of the most efficacious way of exorcising them should they become aggressive.

[119] Detienne and Vernant 1978: 271–72. This point is already noted in Delcourt 1957:
111.

[120] Faraone (1992: 56) also comments on the frequent coalescence between the apotropaic
and the comic.

[121] Detienne and Vernant 1978: 272–73.

[122] Very early conceptions of Hephaistos may have figured him not so much as the crafts-

Hephaistos capable of traveling in two directions, image-makers declare the rapidity and volatility of fire, while accounts of the god as lame suggest the necessary containment of the element and the restraints it must observe if men are to harness it to their domestic and artisanal ends. The statues or protomes of Hephaistos that Athenians set up before household hearths, commercial kilns, and foundries call upon the god in his twin capacity as instantiation and master of fire:[123] equipped with all the properties of the flames, he is also ideally suited to keep them within bounds, to fight fire with fire.

One final impetus may dictate the application of bonds, shackles, and other crippling devices to representations of both Hephaistos and several fellow gods. In a turning of the tables, the craftsman deity must be lamed or hobbled because he is the binding god par excellence, the figure whom poets and mythmakers describe fashioning the invisible net that pinions the adulterous Ares and Aphrodite to the marriage bed and the bonds that immobilize Hera when she sits down on a throne of his design. In the Aeschylean episode where Hephaistos acts more as metalworker than magician-artist, the god reluctantly chains Prometheus to the rock with fetters of his own making.[124] Other gods prone to bind, paralyze, or strip mortals of their capacity for motion experience, in the person of their statues, chaining or hobbling in their turn.[125] Fetters and other inhibiting devices used for images of Dionysus—Dionysus on Chios, Dionysus Aisymnetes, and Dionysus Phallen among them—respond to the god's own skilled manipulation of these same stratagems.[126] Myth and drama repeatedly describe Dionysus as Lysios, the figure who can dissolve and escape the restraints that others would impose on him and his followers,[127] and these very "loosening" powers presuppose his

---

man deity, but as an instantiation of fire and as the fire god, the one who does battle with the river Xanthos in the elemental conflict described in *Iliad* 21 (cf. *Il.* 2.426, with Faraone 1992: 54). For Hephaistos as a fire demon in Corinthian belief, Faraone 1992: 134.

[123] For these protomes, see Delcourt 1957: 113; Faraone 1992: 55–56. Faraone cites the comment of a scholiast on a line in Aristophanes that instructs a character to place his shield "upon the hearth near the *epistatēs*" (*Av.* 436–37); the gloss explains that this *epistatēs* denotes "the clay [statue of] Hephaistos set up before the hearth as an overseer (*ephoros*) of the fire" or "depicted in relief on kilns." The terms *epistatēs* and *ephoros* both indicate the protective role of the images, whose placement at the hearth or kiln constrains the action of the fire.

[124] Delcourt (1957: 12) suggests that in Aeschylus's drama we witness the shift from Hephaistos as magician to Hephaistos as patron of metal-workers.

[125] A reciprocity observed by Delcourt (ibid.: esp. 25–26).

[126] For these bound images of Dionysus, see Meuli 1975: 1066. Meuli also suggests that the Athenian Lenaea began with a chained image of Dionysus being born in the ship-wagon.

[127] Most notoriously in Euripides' *Bacchae*, where the god frees both himself and the

mastery over bonds, his capacity to arrest life and motion in those who oppose his divinity.[128] Able to impose impotence or a state of frozen arousal on his victims (or so a scholion to Aristophanes attests),[129] he can also manifest himself as Dionysus Sphaleotas, the one who causes you to trip and fall.[130] The chained images of Kronos cited in late sources may similarly answer to much earlier myths that describe the god as binder of his enemies (*Theog.* 718, 501–2);[131] and Death and Sleep, whom the artist of the chest of Kypselos takes pains to show with their feet twisted round about, are also forces notoriously able to shackle their victims.[132]

But for Athenians of the classical period, binding is the province of one particular god. Addressing him in his capacity as "restrainer" (*Katochos*), Attic curse tablets repeatedly invoke Hermes and call upon him to hold fast the object of the imprecation (*Hermē kateche ton deina*), to arrest his motion and vital faculties, and to pinion his limbs.[133] As guardian of the door and the inner-city boundary, Hermes exercises analogous powers of restraint, keeping off the unwanted visitor by stopping him in his tracks. Unwilling to allow so potent a figure to deploy his prerogatives unchecked, the Athenians devise a form of representation that simultaneously declares Hermes' potency and keeps his interventions within bounds: no more than a head stuck on a squared off, aniconic block complete with erect phallos, the legless herm fixes this supremely peripatetic and boundary-crossing god in place, and visualizes the very immobilizing powers that he is called upon to practice.[134]

Divine Sight

No less distinctive and potent than their modes of locomotion are the visual forces deployed by the gods. Immortals in Homer possess eyes so

---

Bacchants from chains (447–48, 498, 615, 633–34, 643); note, too, *Hymn. Hom. Bacch.* 12–14. Even the story of Dionysus's gestation, bound in the thigh of Zeus, suggests an attempt to restrain this most irrepressible of gods.

[128] The vines that Dionysus causes mysteriously to grow (*Hymn. Hom. Bacch.* 38–41; Aelian *VH* 3.42) could perhaps be seen as binding and certainly as immobilizing devices.

[129] Schol. ad Ar. *Ach.* 243.

[130] Frontisi-Ducroux 1991: 197.

[131] On this and other examples, see Delcourt 1957: 21–22.

[132] Ibid.: 22, 119.

[133] For discussion and examples, see Faraone 1991a and 1992: 87 n. 9. When an oracle bids the people of Syedra to erect a bound image of Ares, the fetters are described as "the iron bonds of Hermes" (cited Faraone 1992: 75). Hermes is ideally suited for this binding task as myth imagines him master of the arts of both binding and loosening (see *Hymn. Hom. Merc.* 409–11; also Serv. ad Verg. *Aen.* 6.42).

[134] Here I follow the suggestion in Faraone 1992: 118–19.

brilliant and radiant that they betray even divinities who have concealed themselves in mortal guise. For all that she has assumed the appearance of an aged wool-worker when she approaches Helen, Aphrodite cannot dim her *ommata marmaironta* (*Il.* 3.397), and Achilles discerns the presence of Athena when he perceives the flash in his patron's eyes (*Il.* 1.200).[135] A warrior momentarily possessed by a supernatural force exhibits the features of the god who inspires his *menos*, and at *Iliad* 8.349 Hector looks with the burning eyes of Ares. For the authors of the *Homeric Hymns*, such is the brilliant quality of the immortal gaze that men cannot sustain its power. In the tale of Aphrodite's seduction of Anchises, the goddess first turns her "fair eyes" aside (*Hymn. Hom. Ven.* 156) as in a single move she apes the behavior of the modest maiden and prevents a premature disclosure of her identity, and Demeter must lower her *ommata* when she enters the house of Metaneira, and draw her veil so as to hide her countenance (*Hymn. Hom. Cer.* 194, 197).[136] This larger face or *prosōpon*, conceived as the site from which the look is emitted, which allows the looker to be seen in turn,[137] shares the same dazzle that the eyes possess, and Ion instantly knows himself in the presence of the divine when, confronted by the epiphanic Athena on the temple roof, he seeks to identify the god who shows a "face bright like the sun" (Eur. *Ion* 1550). Distinctive, too, are the properties of the gods' vision. If their limbs are never wearied, then immortals enjoy a surpassing keenness of sight, and an ability to apprehend what remains hidden from men's view. Helios is panoptic, Hermes can see in the dark, and Zeus's sight never flags as his eyes remain ever vigilant and unsleeping; Athena's epithet *oxuderkēs* acknowledges both the acute and the fascinating qualities of her gaze.[138]

As these last examples attest, gods not only reveal their presence through their eyes, but use the organs in their displays of power. On the Iliadic battlefield Poseidon charms Alkathoos with his shining eyes, paralyzing his victim so that he can neither advance nor retreat (13.435). In his own descent into the fray, Apollo casts his witching powers more broadly:

> So long as Phoebos Apollo held unmoving in his hand the aegis, so long the thrown weapons of both took hold and men fell. But when he stared straight

[135] Indeed, it says much about these two individuals that they can look on a god directly; normally mortals look away from a divinity's face.
[136] As the disguised Dionysus effects his miracles on board ship, he sits with a telltale smile in his dark eyes (*Hymn. Hom. Bacch.* 14–15). For discussions of these and other examples, see the comprehensive treatment in Malten 1961: 12, 14.
[137] Arist. *Hist. an.* 1.8.491b; *Part. an.* 3.1.662a, with Frontisi-Ducroux 1995: 19–20.
[138] For Helios, *Hymn. Hom. Cer.* 69–70; Hermes, Aesch. *Cho.* 816–18; for discussion of Zeus's gaze, Detienne and Vernant 1978: 79; for Athena, Delcourt 1957: 142–43.

into the eyes of the swift-mounted Danaans, and shook the aegis, and he himself cried out very mightily, then he bewitched (*ethelge*) the spirit in their breasts, and they forgot their warrior might. (*Il.* 15.318–22)

The aegis brandished by Apollo here works in tandem with the deity's own visual faculties; it carries at its center the face of the Gorgon, the monster who "glares terribly" (*Il.* 11.36–37) and may freeze a man with her glance (*Od.* 11.633–35).[139]

Beyond the Homeric songs, and in the realm of Attic drama, the eyes of the gods effect still more radical changes. Immortals look in order not only to paralyze, but also to blind, madden, or lastingly transform their victims in shape and form. In the attacks that Zeus launches on renegade morals, the deity actually hurls the blasting thunder and lightning bolt from his eyes (Aesch. *Ag.* 469),[140] and elsewhere he directs these same powers against the most fearsome of his immortal opponents, the monster Typhoeus. The account of the encounter between the god and rebel in *Prometheus Bound* imagines the weapons wielded by the two antagonists as properly visual ones: Typhoeus comes armed with the *gorgōpon selas* (356)—perhaps an echo of the fire that the Hesiodic monster had flashed "from under the brows of his eyes in his marvelous heads" and that burned from these heads as he glared (*Theog.* 826–28)—while Zeus brandishes the *agrupnon belos* (358), the lightning whose epithet recalls the god's unceasing visual guard.[141] The devastation that this missile works on the first challenger anticipates the impact it will have on a second: the bolt that leaves Typhoeus maimed and buried beneath the ground also threatens to hide Prometheus in the earth's depths, deprived of vision-granting light (Aesch. *PV* 1016–21).

Mental as well as physical impairment may be the consequence of encounters with the gods and the exposure to their eyes that the fifth-century dramatists like to document. Sophocles' Ajax calls Athena by the title Gorgopis at the moment when he accuses her of having robbed him of his sanity (*Aj.* 450), and earlier in the drama the goddess announces her blinding powers when she promises Odysseus that he will remain unseen by Ajax: "I shall darken his eyes, (keen-) sighted though

---

[139] At *Iliad* 11.36–37 the face of the Gorgon stands appropriately flanked by Deinos and Phobos. As noted earlier, a mortal warrior, when inspired by the gods, can briefly assume the visual powers that belong to these immortal and daemonic beings: when Hector manifests himself at his most fearsome, he unites the fascinating gaze of the Gorgon with Ares' glaring eyes (*Il.* 8.349). The combination of the two succinctly signals the momentary invincibility of the warrior; while the eyes of the Gorgon paralyze a man and prevent his flight, Ares deals the killing blow. See Lonsdale 1989 more generally for the way in which an antagonist paralyzes his victim by his hypnotizing stare.

[140] See Fraenkel 1962: ad 469 and 947 for this reading.

[141] For this parallelism, see Detienne and Vernant 1978: 101 n. 99.

they are" (85). Heracles suffers the same confusion, again in mind and eyes both, as a result of the visit of the daemonic being dispatched by Hera: identifying the source of the enraged madness attacking the hero, the chorus of the drama declares: "It is the Gorgon, daughter of Night, and her vipers with their hundred clamorous heads; it is glittering-eyed (*marmarōpos*) Lyssa" (Eur. *HF* 882–83). As the frenzy takes possession of him, Heracles assumes the same appearance and powers as the invading force: issuing "terrifying looks," he rolls his Gorgonlike eyes (*gorgōpas koras*, 868; cf. 990) about.

A divinity's larger *prosōpon* can also work this maddening effect, and nowhere more than in the case of Dionysus. Through the course of his *Bacchae*, Euripides draws his audience's attention to the peculiar quality of the countenance exhibited by the god (a quality reinforced by the distinctively nontragic mask that the actor would probably have worn), which seems to have escaped the disguise transforming the remainder of his body into human shape:[142] the Lydian Stranger, preserving his wine-colored cheeks, does not pale with fear when his antagonists approach (438–39), and as the epiphanic Bacchus, has the same smiling look upon his *prosōpon* (1021) that he maintains in his mortal guise. These invitations to focus on the god's face complement the play's emphasis on visual encounters between Dionysus and men, and on the changes that an exchange of divine and human glances can instigate: as the Stranger reveals, the individual who confronts the divinity face-to-face is also seen, *horōn horonta* (470), as though viewing the *prosōpon* of Dionysus means seeing yourself reflected back, albeit in altered fashion, in his gaze.

For those who willingly submit to the god's power, this conflation of gazes and personas, and the transformations it effects, can produce the deeper insight and more acute vision that the chorus of Bacchants enjoys; but for those who resist Dionysus and insist on viewing the god and his mysteries in unmediated fashion, with their own eyes (502), the visual and mental confusion that overcomes Pentheus in the drama's second half follows.[143] Just as the mortal hero "sees double" (918ff.) in the moments when he wavers between a supposedly normal perception and a more visionary one, so, too, Agave, punished by the illusions and inauthentic shapes that Dionysus has inflicted on her, mis-sees what stands before her eyes. The instrument that draws her from her blindness and transports her back to the everyday world is none other than

---

[142] Note that in the prologue, the speaker makes no explicit reference to his face, referring only to the *skeuē* (34), *eidos* (53), and *morphē* (54) that he has assumed. For discussion, Frontisi-Ducroux 1991: 226.
[143] Note especially 918–22 and 1075.

the sobering *prosōpon* of her dead son (1264–80).[144] To look on a man's face rather than that of a god is to regain conventional modes of perception, to apprehend things as they appear to mortal viewers.

For one final expression of the intimate connection between the powers of gods or supernatural creatures and their visual faculties, there are the tales that epic and drama include of deities blinded or more momentarily deprived of sight. Like binding, hobbling, and incarcerating, robbing a divinity or daemonic creature of his visual faculties renders him inoperative. In the Hesiodic theomachies, gods seeking to defeat their antagonists not only immobilize them, but sometimes blind them as well. Zeus's thunder and lightning are the source of the darkness that claims the Titans, robbed of their vision by the weapons' too-brilliant glare (*Theog.* 698–99),[145] and elsewhere in the story paralysis and blindness jointly claim those who fight on the losing side: the rebels are pinned beneath stones and "put in the shadows" by the Hundred-Handers, where they lie fettered in painful bonds (716–18). Zeus figures again as the source of the blindness from which a deity suffers in Aristophanes' *Ploutos*, where the infirm god of wealth must visit the shrine of Asklepios in search of a cure for his visual disease; for as long as the illness lasts, Ploutos proves unable to exercise his prerogatives, and human affairs go consequently awry. Blindness also puts a stop to the activities of one final immortal, but monstrous, being. The special *kibisis* or pouch with which Perseus comes equipped serves expressly to cover the Gorgon's fearsome head, which from the *Iliad* on features eyes that glare terribly from the monster's face,[146] and to keep its visual powers in check; a fifth-century hydria evoking the moment following Medusa's decapitation doubly determines the fact of sightlessness, portraying the head poking out of the bag with its eyes closed.[147]

Image-Viewing

Among the 250 figures on the François vase of c. 570, only three are shown frontally, directly engaging with the audience's gaze, imposing themselves on its vision; and two of these, the Gorgon and Dionysus, display faces in the form of masks. The conventions used by the artist,

---

[144] Here, as many note, Euripides also sounds a metatheatric note as he reminds the audience that they, too, have been experiencing altered vision in viewing an actor's mask as the individual whom it represents. For this confusion, see note 168.

[145] As Detienne and Vernant (1978: 78) note, the expression used by Hesiod corresponds very closely to the description of how the flash of bronze at *Iliad* 13.340–41 blinds the eyes of the warrior.

[146] *Il.* 5.741–42, 8.348, 11.36–37.

[147] *ARV*² 555, 96, with discussion in Frontisi-Ducroux 1995: 70.

both the frontal position and the face-as-mask, reappear in three-dimensional accounts of the monster and the god[148] and suggest that the efficacy of these representations, no less than that of the divine and daemonic beings themselves, depends on face-to-face confrontations, on the viewer both seeing and being seen. While these out-staring masks supply the most signal instance of the powers that images' faces and eyes inherit from their immortal archetypes, other artistic stratagems may also be calculated to enhance and emphasize the features, making the artifacts capable of producing the same impact as the radiant-eyed, keen-sighted, and visually potent divinities; to fall beneath the gaze of an image, both artists and myth-makers would have us believe, is tantamount to an encounter with the eyes of the god himself.

Although not the recipient of any cult activity, plastic accounts of the Gorgon play a critical defensive role in Greek life at least from the archaic period on. Designed to operate as apotropaia, or more specifically as "terror masks," which can ward off evil and protect the object to which they are affixed, they are found on temple façades or as akroteria and antefixes, as blazons on shields or ships, as charms in artisans' workshops and kilns, and even decorating common household utensils, bowls, and amphoras.[149] As the Iliadic examples cited earlier show, the heads and wide-open glaring eye that these *gorgoneia* possess operate together to terrify and induce panic and paralysis in the victim; a Medusa whom the viewer does not confront head on, her eyes holding his, is not the Medusa at all.

Vase paintings from the decades following the creation of the François vase reaffirm the link between Dionysus, the mask, and eyes. The prophylactic eyes that first appeared beneath the handles of vases from the seventh century now flank Dionysus displayed as a head or mask on Attic cups from around 520, and the reduplication of the visual organs on the surface of the vessel makes emphatic the conceit of seeing and being seen. Evidence that Dionysus was worshiped as a disembodied face comes from many different parts of Greece, and from the late archaic and classical periods on; the Athenians venerated the god as the mask-and-pillar image featured on the so-called Lenaea vases with its entourage of female celebrants,[150] the Methymneans made regular sacrifices to the *prosōpon* of Dionysus that fishermen had recovered from the sea (Paus. 10.19.3), and Eusebius, citing the Cynic philosopher Oenomaos, suggests that other cities similarly honored the god in the

---

[148] Even when artists depict her body and legs in profile, the Gorgon's face is always shown facing front.

[149] Faraone 1992: 38; Vernant 1991: 112.

[150] For extensive treatment of these, Frontisi-Ducroux 1991.

form of heads fashioned out of stone, bronze, and gold (*Praep. evang.* 5.36.1).[151] A terracotta Dionysus from the very end of the sixth century, its face painted red and beard and hair yellow, is designed to be hung up, and ex-votos dating from the 470's and perhaps modeled on the design of the cult images themselves take the form of marble masks of the god with holes at the back for suspension.[152] Like the Gorgon, Dionysus assumes the guise of a mask because his impact on the celebrant depends critically on the fact of reciprocal vision; as one account explains, "It is impossible to look at him without falling beneath the fascination of his gaze, a gaze that drives a man out of his own mind."[153]

Even where statue-makers equip Dionysus with a body, they frequently privilege the face, and announce its special status in the plastic ensemble. Describing images that belong, in his account at least, to remote antiquity, Pausanias cites the *xoanon* of Dionysus dedicated by one Polydios in Megara, the body of which is hidden while the *prosōpon* remains clearly visible (*phaneron*, 1.43.5); so, too, the lower part of a Dionysus Akratophoros worshiped at Phigaleia in Arkadia is covered over in laurel leaves and ivy, but the upper part is painted with cinnabar "so as to shine" (8.39.6). A partially concealed Dionysus figures once again, this time in company with Demeter and Kore, in a sanctuary some distance from Sikyon where all three *agalmata* show nothing but their faces (2.11.3), and particularly remarkable are two *xoana* of Dionysus in Corinth, supposedly carved from the very tree that Pentheus climbed prior to his dismemberment, the bodies of which are covered in gold and faces painted in red (2.2.6–7).

While Dionysus stands alone in his possession of this uniquely uncanny countenance,[154] other cult images also display faces and eyes marked out for special treatment. Sometimes a more precious or visually arresting material may underscore the countenance's particular potency, drawing the viewer's attention to this area of the body: an *agalma* of Zeus at Megara is fashioned in terracotta and gypsum, but the *prosōpon* is of ivory and gold, and several of the Parthenon inventories refer to a *prosōpon huparguron* or *katachruson*, which suggests a gilding and refurbishment of Pheidias's image's face.[155] Where precious

---

[151] For discussion, ibid.: 195 and 199. As Frontisi-Ducroux notes, the plural may be a case of Christian polemicizing.

[152] Ibid.: 203–11, for these and other examples.

[153] Vernant and Frontisi-Ducroux 1988: 202.

[154] Frontisi-Ducroux (1991: 189–92) would single out Dionysus for this special treatment, and she suggests that the attention paid to the faces and heads of other images carries a different significance. While granting that visual dynamics are particularly crucial where the figure of Dionysus is concerned, I believe that the faces of all (images of) divinities were perceived as particularly charged areas.

[155] *IG* I^2 277, 25; 279, 58; 280, 76. These are dated to the last third of the fifth century.

stones give to the eyes of the Parthenos and other fifth-century chrys-elephantine works the requisite sparkle, inserts of painted or gilded glass lend a heightened radiance to these features when they appear on images cast in bronze.[156] Sculptors could also turn to the painters who worked along with them in the finishing process to achieve the desired effect: in his account of the image of Athena standing in the Temple of Hephaistos in Athens, Pausanias singles out the eyes and their colora-tion for special note (1.14.6),[157] and several ancient viewers remarked on the liquid luminosity of the Knidian Aphrodite's gaze.[158]

Framing these images and enhancing their impact are indications of the remarkable powers of sight that idols, no less than the immortals for whom they stand in, are believed to possess. Fifth-century drama already includes the motif: the guardian figures "facing the rising sun (*antēlioi*)" that stand outside Agamemnon's palace convey their joy at the king's return with shining *ommata* (Aesch. *Ag.* 519–20),[159] while the statue presided over by Iphigenia at Tauris announces its displeasure at the projected sacrifice of the Greek strangers through the closure of its eyes: *opsin d'ommatōn sunērmosen* (Eur. *IT* 1167).[160] In later sources these marvels proliferate and cluster around many of the most famous images in antiquity. Statues that avert their eyes at some unsightly deed committed in their presence include the Palladion and the Athena of Siris,[161] and so common is the phenomenon that Plutarch, in an editorializing aside, includes it as a standard element in the miracle-working repertoire: recording the supposed exchange between the Ro-man general Camillus and a statue, he notes that "those who insist upon and defend the marvel . . . also bring up similar things, such as the frequent pouring out of sweat of *agalmata*, or *xoana* being heard groaning and being seen turning away and closing their eyes" (*Cam.* 6.3). Lucian records of a *xoanon* of Hera, "If you should stand over against it, it looks you in the face, and as you pass it the gaze still follows you, and if another approaching it from a different quarter looks at it, he is similarly affected" (*Syr. D.* 32).[162] No less curious is a

[156] Stewart 1990: 40.

[157] This, Delcourt (1957: 192), suggests, may be the same image that Sophocles evokes in a reference to the figure of Athena Gorgopis venerated in the Chalkeia.

[158] Lucian *Eikones* 6. Images of Alexander also possessed eyes characterized in similar terms (e.g., Plut. *Alex.* 4.2, *Pomp.* 2.1). For this, see the discussion of L'Orange (1982: 22), who argues that the conceit formed part of the depiction of the ruler in divine terms.

[159] The same term *antēlios* is used of the living Athena at Eur. *Ion* 1550.

[160] See Platnauer 1984: ad loc. for other examples of the same phenomenon in later sources.

[161] For the Palladion, Strabo 6.1.14. For Athena of Siris, Nilsson 1967: 83.

[162] A close parallel exists with the ocular activity ascribed to saints' images in later Chris-tian sources. Bernard of Angers writes of the statue of Sainte Foy at Conques, "So strikingly was the face of the human figure portrayed that it seemed to several people as if

sixth-century image of Artemis on Chios that supposedly changed its expression to denote emotion, looking severe when a viewer entered and glad when he departed (Pliny *HN* 36.13).[163]

The seeming animation of these images' eyes tells only half the story, and more extraordinary still are the changes that the organs can work on those whom they encounter. Taking their lead from the living gods and daemonic creatures, statues paralyze, blind, and madden men who enter their line of sight. Travelers freeze in their tracks when they confront the "terrifying look" (*phobon blepōn*) directed at them by the satyr-head protomes cited in Aeschylus,[164] and other apotropaia, Gorgon's heads among them, possess distended eyes, perhaps in order to magnify the source of their power, and the better to immobilize and fix the viewer to the spot. While other communities gave Athena epithets expressive of her ocular powers (she is dubbed Oxyderkes, sharp-eyed at Argos, and Narkaia, the petrifying one, at Elis),[165] the maker of the Athena Polias chose to emblematize the goddess's visual potency by placing the Gorgon's head on his image's breast. The tragic sources, which regularly describe the statue as terrifying to behold,[166] detail the particular blend of apotropaic and protective powers that this blazon exercises; while the goddess wards off the Furies with her frightful serpents, the *gorgoneion* can simultaneously protect fugitives (Eur. *El.* 1254–57).[167]

Again like the gods whom they re-present, images of divinities use their visual faculties to impair or rob a viewer of his sight, leaving altered vision, blindness, and its corollary, madness, in their wake. While Dionysus enters Euripides' *Bacchae* as a living protagonist, the text imagines his countenance in ways perhaps calculated to put an audience in mind of the god as he manifested himself in contemporary worship. The smiling *prosōpon* or mask on the character's face (referred to at 1021) would have looked much like one of the faces exhibited by the mask-and-pillar images used in cult activities and featured on the

---

it were fixing its beholders with a piercing gaze, as well as sometimes graciously granting the petitions of her suppliants with a twinkle of the eye" (cited in Dahl 1978: 188). For other instances, Freedberg 1989: esp. 51–52; Belting 1994: 62.

[163] The notorious "singing" statue of Memnon also has a place in this company: no sooner did the sun fall on the lifeless-looking body than "its eyes appeared to gaze cheerfully at the light, as the eyes of sunbathers do" (Philostr. *VA* 6.4).

[164] Fr. 78a Radt, with discussion in Chapter One. The expression, however, depends on a conjecture.

[165] For these epithets, Delcourt 1957: 142.

[166] Eur. *HF* 1002–4; *Ion* 989, 993–97.

[167] In a tale preserved by Pausanias (9.34.1), the priestess of Athena Itonia in Boeotia goes into the sanctuary at night, where she encounters the goddess and sees the head of the monster worked on her tunic; petrifaction instantly follows.

Lenaea vases. As the mask worn by the actor oscillates between its theatrical and cultic identities, the visual and mental confusions that it
prompts and the questions of identity that it raises might recall for the
theater goer something of his own experiences with Dionysus and the
images that channeled his power: performing the rites that accompanied
the display of the god as mask and looking at it face-to-face, he, too,
would undergo a dizzying disorientation, his normal powers of perception heightened, distorted, and changed, his sense of self made as fluid
and distended as that of Pentheus.[168]

More explicit references to the ability of images to trouble or destroy
men's powers of sight would multiply in later sources. Visiting the sanctuary at Lykosura, Pausanias notes the curious phenomenon that follows from looking at the statue group displaying a highly revered divinity named Despoina alongside Demeter, Artemis, and a Titan: "On the
right as you go out of the temple there is a mirror fitted into the wall. If
anyone looks into the mirror, he will see himself very dimly or not at
all" (8.37.7).[169] More potent still are images that blind their viewers. No
sooner did the Greek Ilos seize the Palladion from Athena's shrine at
Troy and lay hands on an object that "might not be looked upon by a
man" than he lost his sight, and the same penalty subsequently claimed
Antylus (or Metellus), who took the statue from the Temple of Vesta at
Rome.[170]

An emphasis on visual exchange also characterizes several of these
stories describing statues that madden their unwary viewers, and the
reports provided by the sources suggest that the mental impairment results directly from encountering the idol's eyes or countenance, from
seeing and so being seen.[171] The people of Pellene are safe as long as no

---

[168] Issues of theatrical representation reinforce the problematic nature of the *prosōpon*. As
the mask that the actor wears, it declares the individual the Lydian Stranger whom he
claims to be. But the audience, party from the start to the plans of Dionysus, knows that
the characters within the drama who assume that face and mask are one (as the theatrical
convention requires) effectively mis-see. Instead, for them, the patently nontragic *prosōpon*, distinguished by its smile and anomalous ruddy hue, declares the character a god,
or an image of the same. Euripides reminds his spectators of the two meanings of the
prosōpon at 1277 when Kadmos applies the term to the "face" of the dead Pentheus as
Agave cradles the actor's mask in her arms.

[169] For more on this, see below. Fragments of the cult statue show that her drapery figured
masked worshipers.

[170] For both stories, see Plut. *Mor.* 309f–310a. For the Roman incident, Courtney 1980:
ad Juv. 6.265 (the two stories are clearly duplicates of one another). As Buxton (1980: 30)
demonstrates, blindness can also claim those who enter a sanctuary that should not be
entered.

[171] For individuals who are maddened by images, but not explicitly as a result of visual
contact, there are the Athenians who tamper with the statues of Damia and Auxesia (Hdt.

one "looks directly" (*enantion*) at the statue of Artemis Soteria, which causes trees to become barren and cast their fruit as it passes in its annual procession; but when the priestess brandishes the goddess "in the face" (*antiprosōpon*) of an attacking Aetolian army, the aggressors instantly lose their wits (Plut. *Arat.* 32).[172] Pausanias's tale of the Trojan hero Eurypylos, who no sooner opens a chest enclosing the image of Dionysus Aisymnetes than he goes mad, twice calls attention to the viewing that goes on: "He saw (*eide*) the *agalma* and was straightaway mad after the sight (*thean*)" (7.9.6–9).

As the box hiding Dionysus indicates, safe encounters with potent images require a variety of protective measures; just as epic heroes shield their eyes in response to divine epiphanies (Telemachus turns his head aside when he thinks that Odysseus is one of the immortals, and Anchises performs the same gesture when Aphrodite reveals herself, flashing eyes and all), so, too, viewers of divine images in real-world shrines and sanctuaries avoid unmediated face-to-face exchanges and take special pains to safeguard their eyes. While the people of Pellene "turn their gaze away" so as not to see Artemis Soteria, sacristans introducing visitors to the opsithodome of the Temple of Artemis of Ephesos, where the statue of Hera resides, warn viewers "to be careful of their eyes" (Pliny *HN* 36.32). The explanation that Pliny or his source provides for the admonition, "so intense is the glare of the marble," may be a rationalizing gloss grafted onto an older tradition that recorded the devastating impact of the idol's glance. The mirror at Lykosura cited by Pausanias can perhaps shield the visitor from the untenable radiance of the divinities (a direct encounter might cause more lasting damage to his eyes),[173] and at Olympia the periegete learns of the image of the goddess Sosipolis whom the priestess may only approach with her head and face covered in a veil (6.20.3).

The overly efficacious gaze of idols may also elicit a more radical response. If the object deploys its influence through its eyes, then by manipulating, impairing, or removing those features altogether men

---

5.82), the finders of the image of Artemis Ortheia (Paus. 3.16.7–11), and the daughters of Proetus, who mock a *bretas* of Hera (Apollod. *Bibl.* 2.2.2). Note, too, Dem. 24.121.

[172] As Frontisi-Ducroux (1995) amply demonstrates, the term *prosōpon* necessarily involves reciprocal visual activity: "le *prosōpon* s'entend comme *devant* par rapport aux *yeux* d'un sujet regardant" (20; "*prosōpon* is understood as *in front* in relation to the *eyes* of the one who is seeing"; italics in original).

[173] But note my discussion of the incident below. In Apuleius *Met.* 11.9, the female devotees of Isis hold mirrors behind their backs to face the statue of the goddess while they look ahead as they walk in procession. The doors, curtains, and other devices discussed in chapter 2 supply additional screens that limit the exchanges between the celebrant and god.

might control the nature of its (and/or the god's) interventions in their own lives. Prayers to divinities suggest a model here: the deity, the petitioner specifies, should adopt a kindly and protective rather than inimical expression, and should come not only with a gentle motion, but with a smile and benevolent countenance;[174] a steady and pitying look, denoting favor and protection, is what the suppliant most wants, while the angry, destructive, and bloodshot glance deities may emit should be directed against an enemy.[175] The same persuasive and coercive "rhetoric" informs the design and deployment of sculpted images; both the mode in which the artists choose to depict the deities' eyes and the devices communities adopt to predetermine the quality and impact of the gaze serve as means of directing the influence that the image exercises over the affairs of men.

A small number of ancient images allow us to match facial expression, and most particularly the representation of the eyes, with the object's broader functions. As noted earlier, Gorgon faces and other "terror masks" come equipped with the wide open and exaggerated eyes that maximize the efficacy of the apotropaia. The equally prominent features of Dionysus in some depictions of his mask images on Attic vases may be calculated to promote the vision- and mind-altering impact of encounters with the god, and the use of two heads affixed to a single pillar (if the vases reflect actual practice) again guarantees that at no point does the celebrant escape from the god's gaze.[176] For the rest we can only speculate. Does the brilliance that precious stones and gilded or painted glass give to divine features enhance the celebrant's sense that the god's power is at work, and even acting on his behalf, and might an artist give his statue downturned eyes, a steady gaze, or an expression suggestive of kindliness or ferocity because he hopes to determine the mode in which the deity manifests himself, and the role that he comes to play? The notion familiar in antiquity (so Strabo 8.3.30) that Pheidias sought to reproduce in his Zeus at Olympia the countenance that Homer assigns to the god at the moment when he "nodded his dark brow" in consent to Thetis's petition (*Il.* 1.528–30) suggests that the sculptor aimed to grant his image the potency celebrated by the epic poet: much of the subsequent action of the poem results from that single gesture of acquiescence.

Support for this reading comes from the measures taken to inhibit, or

[174] Among the many possible examples, Sappho fr. 1.14 LP; Aesch. *Supp.* 1–2 (cf. 207, 811–13), *Sept.* 106, 110; Soph. *Aj.* 854. For these and other instances, Malten 1961: 22–23.

[175] For the angry, malevolent gaze, Aesch. *Sept.* 485, *Cho.* 1058. For other examples, Malten 1961: 23.

[176] Frontisi-Ducroux 1991: chap. 5 for discussion.

even to destroy, the visual powers of images of potentially inimical or dangerous divinities. Just as an immortal who undergoes blinding or lies banished from the light loses his usual efficacy and sphere of influence, so, too, a statue allowed only partial vision or robbed of its eyes suffers a reduction or annulment of its (and hence the divinity's) prerogatives. In addition to the immobilizing chains that the Aphrodite Morphe encountered by Pausanias wears about her feet, she has her face covered over with a veil (3.15.10). If, as local tradition suggests, Tyndareos sought to punish the goddess for her role in Helen's flight, then the aggrieved father has not just directed his attack against the two regions where an image's potency chiefly clusters, but has chosen to strike a blow against the particular mode in which Aphrodite deploys her influence: since the goddess, or rather the sexual passion that she instantiates, works through an exchange of gazes, an Aphrodite who can neither see nor be seen finds herself deprived of her usual love-inducing powers. Pausanias's anecdote echoes a motif already implicit in a much earlier source. The inability of the *kolossoi* of Aeschylus's *Agamemnon* to console Menelaus, and to double for the absent Helen, rests principally with their want of eyes, prompting the chorus to remark, "In the absence of eyes, gone is all Aphrodite" (418–19). The conclusion of Aristophanes' *Ploutos* reverses this scenario, reendowing a blind godcum-image with the ability to see. As the drama ends with a grand celebration of the god's cure, and Chremylos prepares to conduct Ploutos back in procession to the city treasury where he presides, the figure to be reinstalled is not so much the living god who has appeared onstage, but an image of the same.[177] Its visual powers restored, the idol has recovered all its former influence.

The archaeological record includes some faint but suggestive indications that these now blind, now resighted images may be more than pure literary conceits. Earlier I mentioned the figures found at the site of graves at Kyrene, some shown with stone veils obscuring their face, and others whose want of eyes appears the more startling for the carefully modeled hair on either side of the vacant countenance. Images discovered at Agrigento and Selinunte exhibit the same anomaly: the first take the form of terracotta columns equipped with hair and ears but no eyes, and the second lack both eyes and mouths. If, as several readings suggest,[178] these depict a funerary deity, or even some figuration of Death

---

[177] As made clear by the scholiast ad 1197 as well as the language of the drama.
[178] Deonna 1930: 324; see, too, Frontisi-Ducroux 1975: 109. Deonna has suggested that the Greeks, like many other cultures before and after them, modeled some images without eyes in order to avoid the damage that the features could inflict, and interprets traditions describing blind or eyeless statues as enduring traces of these beliefs.

itself, then are the representations so many attempts to render the god/goddess inoperative, and perhaps to hinder that acuteness of vision which allows the infernal power to claim its victims?[179]

Talking Heads

In contrast to their powers of locomotion and of sight, the vocal powers of the gods receive little attention, and the sources neither particularize divine voices nor equate a god's ability to speak with his broader efficacy.[180] On one occasion alone Hesiod includes voicelessness as part of the impotence that can afflict a deity, but in this instance the penalty results naturally from the verbal perjury of which the victim stands convicted: the god who swears a false oath by the waters of the Styx must lie "spiritless and voiceless on a strewn bed" for a year (*Theog.* 797–98). But for the sake of completeness, I want briefly to note how voice, as one of the three key life indicators, takes its place in the miraculous doings ascribed to divine images and belongs together with motion and sight in the accounts of the activities that classical authors supply.

In Attic comedy, the gods who appear in the form of idols onstage enter into conversation with the living participants in the scene, and although the audience does not always directly hear their words, the partner in the dialogue clearly registers and responds to their voice. Hermes seemingly speaks with (the image of) Peace, whose answers he reports to the audience (Ar. *Peace* 661, 682–83), and the herm to which Strepsiades turns after seeing the folly of his ways in Aristophanes' *Nubes* advises the protagonist in answer to his request.[181] In a fragment of the comic dramatist Plato (fr. 204 KA), another herm audibly answers the questions asked of him, and it is a Hermes statue once again that enters into dialogue with an unnamed interlocutor in the comedy by Phrynichos cited by Plutarch (*Alc.* 20.5 = fr. 61 KA). But in these several instances, voice serves simply to indicate the animate character of the image and to mark it out from the more humdrum objects encountered outside the topsy-turvy world described by the comic stage.

---

[179] Glossing Hades' name as the "unseeing one" would offer a similar apotropaic gesture. Attacks on images believed malevolent in both the Byzantine and later periods have frequently taken the form of attempts to damage or deface the objects' eyes. Freedberg (1989: 415–16) supplies numerous examples of such mutilations, and Camille (1989: 18) records how, during Otto of Bamberg's mission to convert the Pomeranians in 1123, an idol at Gutzkow had its hands and feet cut off and its eyes gouged out. For the late antique view that daemons operated through the eyes of images, see Mango 1963. For additional examples, Deonna 1930: 329–30.

[180] Although on occasion they can shout terribly (so Apollo at *Il.* 15. 321), or speak in particularly persuasive fashion.

[181] For this, see pp. 129–30.

Evidence for cult images that speak with their worshipers and viewers comes only from postclassical sources, where the phenomenon occurs repeatedly. Here representations of divinities regularly emit sounds, speech, and oracles, and answer the questions put to them. So Dionysius of Halicarnassus describes several speaking *agalmata* and *xoana* (one of which "uttered some words . . . in a voice both distinct and loud," 8.56.2–4) and includes the story of an image of Hera that twice repeats, when questioned by some Roman soldiers, that she wishes to move to Rome (13.3.2).[182] The same incident appears in Plutarch accompanied by a dismissal of the whole conceit (*Cam.* 6), and on a second occasion, too, the author tries to rationalize the otherwise foolish notion: "It is possible also that *agalmata* may emit a noise like a moan or a groan by reason of a fracture or a rupture, which is more violent if it takes place in the interior. But that articulate speech and language, so clear and abundant and precise, should proceed from a soulless thing is altogether impossible" (*Coriolanus* 37.3–38). Lucian has several additional examples to contribute, among them the *xoana* in Syria that sweat, move, and give oracles (*Syr. D.* 10), and most notorious of all is the singing statue of Memnon that figures in so many late-antique travelers' tales.[183]

Perhaps because the efficacy of a god does not reside especially in his voice (except where the business of declaring oracles is concerned, and even then deities tend to use a human mouthpiece or some other vehicle rather than address their petitioners directly), neither the design of divine images nor the modes in which they are deployed place particular emphasis on their speaking powers. Instead, respecting the immortals' preference for communicating through a simple motion, whether a nod or shake of the head or an extension of the arm, a statue's facial expression and pose may carry much more weight. Although Dio Chrysostom does entertain the fantasy that Pheidias's Zeus is actually speaking (12.85),[184] it was the divinity's silent gesture of consent that the statue-maker supposedly sought to reproduce. And while several of the funerary images cited earlier lack a mouth as well as eyes, the feature may be omitted simply on the grounds that it is part of what differentiates the inanimate from the living, and not because it pertains to the prerogatives that the divinity exercises.

The contrast between the animate and the still underscored by these speaking images looks back to the broader issue with which my discus-

[182] The conceit of the statue willing to move forms a conventional part of the Roman practice of *evocatio*.
[183] See Aelius Aristides *Sacred Tales* 4.50–51 for a speaking statue of Asklepios; also Diod. Sic. 17.50–51; Strabo 17.1.43.
[184] See p. 125.

sion began: the twin capacities of the statue both to define and to transcend the divide between the categories of the living and the lifeless. But when set alongside the impact that divine idols can have on men, and the measures that communities take to contain their potency, the distinctions explored in the earlier part of the chapter take on a fresh significance. Just as a curious set of exchanges went on between the viewer of the grave monument and the statue or stele standing in for the dead, so, too, reversals occur when mortals confront representations of the gods. With their power to paralyze, transfix, blind, and madden those who enter their charged space, the idols strip the observer of his ability to move and see, and render him as lifeless as images themselves are normally supposed to be. And in chaining, confining, veiling, or blinding their images, individuals and communities respond in kind, limiting or annulling the objects' capacity for hostile activity by attacking the chief loci of their life and potency, and (to a partial degree) returning them to the class of inanimate objects whose bounds they have transgressed.

Very much in accord with the tales the ancient sources have to tell, contemporary explorations of the conceit of the "living image" in novels, poetry, film, and other media have described the kinds of confusion and inversion that occur when men encounter and contemplate sculpted bodies, and have observed the reassignment of properties that frequently takes place:[185] the viewer adopts the fixity, insensibility, and silence of the stone, while the statue borrows all the dynamism that should belong to the living form. But for the images that populate Greek sanctuaries and shrines, I would propose a different reading of the paradox. The figures, together with the uncanny powers ascribed to them, supply visualizations and expressions of the gap between mortals and divinities, and a means of contrasting two entirely distinct modes of being.

For this I go back to Pausanias's report of events at Lykosura. The description of the visit to the sanctuary contains an anomaly beyond that earlier observed. Even as the viewer finds his own reflection becoming indistinct, the figures of the gods and the thrones supporting them show up with surpassing brightness in the mirror, and can be seen *enargōs*, with clarity (*ta de agalmata tōn theōn kai auta kai ton thronon estin enargōs theasasthai*, 8.37.7).[186] The account introduces two reflections side-by-side, the one divine, invested with all the brilliance and radiance that characterizes epiphanies, the other mortal, blurred, and unclear. Although Pausanias provides no gloss on the phenomenon, we

---

[185] The seminal treatment is Jakobson 1987b. See, too, the discussion of that work, and additional reflections, in K. Gross 1992: esp. 125–36.

[186] For the "logic" behind the seemingly paradoxical intensification of the "image in the image," see the discussion of Vernant (1991: 141–43), from whose remarks I have drawn.

might speculate on its meaning: a man cannot perceive both himself and a god in a single instant because when the two figures appear in immediate proximity, the divinity so casts a mortal into the shade that he becomes virtually invisible. Earlier Greek poets anticipate this imbalance when they imagine a "top-down" look and attempt to apprehend men from an Olympian point of view. In Pindar's famous phrase, a mortal is nothing more than "the dream of a shade" until the *aigla*, the particular radiance the gods briefly lend to those whom they favor, illuminates him with its brilliance and gives him a comparable luminosity (*Pyth.* 8.95–97). Odysseus, whom Athena has endowed with the momentary ability to look at his fellow men from the site a god regularly occupies, comments: "I see that we mortals are nothing but phantoms and insubstantial shadows" (Soph. *Aj.* 125–26).[187] For a man to view a divine epiphany — whether it takes the form of a living god or a sculpted version of the same reflected in a polished surface — is similarly to realize the spectral quality of his own existence.

But the transmutations that the Lykosura sanctuary effects present an even more negative account of the state occupied by living men. The term that Pausanias selects for the blurring of the viewer's reflection, *amudrōs*, recalls the kindred expression *amauros* (dim or sightless) used by archaic poets for phantoms and the dead.[188] In the moment when he witnesses the mirror images and loses clear sight of his own person, the visitor to the sanctuary finds himself reduced to the facelessness and invisibility that are more normally restricted to the inhabitants of underworld realms. Confronted with the particular self-knowledge that contemplation in a mirror can engender, the viewer glimpses his own life in comparison to that of the gods: set against the richness and plenitude of divine existence, men occupy a condition little better than that allotted to the dead. To contemplate the statues of the gods reflected back and enhanced by a second imaging device is thus to suffer the reversal that occurs on many other occasions: it is the statue-viewer who finds himself relegated to the category of the inanimate block of stone.

---

[187] See Buxton 1980: 23 for a very suggestive discussion of this episode.

[188] *Od.* 4.824, 835; Sappho fr. 55 LP. For this point, see Vernant 1991: 142.

CHAPTER FOUR

For Love of a Statue

AT THE ORIGINS of image-making, if we follow Pliny's tale of the Corinthian potter Boutades and his daughter, stands a maiden about to be separated from her loved one, and seeking to assuage the unhappiness his departure will bring (*HN* 35.151).[1] Although the story appears in a source belonging to the imperial age, it features a link between images and eros visible in texts from many centuries before. The statues that populate Greek myth, poetry, and drama are from the first intimately bound up with sentiments of love and fervent longing (*pothos*), and offer ways of exploring the pathology of desire, its impact on lovers and the instigators of their passion. Nor does iconophilia (or more properly, *agalmatophilia*) remain the province of poets and myth-makers alone; matching and fueling the stories told by the sources are the figures that statue-makers of the late archaic and classical age build, and that regularly feature individuals endowed with the very roles and appearances that contemporary society deemed most likely to stimulate desire. Placing the audience in the role of the protagonist in the text, they, too, seem designed to engage and arouse, and endlessly to reenact the frequently vexed relations between the lover and beloved. More than that, the images visually realize the conceit that the written sources spell out: inviting the viewer to elide the representation with a living object of erotic longing, they chart just how far that slippage can proceed. Read together, the texts and statues allow us not only to suggest something of the reactions that the works of art would have provoked in their audiences, but also to understand their place within a particular historical context. As I propose, these visual discussions of desire play centrally into some of the larger social and political currents in late sixth- and fifth-century Greece, where eros, and its proper objects, limitations, and role in the lives of citizen-viewers, become a matter of public as well as private concern.[2]

---

[1] See chapter 1 for detailed discussion of the story.
[2] For discussion of the term "desire" and warnings against using it in any transhistorical sense, see Kampen 1997: 267–68.

IMAGE LOVE IN LITERARY ACCOUNTS

Pandora

Many centuries before Pliny's mention of the terracotta work fired in Boutades' kiln, Greek myth devises a tale that places desire at the heart of the fashioned image and casts the statue as partner in an erotic relationship. In his two accounts of Pandora, Hesiod already introduces the motifs to which later authors will return in their evocations of love-instigating artifacts, and sounds the question central to subsequent treatments of the theme: why do the gods choose to create by way of most irresistible amorous lure not a living being, but an animated piece of craftsmanship, and what is the connection between Pandora's status as an image and the desire that she incites?

Pandora's artificial, fabricated character determines and informs both her nature and her function. As a substitute and as a figure whose arrival heralds man's entry into a symbolic rather than an immediate sphere, she aptly comes in the shape of a manufactured good that replaces the organic element, fire, that Zeus has withdrawn.[3] But on at least two counts, her status as work of art also looks directly to her erotic powers. First, as Hesiod suggests, and other sources will go on to demonstrate, the finely crafted object generates desire in and of itself, eroticizing the viewer's look through its capacity to externalize and show in concentrated form whatever gives the human form its prime appeal; and second, the painful longing (*pothon argaleon*, *Op.* 66) that regularly afflicts lovers repeatedly directs itself toward representations and replacements existing at several removes from an original beloved, and constituting their own independent but no less unattainable reality.

To begin with the first point, "facture" declares itself from the very start of the myth that privileges *technē* over biology.[4] Pandora owes her genesis not to an act of sexual procreation (or even to a male-slanted variation on the same such as the gods of the *Theogony* can perform),[5] but to a notion first conceived by the mind of Zeus (*Op.* 49), then

---

[3] For this, see chapter 1.

[4] I borrow the term "facture" as a translation of the Greek *technē* from Stewart 1997: 43.

[5] Each in his own different way, Hesiod's Ouranos, Kronos, and Zeus all succeed in simulating the biological processes of pregnancy and birth: Aphrodite appears from the semen of Ouranos, and the Erinyes emerge from the blood that drips from his severed genitals onto the earth (*Theog.* 183–200); Kronos first swallows the children that Rhea has conceived, and then, when Zeus's trick compels him to release the offspring now occupying his womb or *nēdus*, the god gives birth through his mouth (*Theog.* 453–500); going one better than his father, Zeus ingests the pregnant Metis and bears Athena from his head (*Theog.* 886–95). For more detailed discussion of the significance of these episodes, see Zeitlin 1996: 79–83.

translated into speech, and finally realized with the help of craftsmen deities. Pandora may be molded from the living earth, but the poet's tale—unlike some vase representations—omits any hint of autochthony.[6] Instead, Hephaistos models Pandora deploying his strictly artisanal powers (*Theog.* 570–71; *Op.* 61, 70). At his side, in both the Hesiodic story and artistic visualizations, stands Athena, herself patron-goddess of workers in metal and in stone, and a divinity generated, if not conceived, by technical, almost metallurgical means.[7] Just as Pandora belongs outside the normal sequence of gestation and birth, so, too, she experiences nothing of the growth and development that characterize properly biological offspring,[8] and like the "new-born" Athena once again, she appears already fully formed, equipped with the shape and dress she permanently preserves.[9] Her very completeness, and her separation from the natural cycles of evolution, maturation, and decay, confirm her affinity with the unchanging products of potter, sculptor, and smith.[10]

Also indicative of the artistic, artificial aspect of the woman is her divorce from an original to whom she might stand in organic relationship. Biological birth requires progenitors, producers of offspring who, as Hesiod himself observes (*Op.* 235; cf. 182), offer replicas of the parental model.[11] But the Pandora of the *Works and Days* has a multiplicity of parents, and she exactly resembles none of the company. In an act

---

[6] Loraux 1993: 78. For artistic accounts in which Pandora/Anesidora rises from the earth, *LIMC* s.v.

[7] The earliest artistic portrayal of the scene appears to introduce Hephaistos in the role of craftsman-cum-midwife positioned near the throne of Zeus, while a second figure, possibly Daidalos, floats above (for discussion, S. P. Morris 1992: 84; Loraux 1993: 131). Athenian vase-painters would later equip Hephaistos with a double-axe in order to release Athena from her father's head. The same god also attends the birth of Pandora, this time carrying a mallet.

[8] Zeitlin (1996: 57) makes this point, contrasting Pandora with Hesiod's account of man, who evolves in stages in the parallel tale of the five ages in the *Works and Days*.

[9] Loraux 1993: 133 n. 100.

[10] Note the conceit of the sophist Onomarchos of Andros, who, in a patent *adunaton*, curses a beloved image by wishing on it old age in a speech entitled "The Man Who Fell in Love with a Statue" (Philostr. *VS* 2.18).

[11] Look at a child, and the father stands before you, identical in hands, feet, voice, and countenance (so *Od.* 1.208–9, 4.149–50). Classical sources would, however, use artisanal terms to describe this process of reproduction, presenting the child as the *ergon* of the parent and employing the vocabulary of molding and imprinting to describe how offspring take on the form of their (male) progenitors. For this, see Aesch. *Supp.* 282–83; Hdt. 1.116.1; note, too, Pind. fr. 34 Snell-Maehler for the association of childbirth with metallurgy. In Aristotle's account of sexual reproduction, illustrations from the realm of craftsmanship proliferate (e.g., *Gen. an.* 729a12–14, 730b25–32, 738b25, 740a13–16). For more detailed discussion, Dean-Jones 1994: 184–99; Laqueur 1990: 42.

that simulates but does not reenact the genitor's transmission of his appearance and nature to his child, the gods endow and "fill" (*enti-thēmi*, 61, 67, 79–80) the vessel with their particular powers and properties. Likeness does inform the creation of the woman, but the embarrassment of referents complicates the tale and turns Pandora into an amalgam on several counts: at once an exemplary instance of that brilliant mixture of colors, materials, and textures that the Greeks termed *poikilia* and prized so highly in their works of art, she is also a hybrid, a composite of divine, human, and animal traits, whose different attributes form the entirely novel and unprecedented ensemble that works of *poiēsis* can uniquely achieve.[12]

But far from diminishing her appeal, the process of manufacture defining Pandora only heightens her love-inspiring powers. As Hesiod's account demonstrates, the charm or *charis* that mortals exhibit, and their ability to manifest a loveliness that approximates them to the perfectly beautiful divinities, depends on the superaddition of qualities from without, and on a process of artistic ornamentation, embellishment, and "making like";[13] the body must be "worked" and enhanced from the outside in order to achieve maximum appeal and to acquire the status of an *agalma* or thing that gives delight. This artisanal idiom informs the creation of Pandora through and through, whether the poet is describing her external or internal properties. In the *Theogony*, linguistic echoes connect the living woman to her more patently ornamental aspects,[14] and the omission of any overt reference to what lies beneath the garments and ornaments turns Pandora into a composite of the coverings, jewelry, and crown that she wears, all decorative allure.[15] The *Works and Days* presents the snare covered with the *charis* that Aphrodite sheds on it (65), but this same surface attribute functions as

[12] Nor does Pandora match either the goddess or the chaste *parthenos* whom Zeus cites as models for Hephaistos's work (*Op.* 62–63, 71). As I argued earlier, in both accounts Hesiod's phrasing suppresses the subject to whom the "modest maiden" stands equivalent (*Theog.* 571–72; *Op.* 70–71) and signals that this is no replica but an entirely new being. Here the paradox of the technical act of (re)production emerges most clearly; as Vernant (1996: 383) remarks, "L'identité de Pandora . . . s'établit par et dans la semblance à ce qu'elle doit être pour être elle-même" ("The identity of Pandora is established by and in the semblance to what she must be in order to be herself").

[13] For this argument, Saintillan 1996: 343–44.

[14] Zeus directs Hephaistos to fashion (*teuchein*) the "evil thing" (570), and the verb is used again of the *daidala* that decorate Pandora's crown (581). The same notion of semblance that describes the creatures on the headdress (*zōoisin eoikota*, 584) earlier informs Pandora's approximation of the bashful maiden (572). Just as the embroidered veil provokes *thauma* in its viewers (575), so, too, does the ensemble of woman and adornment when the work is done (588).

[15] Loraux 1993: 81.

the quickening property that turns the artifact into a properly sentient and animated being.[16] Desire for Pandora on any count means desire for the product of *technē*.

But Hesiod does not end things there. Although the story holds out the hope that woman will bring men delight as well as grievous cares, and that she will satisfy the longing she incites, that fulfillment remains, at least for the purposes of the Hesiodic texts, endlessly deferred; in an enigmatic twist on the expected scenario, the creature who imposes on men the necessity of sexual reproduction seems neither to consummate her marriage nor to give birth.[17] At most points in the tale, the link between these failures and Pandora's artisanal origins remains implicit,[18] but the concluding event in the version related in the *Works and Days* brings the elements into particularly close proximity. No sooner has Epimetheus received the baneful gift than his bride reappears equipped with the *pithos* whose artificial manufacture, function, and shape so patently recapitulate her own genesis and form.[19] For a moment Pandora seems ready to realize the metonymic relation in which the jar stands to her body, and in so doing to take on her proper marital and maternal functions: like the *pithos*, she can be breached, filled, and finally sealed so as to keep safe the seed of Epimetheus's future child. But the husband never appears to claim his prerogative. Instead, Pandora removes the stopper with her own hands (94) and allows the contents to scatter abroad.[20] No longer equivalent to the female body, which typically closes up to safeguard the male seed that it has received,[21] the jar, an inanimate and nongenerative object, instead recalls the artisanal quality that its bearer originally possessed. No wonder that this account

---

[16] On this latter point, Saintillan 1996: 320.

[17] As argued in detail in Zeitlin 1996: esp. 57–61. In addition to the points Zeitlin makes, note how in *Works and Days* Zeus charges Aphrodite with a leading role in the manufacture, but in one of the several uncouplings that occur between the original injunctions and the actual course of events, others fill in for the goddess named. Athena dresses Pandora as virginal bride, while the Charites and Peitho place golden necklaces about her, and the Horai garland her in spring flowers (72–75). The Graces, Peitho, and the Horai can be read as Aphrodite's surrogates and supplements here, but the substitution also indicates the character of the eros that Pandora will arouse. While Aphrodite's presence would spell a desire that achieves its goal—witness the goddess's progress in her *Homeric Hymn*, where she leaves the desire-struck wild beasts mating with one another in her train (*Hymn. Hom. Ven.* 69–74)—the gifts that these deities contribute emphasize the creature's ability to entice rather than to satisfy.

[18] Note, for example, the leading roles of Hephaistos and Athena, deities who both stand in hostile or tendentious relations to the spheres of sexuality, marriage, and parenthood.

[19] Zeitlin 1996: 64–65; duBois 1988: 76–93; Sissa 1990: 154–55; Dean-Jones 1994: 78.

[20] Zeitlin (1996: 71) reads the incident as a means of glossing over men's part in the sexual act, and so freeing them from responsibility for any evil effects it may have had.

[21] On the closure of the woman's body, Hanson 1990: 324–30; Sissa 1990: 158–60.

omits all mention, direct or elliptical, of Pandora as the mother of her husband's offspring; the race of women is in every way a race apart.[22]

As vivified bride, Pandora not only continues to act in a manner that harks back to her mode of production, but also displays the behavior that subsequent sources will repeatedly ascribe to statues assuming the role of objects of desire. In Hesiod's two presentations of the single episode, the manufactured article exists as nothing more than the recipient and vehicle for what others have put into and onto it, in both literal and symbolic fashion, and cannot reciprocate in and of its own. Consumer of others' substance, not producer of goods, it lacks the generative ability necessary for (re)production. The lover's behavior in the face of such an object is the matter that later tales of *agalmatophilia* take up.

The Absent Beloved

Although the concept of "imitation of an absent model" cannot be applied to Pandora in any straightforward fashion (since the object follows no single or existing archetype and possesses an autonomy and life energy of its own), Hesiod equips his maiden with a property that aligns her with other representations more obviously standing in for something missing or forever lost. According to Zeus's injunctions, the fabricated object should afflict men with "painful *pothos*" (*Op.* 66), and *pothos* already in archaic song may be defined as a fervent longing to make the absent present.[23] While Hesiod does not follow through on the implications of the term, the motif of absence, of a quest for an antecedent reality and referent more real than the representation itself, figures centrally in tales of lovers who have recourse to images, and who use the objects in attempts to "presentify" the missing beloved. The problematic relations between the model and the imitation, and the mismatch between the image and the double, fascinate storytellers who endlessly compare and contrast the two. Building on the notion of dis-

[22] The *pithos*, of course, does not scatter quite all its contents. Zeitlin understands the continued presence of Hope as a figuration of the child yet to be born, an indication that procreation has in fact occurred: "To close the jar upon the Elpis that remains within marks the beginning of pregnancy, not yet brought to term" (1996: 66). But the Hope that lingers within the jar might also function more literally; it signals the expectation that Pandora's body continually holds out, the promise of satisfaction that the object of desire has yet to grant.

[23] See Vernant 1990a: 41–45 for a detailed study of uses of the term in Homer and beyond, and the development of many of his suggestions in Bettini 1992: chap. 1. In *Eth. Nic.* 1187a6, Aristotle comments, "One is in love whenever one longs (*pothei*) for the beloved when absent, and eagerly desires his presence." Note, too, how Gorgias (*Encomion to Helen* 18) uses the term *pothos* in reference to sculpted images—they provoke *eros* and *pothos*.

similarity, which Greek thought of the classical age ascribes to the act of artistic *mimēsis*, these tales of iconophilia pin the nonfulfillment of the lover's search to the nature of the object to which he turns.

No lover ever erects an image or directs his passion toward the figurine when the living object of desire is close at hand. Instead the real and notional statues that appear in classical texts repeatedly serve to fill an absence, to act as substitute for a missing beloved. Menelaus looks to the *kolossoi* in his palace to appease his longings for the departed Helen (Aesch. *Ag.* 416–19), and in Euripides' *Alcestis*, Admetus proposes having a statue made to replace his dead wife in the marriage bed (348–54). In Euripides' lost *Protesilaus*, Laodamia actually effects the consolation that Admetus intends, and has an image built when she discovers her husband's death at Troy.[24] Nor is it fortuitous that the frustrated Alcibiades compares Socrates to an *eikōn* at the beginning of his description of the philosopher (Pl. *Symp.* 215a–b). For all the living presence of Socrates occupying his couch at Agathon's party, the beloved remains as unattainable as though he were at many miles' remove.[25]

Where mortal lovers fashion real and metaphoric statues in their abandoned states, gods create beguiling copies or *eidōla* when they wish to ward men off from the targets of their transgressive passions. Paris embraces the plastic simulacrum of Helen modeled by Hera's craft in place of the living queen (Eur. *Hel.* 31–36),[26] and several myths—those of Ixion and Iasion to name but two—detail how deities fabricate and deploy artificial replicas of themselves or other immortals in order to frustrate men bent on satisfying their illicit longings for the bodies of the gods.[27] In these episodes the more generalized problem of how to

---

[24] For more complete accounts of the story, Apollod. *Epit.* 3.30; Hyg. *Fab.* 104; Ov. *Her.* 13.

[25] To glance at the later sources is to find the same conceit: Apuleius's Charite will comfort herself by lavishing attention on a fabricated mask of her dead spouse (*Met.* 8.7); and note, too, the *xoanon* that Zeus has made to stand *anti numphēs*, in place of his actual wife Hera, from whom he is estranged (Paus. 9.2.7–9.3). In this instance the creation of the image actually prompts a reconciliation between husband and wife when Hera is delighted to discover that the "Plataea" whom she thinks Zeus in the act of wedding is nothing more than a wooden object. For discussion of the story, S. P. Morris (1992: 54–58), who suggestively connects it with the Pandora tale. Of course Ovid's Pygmalion story, with its own many echoes of the Hesiodic myth (so Sharrock 1992: 175), caps all previous versions. Pygmalion creates a being who, like the manufactured Pandora, corresponds to no mortal creature and displays a beauty "more perfect than that of woman ever born" (*Met.* 10.248–49).

[26] According to a variant, Paris receives not a plastic double of Helen, but an image *en pinaki . . . gegrammenon* (schol. ad Aelius Aristides 1.131.1 Dindorf).

[27] For a full accounts of these, see Kannicht 1969: 1:33–38.

give visual and tangible presence to powers that lie beyond mortal apprehension takes on an explicitly erotic cast as it melds with the motif of an amorous pursuit; now individuals seek not merely to see immortals face-to-face, but to enter into the most intimate relations of all. The impossible nature of the quest, whether for the human or for the divine (and Helen, of course, occupies a place intermediary between the two), finds expression in the final outcome of these stories; no more than phantom presences, the cloud *eidōla* must melt away to nothingness.[28]

The evanescence of these airy simulacra corresponds to the void that so frequently lies behind the surface of the image, and that further hinders the lover's search for the living presence he desires. Already in the *Theogony*, Pandora is no more than her garments and ornamentation, and the text teases its audience with the absence of a body underneath. The departure of Aphrodite from the *kolossoi* that momentarily beguile Menelaus signals the vacancy that lies within these seemingly living statues (Aesch. *Ag.* 419), and Admetus's reference to the "cold" comfort that he will derive from the Alcestis-image's embrace (Eur. *Alc.* 353) reminds the audience of his inability to pass beyond the hard surface matter.[29] The relation between the appearance and the interior of such a passion-inciting object builds on another problematic that the split-leveled statue manifests: now combined with the erotic nature of the lover's quest, commonly imagined as an attempt to open up, uncover, or enter the closed vessel of the body, the lover's inability to penetrate the image and to lay hold of its (missing) depth figures the frustration of his sexual desires.[30]

Even as the statues refuse to re-present or yield up the absent beloved, they can further declare their distance from the model by taking on a life and identity of their own, and even by displacing the prior object of

---

[28] So Nephele, who replaces Hera in the tale of Ixion, and the *eidōlon* of Helen, which rejoins the aether (Eur. *Hel.* 605–6).

[29] When Alcestis returns at the end of the play, she, too, seems a thing of pure externality; the maiden is a composite of clothing and ornaments (1050), and the veil that covers her face, together with her lack of voice, strip the figure of the conduits that serve to convey inner life to the surface. For the relations between the statue trope and the heroine's final appearance, see chapter 3.

[30] Postclassical texts are no less preoccupied with the problem of what lies beneath the surface of the image as beloved. In the several accounts of the youth enamored of the Knidia, the sources often frame the anecdotes as *aitia* for the stain on the otherwise flawless marble surface, a confirmation of the "lustful act" (Pliny *HN* 36.22; cf. *HN* 36.23) that the individual driven to distraction finally performs; but the disfigurement also offers visual affirmation that the idolater remains restricted to the exterior of the object. Ovid's Pygmalion offers the exception that proves the rule: the narrative highlights the paradox of this image's possession of inner life and depth when the happy denouement takes the form of the conception of a child, nourished within the body of the artist's bride.

eros. When Euripides' Menelaus unwittingly pursues the plastic *eidōlon* of Helen, he goes in quest of a creature whose nature radically differs from that assigned (in this rewriting of the story) to the living queen; as the "true" Helen takes such pains to point out, she remains chaste and guiltless, while the phantom stands convicted of betrayal and adultery. But so compelling is the version of events embedded in the *eidōlon*, which for all its crimes stands proof of Menelaus's victory in the Trojan War, that it threatens to derail the reunion between husband and wife halfway through the play; only the disappearance of the simulacrum, together with its declaration of its origins, makes Helen the winner in the struggle between the two. And in Laodamia's suicide after the destruction of the image she has made, should we understand that the wife immolates herself through grief for the dead Protesilaus, or because she cannot live deprived of the representation of the same?[31]

These disjunctures between the model and the plastic copy find renewed emphasis in the other phantasmagoric and secondary phenomena, the dreams, daytime visions, and ghosts, which the fifth- and fourth-century sources place alongside the statue in the lover's home.[32] In the first stasimon of Aeschylus's *Agamemnon*, a *phasma*, statues, and dreams follow one another in rapid succession (415, 416, 420), and Euripides will borrow the device when Admetus turns from his evocation of an image to thoughts of the nighttime visions of his wife that will visit his bed (*Alc.* 354–55). In each instance, the vexing intangibility and evanescence of the apparitions underscore and invert the no less distressing materiality characterizing the statue that has gone before. The sources even suggest that one form of "double" may generate another. Confronted with the woman who so closely resembles (the statue of) his wife,[33] Admetus charges Heracles with dabbling in necromancy and bringing back a ghost from the dead (*Alc.* 1127–28), and Menelaus reacts in identical fashion to the "apparition" of Helen whom

---

[31] There is no knowing whether Euripides included the motif in his *Protesilaus*, but later iconographical renditions of the myth suggest a possible conflict between the original and the model, and their simultaneous claims on the widow's affections: a cameo from the Hellenistic age and the well-known Vatican sarcophagus picture show Laodamia embracing (the ghost of) Protesilaus, whom the gods have released from Hades for a stipulated time, while a portrait image of the husband stands close by. See Bettini 1992: 14–15 for details of these, and his discussion of the larger problems generated by the copresence of image and original in the final chapter of his study.

[32] For the larger affinities between these "doubles," Vernant 1983: 309–10 and 1990a: 34–41; Brillante 1988: esp. 17–18; Bettini 1992: esp. 28–29. The affinity acquires a new twist when gods manifest themselves in dreams in the form of their cult images; as Brillante (1988: 18) points out, because the dream is already by its nature an image, it makes scant difference whether it features the deity himself or shows him in the form of a statue.

[33] For this, see chapter 3.

he encounters in Egypt (Eur. *Hel.* 569). Even as the enamored Kritoboulos boasts of the clarity of the *eidōlon* of Kleinias that he preserves in his soul, his subsequent equation of one type of secondary representation with another betrays the fact of the *erōmenos*'s absence: so *saphēs*, or apparent, is the double that a sculptor or painter could fashion as good a portrait of Kleinias by looking on the *eidōlon* as on the original (Xen. *Symp.* 4.21–22).

Like the statue, these dreams, ghosts, and *eidōla* have their genesis in the *pothos* that afflicts the grieving individual, and like the statue, too, they leave only more fervent longing in their wake. The visit of the insubstantial *eidōlon* of Patroklos in *Iliad* 23 complements the *pothos* that Achilles has suffered since the death of his *therapōn* (19.321), and *pothos* troubles Menelaus surrounded by dream visions, ghosts, and the *kolossoi* of Helen in his palace (Aesch. *Ag.* 414); so, too, Kritoboulos experiences *pothos* for the absent Kleinias, whom he entertains as no more than an *eidōlon* in his *psuchē* (Xen. *Symp.* 4.22).[34] But because it is predicated on an absent original, neither dream nor statue nor *eidōlon* can satisfy the longing the lover feels, and Socrates names the only possible cure for his friend's distress: rather than seeking solace in secondary manifestations, Kritoboulos should go off and see Kleinias himself. In a second sounding of the motif by Xenophon, this time in reference to a painted rather than a plastic work of art, Socrates and his companions pay a visit to the famous *hetaira* Theodote, who happens to be posing for her portrait as the visitors arrive (*Mem.* 3.11.2–3). Although Socrates uses the encounter to illustrate a very different point, viewing the woman-positioned-as-image generates the usual desirous response and will put those who then quit the scene in a state of longing for the absent: as Socrates remarks, "We already desire to touch what we have seen; we shall go away excited, and when we have gone we shall feel an unsatisfied longing (*pothēsomen*)."[35]

Surface Appeal

The power of the image, whether statue, painting, or other kind of double, to inspire longing does not derive solely from the object's representational

---

[34] See the treatment in Vernant 1990a: 41–45 for these and other examples.

[35] Hugh of St. Victor's later account of the sensations aroused by the beauty of visible objects, similarly divorced from a prior reality, closely corresponds to the suffering that *agalmatophilia* involves: "When we admire the beauty of visible objects, we experience joy, certainly, but at the same time we experience a feeling of tremendous void. Forms excite our desire but do not gratify it. In addition they do not permit us to be satisfied with them; they incite us to a continual desire for more and better, they urge us to proceed from the image to the reality" (quoted in Camille 1989: 53). For this scenario in relation to the Pygmalion tale, Elsner 1992: 165.

claims. The *charis* that Menelaus observes in the *kolossoi*, the *terpsis* that Admetus expects from his Alcestis image, and the *pothos* that Socrates and his companions experience at the sight of the "painted" Theodote hark back to a different facet of the Pandora tale, where the woman's irresistible allure depended on her character as a fabricated object, one modeled through the *technē* that gave the creature not just her surface but her more wholesale charm. Exploring anew the capacity of the skillfully made artifact to engage and arouse on its own count, archaic and classical sources pick up on and develop the suggestion present in the Hesiodic myth: a work of art does not owe its appeal to its resemblance to a living beloved, but the beloved instigates passion precisely because he or she displays the properties that belong to finely crafted objects.

To anticipate and even to predetermine the amorous response that an individual elicits, and to signal his or her coming role as an object of erotic yearning, Homer twice compares or conflates the protagonist with a finely crafted artifact, and shows how the "technical" patina that the body has assumed constitutes a cardinal element in its powers of attraction. When Nausikaa first encounters Odysseus down by the seashore, he appears naked, disheveled, and so wild in aspect that he puts all the maids to flight. But then the hero undergoes a metamorphosis. Once bathed, anointed, and clothed, he becomes the object of Athena's artistic attentions, as she makes her protégé into a figure taller, broader, and more radiant than before. To describe the goddess at her task, Homer likens her to a skilled artisan building a silver image overlaid with gold (*Od.* 6.232–35). Three times the poet repeats the term *charis*, first to describe the products of the craftsman (234), then to pinpoint the property that the goddess "pours down" over the hero (235), and finally to present the completed figure:

> ὡς δ' ὅτε τις χρυσὸν περιχεύεται ἀργύρῳ ἀνὴρ
> ἴδρις, ὃν Ἥφαιστος δέδαεν καὶ Παλλὰς Ἀθήνη
> τέχνην παντοίην, χαρίεντα δὲ ἔργα τελείει,
> ὣς ἄρα τῷ κατέχευε χάριν κεφαλῇ τε καὶ ὤμοις.
> ἕζετ' ἔπειτ' ἀπάνευθε κιὼν ἐπὶ θῖνα θαλάσσης,
> κάλλεϊ καὶ χάρισι στίλβων.   (*Od.* 6.232–37)

And as when a skilled man pours gold on silver, he whom Hephaistos and Pallas Athena have taught in every skill, and who completes grace-filled works, so Athena poured grace on his head and shoulders. And afterward, going to the shore of the sea, he sat a little apart, gleaming with beauty and grace.

The quality originally added from without has become an emanation from within as the two facets of *charis* coalesce: both the radiance and charm that result from a process of manufacture, and the brilliance that issues from a living body, *charis* can be either an artificial or an organic property. Once Odysseus has been invested with the likeness of an artifact, Homer describes Nausikaa's much-altered response. She gazes admiringly at the stranger[36] and desires to have him for her own: would that she could find a husband such as this man.[37]

Desire is written still more broadly into the complementary episode later in the song where a second "makeover" occurs. Now in Ithaca, Athena visits Penelope in order to transform the tear-stained, aging wife into a rejuvenated and alluring bride-to-be. In a passage that recalls the Hesiodic account of the fabrication of Pandora on several scores, Athena endows Penelope with the gifts of the gods and anoints her with the ambrosia that belongs to Aphrodite. Then, in actions reminiscent of the attentions she paid to Odysseus on the Phaeacian shore, the goddess makes the heroine larger and fuller than before, and, in a rapid nod to the activity of the artisan who fashions precious *agalmata*, "whiter than sawn ivory" (*Od.* 18.187–96).[38] The aftermath of the scene confirms the several parallels. Just as Pandora and Odysseus were designed to attract those who looked on them, so, too, Penelope, positioned and framed as the object of the suitors' contemplation as she takes her stand between her maids in the *megaron*, instantly charms her audience and incites their limb-loosening (and unsatisfied) longings (18.212–13). Athena's goal, to make the Achaeans gaze at the woman with admiration-cum-desire (*thesaiat' Achaioi*, 191), has been amply realized, and Penelope's heightened erotic allure, like that of her husband, follows from her refashioning in the manner of an artifact, endowed with charm from without.

Ivory features again in a third, more literal sounding of the motif of the beloved-to-be embellished and invested with the likeness of a work of art. In Pindar's turn to the myth of Pelops that will occupy the midsection of his first *Olympian*, he introduces the hero as the boy with whom Poseidon "fell in love" (*erassato*) at the moment when Klotho drew him out of the cauldron "furnished with [or 'excelling in respect to'] a shoulder brilliant with ivory" (25–27). Although the poet will go on to amend this particular version of the myth, suppressing the embar-

---

[36] The term *theaomai* used at 237 carries many different meanings in Homer, but among them is the spectatorship that works of art inspire; so *Od.* 19.235.

[37] Nausikaa's desire for Odysseus is, of course, destined to remain unsatisfied.

[38] Cf. the ivory cheek-piece in *Il.* 4.141–45, whose decoration is described and which earns the term *agalma*. Ivory is closely associated with the figure of Penelope both here and at 19.562–67 and 21.7, and may look to the larger issues of beguilement and deception that surround the behavior of this figure, properties very apparent in the solicitation of gifts from the suitors about to occur.

rassing facts of divine dismemberment, cannibalism. and prosthetic sur-
gery that it presupposes, his opening account links Poseidon's suddenly
conceived passion to the beloved's manifestation of his distinctive and
embellishing mark, and even suggests a causal connection (*epei*) between the two.[39] The term *phaidimos* further draws attention to the
special quality of the artificial element, as Pindar's phrase pinpoints it as
the source of the youth's seductive radiance or gleam. While Homer
uses the adjective for his heroes and their body parts (particularly their
shoulders and limbs), here the formula declares the generator of the
brilliance something not intrinsic to the body, but added from without.[40]

The same coalescence of a body's display of 'artistic' and supplementary qualities, and its desirability, figures in Attic drama. When Perseus
first catches sight of Andromeda, bound to the rock and about to be
devoured by the monster coming from the sea, the hero's amorous look
perceives the maiden as a statue: "Well, what hill is this I see, with sea-
foam floating around it? And there is some *eikōn* of a maiden, chiseled
from the very foam of the rock itself, an *agalma* made by a skilled
hand" (fr. 125 N²; cf. Eur. *Alc.* 348).[41] A fragment from Chairemon's
Alphesiboea (fr. 1) confirms a maiden's appeal by comparing her to "a
wax-colored fashioned statue," and the simile forms a natural pendant
to the earlier suggestions of the "artificed" and spectacular quality of
the figure held up for show. In the lines preceding the conceit the
speaker, inviting his interlocutor to look on the vision of beauty (*op-
seis*), calls attention to the polished gleam (*stilbōn*) of the maiden's skin;
the blush of modesty that contributes to her allure is, like the *charis*
poured down on Odysseus, added to the surface as a final element in
the *kosmēsis* of the whole. The comparison to an image may also more
discreetly signal the erotic charge latent in a scene and the presence of
an audience that directs its often fetishizing scrutiny to the body-object
on display. For all the pathos of her situation, there is no mistaking the
desirability of the semi-clad Polyxena as she prepares for her sacrificial
death; placed before the ranks of the assembled army, her dress torn
away and the separate portions of her anatomy, breast and chest, bared
for the knife, she appears "like an *agalma*" (Eur. *Hec.* 558–61).[42]

---

[39] On the question of whether *epei* in line 26 should be read as temporal or causal, see
Gerber 1982: ad loc. My reading obviously tends toward the latter interpretation, for
which see, too, Köhnken 1983, and Mullen 1982: 171–72 and n. 26.

[40] For more detailed discussion of the passage, see Chapter Five.

[41] Later versions of this same instant repeat and embroider on the motif; for Ovid's Perseus, Andromeda appears a *marmoreum opus* (*Met.* 4.675; see Barkan 1986: 53 for discussion), while Achilles Tatius adds an additional framing device when he presents the
heroine in the form of a tableau, which he then likens to a statue (3.7.2).

[42] Collard (1991: ad 559–60) suggests that Euripides may have been inspired by the scene

From these and other episodes, a more complex account of the relation between the work of art and a loved object emerges: for all the failure of the image to re-present the absent or missing beloved and the persistent gap between the original and copy, the fact of *poiēsis*, the material and technical aspects of the statue, need not stand in the way of the act of elision or substitution that the lover strives to perform.[43] Instead, the object suggests itself because it offers a paradigmatic instance of that *charis* which the supremely attractive body also displays, and of the work of supplementation and embellishment from without that the most desirable human form has undergone. As Pindar's sixth *Olympian* affirms, *charis* is not only the outcome of this process of ornamentation but, as the property of grace personified, the prime practitioner of the transformation: the goddess Charis herself appears in the song, where, much in the manner of the artist who gives his product its final polish, she "distills" (76) a celebrated *morphē* onto the athlete as he gains his triumph, and in so doing makes him the cynosure of all eyes.

Relations of Reciprocity

Episodes where Penelope, Andromeda, and the rest assume the likeness of artifacts before their smitten viewers might invite a different reading. According to current theories of spectatorship, the transformation of the living body into (the likeness of) a pictorial or plastic representation follows not from qualities particular to the "imaged" person, but from the stance that an audience adopts. Positioned as the target of another's desiring look, the object of the gaze is reified, stripped of its subjectivity so as to allow the (male) viewer to construct his own.[44] Within the realm of verbal and visual representations, depicting a body in a manner that emphasizes its "to-be-looked-at-ness," which codes its appearance for strong visual and erotic impact, turns that body from autonomous subject into spectacle and signals its position as the passive, "lithified" object of the viewer's gaze.[45] But on several counts Greek

---

as shown in Polygnotos's *Ilioupersis*, painted for the Stoa Poikile in Athens c. 460. See, too, *Anth. Plan.* 16.150.

[43] Pace Stewart (1997: esp. 43), who argues that ultimately *technē*, for all its independent appeal, prevents the lover/viewer from conflating body and statue and maintaining the passing fantasy that stone and flesh are one.

[44] For the original statement of this dynamic, see Sartre 1966: esp. 316ff., and the very lucid exposition of Sartre's position in Jay 1993: 287–98. For Sartre, this process is explicitly that of turning the body of the other into a statue: "The Other's look fashions my body in its nakedness, causes it to be born, sculptures it" (1966: 445).

[45] For an early statement of this, Berger 1972: 47; both Berger and others who have built

tales of *agalmatophilia* run counter to this reading; not only do they propose that the living body's affinity to an artifact can stand prior to, and even form the precondition for, the eros that it inspires, but they also imagine this process of objectification as reciprocal rather than unilinear. As a series of conceits and episodes probing the nature of amorous desire reveals, the lover who views the beloved in the form of an image may be reflected back in equivalent form, and may himself undergo metamorphosis into a second representation or thing of stone.[46]

Present a viewer with an *agalma*-like beloved and he rapidly finds his own body rigidified. When Hephaistos and Athena finish their task and the deity leads Pandora before the mixed company of gods and mortals, the fabricated woman elicits an instant response: "*Thauma* held (*eche*) the immortal gods and mortal men" (Hes. *Theog.* 586–88). While *thauma* in epic song may refer quite simply to the astonishment provoked by fabulously crafted objects,[47] Hesiod's phrasing anticipates the more properly physiological reaction that later texts describe, imagining the "wonder-struck" viewer rooted to the spot and unable to escape the object's appeal. Euripides' Helen, a figure who already in epic sources possesses the ability to generate a chilling, paralyzing sensation,[48] leaves Menelaus "thunder-struck" and deprived of speech at the moment of their reencounter (*Hel.* 548–49), and Admetus experiences much the same, and in still more explicit fashion, in his own reunion with an "image" of his wife: confronted with the revenant whom Heracles has brought to his home, he will not look directly at her lest, in meeting her eye, he find himself transformed to stone (Eur. *Alc.* 1118). When Charmides enters the gymnasium, Socrates also feels *thauma* at the sight, and notes how all those gazing at the youth "like a statue" are dazed and astounded (*ekpeplēgmenoi*, Pl. *Chrm.* 154c) in his presence.[49]

---

on his ideas focus chiefly on the female body as the bearer of the male gaze (see particularly Mulvey 1992 [originally published in 1975] and other articles in Caughie and Kuhn 1992), but as Neale (1992) and Hatt (1993) argue, the male body can also fulfill this role. Following Solomon-Godeau (1988: 2), "The position of subject-made-spectacle can be filled by any(body)."

[46] Sartre's account of the dialectic of the look exchanged between the two parties to the love relationship makes the first of these points; each seeks to possess the other, robbing him of his freedom and autonomy (1966: 452). Relevant to the second point is Jakobson 1987b: 326.

[47] E.g., *Il.* 18.377; *Od.* 19.229; Hes. *Theog.* 581.

[48] Clader 1976: 18–23 documents this.

[49] Although the philosopher experiences desire as a flame when he glimpses the youth's body beneath his cloak (155d), he later describes his recovery of his wits and restoration to himself as a process whereby his frozen person regains its vital heat (156d). Later sources ascribe the same paralyzing impact to love-inspiring images, whether they take the form of actual statues or of maidens depicted as representations of the same. Among other

For a more sustained exploration of the statuefied beloved's reciprocal capacity to petrify, there is Alcibiades' comparison of Socrates to the
Silenus *eikōn* (Pl. *Symp.* 215a–b). While the simile anticipates the
"stony" character that Alcibiades will attribute to the object of his amorous quest, looking forward to his later account of Socrates' feats of
endurance, his immobility, his imperviousness to hunger, cold, and even
desire for the most beautiful of Athenian youths,[50] the analogy also suits
its target because Alcibiades knows that Socrates can calcify in turn.
The speaker goes on to signal this power when he equips the *eikōn* with
a syrinx,[51] then adds a second term to his initial conceit: Socrates is like
the satyr Marsyas, notorious for the enthralling quality of the sounds he
produces with his flute (215b–c). Socrates' words, Alcibiades remarks,
act the part of that flute, holding the philosopher's listeners stunned and
fastened to the spot (*ekpeplēgmenoi esmen kai katechometha*, 215c–d).

Behind the speaker's careful choice of analogy lies the larger "history" of this flute, and an acknowledgment of the transformations that
it could effect. According to the myth framing its discovery, the instrument could petrify not only those who heard its music, but the player,
too. The first victim of its power is none other than the flute's inventor,
Athena. As she strains to produce sound from her newly created object,
the goddess stands with her mouth outstretched, her cheeks swollen and
face grimacing with the strain. Her unlovely appearance prompts Marsyas, who intrudes on the scene, to bid her put down the instrument
and unclench her jaws. But it is only after the goddess glimpses herself
in the waters of a river and perceives the distortions in her divine countenance that she heeds the satyr's warning, and throws away the flute.[52]
The satyr, who then claims the instrument, is ideally suited to issue the
warning: the image that the goddess sees reflected back from the water's
surface too powerfully recalls the beast's physiognomy, which has offered itself as a mirror to her own.[53] Nor can the capacity of the *aulos* to
decompose the player's face, to fix it into a representation of a being
alien to the self, be divorced from the origins of the sounds it creates.
Invented by Athena in an attempt to imitate the cries of the many-
headed Euryala, sister of Medusa, both the flute and its music preserve
something of the monster's petrifying powers; while the listener finds

examples, Achilles Tatius 1.4.4–5; Chariton 2.5.3; [Lucian] *Amores* 13–14. Cf. Ov. *Met.*
4.675–76, where the two countersensations, burning and paralysis, claim Perseus looking
on the monumentalized Andromeda: *trahit inscius ignes et stupet.*
[50] See 219e–220d; 214a.
[51] Cf. Eur. *Hel.* 169–71, where the imagelike Helen appeals to the Sirens and imagines
herself accompanied by a syrinx.
[52] For this version of the tale, *Trag. Adesp.* 381 = Plut. *Mor.* 456b; Apollod. *Bibl.* 1.4.2.
[53] As noted in Leclercq-Neveu 1989: 255.

himself immobilized by the melodies the instrument sings, the satyr and all subsequent players have become things of stone, *gorgoneia*, their faces frozen in the monster's rictus.[54]

In order to resist the flute-playing Socrates' calcifying powers and his own transformation into a second thing of stone, Alcibiades has made repeated efforts to escape the philosopher's "music"; emulating the heroics of Odysseus, he stops his ears and tears himself away by force from the Siren song that threatens to keep the listener fixed at the speaker's side until the moment of his death (216a–c). But the very metamorphosis that Alcibiades fears is, paradoxically, the one that another pair of lovers described in the course of Agathon's dinner party most fervently desire. In the myth of the circle-men earlier related by Aristophanes, Zeus punishes mankind by dividing the original spherical creatures into two equal and complementary halves, and so condemns each and every one to a lifelong, random, and often fruitless quest for his missing, mirror-image pair. At first there is little to anticipate the statue motif that Plato will use later on as Aristophanes draws on sorb apples and eggs split in two, and on cobblers fabricating shoes, to visualize the strange scenario his words describe (190d–e). But when the speaker comes to imagine the still more awful fate that Zeus would inflict on these diminished individuals should they assert themselves a second time, he introduces an incised figure onto the scene: "There's a danger that if we don't behave in orderly fashion before the gods, we will be split in two again, and then we will go walking about in the condition of people carved on grave stones in bas relief, sawn apart between the nostrils like half die" (193a).

The caution that Aristophanes includes follows closely on his evocation of the dream cherished by these sadly bifurcated creatures. Those fortunate enough to find their missing halves want nothing so much as to remain eternally together, intertwined in a lasting and loving embrace. But, the speaker reveals, this constant cleaving means more than a pursuit of the pleasures of sexual intimacy, and through the words supplied by Hephaistos, the lovers articulate their unspoken and almost ineffable heart's wish:

> Is this your desire then — for the two of you to become parts of the same whole, as near as can be, and never to separate day or night? Because if that

---

[54] A point elaborated on by Vernant (1991: 125) and Frontisi-Ducroux (1994: 245–46). According to these analyses, the deformation of the face creates a homology between the flute-player, the satyr, and the Gorgon. Particularly evocative is an early fifth-century Attic vase showing Perseus on one side, holding Medusa's head in front of him, and a flautist playing on the other (*ARV*[2] 554, 85). See, too, Wilson 1999: 70–72.

is your desire, I'd like to weld you together and join you into something that is naturally whole. (*Symp*. 192d)

Of all the Olympians, Hephaistos stands best qualified to perform the task. Not only does he act as binding god par excellence, notorious for having joined a less willing pair of lovers in an immobilizing embrace,[55] but he is artist and metallurgist, the deity who designs images for gods and men.[56] It is as metal-worker and even statue-maker that Hephaistos enters Aristophanes' tale. The god comes equipped with his craftsman's tools (192d), and the fusion he imagines corresponds to the techniques of the fifth-century worker in bronze, who would prepare the sections of the statue separately, and then solder or rivet together the individual pieces so as to form the whole.[57] The composite creature that Hephaistos proposes to build displays all the properties of an image, immobile, inviolable, placed outside the vicissitudes of time and change, the very attributes that the reunited pair seek to possess. But as Martha Nussbaum observes, the dream the craftsman god holds out has described not so much the final word in erotic intimacy as a passion that negates and ends all passion:[58] self-generated, self-directed, self-sufficient, and complete, this is the eros that the lover purchases at the price of becoming a metallic artifact; and this alone can satisfy his "longing for an end to longing."[59]

While Aristophanes marks his wish as impossible, Socrates, in the speech immediately preceding Alcibiades' own, returns to the problem of how the lover might escape from the torments that eros so frequently inflicts. In his ascent from the body of the individual beloved to the sphere of the immutable, everlasting Forms, the *erastēs* effectively frees himself from bondage to a particular *erōmenos*, one who dwells in a

[55] *Od*. 8.299.

[56] On these, see Faraone 1992: 18–21.

[57] For a full account of this "indirect" method of casting, see Stewart 1990: 38–39. Intriguing for its echoes of Aristophanes' tale is Diodorus Siculus's account of two sixth-century sculptors, the brothers Theodoros and Telekles, who each completed their half of an image of Apollo in such a way that "when the parts were fitted together with one another, they corresponded so well that they appeared to have been made by one person" (1.98.5–8).

[58] Nussbaum (1986: 176) imagines the mode of existence that would result as the pair recapture their primal unity in terms that exactly evoke the (non)experience ascribed to statues in Greek thought: "What they thought they most wanted out of their passionate movement turns out to be a wholeness that would put an end to all movement and all passion. A sphere would not have intercourse with anyone. It would not eat, or doubt, or drink. It would not, as Xenophanes shrewdly observed, even move this way or that, because it would have no reason; it would be complete (B25 DK)." See, too, K. Gross 1992: 133 for a discussion of the same ideas in explicit reference to statues.

[59] I borrow the phrase from Nussbaum (1986: 183).

world of flux, who constantly changes and must eventually pass away (207d–e). The speaker concludes his account by touching on the impact that constant viewing of and "being with" the Beautiful itself has on the initiate (read Socrates): by virtue of his contact with this higher realm, he acquires something of the character of the Forms, achieving his own version of their immortality and enjoying the same imperviousness to external influence and change (212a–b). It is Alcibiades who follows through on these suggestions and who shows, with the aid of the statue conceit, how very closely Socrates has come to resemble the objects of his erotic-cum-philosophic quest: like a Form in his hardness, his inviolability, and his steadfast nature, he supplies a fixed object of contemplation whom others look upon and with whom they seek to have intimate and constant communion.[60] Nor does the "imaging" effect end there. Individuals wanting to "be with" Socrates, in a spiritual rather than physical sense, are inspired to model themselves after him, and to make of themselves fresh imitations that replicate their master on every count.[61]

Included in the *Symposium* are hints of a physical mechanism behind this reflexivity and the transformation that the objectified beloved works on the person of the lover. As Diotima explains, the individual who has undergone initiation into the mysteries of eros will enjoy a properly visual revelation at the end of his quest: "He will suddenly perceive (*katopsetai*) a certain beauty, marvelous in nature" (210e), and intimacy with "beauty in itself" will take the form of that eternal spectatorship (*theasthai*) which the earthbound lover seeks to practice on the mortal body of his beloved (211d). That the erotic experience depends on the faculty of sight a second Platonic text spells out, as it details how lover and beloved both act as mirrors for one another, each partner discerning his own reflection or image in the other's eye and making that the object of his desire.[62] At the moment when passion fills the soul of the *erōmenos*,

ἐρᾷ μὲν οὖν, ὅτου δὲ ἀπορεῖ· καὶ οὔθ᾽ ὅτι πέπονθεν οἶδεν οὐδ᾽ ἔχει φράσαι, ἀλλ᾽ οἷον ἀπ᾽ ἄλλου ὀφθαλμίας ἀπολελαυκὼς πρόφασιν εἰπεῖν οὐκ ἔχει, ὥσπερ δὲ ἐν κατόπτρῳ ἐν τῷ ἐρῶντι ἑαυτὸν ὁρῶν λέληθεν. καὶ ὅταν μὲν ἐκεῖνος παρῇ, λήγει κατὰ ταὐτὰ ἐκείνῳ τῆς ὀδύνης, ὅταν

---

[60] Note the emphasis on viewing Socrates, in fixed position, at 220b–c; cf. 221a.

[61] His disciples Apollodoros and Aristodemos are willing to emulate his behavior down to its very last eccentricities, succumbing to precisely the petrifying power that Alcibiades would resist. On this, see Halperin 1992: 110–11; Steiner 1996: 104.

[62] Cf. Pl. *Alc.* 1.132e–133a: "Have you noticed that the face of a person looking into another's eye is reflected there as in a mirror? We call that part the pupil because a person looking there sees his own *eidōlon*. . . . Then an eye, seeing another eye, and looking into the best part of it, the part with which it sees, will see itself."

δὲ ἀπῇ, κατὰ ταὐτὰ αὖ ποθεῖ καὶ ποθεῖται, εἴδωλον ἔρωτος ἀντέρωτα
ἔχων. (*Phdr.* 255d)

> He is in love, but with what he is at a loss to know, nor is he able to under-
> stand what he has experienced; but as if having caught the infection of blind-
> ness from another he is not able to say, and is unaware of himself seeing
> himself in the lover as in a mirror. And when the lover is present, he ceases
> because of that from suffering on his account, but when the lover is absent,
> for the same reason he desires and is desired, possessing an *anterōs* that is a
> double of [sc. the *erastēs'*] eros.

The scenario whereby the amorous gaze reifies the object of desire has
here undergone a signal change. Because vision is reciprocal, and seeing
involves being seen, the individual whom the looker observes transformed into a mirror image is none other than himself; and his own
person, now in the form of an *eidōlon*, has become the target of his
longing. To gaze longingly at a beloved image is to engage not only in
scopophilia (the pleasure that arises from using another person as the
object of erotic stimulation through sight), but in narcissism, too, as the
double or other object provides a reflective device re-presenting the lover,
often in idealized or inverted form, to himself. In these instances, the
replacement theme so central to all tales of *agalmatophilia* takes on a
reflexive twist; rather than substituting for the absent beloved, the object becomes a site where the lover might rediscover his own self. The
pothos suffered by the beloved in Plato's account registers the shift: the
painful longing that this secondary image, like all others, generates now
takes the form of a desire for the absent self.[63]

The Impervious Beloved

But even in the quite literally mirroring passion that Socrates imagines,
an imbalance remains between the lover and beloved. Although the *an-
terōs* is an exact replica of the lover's *erōs*, the youth thinks it different:
he "calls it, and believes it to be, not *erōs* but *philia*" (255e).[64] The
disequilibrium between the original sentiment and its double noted here
exists in a much more pronounced form in the asymmetry that so fre-

---

[63] Other images featured in postclassical sources, several expressly designed to still a lover-
cum-griever's *pothos*, retain this reflexive property and describe how love for the representation necessarily involves desire for reunion with some missing part of the self. See
particularly Apollod. *Bibl.* 3.12.3 with Bettini 1992: 118–19, and the Narcissus story,
both in its canonical form and in Pausanias's alternate version at 9.31.8 (where the youth
is initially in love with his twin sister, and seeks to recreate her after her death by gazing at
an image of himself).

[64] Dover 1978: 52.

quently divides the beloved from his or her admirer. According to Greek accounts of the erotic relationship, sought-after youths and maidens usually answer the pursuer's desires with their lack of passion, his eagerness with their reticence, and his heat with their frigidity. The statue trope supplies a way of signposting this disharmony, and of expressing the grander problematic of erotic passion as classical sources, visual and textual both, so frequently construe it. Making quite literal the impenetrable and impervious surface that the living beloved typically displays, the image simultaneously declares the allurement that rests with the form that, to the lover's eye, the object of passion has assumed; supremely engaging without itself being engaged, the artifact emanates a desirability to which it is singularly ill-suited to respond.

The late archaic poets and classical texts reflect repeatedly on the lover's failure to inspire a passion that equals his own, pairing his (or her) chase with the beloved's indifference or flight. In fifth- and fourth-century visual and written accounts, the *erastēs* shows himself the creature aflame, in relentless and ever-active pursuit of his goal; but the *erōmenos* (Plato's version excepted) typically remains unmoving and unmoved, the passive or unwilling recipient of the attentions another directs at him.[65] Anticipating Xenophon's succinct formulation of the relationship — "The boy does not share in the man's pleasure in intercourse as a woman does; cold sober, he looks upon the other drunk with sexual desire" (*Symp.* 8.21) — both black- and red-figure vase paintings visualize the lover's plight. Some contrast his state of arousal with the flaccid condition of the youth whom he solicits and caresses,[66] while others show the beloved gazing off vacantly into space, apparently ignoring the older man, who bends or raises his head toward him and gazes intently into his eyes.[67] The cloak enveloping the sought-after youth or maiden in a number of courting scenes provides artists with another means of articulating both the passivity and the imperviousness adhering to the object of desire.[68] Muffling the figure from head to toe, it keeps the lover from the longed-for body, and so effectively hinders any motion or response that the wearer can perform only the most restricted and awkward of gestures.

To liken the instigator of eros to a statue is to reflect on the same discomfort the lover experiences, transposing the passivity, immobility, and want of sensation associated with the work of art to the unwilling

---

[65] For a succinct statement of this dynamic, Halperin 1990: 130. The beloved may also be portrayed more actively, in actual flight from his pursuer.

[66] For these, Dover 1978: 94–97.

[67] E.g., Beazley, *ABV* 315; *ARV*² 471, 196.

[68] For these, Ferrari 1990. For a clear instance of the seductive power of the muffled youth, *ARV*² 322, 37; 188, 67; 437, 116.

and unresponsive beloved. While the lover, in Pindar's phrase, "melts like the wax of sacred bees" when confronted with the *erōmenos* (fr. 123.10–11 Snell-Maehler), the beloved-as-image remains obstinately rigid and cold. Admetus's reference to the chilly delight that he would derive from the replica Alcestis looks to the unyielding and unresponding quality common to the artifact and dead woman both, and the absence of motion and sight that regularly characterizes the image supplies Xenophon with the means of underscoring the chastity of Spartan youths and their unwillingness to return a would-be lover's look: "It would be easier," he remarks, "to make the eyes of bronze statues turn" (*Lac.* 3.5). Euripides' appeal to the *agalma* to describe Polyxena's bared breasts and upper body ("lovely as that of an image," *Hec.* 560–61) not only positions the maiden as the target of the Achaean soldiers' fetishizing look and evokes the erotic impact of her self-display, but also anticipates the virginal and unbreachable quality that the victim will preserve despite her exposure on the sacrificial altar. Even after the blow falls, Polyxena remains intact, unmarked by the bloodletting that, in the vocabulary of Greek tragic drama, stands equivalent to a loss of maidenhood: instead, her body folds back on itself as it falls, and acquires the fresh covering of leaves, garments, and ornaments that the soldiers reverently bring (574–78).

But as the written and visual sources also affirm, the beloved's resistance or remoteness does nothing to lessen the charms of his or her person. Instead, in a variety of ways, authors and artists highlight the enticement that lies in a (sometimes calculated) display of reticence and indifference, commonly describing it with the term *aidōs*. Theognis looks for *aidōs*, respect, youthful shyness, and modesty, too — in his *pais* and links it closely to the erotic *charis* that he seeks;[69] the *erōmenos* of black- and red-figure vase painting often inclines his head and eyes to the ground, observing the dictates regulating the bodily posture and conduct of the young, and the cloak surrounding the object of solicitation allows artists another means of translating into visual terms the proper modesty, serving as a conventional signifier for *aidōs*.[70] *Aidōs* naturally accompanies the statuefied beloved, and again forms a potent ingredient in its overall allure. In both Hesiodic accounts, Pandora is fashioned in the likeness of a "modest *parthenos*" (*Theog.* 572; *Op.*

---

[69] Thgn. 1331: "Show me *aidōs*, boy, giving me *charis*"; elsewhere the poet describes a refusal of sexual favors as tantamount to a want of *aidōs* (1263–66). As Pind. *Pyth.* 9.12 shows, far from obstructing eros, *aidōs* seems able to work with it right up to the moment of consummation.

[70] Ferrari 1990; Frontisi-Ducroux 1996: 82 and 90.

71),[71] and the maiden's *aidōs*, carried over from Zeus's original blue-print to the actual design, should be reckoned integral to the workings of the snare. At once the virginal modesty that any bride must possess (a property recapitulated by Pandora's veil at *Theog.* 574–75, which shrouds even as it begs to be removed), it forms a central component in the "cruel longing" and desire that the fabricated woman instigates. No less charmingly chaste in her self-revelation, the *agalma*-like girl from the fragment of Chairemon's *Alphesiboea* presents herself for the audience's scrutiny: "And modesty tempered a gentle blush that she added to her brightness of color" (fr. 1).

While seemingly an ethical quality proper to the inner person of the youth or maiden, *aidōs* appears in these accounts as a feature contributed from without. Whether in the form of a blush "added" on or an embroidered veil, it forms part of the erotic appeal that issues from the surface of the body and ranges itself alongside those other properties with which a skilled craftsman endows his products. But even as it enhances the figure's allure, the *aidōs* characteristic of the statuefied beloved simultaneously reinforces the barrier that the image sets up: supplying yet another external surface blocking the lover's access to the object of desire, it reiterates the impenetrable quality of the work of art. The individual displayed in the manner of an artifact, whether self-fashioned or the product of others, presents "the occasion for transgressive desire, but not for actual transgression."[72]

REAL-WORLD VIEWING

The Images in Context

The statues cited above remain bounded by the theatrical stage or by the imaginary worlds that poets and myth-tellers contrive. But beyond the texts stand the actual works of art that, through the course of the late archaic and classical age, came to populate the secular and religious sites of Greece: in the city agora and other public spaces, on the parapets of temples, in shrines, sanctuaries, and graveyards, stood evocations of beautiful bodies, and most particularly of youths and maidens

---

[71] Ovid may be picking up on the term when he describes the *reverentia* Pygmalion must overcome—the sexual restraint, modesty, and even religious awe that stands between him and his desire (*Met.* 10.251). As so much in this story, the term carries several possible referents; it may belong to Pygmalion as viewer of the image, to the audience as reader of the text (250), or to the maiden herself, who, should the chaste modesty proper to a virgin be dispelled, would wish to move/be moved (*moveri*, 251). On the ambiguity of the middle voice here, see Sharrock 1992: 171–72.

[72] The expression belongs to Elsom 1992: 221.

exhibiting the properties that the sources have specified as most likely to charm.[73] Because, as the texts repeatedly inform us, what is beautiful is also most desirable, and because these images, set up expressly as objects to be looked upon, seem to invite the visual exchange that forms the basis of erotic engagement, they offer themselves as possible analogues and even sources for some of the statues introduced into contemporary texts. And while no archaic or classical author describes how viewing a real-world sculpture produces sensations of desire,[74] the frequency of the equation of eros and *agalmata* in their accounts suggests an audience alive to this dimension of the image.

To illustrate the coherence between the visual and textual material, I propose singling out a handful of statues or statue types that, among their diverse roles and functions, seem most likely to solicit and garner an amorous response.[75] Whether through their subject matter, their context, their pose, adornment, or other attributes, these works match the literary conceits on several scores; they not only invite the viewer to "slide" from the person of the image to the body of the beloved, but also demonstrate that *technē* can enhance the desirability of the figure in the work, and so promote the "cathexis" that occurs; apparent, too, is the capacity of a manufactured image to occupy precisely the position that the living beloved assumes, sometimes rejecting the advances the viewer would make, sometimes presenting him with a reflection or inversion of his own desire.

But these engaging and arousing images also belong within a particular and changing historical milieu, one that late archaic and classical Athens allows us most closely to document. As Attic visual and written sources both indicate, desire, its proper targets, and the modes in which it may be exercised within the parameters of city life not only are the subject of evolving legal strictures, but also depend on a series of sometimes conflicting social norms and patterns of social control that writers and artists can echo, challenge, and manipulate to suit their ends.[76] More specifically, eros, viewing, and the relations between them in the democratic polis become a topic of particular concern in sources dating from the fifth century's second half, perhaps testament to the city's

---

[73] For recent discussions of the "desirability" of many of these historical images, see particularly Osborne 1994a, Havelock 1995, the essays in Kampen 1996, and Stewart 1997.
[74] But this forms part of the larger reticence concerning the experience of looking at art. Note, however, Arist. *Eth. Eud.* 1230b30–36, which suggests that a man could become so absorbed in looking at a statue as to lose his appetite for lovemaking.
[75] Unless otherwise specified, I assume an adult male viewer, although some of the points I make are relevant for a female audience, too. A more extended treatment would properly consider both perspectives.
[76] For these issues, see particularly D. Cohen 1991; Winkler 1990; Foucault 1985.

transformation into a place "in which the roles, statuses, positions of the democratic actors were constantly being structured in and through the gaze of the citizens."[77]

Several moments in Thucydides' text can illustrate the ways in which the act of desirous looking becomes aligned, for better or for worse, with participation in civic life and with the enterprises that the collectivity of citizens undertakes. Dismissing the need to remind his audience of the benefits to be derived from repelling the enemy, Perikles exhorts the Athenians to be spectators of their city, and by their act of contemplation (*theōmenous*) to become Athens's *erastai* (2.43.1); as lovers, they will be willing to hazard their lives on the polis's behalf. This same state of desire, again combined with the gaze, can also prove destructive to the body politic. What goads the Athenians into embarking on their ill-judged Sicilian expedition is, in Nikias's words, a hopeless passion for the absent (*duserōtas . . . tōn apontōn*, 6.13.1), and Thucydides glosses the general's speech by acknowledging that all succumbed to the *erōs* to set sail (24.3); among the most passionate are the young, infected with *pothos* for "sights and spectatorship" (*pothōi opseōs kai theōrias*, 24.3). The subsequent grand account of the launching of the venture makes patent the desire for agonistic self-display, spectacle, and "viewership" motivating the Athenians. Strangers fill the city to enjoy the sight (*thean*) of the assembled fleet, and this vision or *opsis* simultaneously inflates the spirit of the citizens themselves (31.1). The vocabulary of viewing and visual display returns repeatedly in the passages that follow, and as the historian draws his description to its close, he remarks that what makes the expedition so famous is the very brilliance of the show that its participants have taken such pains to mount (31.6).[78]

This cautionary account of the impact of the visually brilliant and beautiful, and of the disorder that the eros accompanying it provokes, anticipates fourth-century texts that issue still sterner warnings concerning the place of desire within political life, and that turn their attention to the need for regulating encounters with potential instigators of passion inhabiting the city. According to Plato, Xenophon, Aristotle, and others, an unchecked and rampant eros proves incompatible with the self-mastery that the citizen was bound to achieve and renders a man unfit not only for the regulation of his private life, but also, no less critically, for office-holding in the democracy. Nor are these strictures mere philosophical musings. Those who indulged, or permitted others to indulge, a misdirected eros paid the penalty: one statute partially

---

[77] Goldhill 1998: 108.

[78] Note, too, the emphasis on the attention paid to the fittings of the ship, each captain wanting his vessel to stand out from the rest due to its fine looks (31.3).

disenfranchised an Athenian citizen charged with engaging in homosexual intercourse for gain, whether as a boy or as an adult, and the law of *hubris* (a term that covers sexual abuse) may have been applicable to cases where an adult male had persuaded or forced a boy to submit to his sexual advances;[79] so, too, the individual caught in the act of adultery could be put to death by the offended husband, and the adulterous woman could be barred from participation in religious rituals.[80]

Alongside the statutes regulating sexual conduct (although questions remain concerning the frequency with which they would have been applied) are the laws and less formalized conventions dictating that the objects of men's attentions be spared unnecessary exposure and abstain from the provocation that accompanies visual encounters. Since youthful nakedness was considered sexually stimulating,[81] opportunities for viewing unclad boys were circumscribed (largely limited to the gymnasium and athletic games), and only men above the age of thirty might participate in the Athenian Council's scrutiny of youths' bodies to determine whether they were eighteen.[82] One category of laws concerning education featured detailed prohibitions aimed at shielding schoolboys from the attentions of adult men, and Aeschines cites a statute regulating the times at which schools might open and close, and determining who might enter the building and under what circumstances (1.9–14). More generally, social practice required that, through the carriage of the body, the quality of the gaze, and other such visible indicators, youths should avoid any behavior likely to invite the notice of those whom Aeschines calls "hunters of boys," and an adolescent's future standing in the city would be determined by the inferences drawn from his public deportment when in the company of older men.[83] A similar decorum surrounded the appearance and actions of young girls and married women, who, in theory at least, were bound to avoid all encounters with men from beyond their immediate family: those who show themselves at the door of their houses, Lycurgus comments, engage in unworthy behavior (*Leoc.* 40), and Lysias underscores the honor of women who have led particularly well-ordered lives by styling them "ashamed to be seen even by their kinsmen" (3.6–7).

And yet, as discussions of social mores in Athens regularly acknowledge, these legal and social sanctions tell only part of a "many-hued"

---

[79] For discussion, see particularly Winkler 1990: 54–63; D. Cohen 1991: 175–80.
[80] D. Cohen 1991: 98–132 for detailed treatment.
[81] Ar. *Nub.* 965; cf. *Av.* 137–42.
[82] Ar. *Vesp.* 578.
[83] See particularly Dem. 61.17–21.

story.[84] While adult men were deemed inappropriate targets of desire and should not submit to being such objects, the courtship of boys was so institutionalized as to be governed by its own set of widely acknowledged *nomoi*, or conventions; correctly pursued, it could be an honorable mode of conduct for lover and beloved alike. While the laws registered an evident concern about pederasty and saw it as a threat to the well-being of the polis, no statute absolutely forbade it, and nothing prevented an adolescent (or even a more mature individual) from being the recognized *erōmenos* of an older man. The ideals concerning the activities of women sit no less uneasily with actual social practices and the realities of women's lives as the sources describe them; economic, religious, and social functions would take both young girls and their mothers outside the confines of the home, and their daily activities, whether fetching water, washing clothes, participating in weddings, funerals, and the like, would bring them into the public spaces of the city, where they would have contact with men.[85] In the world that Aristophanes portrays, maidens and wives regularly engage in premarital and adulterous courtship routines,[86] and the daughter who accompanies her father and mother to a sacrifice in *Acharnians* 252–58 knows very well that she is on display to potential suitors.

Read against the background of these strictures surrounding desire, its proper objects, and the boundaries it must observe, the statues of beautiful bodies decorating the Athenian polis pose questions that reach beyond their potential for eliciting eros. If viewing, as Thucydides and others suggest, makes men lovers of the object of their gaze, then how might these patent displays of the desirable, some of them erected at state expense, affect citizen viewers, and how should individuals respond to representations of those whom law and normative values often deemed out of bounds? Can these images fall in with the larger agenda shaping so much of the public art in the polis and dictating that it be used for properly democratic, civically beneficial ends, or are they witness to those divergent views of city culture which the written sources reflect, and to the ambiguities and conflicts informing sexual morality and a man's ability to pursue the object of his desires? These questions hold good not for Athens alone, but, I suggest, for images adorning other public sites and sanctuaries in classical Greece.

---

[84] The expression is that which Plato puts in the mouth of Pausanias when describing the status of pederasty in Athens at *Symp.* 182a. D. Cohen (1991: 202) aptly uses the term to characterize the complex social reality surrounding the practice.

[85] As argued in D. Cohen 1991: esp. 133–70.

[86] E.g., *Peace* 978–85, *Thesm.* 797–99, *Eccl.* 911–14.

Kouroi

Long antedating the evolution of democratic Athens, and exemplary of
the aristocratic culture that that city would both challenge and seek to
incorporate into an idealized image of its own "citizen body," stands
the paradigmatic representation of the beautiful youth. From its first
appearance in Greece around the mid-seventh century to its disappearance some 150 years later, the *kouros* proved endlessly popular; according to one reconstruction, perhaps as many as several thousand such
works populated the Attic landscape by the end of the sixth century,[87]
lining the major roads in and out of the city and standing in sanctuaries
and burial grounds. Among the varied sources of the *kouros*'s success,[88]
I single out just one facet of its evident appeal, detailing its possession
of those properties best calculated to engage and even seduce the viewer.
The *kouros*, I suggest, not only looks forward to later images of beautiful young men through its display of nudity, youth, surface luster, and
other allure-promoting attributes, but also anticipates future works by
virtue of the position that it imposes on the viewer; already here pose,
demeanor, and context complicate the response that the statue seems to
invite, and leave a spectator uncertain of his relationship to the youth
on display.

When Greek sculptors began to fashion *kouroi*, they rid the Egyptian
prototype of its loincloth and let it stand free of any clothes. But what
are we to make of this choice to show the figure naked when other
options existed in post-Mycenaean art?[89] The protean debate surrounding the origins and significance of nudity in Greek sculpture and painting offers a number of possible readings. In geometric art, and through
the seventh century, nudity seems a matter of convention, useful chiefly
for gender differentiation, and it comes without the various divinizing,
heroicizing, or eroticizing charges it would acquire later on. In the case
of the *kouros*, the lack of clothing might look to the normative and
generic quality of the object, and to that lack of particularity or specific
context that makes it so versatile an image type. As Andrew Stewart has
argued, the naked male would represent the "natural" gender, while the
clothed woman occupies the marked category: "A 'real' man is man in

[87] Stewart 1997: 63–64.
[88] For other dimensions of its popularity, see the discussion in chapter 1.
[89] Everything the sources tell us of archaic and classical Greece suggests that men did not
normally walk about without their clothes, and that their depiction in painting and sculpture does not offer an accurate reflection of real life. For this and what follows I have
drawn particularly on the discussions in Bonfante 1989; Himmelmann 1990; Osborne
1997; Stewart 1990: 105–6 and 1997: chap. 2.

his natural state."[90] It is the clothed rather than the unclothed male who begs for explanation.

But the nudity of the figure may come to carry connotations that lie outside its generic and archetypal status and its embodiment of an untrammeled masculinity. While viewers accustomed to unclad men in art would accept the "naturalness" of the nakedness, *kouroi* variously equipped with boots, cloaks, hairbands, and caps on their heads argue against a simple tie between this image type and an absence of all clothes.[91] Also telling against the normative quality of the images are other sixth-century Attic funerary monuments featuring young draped males, which suggest that the unclad *kouros* was only one among a series of possible idealizing or generalizing modes of depiction, and a matter of deliberate artistic choice.[92] So, rather than offering the naked body as the unmarked category, the absence of clothes can be a more loaded device, designed to focus the viewer's attention on the physique whose unhindered display it allowed. The unclad figure that the *kouros* exhibited was not so much generic in character as supremely beautiful, and a paradigm toward which all other lesser bodily forms might hope to aspire. Each region put on show its own ideal of masculine perfection in its version of the monument: Boeotia favored the vigorous and angular, Naxos the lithe, undermuscled, and curvaceous, and Samos a rounder and more muscular body.

If the nudity and beauty of the *kouros* form a pair, then they must inevitably accommodate a third term. All *kouroi* are unbearded youths, positioned precisely at that "ripening" springtime age which finds celebration in songs coeval with the images, and which composers of epitaphs frequently highlight in the inscriptions accompanying the figures standing astride the grave. That youth and beauty go hand-in-hand needs no demonstration; the archaic and lyric poets endlessly rehearse the combination and mourn its rapid passage.[93] Youth and nudity are no less closely intertwined: once the individual has passed his brief moment of bloom and no longer boasts the unblemished body that the statue displays, he must cover up. Grave markers designed for older men tend to replace the *kouros* with a seated figure fully clad, while on fifth-century Attic funerary monuments, only the young would be shown naked, while fully mature men inevitably appear clothed.[94]

[90] Stewart 1997: 40.
[91] On clothed *kouroi*, see Barletta 1987.
[92] Sourvinou-Inwood 1995: 231–32.
[93] E.g., Mimnermus frs. 1, 2, and 5.
[94] Osborne 1997: 520 and n. 45. The beardless *kouros* also suggests a calculated attempt to prolong this most lovely of all periods: implausibly smooth cheeks and chins belong to *kouroi* decorating tombs of men of ephebic and postephebic ages. As Stewart (1997: 66)

As authors contemporary with these statues remind us, youth is also characterized by that particular radiance which the term *aglaos* describes.[95] The marble chosen by the artist not only broadcasts the donor and/or mourner's wealth, but also ensures that the *kouros* reiterates this brilliant quality; the term *marmaros* used by the Greeks for the material encapsulates the shine and sparkle (*marmairein*) singled out as its defining property, and the practice of polishing the finished image would enhance the luminosity of the work.[96] The stone's radiance is one of the points where *technē* allows the *kouros* to realize the attributes that viewers sought in the living body. If poetic celebrations of shining youths with gleaming limbs reflect the way in which their subjects were ideally thought to be, then the statue can make literal and visible the patina. Far from obstructing an approximation between the image and the admired living reality, the surface of the *kouros* celebrates the youth's affinity to an *agalma*.

Nor are these images reticent about declaring their charms. Instead, the inscriptions on the statue bases, or sometimes on the bodies of the *kouroi* themselves, invite the viewer to recognize their loveliness and respond to their appeal. A *kouros* base from the Piraeus gate of Athens ascribes *charis* to itself: "This is the marker of the boy Nelon son of Nelonides, and it was he who had this delightful (*charien*) memorial made to a good son" (*CEG* 42); and other images regularly call themselves "beautiful" and "beautiful to look upon."[97] In one instance a statue explicitly declares itself a "very beautiful *agalma*" (*CEG* 423), an object capable of producing visual pleasure in its beholder. The loveliness characteristic of the youth on whose grave a funerary *kouros* stands becomes elided with that of the marble figure (e.g., *CEG* 68), and the monument offers a worthy substitute for the missing body.

That its several properties might make of the statue not just a thing of beauty and charm but an object of desire, too, texts from the archaic period to the early classical period attest. The Homeric songs already qualify shining youth and beauty with the epithet *eratos*, and in Theognis's straightforward formulation, "What is beautiful is loved" (17);

---

points out, the inscription accompanying the Kroisos monument (*CEG* 27, see fig. 1) celebrates the dead man for his place among the *promachoi* where the valiant fight, but in order to occupy this position, he would have been a hoplite, and so over twenty years of age and doubtless bearded. See Sourvinou-Inwood 1995: 262 for one way of meeting this objection.

[95] Tyrtaeus 10.28; Thgn. 985. In Homer, the formula *aglaos hēbē* already occurs, and the limbs of warriors are regularly qualified by the term.

[96] Stewart 1997: 46.

[97] E.g., *CEG* 161, 165.

according to the same poet, the fairest of boys necessarily ranks as the most desirable of all (*kalliste kai himeroestate*, 1365). For Mimnermus, the gifts of Aphrodite cannot exist apart from the "flower of youth," and the advent of maturity makes an individual repugnant in all respects (fr. 1). So, too, Pindar celebrates youth as the season for eros ("One must, my heart, pluck love's fruits in due season, with the ripening of youth," fr. 123.1–2 Snell-Maehler), and in the same snatch of love song he notes the irresistible power of the gleam emanating from the beloved:[98] very much in the manner of the dazzle of marble, rays of light come flashing (*marmaruzoisas*, 3) from Theoxenos's eyes. Radiance and youth are also prime ingredients in the heady erotic amalgam described by the umbrella term *charis*. For Anakreon, "Youth is full of *charis*" (fr. 395.3 *PMG*; cf. *Od.* 10.279), and the attribute declares itself only when the individual occupies that brief flowering season, his *hōra* and *hēbē*, which is suitable for love;[99] in Theognis's sobering reminder, his *pais* should give him *charis*, "since you will not long possess the gift of violet-crowned Kypris" (1303–4).[100]

Invested with youth, beauty, brilliance, and charm, the *kouros* seems ideally positioned to address itself to one particular audience; if familiarity with the type did not render viewers impervious to its appeal, then the lovely, muscular, and unbearded youth might appear ready to model the *erōmenos* whom the adult *erastēs* pursues.[101] The particular attributes that *kouroi* display match those of such "beloveds" in the visual and literary sources from the late archaic to the classical age. Their broad shoulders, deep chests, pronounced pectoral muscles, slim waists, jutting buttocks, stout thighs and calves, and small sexual organs not only are the requisite elements of any attractive male physique, but they reappear in the adolescents whom black- and red-figure artists portray in homosexual courting scenes[102] and whom homoerotic texts regularly cite as their ideals.[103] *Hōraios*, the adjective descriptive of the "seasonability" that the smooth-cheeked *kouros* incorporates, must also

---

[98] Without the brilliance cognate with the Grace Aglaia herself, women as well as men lose much of their allure. Penelope describes the beauty that was hers as a young bride as her *aglaiē* (*Od.* 18.180), and the advent of age means the dimming of that youthful luster.

[99] At Thgn. 1275, Eros is himself *hōraios*.

[100] See MacLachlan 1993: 58 for this and other examples.

[101] Stewart 1997: 67.

[102] These properties, as Dover (1978: 70) documents, persist to the middle of the fifth century.

[103] E.g., Solon fr. 25; Aesch. fr. 135 Radt; cf. Soph. fr. 345 Radt. Note, too, the evocation of a physical type now lost, but the object of any normal man's predilection in the bygone Marathonian days, by Aristophanes' Right Logos: big shoulders, ample buttocks, a well-rounded and sleek chest, lustrous skin, and a small penis (*Nub.* 1011–13).

characterize the beloved,[104] and no sooner has the adolescent begun to grow a beard than he is already on the brink of quitting his *erōmenos* role. Theognis declares that he will never cease to celebrate his beloved so long as the boy's cheek remains hairless (1327–28), and Pindar's Pelops, selected as the beloved of Poseidon, must return to earth once his beard begins to grow (*Ol.* 1.67–68).[105]

In one site at least, the social milieu surrounding the *kouros* would also have proved particularly accommodating to its homoerotic potential. Although the type first appears in seventh-century Greece, sculptors working in Attica do not take it up before c. 600, and they abandon its production almost exactly a century later. During this period pederastic relationships seem to have enjoyed a particular status and acceptability, and seem to have been the object of approving attention from artists, poets, and lawmakers alike.[106] Solon, himself the author of verses evoking the desirable thighs and lips of youths (fr. 25), is credited with a series of laws on male prostitution and homosexuality designed to regulate what must have been an already well-established practice, and one measure attributed to the statesman in particular grants it a constructive civic role: Solon, Aeschines reports, prohibited slaves from making freeborn youths their *erōmenoi*, and Plutarch explains that his aim was not so much to restrict the practice as more actively to promote relationships among citizen men and youths (*Sol.* 1.3).[107]

No less accommodating were the tyrants who subsequently assumed control of the city: Peisistratos (supposedly the object of Solon's own attentions as a young boy) dedicated a statue of Eros in the Academy to commemorate his love for Charmos (Plut. *Sol.* 1.4), and Hipparchos's subsequent amorous imbroglio would notoriously provoke the downfall of the dynasty. Anakreon, whose infatuations with one boy or another supply endless matter for later writers, found a warm welcome at the tyrants' court, and there became associated with the cultivated Ionian mores and luxuriant lifestyle, itself including pederasty, adopted by the eastward-looking Athenian elite of the time. Also suggestive of the distinction and popularity adhering to homosexual attachments is the sudden abundance of images of men courting youths (and youths courting youths) on black- and red-figure vases, a genre scene that proliferates c.

---

[104] Later the term *hōraios* would describe the appeal of Timarchos, the individual whom Aeschines charges with having prostituted himself as a youth (Aeschin. 1.42; cf. 126).

[105] So, too, a friend of Socrates remarks apropos of Alcibiades: "I thought he was a handsome man—but a *man*, Socrates, between ourselves, and getting quite a beard now (Pl. *Prt.* 309a). Cf. Bion's witticism cited in Plut. *Mor.* 770b–c, where the beard appearing on the *erōmenos* "liberates the *erastēs* from the tyranny of eros."

[106] As argued in Shapiro 1981, on whose treatment I have drawn.

[107] For this, ibid.: 135 n. 19.

550–500.[108] Like the *kouroi* whom the statue-makers design, the *erō-menoi* portrayed by the artists show marks of high social status, often displaying elaborate coiffures and imagined participating in those athletic and intellectual pursuits exclusive to the *kaloikagathoi* (Athens's "beautiful people"). Like the *kouroi*, these images disappear in the early decades of the fifth century; following the overthrow of the tyranny and the implementation of the Kleisthenic reforms, the modes of behavior and elite existence that the vases held up for show seem no longer to have commanded the same public prestige, and if beautiful youths were to be featured in works of art, they would perhaps have to be incorporated within a more pronouncedly civic context.

But for all the erotic potential of the *kouros* and its affinity to the living beloved, the figure's two chief functions complicate this reading of its role, and might incline a viewer to construe its loveliness in quite different ways. Where the image serves as votive offering, as in the sanctuary full of *kouroi* dedicated to Apollo Ptoios in Boeotia, it stands marked as divine property, and its capacity to delight, as the accompanying inscriptions so often affirm, directs itself to a divine rather than a mortal audience. Particularly emphatic declarations of immortal ownership issue from the *kouroi* that carry these messages on the surface of their bodies: one marble youth (fig. 17) bears its dedicatory text carved into its left thigh, while a *kouros* from Samos exhibits the name of the deity for whom it is destined on its leg ("Charmeus dedicated me to the goddess, a very beautiful *agalma*," *CEG* 423). Here the self-proclaimed beauty of the *agalma* does not so much align it with a mortal youth as recall the inimitable loveliness of the gods themselves, and most particularly of that prototypical perfect young divinity Apollo, who is the recipient and even the subject of so many of the images.

Equally high barriers go up around the funerary *kouros*. Now the statue's beauty appears inextricably linked with the fact of death, and with the freedom from the depreciating impact of passing time that a young man cut off in his prime uniquely shares with his marble image. And though death in no way diminishes its victim's allure, but rather enhances the same (in Sparta, Pausanias reports at 3.18.1–2, images of Sleep and Death stood next to Aphrodite Ambologera, the one who postpones old age),[109] it sets that beauty outside the reach of those who must still live and change.

More than just the outcome of their subjects' untimely demise, the images' paradigmatic loveliness may additionally depend on the particu-

---

[108] Shapiro 1981 and Hupperts 1988 for these.

[109] For the links between eros and death, and the later suggestion that the gods claimed youths for their beauty, see Vermeule 1981: chap. 5.

lar manner in which Thanatos has claimed his victim. In the words that Priam addresses to Hector, "For a young man all things are decorous when he lies slain in battle, torn with the sharp bronze. And everything is beautiful although he is dead, whatever may present itself" (*Il.* 22.71–73).[110] Hector's subsequent heroic fall proves the truth of his father's remark: no sooner has Achilles stripped his enemy of his armor than the Achaeans gather to view the corpse, wondering at the beauty of the lifeless form: *thēēsanto phuēn kai eidos agēton Hektoros* (22.370–71).[111] The marble youths who top the real-world graves celebrate their residents' own valiant deaths and position them through visual and verbal signs in this elite and heroic company: the inscription on Kroisos's grave declares in epic style that Ares slew him as he stood "in the front rank" (*CEG* 27; see fig. 1), and another monument bids the passerby shed a tear while "looking upon the memorial of Kleitos the deceased son of Menesaichmos . . . he died a *kalos*" (*CEG* 68).

Hindered from placing the *kouros* in the role of *erōmenos*, the viewer might attempt a different relationship with the figure on display. If image love, as the literary tales suggest, involves a form of self-love and an act of self-projection, then the statue could prompt a response more tinged with narcissism, providing an idealized reflection of the audience's own person.[112] But here, too, the *kouros* refuses to lend itself to such self-scrutiny. The fact that it neither returns nor mirrors the viewer's gaze prevents its assuming the function of reflector of the observer, and although the figure's lack of particular action and obvious individuality rid it of those elements which would markedly distance it from its audience,[113] the very generic quality of the work might constitute a barrier in and of itself. Confronted with the fact of his own particularity, the viewer is forced to recognize the distance between himself and this normative being whose physical perfection so surpasses his own, and whose proximity to the world of the gods or the dead he cannot and should not seek to match.

---

[110] Here Priam is explicitly contrasting the death of a young man with the shame and ugliness that attends an old man's violent slaughter in the home. For the same sentiment see Tyrtaeus 10.27–30; for discussion, Loraux 1982; Vernant 1982. Note, too, d'Onofrio 1982: 164–65, which emphasizes the affinities between the *kouros* and the young Homeric warrior.

[111] In Vernant's reading of the scene (1982: 58–62), it is only at the moment of death, when movement and action have ceased to distract witnesses from his body's more essential properties, that the warrior achieves this formal beauty.

[112] The capacity of the *kouros* to reflect back the viewer is argued in Osborne 1988: 7–9 and 1994a: 88; contra his position, Stewart 1997: 66.

[113] Osborne 1988: 7.

Harmodios and Aristogeiton

If the *kouros* resists specific contextualization, then a very particular and markedly eros-tinged event frames Kritios and Nesiotes' images of Harmodios and Aristogeiton, set up in the Athenian agora in 477/76 (see fig. 6). As Thucydides preserves the tale, the Tyrannicides' heroic deed was motivated by Hipparchos's failed attempt to seduce the youthful Harmodios away from his *erastēs*, and by the insult that the disappointed suitor then addressed to Harmodios's sister by way of retaliation (1.20.1 and 6.54–59). While Kritios and Nesiotes' original work is lost (and nothing is known of the still earlier group by Antenor that the Persians stole from the city in 480), extant copies and imitations in other media suggest that the images would quickly have clued viewers into the love relationship between the two heroes, and would even have presented the bond as integral to their action. But to square that eros with the new democratic ideology that the images are also bound to serve requires that the sculptors incorporate a series of potentially conflicting stories into their portrayal, and the various readings that the figures and their deed can (and seemingly did) invite stand testament to some of the juxtapositions and resolutions that the monument holds up for show.

Standing over six feet tall, and both unclad but for the cloak that Aristogeiton wears draped about his arm, the two heroes stride forward to claim their victim. No longer the wholly "natural" nakedness of earlier centuries, their want of clothes now looks for explanation. Early fifth-century sculptors and painters are generally careful and deliberate in their choice of the device, using it not only to situate figures in the real-life contexts where nudity might be practiced (most typically athletics), but also to invest the body with a markedly sexual edge.[114] If this is the artists' intention here, then the absence of clothes would jibe with other dimensions of (copies of) the group that make the love relationship central to its meaning. Aristogeiton, his maturity signaled by his beard and his more massive physique, clearly plays the *erastēs*, while the more delicate, unbearded Harmodios exactly matches the individual whom Thucydides' later account terms *lampros* and imagines in the full bloom of his youth (6.54.2). The similarity of copies of the head of the Harmodios figure to that of the so-called Kritian boy suggests that the artists may have given the young man the same ripening sexual maturity and delicately evoked youth that Kritios's still-extant work possesses.

But the sexual charge that emanates from these bodies, and that can

[114] Osborne 1997: 512–14.

implicate not only the two lovers, but also the viewer, runs counter to the more public or official meaning informing the monument.[115] For all that a speaker in Plato's *Symposium* makes the love of Harmodios and Aristogeiton responsible for the Peisistratids' overthrow, and declares such intimacies antithetical to tyrannical regimes (182c–d),[116] this account of their enterprise might have won scant approbation at the time of the statues' creation. In early fifth-century Athens, pederasty seems to have lost the socially positive charge that it had carried in earlier decades. Perhaps deemed overly elitist in the new democracy, and tainted by its association with the mores of the Peisistratid court and society, it no longer supplied a popular topic for poetic or artistic celebrations and was chiefly relocated to the divine and mythological sphere.[117] Rather than presenting the Tyrannicides as lovers, supporters of the current regime would instead have wanted to promote the view that their motives had been political from the start, and would have cast them as proto-democrats, citizens willing to sacrifice their lives on their city's behalf.[118]

The group that Kritios and Nesiotes create readily accommodates this very different interpretation of events. Although the unclothed body can be sexualized in early fifth-century sculpture and painting, it may also place the figure in a long artistic tradition, and highlight the subject's affinity to characters featured in earlier painted and plastic scenes. In this instance, the glance back to earlier conventions serves the sculptors' aims very well: even as Harmodios and Aristogeiton call to mind the noble Athenians who had recently hazarded their lives against a fresh tyrannical threat (this time from without), in their outsized stature, beauty, and bravery they also recall the heroes of bygone ages.[119] The bronze used to cast the statues contains a further backward reference to a mythical and heroic period: closely linked with the world of the Hesiodic Bronze Age fighters,[120] it emphasizes the rigor, hardness, and sharp contours of these bodies, proclaiming the individuals first and foremost

[115] Here I would nuance Stewart's suggestion that the group "placed the homoerotic bond at the core of Athenian political freedom" (1997: 73).
[116] Cf. Aeschin. 1.132.
[117] Shapiro 1981: 141–42 documents the shift.
[118] Accounts in fifth-century historians also register this change: Herodotus, writing in the middle of the century when the radical democracy was still going strong, gives the "official" version and says nothing of the romantic quarrel behind the attack. Thucydides, witness to the unraveling of some of the central institutions of the city and ever quick to display the cracks and fissures in the system, presents the act in a very different light.
[119] This argument need not presuppose, as Himmelmann (1990) most forcefully does, that nakedness implies heroization. However, the Tyrannicides were elevated to hero status and received cult worship in the city.
[120] Stewart 1997: 52–53.

warriors. Also pointing toward the martial and heroic role that the Tyrannicides have assumed, and investing that role with a particularly Athenian dimension, are the characteristics that the two figures hold up for show: together they display the contrasting but coexisting virtues of boldness and moderation, of uncalculated bravery and caution, of aggression and defensiveness, which Perikles' Funeral Oration would later famously describe as unique to citizens of Athens and the source of their particular excellence in the face of their enemies (Thuc. 2.39–41).

A viewer's response to the group would follow from the facets of the images on which he chose to focus. For the individual seeking an erotic charge, Harmodios, advancing forward with his eyes directed toward the audience, with his supremely "seasonable," naked, and unblemished physique on full display, might arouse desire and even seem ready to respond to the sensations he provokes.[121] But to treat Harmodios as a potential *erōmenos* casts the viewer in so uncomfortable a role that he might quickly turn toward the more properly heroic and civic dimensions of the work: to seek the attentions of Harmodios while standing before the pair is quite literally to occupy the position of Hipparchos, and to become the target of the young man's raised sword. Aristogeiton's protective pose delivers another warning to the intriguant who would seek this beloved for his own, as it declares the youth already spoken for. Better to regard the two bodies as paradigmatic of the physical, ethical, and political virtues that the Athenian citizen should ideally combine.

An integral part of the statue, and a reiteration of its several messages, is the inscription on its base:

> ἦ μέγ' Ἀθηναίοισι φόως γένεθ' ἡνίκ Ἀριστο-
> γείτων Ἵππαρχον κτεῖνε καὶ Ἁρμόδιος.

> Surely a great light for the Athenians came into being when Aristogeiton and Harmodios killed Hipparchos.

The author, supposedly Simonides (1 *FGE*), follows the artists in allowing both erotic and civic elements to coexist. Beginning with an assertion of the political and proto-democratic dimensions of the deed, the couplet goes on more implicitly to acknowledge the love intrigue that impelled the men to take up arms. Inserted between the names of the two lovers, Hipparchos occupies the space in the text that corresponds to the place that he (and the present-day viewer/reader positioned before the group) vainly sought to occupy. Also included in the lines' design is an indication of the consequences of this attempted breach. As

---

[121] According to Stewart (ibid.: 73), Aristogeiton supplies a figure with whom the adult male spectator could happily identify.

Anne Carson suggests, the epigram's deliberate contravention of the cardinal rule of elegiac verse, that word boundary should coincide with verse end, reflects the uncheckable motion that will drive Aristogeiton to his beloved's defense and to strike down any individual who would break into their partnership.[122] The salvation that the Athenians enjoyed seems, in retrospect, to depend on this purely private rather than public impetus.

The differing interpretations that the group hosts not only correspond to fifth- and fourth-century sources' divergent accounts of the Tyrannicides' act, but also recall the tensions and possible accommodations that exist between the new democratic priorities and an elite institution that, civic ideology, changing social norms, and perhaps even the threat of prosecutions notwithstanding, continued to play a central role in the lives of Athenian men and boys. Reflecting the Athenians' own differentiated view of their politics and culture, the artists, like some of their literary counterparts of the time,[123] have created a monument that affirms the collaborative and community values preached by the democratic city even as it displays an idealized account of the social realities still prevailing at the time. While it proves possible to enjoy the youthful and unclad masculine physique in this politically sanctioned account, the viewer is prevented from claiming that body for his own, except perhaps at the cost of his own self-sacrifice to freedom's cause.

Athletic Images

For the makers of the Tyrannicides, the politics and erotics of Harmodios and Aristogeiton are potentially at odds. Contradictions of these and other kinds inform the monumental images of youthful athletes and victors in the games that Greek sculptors of the late archaic and classical age created and put up in the civic spaces of the polis and at panhellenic shrines. Placed in the public eye, and necessarily involved in the risks of provocative display, participants in athletics and the games are bound to maintain a particular modesty and even to practice a sexual abstinence thought to improve performance;[124] but the boys' nudity, their exposure to the gaze, and their very presence at the gymnasium, palaestra, and sites of the games also makes them a target of the adult man's quest, and positions them as well-recognized objects of his voyeurism, courtship, and seduction. Makers of athletic statues seem to play off this particular blend; even as they fashion works that incorpo-

---

[122] Carson 1996: 11–12.
[123] See Griffith 1995 for a reading of Aeschylus's *Oresteia* that recognizes this variegated view.
[124] Pl. *Laws* 840a.

rate the youths' own role as instigators of the desirous look and sources of pleasurable viewing, and encourage an audience to "slide" from the image to the living body, they temper their subjects' patent seductiveness with the requisite degree of reticence, self-control, and even a hint of asexuality. The delicate balance that informs the representations also answers to the ambivalent status of prize-winning athletes within some of the fifth-century city-states: outsized individuals, and practitioners of what remains a chiefly elite activity among a populace that may espouse the virtues of more collective and "middling" modes of conduct, victors can be depicted in a manner designed to mitigate the claims to singularity and individualized prominence that the monuments might otherwise broadcast.

A familiar series of late archaic and classical texts signals the links between erotic intrigues and athletic activity, and presents the gymnasium and palaestra as sites particularly accommodating to "homosocial" and homoerotic relations.[125] Theognis first declares happy the man who "is in love while he exercises (*gumnazetai*), and returning home sleeps with the beautiful boy the whole day through" (1335–36), and comic poets will later suggest that only the most faint of heart or outstandingly restrained can resist the opportunities for pederastic affairs that the gymnasium and wrestling school so richly supply.[126] With little success, Alcibiades employs the ruse of a wrestling bout in his attempt to attract and embrace the longed-for body of Socrates.[127] Less well-documented, but no less common, are the instances in which victors in local or crown games become the focus of amorous desire. Pindar hopes for a second occasion on which to make the youthful subject of *Pythian* 10 a *melēma*, a darling or beloved, to those who witness his triumph (59),[128] and he underscores the erotic charge surrounding his subjects by styling them recipients of the powers of seduction that Aphrodite and

[125] I borrow the term "homosocial," which encompasses but extends beyond homosexuality, from Sedgwick (1985). For an application of the notion to painting, see the very illuminating discussion in Solomon-Godeau 1993: 288–89.
[126] Ar. *Vesp.* 1023–25, *Peace* 762–63. Cf. Aeschin. 135, 138–39; [Lucian] *Amores* 9; for good-looking boys in wrestling schools, see Pl. *Chrm.* 154a–c, *Euthydemus* 237a, *Lysis* 206e. Dover (1978: 54) briefly sums up the situation: "The gymnasium as a whole or the wrestling school in particular provided opportunities for looking at naked boys, bringing oneself discreetly to a boy's notice in the hope of eventually speaking to him . . . and even touching a boy in a suggestive way, as if by accident, while wrestling with him."
[127] Pl. *Symp.* 217c. For an explicit statement of the link between the institution of the gymnasium and homoeroticism, see Pl. *Laws* 636c.
[128] The term *melēma* used by Pindar in other contexts makes quite plain its erotic connotations; on one occasion he styles his subject *melēma Charitōn* (fr. 95 Snell-Maehler), on another *melēma Kupridos* (fr. 217 Snell-Maehler). It should be noted that in *Pyth.* 10 the audience is made up of women as well as men.

the Graces bestow.[129] Leagros, a famed beauty of his age, may be the individual shown as a wreathed pentathlete victor and acclaimed as *kalos* on a red-figure kylix from the start of the fifth century (Fig. 18),[130] and Xenophon's *Symposium* opens with Kallias, the devoted admirer of one young victor in the Panathenaic games, issuing invitations to a party in honor of his beloved: Autolykos's dazzling beauty proves quite spellbinding to all who gaze on him, "like a light appearing at night" (1.8), and Kallias's predilection raises no eyebrows among this select company.[131]

Within the space of the gymnasium or the athletic games, several factors would foster an erotic atmosphere and concentrate spectators' attention on the participants' physical charms. First and foremost, athletes exercised and competed without their clothes,[132] and there seems little doubt that this rare opportunity to gaze on youthful unclad bodies would form part of the attraction of the gymnasium, palaestra, and local or panhellenic contests.[133] Laws, operative at least by the fourth century and ascribed to Solon in fourth-century sources,[134] acknowledge the pulling power of these displays as they seek to protect boys at gymnasia from unwanted attentions. One event included at some games, on occasion called the *euandria*, even made the participants' attractive and unclothed physiques the focal point of the competition: here youths would parade before the judges, and the prize probably go to those outstanding in beauty and in strength.[135]

[129] E.g., *Pyth.* 5.45, *Ol.* 6.76, *Nem.* 6.37–38.

[130] *ARV*[2] 177, 3. For more on this depiction, see pp. 226–27. Leagros also appears on the Getty psykter (82.AE.53), which shows the vase painter Euphronios embracing the semi-clad youth among other named courting pairs in the palaestra or gymnasium.

[131] The beloved, Autolykos, pankration victor in 422, was later celebrated by a statue by Leochares, raised in the Prytaneion. The quasi-Pindaric terms used by Xenophon to evoke his beauty are perhaps deliberate. Note, too, *Anth. Pal.* 12.123, whose anonymous author boasts of kissing a beloved boy "smeared all over with blood" after victory in the boxing.

[132] The convention of athletes competing naked was a practice thought singular enough to merit discussion in fifth- and fourth-century authors, who cite it as a distinctively Greek custom (so Hdt. 1.10.3; Thuc. 1.5–6; Pl. *Resp.* 452c; cf. Paus. 1.44.1; Dion. Hal. 7.22.2–3; Isid. *Etym.* 18.17.2). For recent views on the origins and dating of athletic nudity, McDonnell 1991; Bonfante 1989: 552–58; Himmelmann 1990; Stewart 1997: 24–42.

[133] As Stewart (1997: 27) points out, public nakedness was permitted only in the context of bathing and athletics. The taboo surrounding displays of the naked body elsewhere would have given the sites where it was sanctioned a marked quality.

[134] Aeschin. 1.9–11.

[135] For details of these contests, Crowther 1985. Boegehold (1996: 97–103) takes issue with the interpretation of the *euandria* as a beauty contest, but the definition is endorsed in Neils 1994. According to her reading, the youth depicted on an amphora by Douris in St. Petersburg (*ARV*[2] 446, 263), who wears a cap carrying a banner inscribed *Ho pais kalos*, represents a winner in the *euandria*.

But the best evidence for the allure of athletes both at home and at the games belongs to the visual medium, where vase painters employ a variety of motifs to highlight their desirability, and to position them as the targets of would-be *erastai*.[136] Mature, bearded, and clothed men regularly play the role of trainers or admiring spectators at the gymnasium,[137] and an early fifth-century column krater pairs naked jumpers with a trainer on one side, and a fully muffled youth (no less provocative for his enveloping cloak) being courted by an older man on the other.[138] Wine cups frequently depict the young nude athlete with his body fully turned to face the drinker, and the *kalos* inscription that accompanies one such *apostrophē* plainly indicates the appropriate response.[139] The circulation of these vessels at the symposium, a second prime homosocial space, melds in one the heady erotic atmospheres of the athletic field and the drinking party.[140] The same semantic devices used to frame the youths at their exercises reappear in representations of contestants at the games:[141] again the different events allow the painters to show the unclad bodies to advantage, while the crowning ceremony matches the still-naked youth, his body sometimes presented in profile, sometimes positioned so as fully to face the user of the cup, with an older, bearded man,[142] or a maiden,[143] or even the goddess Nike standing with a ribbon or wreath in hand ready to invest him with his prize.[144]

---

[136] As Bérard (1986: 195) comments, the different activities the athletes perform "sont autant de prétextes à mettre en scène des corps juvéniles nus pour en exalter la beauté séductrice" ("are so many pretexts for exhibiting naked young bodies in order to promote their seductive beauty"). Note the observations of Bonfante (1989: 555–56) on the rare depictions of ugly athletes in vase painting, and for the exception that proves the rule, ARV^2 401, 3.

[137] ARV^2 1648 and 1705, 36 *bis*; 815, 4. In the last instance, as Frontisi-Ducroux (1995: 128) suggests, the viewer is encouraged to identify with the older man who looks outward at the drinker, inviting him to judge the youthful beauty on display. For more on the homoerotic implications of this pairing of the mature, bearded man and the youth, see Stewart 1997: 7 and chap. 4 passim.

[138] ARV^2 274, 43.

[139] ARV^2 322, 37 with discussion in Frontisi-Ducroux 1995: 125. See, too, ARV^2 117, 6; 321, 23; 322, 28.

[140] Lissarrague 1990a: 100.

[141] In many instances, there is no telling whether the individual is merely training or is actually participating in competition.

[142] ARV^2 54, 7 offers a particularly fine example. See, too, ARV^2 455, 10.

[143] A Protolucanian pelike from the fifth century (Trendall 467) shows the athlete with his body facing the viewer, while his head turns to the left; on this occasion he is flanked by two maidens shown in profile who give him his crown and other gifts.

[144] For examples, see the relevant entries in *LIMC* s.v. Nike. The occasional presence of Nike in the episodes is suggestive on several counts. First, like the maidens, she may

Key to all these representations are the visual dynamics of the scene, designed to encourage the user of the vessel to participate in the amorous encounter. The presence of an internal onlooker offers him a pair of eyes within the pictorial space and prompts him to assume the painted figure's role as admirer and potential seducer of the youth. The athlete who presents himself full face still more directly implicates the drinker bending to his cup, and invites him to displace any other internal spectators and (if the youth does not look downward or avert his head) to fancy himself the fortunate partner in a reciprocal relationship.[145] The inclusion of the female figures in the scene causes a triangulation of desire: while the women desire the athlete, now doubly figured as the bearer of the gaze, the external viewer can let his fantasies play simultaneously on the nubile maidens (or goddess) and the youthful athlete.

Where athletes serve as the target of the gaze, the artist occasionally uses an additional device to underline the "to-be-looked-at-ness" that stamps them as objects of desire. On two fifth-century vases, the body placed before the amorous viewer internal or external to the scene assumes the likeness of a sculpted image. The first, an early fifth-century kylix, shows in its tondo an older man positioned in front of a young, nude victor, a pentathlete crowned with an olive wreath, who stands equipped with javelin, sponge, and aryballos (fig. 18); an inscription reaching from the top of the older man's head and arching around the body of the youth acclaims Leagros as *kalos*.[146] What distinguishes this vase from myriad other amorous encounters between athletes and their trainers/admirers in the Attic red-figure repertoire is the presentation of the boy on a two-step base, his body frozen in a stiff, *kouros*-like pose. Interpretations of the image dispute the status of the youth. According to some, the painter intends to show not an individual of flesh and blood, but a statue, perhaps even the victory monument dedicated by Leagros; others read the podium as a solution to the problem of depicting the shorter figure of the athlete within a tondo.[147] But the ambiguity

---

supply a second object of desire, particularly in the light of the goddess's patently sexualized character in contemporary visual and sculptural accounts (on which see the later discussion). Second, the winged goddess who approaches with ribbon or wreath in hand closely recalls depictions of the similarly winged Eros, who bestows parallel gifts on youths, maidens, and most particularly grooms and brides (for examples, see the vases discussed in Oakley and Sinos 1993); the common motifs might prompt the viewer to equate the two arrangements and set the athlete within the more explicitly amorous context that the scenes with Eros portray.

[145] On these interactions between viewer and viewed, see particularly Frontisi-Ducroux 1995: 127–30 and 1996; also Clark 1984: 132–33.

[146] *ARV*[2] 177, 3.

[147] For recent discussion, see Neils 1992: 163; Francis and Vickers (1981) simply assume a statue. For another, though less obvious, coalescence between a statue and a living youth,

surrounding the boy may be exactly the goal the painter has in mind. Together pose, pedestal, and inscription realize the impact that eros has on the recipient of the longing look and remind external viewers that they, following the older man in the scene, regard the athlete in the manner of an *agalma*, an object of visual delight and desire. A still more patent "monumentalization" takes place on the surface of a cup attributed to the Antiphon painter, where another nude and youthful athlete, this one unmistakably alive, pours oil into his hand as he relaxes from his exertions (fig. 19).[148] Inscribed on his thigh, exactly as if he were one of the many votive figurines that carry dedications incised on their bodies, or the *kouros* of Charmeus from Samos cited earlier, run the words *Laches kalos*.[149] Again the living body has assumed the likeness of a material artifact set up for display, a surface on which the admiring viewer may place his mark. In both instances, the artist has visualized the moment that poets, dramatists, and philosophers also describe: when the lover contemplates the person of the beloved, he views it as though it were a statue.

If the athlete already serves as an object of spectatorship, and one perceived as an artifact for the aesthetic and sensual pleasure that he supplies, then what happens when his person takes the form of a sculpted image, most particularly that of the victory statue erected on behalf of winners in the games? The monument short-circuits the process that the vase paintings have described, presenting the athlete's body as a beautiful piece expressly set up for public display. In this transformation the individual need lose nothing of his original appeal, and statue-makers not only preserve many of the living athlete's own most potent sources of allure, but additionally use the technical and material aspects of their craft to enhance those charms: seeing the statue *as* the athlete and seeing the athlete *in* the statue form a unified response because the qualities of the piece — its beauty, style, and high craftsmanship — are those that the spectator has admired and desired in the athlete from the start.

On many counts the match between original and image is very close. From what the few extant remains of victory statues and textual ac-

---

see *ARV²* 322, 36; here the athlete, shown full-frontally, his muscles and biceps depicted to full advantage, adopts the exact pose of the figure in victory monuments, one hand raised to touch his head, the other placed on his hip. His companions, meanwhile, gaze on his physique.

[148] *ARV²* 336, 14.

[149] Beazley (*ARV²* ad loc.) comments on the image that the athlete is inscribed "as if he were a statue." The athlete stands in front of a pillar also bearing an inscription: *ho pais / naichi / kalos*. I am most grateful to François Lissarrague, who told me about the image in conversation and gave me the benefit of his interpretation.

counts of the same reveal, the pieces were generally life-sized and life-like, and sought broadly to recreate their subjects as they would have appeared at the various moments of the games. Inscriptions accompanying the monuments promote the identification, regularly eliding the representation with the original and calling on the audience to admire the image and living body in a single glance: so an epigram from the first half of the fifth century urges its audience, "Come to know Theognetos looking upon him, the boy Olympic victor, skilled charioteer of the wrestling, most beautiful to see, and in competing no worse than his form" (Ebert 12 = *Anth. Plan.* 16.2).[150]

Additional details of the victory image would allow the spectator to follow this and other such injunctions, while simultaneously encouraging the desirous element in his viewing. With the exception of monuments raised on behalf of winners in the chariot race, who wear the long chiton appropriate to their event (of which more later on), victors are shown unclothed; and although the depiction of unclad figures in fifth-century painting and sculpture need not always possess an erotic significance, and some view nudity at the games as ritual in origin, the sexual charge surrounding the naked athlete in literary and painted representations would surely carry over into the image. To read the victor statue's nudity as only realistic in intent is to disregard this other register.

No less alluring and "naturalistic," too, was the matter in which the victory monument was cast. By the mid-sixth century, bronze was the material of choice for statue-makers, in part, no doubt, because its gleam so readily brought to mind the burnished, oiled bodies of the athletes themselves.[151] Cleansing regularly followed athletic endeavors, and the use of perfumed oils would give to the tanned skin that satiny appearance which closely jibes with the shining surface of buffed and polished statues.[152] In his catalogue of the physical virtues of the well-exercised *erōmenoi* of bygone Marathon days, Aristophanes' Right Logos nostalgically evokes the youths' sleek chests and lustrous skin (*Nub.* 1012; cf. Pind. *Nem.* 7.70–73), and in more jaundiced vein, a character in Euripides' *Autolykos* grants the resemblance between these glistening living victors and their no less sleek-shining images: athletes "lustrous in youth (*lamproi d'en hēbēi*) lounge like living statues decking the streets" (fr. 282.10–11 N²). This very affinity is what the sculp-

[150] For discussion of this and other examples, see Ebert 1972; Kurke 1993: 141–49.
[151] Stewart 1990: 39. As Stewart's discussion at 1997: 54 explains, it is hard to know what the original color of the statues would have been; some writers of the Roman period speak of bronze images that imitated the tanned flesh of the athlete's body.
[152] Bérard 1986: 196.

tor sought to exploit: the viewer might recapture the sensual pleasure derived from looking at the athlete's oiled physique by gazing on his still more idealized monument.

A further artistic convention would strengthen the bond between model and copy and encourage the transfer of sensations from the living body to its doubling image. As inscriptions, poems, statues, and vase paintings all suggest, the moment when the athlete achieved supreme glory was not the instant of the win but the occasion when he appeared before the audience to claim his crown. This ceremony not only signaled the victor's investment with his talismanic power or *kudos*,[153] but also set his desirability at its topmost mark; now he stood as the cynosure of all eyes, the focus of the concentrated mimetic desires of spectators.[154] The depiction of the athlete just prior to or immediately after the bestowal of the crown is the statue-makers' choice motif[155] and allows the latter-day spectator to confront the burnished body as it radiates the same "epinician" allure that live athletes possessed as they received their prize. Extant inscriptions accompanying lost monuments confirm the popularity of the pose: many not only evoke the act of crowning, but by citing the victory announcement that the herald uttered as the victor stood to accept his prize, they complement the statue's recapitulation of the earlier occasion.[156] The viewer now doubly reenacts the part of those who originally witnessed the event, renewing the visual accolades addressed to the living man with his own admiring and desiring look, and audibly speaking the words that first affirmed the triumph.[157]

Nor does the athlete in the image remain oblivious to the look addressed to him. Both vases and monuments portraying an athlete at the

[153] For this, p. 19.

[154] Vase painters introduce several motifs to convey the heightened sexual charge and to solicit the viewer's own eros-laden look on this particular occasion. I earlier mentioned the use of the *apostrophē*, which turns the victor's body to the external audience, the paradigmatic presence of the judge (note Frontisi-Ducroux 1995: 127), and perhaps a maiden or Nike.

[155] As Hyde (1921: 149) observes, the most common way of characterizing a subject as an athletic victor was to show him with a *tainia*, the band or woolen ribbon that the contestant would either bind about himself or have others place around him immediately when the contest was done; see, too, Kurke 1993: 144–45. Several extant copies of victor statues, and several images described in ancient sources, adopt this pose. Pausanias mentions a statue by Pheidias representing a Boy Binding on a Fillet standing in the Altis (6.4.5), and Pliny refers to Polykleitos's Diadoumenos (*HN* 34.55); for additional discussion of the type, Serwint 1987: 103–4.

[156] Ebert 55, dated to 300 B.C., makes this absolutely explicit: "Standing thus upon the Alpheios, the Pelasgian boxer once showed forth the ordinance of Polydeukes with his hands, when he was heralded victor."

[157] See Kurke 1993: 145 for this reenactment.

crowning ceremony regularly show their subject with his head bowed, or deflecting the internal or external viewer's gaze by glancing aside. When a judge crowns a youthful athlete styled "fair" Epainetos on a red-figure psykter from the late sixth century, the boy averts his eyes, and Roman copies of Polykleitos's Diadoumenos (fig. 4) and the West-macott boy (perhaps originally a dedication at Olympia by Polykleitos from the middle of the fifth century) look downward, their eyes lowered and heads inclined.[158] This gesture of *aidōs* not only indicates the modesty appropriate to a moment of divinely granted good fortune, but also, from the perspective of the artist, sculptor, or viewer of the scene, further contributes to the adolescent's charm; *aidōs* could most easily slide into "a shyness that was homosexually winning,"[159] and written sources contemporary with the images acknowledge the inflammatory power of this (calculated) reticence.

By way of test for the reading proposed so far, I want to turn to one extant early fifth-century image most probably designed to stand as a monument in the victor's native city. In his recent reconstruction of the provenance and identity of the enigmatic Motya charioteer (c. 480–470; see fig. 3), Malcolm Bell persuasively argues that the figure represents a winner in the games and suggests that the statue would originally have been raised in the subject's Sicilian home.[160] Many features of this visually arresting piece accord with what we know of fifth-century victory images. Slightly over life-size (it presently measures about 6 feet), the young, beardless athlete places his weight on his left leg as he stands at rest; the left arm is held akimbo, and the right raised above the horizontal. Bell demonstrates how the position of the now-missing right forearm and hand should be associated with the four bronze nails in the statue's cranium, placed so as to hold a circular object around the charioteer's head; according to his reading, the athlete would be raising his hand in order to hold or touch the *tainia*, or maybe the victory wreath, in the same gesture that appears on contemporary Attic red-figure vase paintings and in the later Westmacott boy and bronze athlete from the Getty museum.[161] Reconstructed in this fashion, the charioteer's attitude exactly echoes that adopted by other victorious athletes, similarly poised at the moment when they prepare to receive their crowns.

---

[158] Other examples include the so-called Motya charioteer (whom I discuss shortly), and the athlete on a marble relief from Sunion where the victor glances downward, his chin almost touching his chest as he raises his hand to his fillet. See, too, *ARV*² 54, 7.

[159] Stewart 1990: 52; see, too, his discussion at 162 and his remarks on *aidôs* in Stewart 1997: 80–82.

[160] Bell 1995.

[161] Ibid.: 9.

Unlike the other images I have cited, but quite in keeping with contemporary painted and sculpted representations of charioteers in the games, the Motya statue wears a long chiton that falls in many flat, shallow folds to ankle length. But this covering does nothing to hide the athlete's physical appeal: virtually transparent, and molding itself against the anatomical forms it drapes, the chiton allows the viewer to trace out the chest, abdomen, legs, thighs, buttocks, and genitals (these emphasized by an additional column of folds) beneath the garment. Because such diaphanous clothing more commonly belongs to representations of women in fifth-century art, some modern viewers have wanted to identify the figure as a transvestite god, hero, dancer, or actor;[162] but as Bell convincingly observes, "Drapery that partially reveals sexual attributes may be sexually charged, whatever the sex of the body underneath."[163] Images that both antedate and follow the Motya charioteer demonstrate his point and illustrate how garments in Greek art (as well as in poetic accounts) may not so much conceal nudity as enhance the loveliness that lies behind, and incite the spectator's longing to gain closer access.[164]

Other elements of the charioteer's design promote his eye-catching appeal. The viewer's attention, already drawn to the lower body by the thumb of the left hand pressed up against the hip and indenting the flesh below,[165] then moves to the contours of the statue's buttocks, a particular source of delectation to homoerotically inclined viewers from the classical to the imperial age.[166] The chest band running tightly around the charioteer's chiton, which causes the material to bunch on top, conveys the strength and vitality of the upper abdomen as it strains against the confines, and recalls the effort just expended in the race. If virility means youth, beauty, and bodily power combined, then the Motya charioteer offers a perfect amalgam of all three. But reticence should also form part of the victor's repertoire of charms: the charioteer holds

---

[162] See ibid.: 7 n. 33.

[163] Ibid.: 7.

[164] For diaphanous clothing as sexually provocative, see Ar. *Lys.* 48, 150–51; on its evolution in Greek art, Stewart 1997: 102 and 128. This is an issue to which I return in later sections.

[165] Bell (1995: 9) observes that the motif of the arm placed on the hip neatly solves the problem of what to do with a limb no longed fixed in its archaic pose, and in early classical sculpture, an arm akimbo and hand on hip signified assertiveness (Stewart 1990: 133 and 145). But the hips also attract the amorous notice of the pederastically inclined Kallikratidas in [Lucian]'s *Amores* (13); more remotely, note, too, how in Ovid's account of Pygmalion, the thumb pressing on the flesh below evokes the "liveliness" of the image (*Met.* 10.285–86).

[166] Ar. *Nub.* 1014; [Lucian] *Amores* 13. The sway-backed silhouette that results in a prominent extrusion of the buttocks is, of course, characteristic of many early fifth-century images, as documented by Métraux (1995: 38–43).

232 • For Love of a Statue

his head very slightly tilted downward, and turned to the left in a three-quarter view when the figure is approached from the front. By refusing to meet the spectator's eye, and by manifesting the appropriate modesty before the fact of victory, the statue tempers his self-display with *aidōs*.

The sexual edge so unmistakable in the Motya charioteer, and no less marked in the painted gymnasia and other athletic scenes contemporary with the image, would undergo some modification in representations from subsequent decades. By the middle of the fifth century, statue-makers seem increasingly to have fashioned figures whose emphatic youth served to undercut the masculinity and virility that their activity would naturally involve, and that the Motya charioteer puts on display;[167] if extant copies of monuments were all the evidence that remained, we might think that none but smooth-faced and unblemished adolescent boys competed in athletic events.[168] While several of the images have bodies whose distinctly mature musculature turns them into something of a biological *adunaton*, perhaps a visualization of the unrealizable pederastic ideal in which only the virile but sexually innocent boy supplies a legitimate target of an adult man's desires, others are invested with a softness and delicacy that accentuate their immaturity; the muscles of the Westmacott athlete are strikingly underdeveloped, and if the copy is to be credited, his face would have preserved all the roundness of boyhood.[169]

While these changing modes of representation could depend on a variety of prompts (social sanctions, new vogues in body types, the promotion of women as objects of desire among them), they might also signal a fresh response to the problems that victors had long been posing to the citizens of their native towns. As the written sources from both the archaic and the classical age attest, the large material rewards athletes garnered and their privileged position in the polis aroused hostility, *phthonos*, and even the more violent measures, which some of the anecdotes surrounding heroized victors and their images describe.[170] By virtue of investing the statue with all the desirability that the living forms of (young) athletes possess, the sculptor not only allows the viewer freely to indulge his taste for the adolescent male physique, but also turns the monument into an instrument for diffusing the more neg-

[167] As Stewart (1997: 80) and Himmelmann (1990) point out, this is a more widespread phenomenon, and involves figures portrayed by vase-painters as well. See, too, Osborne 1999 and 1997: 523.

[168] Vase-painters do show older athletes, but never in implicitly or explicitly erotic contexts.

[169] Osborne 1999: 35.

[170] For these stories, see chapter 1. For critiques of athletes and their veneration, see the material collected in Kyle 1987: 124–41.

ative sensations that the victor's elevation generates, transmuting despite into an amorous delight.[171] No less critically, the artistic account and the respective positions of viewer and the viewed permit the citizen spectator to reclaim some of the status and power that the supremely fortunate living athlete threatens to monopolize. The victor represented in the statue no longer stands in glorious autonomy, distinguished beyond all his fellow members of the polis; instead, his youth, delicacy, and nudity are markers of vulnerability,[172] and his averted eyes acknowledge the spectator's controlling gaze; any fresh *kudos* the athlete earns, as many inscriptions themselves observe with their calls on the audience to stop, look, and "bestow glory," remains dependent on the passerby, who must choose to grant him the requisite admiration and praise and voluntarily respond to his appeal.[173] The modesty that the victor's pose announces perhaps also tempers or causes the viewer to forget the elite nature of his activity, turning the figure into a more generalized and prescriptive account of the demeanor required of all youths still subject to the regulation of mature men.[174]

But for all their attempts to downplay the athlete's bid for power and prestige, the artists have, wittingly or not, adopted a strategy likely to backfire. Even as they encourage the viewer to see the living body and statue as one, they ultimately deny satisfaction to the desires that the elision has aroused, and bring to mind less pleasurable parallels between the boy and his monument. Realizing anew the notion expressed on the red-figure kylix with the "calcified" athlete placed on his pedestal, the victor stands as a sculpted image not simply because he is a statue, but because he is an impassive, impervious, immobile, and infinitely desirable beloved. Just as the living *erōmenos* feels no pleasure in answer to the lover's passion and retains his honor through his disengagement, so, too, the monument preserves its unyielding materiality and remoteness, and the youth victorious in the athletic competition now carries off the prize in the no less antagonistic context of erotic

---

[171] On this, and parallels in poetic practice, see my more detailed discussion in Steiner 1998.

[172] On nudity and vulnerability, Bonfante 1989: 547, 560.

[173] See Ebert 12, 48, 57. Both Pindar and composers of epigrams for victory images insist on the central and even dominant role of the viewer-cum-celebrant of the athlete: without the epinician poet to compose songs of praise, the odes reiterate countless times, victory in the games rapidly fades from view, and only the laudator can give a laudandus his lasting fame; according to the expressions used in epigrams, the athlete remains dependent not only on the sculptor of the image (whose name frequently appears in the inscription), but also on the passerby, who must be exhorted and cajoled into stopping to look and admire.

[174] That the very act of setting up an athletic image in the public spaces of the polis could be politically problematic, the seeming absence of such monuments in fifth-century Athens suggests. For this, see chapter 5.

relations. Through its combination of properties, the image achieves two very different ends, and perhaps articulates a tension implicit in the position of its subject: exactly matching the pederastic ideal as fifth- and fourth-century texts promote it, the monument also accords with the strictures that would deny the older man his youthful beloved.

Korai

So far I have focused on images of men and introduced the adult male viewer in the role of *erastēs* to the youthful *erōmenos*. But the "feminized masculinities" that viewers seem increasingly to have privileged in works of art toward the fifth century's end[175] remind us that images of maidens and women could also instigate desire and offer visualizations of a second source of erotic delight. Just as the *kouros* supplied a point of departure for my earlier selection, I begin here with the *korai* contemporary with the images of youths, which fulfilled the same votive and funerary roles.

The gender of these images dictates one obvious distinction from their male counterparts: *korai* are clothed, and many (the series from the Athenian Acropolis most outstandingly) wear the rich and decorative garments and jewelry that constitute perhaps the cardinal element in their overall charm. In addition to declaring the maidens desirable quite simply on account of the wealth that their clothes, bracelets, earrings, and crowns all advertise,[176] the ornamentation of these images recalls the point that Hesiod's Pandora already exemplified. Just as the statue-woman of the *Theogony* was nothing more than her external adornments and presented a figure attractive from without, so, too, the bodies of the *korai* exist as so many surfaces for decoration, and their appeal depends on what those surfaces display. The Acropolis images wear chitons, mantles, and other garments that would have been brightly painted in many-hued decorative patterns, and some of the clothing features embroidery picked out in red, yellow, brown, and black (figs. 20 and 21). Fresh glitter and color would come from their jewelry and crowns, which could be worked and were often painted and carved.[177] One of the Acropolis maidens (no. 683, sometimes designated "The Dwarf" on account of her abbreviated proportions) shows off her distinctive, and perhaps sought-after, red pointed slippers, and her clothes, too, are most luxurious, with a white painted filigree design still

---

[175] See the remark in Xen. *Symp.* 8.8.

[176] Note how Aphrodite in her seduction of Anchises takes pains to mention her supposed father's wealth, and the dowry of gold and rich cloths she will bring (*Hymn. Hom. Ven.* 139–40).

[177] On these, Ridgway 1993: 85–122; Schneider 1975; Stewart 1990: 123–24.

visible on the chiton's right sleeve. As the inscriptions accompanying many of the works proclaim, these statues are *agalmata*, objects of delight,[178] and that delight derives in no small part from the patently crafted and surface elements of the works.

That the attraction that adheres to clothing and ornamentation can be powerfully erotic in character, the seductive goddesses of epic song already attest.[179] While heroes dress themselves in armor, which enhances their beauty as well as their martial efficacy, female deities (and mortals, too) rely on the woven and embroidered garments that are no less a part of their bodily identity and determinants of their success. Hera painstakingly "arms" and "girds" herself for her seduction of Zeus in *Iliad* 14.170–87, each element of her toilette as calculated as a hero's blows, which loosen a victim's limbs in death rather than desire. So, too, Aphrodite prepares herself for her encounter with Anchises, assuming the garments and golden adornments that will enchant and seduce the mortal viewer with their brilliance. Confronted with the stranger, the hero wonders at the luminous clothing described by the singer in such hyperbolic terms: "A robe outshining the brightness of fire" (*Hymn. Hom. Ven.* 86). The lyric poets confirm that the female figure depends on its external, decorative qualities for its allure. Sappho mourns the absent beloved who appeared draped in the wreaths and garlands that complemented her tender throat (fr. 94 LP), and Anakreon singles out the "motley-colored" sandals (*poikilosambaloi*, 358 *PMG*) the girl from Lesbos wears when listing her particular sources of appeal. The red slippers adorning the marble *korē* cited above may be no less calculated to captivate a viewer: if they are predecessors to the "river-boat slippers" (*peribarides*) that Lysistrata names as one of the weapons deployed by her band to arouse their husbands (Ar. *Lys.* 47), then they form a recognizable part of a woman's seductive toilette.[180]

Just as armor need not so much cover the body as be identical with or even substitute for it, so, too, a woman's garments form one with what lies underneath, as though all elements of her appearance were the outcome of a single manufacturing process. Again, the poet of the *Homeric*

---

[178] E.g., *CEG* 195 and 422.

[179] Havelock 1995: 32–35 for a good statement of this. Fittingly enough, the effeminate Paris owes much of his seductive appeal, from Homer through Euripides' *Troades*, to his garments and lavish ornamentation; see *Il.* 3.371 and 392 (where note the equation of *kallos* and clothing); Eur. *Tro.* 987–92.

[180] See Stieber 1994: 111 n. 49 for the suggestion that the slippers worn by the *korē* may have been called "little boats" (*akatia*) on account of their shape, a term that, Pollux records (7.93), Aristophanes himself used in reference to a type of shoe worn by women. The "river-boat" slippers would also owe their name to their resemblance to a particular kind of ship, perhaps the long, flat barges or *barides* that Hdt. 2.96 describes.

Hymn to Aphrodite dwells on the different items of the goddess's costume, presenting each as an extension and enhancement of the separate parts of her unseen anatomy: her golden robe "shimmered like the moon over her tender breasts. . . . Also she wore twisted brooches and shining earrings in the form of flowers; and round her soft throat were lovely necklaces" (89–91). Much in the manner of the poet describing his seductive goddess, late archaic statue-makers model the *korai*'s garments and ornaments so as to trace the lines of their bodies, minimizing distinctions between the anatomy and the surface drapery and decoration. The triple braids exhibited by the "Lyons" *korē* (fig. 22) frame the young girl's breasts, and the sculptor of *korē* 675 (fig. 20) has spaced the six locks of the girl's hair (the coiffure itself as carefully worked as any ornament) so as to follow the features' contours.[181] As the "Lyons" maiden draws her sheathlike skirt still tighter with her hand, she performs a gesture exactly calculated to accentuate the covered forms of the body, emphasizing her buttocks and thighs. Phrasikleia also gathers her skirts as she steps, and her elaborate coiffure again curves over her shoulders and down her breasts. Nor do the sculptors restrict the viewer's imagination to the external regions of the girls' figures: the multiple folds described by the fall of the floor-length robes and the arrangement of the drapery in the "Lyons" *korē* (fig. 22) and *korē* 594 from the Acropolis give viewing an almost tactile quality and might put an audience in mind of the common equation between the woman's body and the agricultural field whose furrows had also to be ploughed.[182] The beauty of the marriageable form comes additionally to lie in the procreative functions it intimates.

On several counts, these images seem to welcome the viewer's gaze, and to announce themselves willing objects of his scrutiny. Phrasikleia smiles as she steps forward with a slight tilt of the head, and *korē* 674 from the Acropolis also inclines her head downward, acknowledging the presence of an audience and displaying the *aidōs* that any husband might wish to encounter in his future wife. Where *kouroi* generally have their fists clenched and their arms bent slightly by their side, the *korai* place one arm over their breast or, more often, hold it extended in order to present the gift of fruit, flowers, or birds that they carry. Even as the expressions and gestures allow the viewer to engage and interact with the maidens,[183] the offerings themselves are fresh reminders of the still-

[181] A slightly different scheme appears in the "Peplos" *korē* of perhaps some ten years earlier (c. 530; fig. 21) where the locks frame the breasts.
[182] See Stewart 1997: 128 for this suggestion apropos of other images.
[183] A point stressed by Osborne (1994a: 90–93), who contrasts the active, engaged *korai* with the women of high classical sculpture, depicted as passive, nonparticipant figures. In his suggestive reading, the development would have to do with the historical change in the social and economic status of women in matters of marriage and inheritance.

virginal status so central to the *korē*'s appeal: both the objects seemingly offered to the onlooker and those doing the offering are, in the familiar symbolism surrounding eros, ripening fruits and flowers ready to be plucked.[184]

But for all that they are placed in a public site in the polis and exposed to the eyes of strangers, these stone maidens in no way violate the decorum required of young girls in the late archaic and early classical age; rather, they observe all the niceties that their living counterparts' position demands. As votive offerings that lastingly duplicate the gestures of their male and female donors, they participate in the very rituals that featured prominently among the socially sanctioned activities for maidens in Athens and elsewhere; dressed in the finery that daughters from elite families would wear on the occasion of their public appearances,[185] the statues may refer quite specifically to the girls' presence in sanctuaries on the occasion of festivals, choice moments when they might attract and be appraised by prospective husbands.[186] Like their living models, too, these *korai* must temper their self-display with the proper modesty. For all their frontal gaze, the statues mostly refuse to meet the viewer's eye, overlooking him as they stand on their high bases or columns. Some even dominate quite simply on account of their size: the *korē* dedicated by the potter Nearchos and made by Antenor measures some 7 feet, and both her height and massive physique place her, quite literally, outside the spectator's grasp.

The suprahuman proportions of Antenor's *korē* not only prevent direct engagement on the viewer's part, but also serve as an unmistakable reminder of the particular role that both this and the other stone maidens occupy. Just as the perfection of the *kouroi* made them appropriate and *charis*-inspiring gifts for the gods, so, too, the outsized stature, loveliness, luster, and wealth of these self-styled *agalmata* mark them out as destined for immortal recipients. Fresh assertions that these are objects aimed toward the gods, not available to mortal men, come from the inscriptions included on the statue bases, which position the *korai* as objects that circulate,[187] but strictly limit the participants to the exchange. So the message on Antenor's *korē* runs, "Nearchos the potter

---

[184] Note, too, that many of these objects are those which *erastai* present to their *erōmenoi* in contemporary courting scenes.

[185] In Euripides' later *Electra* (175–85), the protagonist would lament her want of rich clothing for precisely such an occasion.

[186] But note the curious disjuncture between the status of some of the donors, and that of the *korai*: as *CEG* 193 and 205 illustrate, the images might be dedicated by those performing trades that kept them out of the top social rank. Should we perhaps read the images as bids for social prestige?

[187] So Osborne 1994a: 89–92 and 93–94, with discussion of the *korē*'s value as symbolic capital and object of exchange.

dedicated me as a tithe of his works to Athena" (*CEG* 193), while another inscription announces that "Naulochos dedicated this *korē* as a tithe of the catch that the ruler of the sea with the golden trident gave him" (*CEG* 266).[188] Still more explicit is *CEG* 205, which names Thebades as maker of the statue and observes that "this *charis*-filled *agalma*" exists for Pallas Athena (cf. *CEG* 422). On one early occasion this statement of divine possession comes accompanied by a listing of the several male kin who surround the donor and declares their continued guardianship over both the woman and her stand-in at the site: the mid-seventh-century *korē* from Delos bears the massage, "Nikandre dedicated me to the far-shooter of arrows, the excellent daughter of Deinodikos of Naxos, sister of Deinomenes, wife of Phraxos" (*CEG* 403).

As funerary images, *korai* also announce themselves to be inaccessible. Phrasikleia holds a lotus at her breast, a symbol of her still-unplucked state and a seeming affirmation of her readiness for marriage. But the words that the figure speaks through the medium of the viewer as he contemplates the monument put paid to any hopes that her maidenhood might arouse, and emphatically declare her fertility not just unrealized but also unrealizable: "I shall forever be called maiden (*korē*), since in place of marriage this name is what the gods have allotted me" (*CEG* 24). Much as the heroic death of the warrior was the precondition for the beauty he displayed when represented in *kouros* form, so the maiden's demise is the price that preservation of her eternally ripening youth, beauty, and chastity exacts, and once again the attributes that earlier were hers have come to reside instead in the lovely, and necessarily unattainable, monument.[189] Written into Phrasikleia and other such funerary monuments are the much-rehearsed ambivalences surrounding a girl's passage from maidenhood to bride and wife: dressed in finery evocative of the garments she would wear for her marriage, she has taken death as her bridal partner in place of the living husband who might seek her for his own.

Nike

The *korai* standing in sanctuaries and burial grounds are testaments to private, particular moments of success or loss. But the images of Nike that sculptors of the late archaic and classical periods create belong very

---

[188] Cf. *CEG* 202.

[189] In another of the few inscriptions that survive from *korai* as grave markers, the image celebrates its own capacity to charm a viewer while distinguishing itself from the dead maiden: "[Philton] (?) set down this memorial of his dead child, a memorial fine to behold, and Phaidimos made it" (*CEG* 18).

much to the communal as well as the individual realm, and are frequently designed to commemorate or encourage triumphs achieved by the polis at large. Heirs to the *korai* on several stylistic grounds, and illustrative of the evolving modes in which female desirability could be publicly represented, these statues also pose a fresh set of questions: what in the nature of the goddess or in the context of the sites where she is set determines Nike's progressive sexualization, and what does the erotic edge so patent within these accounts reveal about contemporary notions of eros in public enterprises?

A rapid glance at the evolution of images of Nike from the sixth to the end of the fifth century shows that artists and sculptors alike invest the figure with growing powers of attraction, and an ever more pronounced femininity. The rather monstrous creature that appears in the Gorgonlike *knielauf* scheme in early sixth-century accounts yields to the graceful floating or flying figure chiefly associated with the Berlin Painter. On one occasion the goddess holds her chiton up to display a very pretty pair of ankles (*LIMC* 14), and on a red-figure cup by Douris (*ARV*² 446, 263) the folds of the garment follow the movements of her body, tracing out the contours of her limbs. Vase painters may even accompany the figure with a *kalē* inscription, indicating the response that the visitation should garner.[190] So, too, at the end of the sixth century, there is a change in the form and appearance of plastic accounts of Nike. Like their painted counterparts, the small-scale bronze figures produced in Athens pick up their dresses with one or both hands in a gesture that serves to emphasize their daintiness and grace, and one such Nike appears holding a small object, probably a bud, that recalls the flowers and tendrils so frequently displayed by the goddess on painted pottery.[191] While earlier marble Nikai from the Acropolis are well under life-size and show a fast-moving, spritelike creature, now the representations become larger, more feminine, and more graceful.

Several of the large-scale figures dated to the turn of the decade additionally incorporate the innovations used to endow the *korai* with their particular appeal. A Nike in the Acropolis Museum (AM 691) displays tresses that curve sharply over the goddess's breast, and, like one of the *korai*, Kallimachos's Nike,[192] dated to c. 490, would have pulled her chiton up with the right hand now missing from the elbow. The treatment of the garment is particularly careful here, and a harbinger of things to come. The artist has arranged the cloth so as to draw the

---

[190] E.g., *LIMC* 113.

[191] For these, see Mark 1979: 36, 46.

[192] On the question of whether the figure depicts Nike or Iris, as some have suggested, see Lippold 1950: 79; Stewart 1990: 131–32.

viewer's attention to the most desirable areas of the goddess's anatomy and to accentuate their contours: the eye is invited to follow the lines of the swallowtail drapery upward, coming to rest on the small, high breast (considered the ideal type of the feature); here the garment loses its former heaviness and solidity, molding itself closely against the curves of the flesh.

Contemporary literary sources supply their own matching conceits, painting a charming goddess capable of existing in close, even amorous, relations with those on whom she bestows her favors. She not only appears as a lovely dark-tressed maiden (Bacchyl. 5.33), but also is a figure who, in the Pindaric formulation, grants both her gifts and her person in the form of what seems an almost erotic consummation. In *Nemean* 5.41–42 Pindar imagines how his Aiginetan subject "twice fell into the arms of Nike and touched the variegated songs," having won a victory in the "lovely armed glen of Nisos" (46), and elsewhere he recalls how the heralds proclaimed the winner "as he fell into the lap of golden Nike" (*Isthm.* 2.25–26). No less suggestive are the poet's personifications of agonistic victory in the shape of a lovely nubile girl whom the victor must woo, cull, and bear off as bride from the site of the games.[193]

In connecting Nike with a sexual felicity either actualized or soon to occur, Pindar points the way toward later fifth-century representations of the goddess. Now many of the images are marked by a still greater degree of sensuality, and nowhere more resoundingly than in the monumental figure of c. 420 (fig. 10) produced by Paionios for the Messenians and their Naupaktian colonists to dedicate at Olympia following their victory at Pylos. Here the statue-maker uses variations in the texture of the deity's garment to exhibit her physique to full advantage. Where the windblown gown billows out from the body, it appears massive and thick, but where it comes into contact with the figure, it clings to the legs and torso, now filmy and thin in character. The folds of the drapery also enable the artist to draw the eye to certain regions of the body. A series of semicircular lines, recalling the shape of the female vulva hidden from view, points to the area between the thighs, while other folds lead upward to the left breast, bared as the windblown draperies open at the shoulder in the course of the goddess's flight. Nor is there any mistaking the erotic character that the motif of the exposed breast would carry.[194] Both the peplos and the chiton that fifth-century

[193] E.g., *Ol.* 1.22 (which Gildersleeve would render as Hieron "brought to victory's embrace"); *Pyth.* 9.71–75; *Nem.* 2.20–22 (note the earlier evocation of the victor culling the fairest bloom of the Isthmian games at line 4); *Isthm.* 2.28–29.

[194] For this and the other examples I cite, see B. Cohen 1997.

women wore were designed fully to cover the female form, and in both visual and literary accounts, a voluntary baring of the breast acts as a sign of sexual willingness and solicitation: so the eager Danae bares both breasts as Zeus arrives in the form of a golden shower on a Boeotian calyx-krater from the late fifth century (Paris Louvre 925), and Euripides famously imagines Helen seeking to rekindle the irate Menelaus's desires after the close of the Trojan War by uncovering her breast (*Andr.* 629). That the flight of Paionios's Nike motivates her own disarray does nothing to lessen the charge of the partial nudity; instead, the viewer may enjoy the sensation of having caught the divinity in accidental dishabille.

Some five to ten years later, the creators of the goddesses on the parapet surrounding the Temple of Athena Nike at Athens would use these and other techniques to endow their figures with equivalent powers of seduction. The sculptor of the so-called Nike Sandal-binder (fig. 23) fashions the pleats of the garment so as to emphasize the point where belly and thighs meet, only then to conceal the area in heavy shadows and many folds of cloth. Like Paionios's goddess, this maiden is caught in a moment when parts of the body are exposed to view: as she bends down to touch her foot, the chiton slips from her shoulder, baring the right breast in its fall. The gesture prompting this revelation allows the viewer's imagination free rein: whether we should understand the figure in the act of removing or of fastening the sandal, the motif reappears on contemporary marriage vases and characterizes the young girl as she prepares for her role as bride.[195]

If the exposure of the breast is no more than the accidental by-product of the goddess's pose, then both the Sandal-binder and her companions advertise the delights of their young, *charis*-filled bodies in more calculated manner. They come dressed in diaphanous clothing that gives an illusion of virtual transparency, and the "ribbon drapery" used to carve their garments is cut in such a way as to enhance the impression of translucency (figs. 9, 23, and 24).[196] Aristophanes provides ample proof of the sexual incitement implicit in this mode of dress: the women in his *Lysistrata* recognize the power they can exercise by putting on their "lawn shifts," clothes made of *amorgis*, an extra-fine, expensive, and diaphanous cloth,[197] which is designed to arouse their husbands and to make the women's abstinence still harder to endure (150–51). Such

[195] Oakley and Sinos 1993: 16, 18 with examples.
[196] On "ribbon drapery," Ridgway 1981: 111–14; Stewart 1990: 166. Cf. the Nereid monument of 390–380, whose figures show close affinities with those of the Nike parapet; all three Nereids wear windblown drapery, and one in particular has a garment transparent over her abdomen and belly.
[197] Schol. ad Ar. *Lys.* 735; Aeschin. 1.97; ps.-Plato *Epistulae* 13.363a.

delicate and transparent clothing even plays a role in Lysistrata's plot from the very start: "That's exactly what I'm counting on to save Greece — our pretty saffron gowns and our perfumes and our river-boat slippers and our rouge and our see-through shifts" (46–48).

Even Athena Nike herself (fig. 24), displayed in a markedly languorous pose on the south side of the parapet, seems touched by the prevailing mood, and appears divested of the virginal and martial character that distinguishes her in other contexts. Although she displays a body more mature than those of her handmaidens, it, too, has a patent sensuality, and once again the goddess's garment slips from one shoulder, baring the breast beneath. Accentuating the figure's allure, and making the partial nudity look like more than mere negligence, is the gesture the goddess performs, holding up her himation in one hand from behind.

But if fifth-century statue-makers did endow their depictions of Nike with markedly seductive powers, why does this particular personification exhibit such pronounced sexuality? What connection might exist between the fact of victory and eros, and what prompts their combination in these several accounts?[198] According to one recent analysis, Nike's teasing sensuousness would signal the tantalizing but elusive quality of the phenomenon that she instantiates. The sandal-binder who calls the viewer's eye to her pubic area, only then to block his gaze, and the Nike at Olympia who floats on high ever beyond the spectator's reach announce that victory, for all its patent desirability, remains eternally outside the grasp, constantly escaping the viewer who thinks to hold it down.[199] But a second discussion notes that a message of inaccessibility ill accords with the context of the representations. Paionios's goddess and the Nikai on the parapet are officially sanctioned works, commissioned by the different city-states and set up to serve as testaments or exhortations to success on the field of battle.[200] Far from expressing the remoteness of victory and visualizing that "eros for the absent" which Thucydides describes, the Messenians' dedication affirms that they have enjoyed the benefits of divine intervention and can lastingly exhibit their signal good fortune in the form of a statue financed from the spoils of their enemies. The very repetition of the Nikai on the Athenian temple parapet (coupled with Athena's own presence on each of the frieze's three sides) emphatically declares the goddesses present,

[198] Note, too, the closely overlapping iconographies of Eros and Nike in vase painting and small-scale bronze representations. While this may have to do with the gods' common connection with fertility (as suggested by Mark 1979), the affinities require additional explanation.
[199] So Osborne (1994a: 86) stresses the unfulfilled nature of the promise Nike holds out.
[200] Stewart 1997: 128, 148, 253.

and might even seek to overdetermine the fact of victory at a moment
in the Peleponnesian War when success no longer seemed assured.[201]
The persuasive rhetoric implicit in the representations should work on the
mortal viewer, too: the citizen soldier who must hazard his life on the
polis's behalf is assured that victory not only is worth striving for, but
lies within his reach. Quite uniquely here, he is invited in a sanctioned
public context to take pleasure in the body that mortal women are
bound to cover up, and to imagine himself the recipient of its divine
owner's favors.

While the public nature of these monuments and their place in peer-
polity interactions at panhellenic sites argue for this second reading, the
single most characteristic feature of the goddess must complicate her
relations to the eros that victory both arouses and satisfies. Initially no
more than traits derived from the larger group of Near Eastern Flü-
gelfrauen (the daemonic and chthonic winged beings from whom Greek
artists first borrowed the type), and indicators of the deity's function as
conveyor of the victory that must be brought from gods to men, Nike's
wings and her power of flight increasingly attract the attention of both
painters and sculptors.[202] The sixth-century figure from Delos, assigned
by some to that same Archermos whom a scholion (ad Ar. Av. 574)
names as the first artist to have endowed Nike with wings, combines the
older pinwheel pose used for the running Gorgon with the winged Artemis scheme, and lifts both her feet off the ground. The Berlin Painter
replaces the goddess in her *knielauf* position with a maiden shown
gracefully flying and floating in mid-air,[203] and several decades later the
maker of the image of Nike from Paros (c. 470) follows suit: his goddess swoops down from heaven, skimming the ground with her left
foot, and the slight twist in the body enhances the illusion of flight.
Toward the century's close, Paionios's windblown figure, equipped with
its vast wings that cut through the air, defies all attempts to obstruct or
arrest its swift passage. Although earthbound, the winged Nikai on the
temple parapet also retain the capacity for rapid movement so pronounced elsewhere: their swirling, rippling drapery invests even the
static figures with a dynamic quality, and the Nike who reaches down to
her sandal may be poised to take her leave.

To possess wings, as the Greek lyric poets already suggest, is to be
deeply implicated in the workings of desire. Well before late archaic

---

[201] For this anxiety, Stewart 1997: 148; see, too, Castriota (1992: 179), who notes the
references back to the successful Persian Wars, which the decorative scheme also includes.
[202] The vast majority of Nikai in both visual and plastic accounts are winged; the rare
exceptions are documented in *LIMC* nos. 370–76.
[203] E.g., *LIMC* nos. 12, 13, 14; 94, 96, 97, 98.

artists begin to portray Eros as a winged creature, Sappho, Anakreon, and others all describe love as the sensation of being winged: the heart flies "like a wing" in the lover's chest (Sappho fr. 31.5–6 LP), *pothos* flutters around the beloved (Sappho fr. 22.9–13 LP), and the *erastēs* rises up to Olympus "on light wings on account of Eros" (Anakreon 378 *PMG*; cf. Ar. *Av.* 1372).[204] Fifth-century dramatists embroider on the conceit: one tragic chorus "shivers in eros" prior to flying upward in delight (Soph. *Aj.* 693), and Aristophanes sounds endless variations on the bond between desire, arousal, wings, and flight in his *Birds*.[205] Vase painters supply images to complement the texts. The winged youth who appears on a series of vessels from the first half of the fifth century in the act of importuning, pursuing, and embracing ephebic boys (sometimes consummating the affair while poised in mid-air) is none other than Eros himself,[206] experiencing the very desire that he arouses and directs. Wings also characterize other gods, goddesses, and mythical creatures whom painters depict regularly or almost exclusively engaged in erotic pursuits: the winged Eos, Boreas, and Zephyros all fly after the objects of their desire, and vase painters imagine a cluster of monstrous hybrids — Sirens and Sphinxes among them — whose wings seem to form a piece with their pronounced taste for pursuing and even raping beautiful young men.

As Nicole Loraux explains the association between eros and flight, "The Greek structure of desire dictates that one needs wings to approach what flies and is ever elusive. But the (Greek) structure of desire also dictates that even as one beholds the winged object, one is painfully deprived of it."[207] This account matches the several positions that visual and plastic representations of Nike allow the viewer to adopt, and whose selection depends on his own changing public and private circumstances. As winged lover, or maidenly bride-to-be, the goddess arrives unsolicited and stands ready to dispense her favors on her protégés; she might even visualize that socially prohibited but no less tempting thought of a woman who actively seeks out the more reluctant male partner, and whose sexuality offers no dangers (as Eos's so notoriously does), but only its delights (fig. 25).[208] To look on the figure in all her beauty and sensuality is to feel oneself sought-after and winged in

[204] See, too, Anakreon 379 *PMG*; Alcaeus 283.3–6 LP.
[205] E.g., 703–4, 793–96. On these and other pairings of wings and eros in the play and beyond, see Arrowsmith 1973.
[206] As persuasively argued by Shapiro 1992.
[207] Loraux 1995: 205.
[208] For this reading of Eos, Osborne 1996. In several painted representations, Nike does take on the role of active pursuer of the victorious youth; see particularly *LIMC* nos. 316, 317, 321, 324, 345.

turn and to experience those sensations of desirability, flight, and erotic consummation that Pindar links so closely with the attainment of a more individualized triumph: at the instant that the athlete takes his prize, he not only mingles with and is embraced by Nike, or claims her in the form of a lovely bride, but he also rises upward on the wings that she and the crown she bears bestow. So at *Ol.* 14.24 one adolescent victor "has garlanded his young hair with the wings of the proud *aethla* [the prize of the contest]," while Aristomenes, having just achieved his own victory, "flies out from hope on wings of manly achievement" (*Pyth.* 8.89–91).[209] Still more explicit is the conflation of marital and agonistic felicity at the very close of *Pythian* 9, where Alexidamos, paradigmatic ancestor of the present-day youthful laudandus, appears as bridegroom and victor both: "Many leaves did they fling on him, and many wings of victory had he received before" (124–25).[210]

But the wings that characterize the goddess also present her to an audience in a second and potentially less satisfying light, one that may undermine the "official" message that the image broadcasts. As the embodiment of the object that the lover eternally pursues, she figures a different facet of victory as the Pindaric songs also construe it. No less rapid in her departures than in her visitations,[211] the goddess and the pleasures she brings may abide for no more than a single moment, and in the words of *Pythian* 8, all mortal delight no sooner shoots up than it falls to the ground (92–93). As Pausanias's (doubtless incorrect) interpretation of the so-called Wingless Victory at Athens would later point out, the only way of keeping Nike by your side is to strip her of the wings on which she would otherwise flee (3.15.7). For victims of the battle of Pylos and members of other defeated city-states who witnessed Paionios's image at Olympia, and for Athenians less and less convinced that victory over Sparta and its allies could be secured, the Nikai conceived by the artists might prove anything but a source of confidence. Like the mortal instigators of the viewers' eros, these goddesses are fickle and shifting in their favors, and exhibit their charm-filled bodies to provoke rather than to satisfy.

---

[209] Note the contrast with the defeated contestants who "slink homeward," and arouse no *charis* at their return (85–87).

[210] For the conflation of *phullobolia* (the leaves thrown at the victor) and *katachusmata* (the shower of foodstuffs and other goods bestowed on the bridal pair) here, see Carson 1982: 123. Note, too, the closing of Aristophanes' *Birds*, which hails Pisthetairos as groom and victor both and calls into play the erotic connotations of wings and flight by suggesting that the desiring husband also raises up the new bride (1760–65).

[211] This is the point argued by Osborne (1996: 69), who suggests that fifth-century artists are "exploiting the parallelism between the impossibility of sustaining the peak of sexual desire and the impossibility of grasping Victory firmly."

The Rape of the Lapiths

The Nikai described above display and even bare parts of their bodies without external constraint. But partial nudity, and most particularly the exposure of the breast, more regularly occurs in monumental art when mortal women find themselves under attack and are cast as the targets of male sexual aggression. Artists in the classical period show no reticence about exploring these episodes (although they relegate them strictly to the mythical domain) and privilege one such scenario on a series of public buildings that span the fifth century and occupy several different sites throughout Greece. Chosen chiefly for the political and ethical issues that the incident can be made to articulate, the rape of the Lapiths additionally allows sculptors to break the taboo surrounding the public display of the nude female body,[212] and in so doing to raise questions concerning men's relations to their own passions and displays of masculinity; for even as these accounts present the viewer with a portrayal of the feminine body calculated to arouse his desires, they prompt a series of reflections that might recall the dangerous and unwanted consequences of acting on the feelings he quite naturally entertains.

The decorations on the Temple of Zeus at Olympia include a depiction of two contrasting episodes.[213] In the frieze on the east pediment, the decorously draped and maidenly Hippodameia (fig. 26) stands drawing the veil from her head, announcing by the gesture her willingness to become Pelops's bride. But on the west pediment, where the Lapith women struggle to resist the assault of the centaurs, the viewer encounters a very different account of relations between the sexes. One beast already has his hand on the new bride's bared breast as she gestures to protect it, and while his right leg presses up against her buttocks, she attempts to push his head away with her elbow (fig. 27). Another Lapith maiden struggles to thrust off the arm of the centaur enfolding her, while a fresh attacker reaches forward to draw her garment away from the already semi-naked form. Her peplos is unpinned at her left shoulder, leaving her breast exposed.

The motif of the body divested in an act of violence returns in the Parthenon's own account of this wedding banquet gone so badly awry. The centaur depicted on south metope 29 carries off a protesting Lapith

---

[212] For discussion of developments in female nudity in painting and statue-making, Bonfante 1989; Sutton 1992; Havelock 1995: 31, 35; Stewart 1997: chap. 2, 101–2. That representations of unclad women could provide titillation, vase paintings of the period unmistakably affirm; for this, see Sutton 1992: 21–24.

[213] For the contrast, Stehle and Day 1996: 103.

woman, her left breast already bared, and on south metope 10, another
young victim under attack may have both her breasts exposed. In a
third and much more brutal evocation of the same event, this time on
the frieze of the Temple of Apollo Epikourios at Bassai in southwest
Arkadia (c. 400), one of the women assaulted by a centaur clearly expresses fear, resistance, and unwillingness in her pose (fig. 28); she has
sought refuge by an unprotecting idol of Artemis and lets her head loll
back in despair as her attacker tears away her ripped garment, laying
bare the naked, heavy body framed against its robe.[214] Just as depictions
of the rape of Cassandra on fifth-century vases like to juxtapose the
half-nude maiden (sometimes shown with her torso or body wholly exposed as Ajax pulls the garment off her fleeing form)[215] with the heavily
draped image of Athena to which she vainly runs or clings, so, too, the
makers of the Bassai frieze contrast the mortal figure in dishabille with
the modestly clad and virginal Artemis. If viewers needed a reminder of
the way women should properly appear, both in life and in the monumental art of the period, then the idol would recall the norm.

But while the figures' partial nudity underscores both their vulnerability and the larger pathos of their situation,[216] the artists also sound a
counternote in these several scenes. Again like the red-figure vase
painters who give Cassandra a voluptuous and shapely body in place of
the diminutive and childlike physique of earlier black-figure accounts,
these sculptors endow the women under attack with a marked sensuality and allure. The Lapith maidens at Olympia have figures that correspond to men's constructions of an ideal femininity, featuring the small,
compact, and firm breasts, broad shoulders, and large calves and thighs
found in women in erotic contexts on contemporary vase representations.[217] And at Bassai, the women's demeanor and pose seem an even
more potent invitation to assault. With breast, belly, and pubic triangle
on conspicuous display, the Lapith bride clinging to the Artemis image
presents her body to the viewer and invites him imaginatively to dwell
on the still more unspeakable acts to come.[218] Other future victims of

---

[214] Evident in these compositions is what Nochlin (1991: 15) has called, in reference to
very different images, the "binary division between male energy, tension and concentration as opposed to female resignation, flaccidity and relaxation."

[215] See particularly the Attic red-figure Nolan amphora dated to c. 440 (Metropolitan
Museum of Art 56.171.41). For detailed discussion of the episode in vase painting, B.
Cohen 1993 and Connelly 1993.

[216] Emphasized by Bonfante (1989: 560, 561). Note that one of the Lapith women at
Bassai carries a baby in her arms, her maternity giving her a particular poignancy; so, too,
the victims' frontal faces make direct appeal to the viewer.

[217] For these, Dover 1978: 70–71.

[218] See Nochlin 1991: 18 on the "fantasy potential" of such moments. Note, too, the

attack on the frieze wear the provocatively diaphanous garments used for the Nikai at Olympia and at Athens, leaving visible their well-fleshed, even meaty bodies in their see-through clothing.

Also complicating the viewer's reaction is the role of the centaurs themselves, and their problematic relation to the "real" men depicted in the scenes. While the creatures act in accordance with the fantasy hyper-masculinity that the myths surrounding them spell out and offer cautionary lessons in what happens when male instincts and desires go unchecked in communal settings, each monument in its own way acknowledges the proximity of the beasts and their human counterparts.[219] The very violence practiced by the centaurs is the necessary precondition for both Heracles' and Pelops's "civilizing" successes on the metopes and east pediment at Olympia, and the Parthenon artists allow no easy distinctions between the assailants and their Lapith hosts, choosing on several occasions (south metopes 30 and 32 most particularly) to downplay the bestial aspect of the former, and to highlight their affinity to those whom they attack. At Bassai, the role assumed by the centaurs as fighters and pursuers of female victims is then transferred to a properly human party in the second episode that the interior frieze displays, where Greek men direct their blows at women as they battle against the Amazons using martial violence in their turn. Looking from one wall of the building to the other, the visitor would see reiterated in the Amazons the bared breasts and transparent garments that characterized the Lapith victims, and perhaps note the links between the erotic and military spheres rehearsed on both occasions. Nor would he enter the temple predisposed to condemn the abduction of women as the act of mere degenerates: instead he would have encountered the porch metopes, where the undeniably heroic Dioskouroi bear off the daughters of the Messenian king Leukippos.

In each instance both the uneasy status of the centaurs vis-à-vis the man or men cast in the hero's role and the Lapith women's erotic appeal confront viewers with questions concerning their own susceptibility to passion, and the costs and benefits of exercising both self-control and collective restraint in the presence of female objects of desire. By manifesting what normally remains hidden from sight, or belongs only to painted images featuring the world of the demi-mondaine, the artist

---

wounded Niobid in the Terme museum, considered a Greek original of c. 440–430; here the maiden bends her right arm back over her head to pull the arrow out, a gesture that causes her dress to fall away and reveal her breasts and naked torso (framed, as usual, by the drapery folds); on the different readings this prompts, some signaling the beauty of the "body that has just blossomed in womanhood," others stressing the mingling of pain, sex, and violence, see Golden 1988: 12.

[219] For this and several of the points that follow, Osborne 1994b.

arouses his audience and prompts him to envision the completion of the action whose commencement he describes. This mode of viewing makes the individual complicit in the deed that the centaur performs and reinforces the affinities between man and beast that the decorative schemes themselves include: both groups represented participate in acts of collective violence, both attempt to tame and subdue women (sometimes in a fully sanctioned form), and both find their instinct for competition or battle stimulated, for good and ill, in the face of the desirable and seemingly available female body. While many representations of centaurs (and more markedly satyrs, too) allow the viewer "sexually to identify with yet at the same time morally to distance himself" from the figures,[220] these several accounts have left distinctions between beast and man sufficiently blurred as to block so comfortable a stance, and instead the individual who responds to the women's erotic appeal must lose something of that superiority that comes with being human, male, and Greek.[221] That this loss and surrender to the "baser" passions is the precondition for the civilizing achievements that the monuments also celebrate is the larger paradox that their sculptural programs exhibit.

Surrounded by alluring bodies, male and female, naked, fully clad, or in their partial dishabille, Greek viewers inhabiting both historical cities and literary sites were invited to respond to images of stone and bronze and to reckon with the consequences of the amorous sensations that statues could provoke. But where the textual and visual evidence most closely correspond is not merely in their demonstration that works of art may be potent objects of desire, turning audiences into *erastai* of what they see, but in their use of statues to sound the nature of eros, and to determine what it is that gives a human body its prime source of appeal.

On two counts, I have suggested, the fashioned image is ideally poised to answer these questions, and to figure and illuminate the sensations that a lover experiences. First, because of the unilateral nature of eros as it so regularly appears in the Greek account, that cruel division between the lover's longing and the beloved's lack of response, the bronze or marble work exactly tropes the dynamic between the two parties. Able to arouse *pothos* but not to satisfy the passion it instigates, it emblematizes both the objectification of the *erōmenos* through the

---

[220] Nochlin 1991: 23.

[221] Contrast the gloss that Nochlin (ibid.) suggests for Gerôme's painting of a lovely nude woman being sold at an Oriental slave market. Gerôme, she proposes, is saying in effect: "Don't think that I, or any other right-thinking Frenchman, would ever be involved in this sort of thing. I am merely taking careful note of the fact that less enlightened races indulge in the trade in naked women — but isn't it arousing!"

lover's eyes, and the power, remoteness, and even representational status with which this transformation endows its original object. And second, because the statue-maker could invest his image with all the enduring and unblemished loveliness that changing, aging, mortal bodies cannot achieve, the depiction of an individual in the form of a statue allows its subject to realize all the qualities that lovers endlessly pursue, and confirms that impossible dream of figures that remain forever young, beautiful, *charis*-filled, and exposed to the viewer's eye.

In the myths and anecdotes that the Greek and Roman writers of the imperial age would go on to relate, the issues sounded by the earlier sources reappear in explicit and exaggerated fashion. The youth who shuts himself in a temple in a vain attempt to satisfy his longing for the marble body of Praxiteles' Aphrodite of Knidos,[222] Pygamalion, whose passion for the work he has carved produces the miracle of vivification, and Narcissus, who pines away in longing for the representation of himself,[223] all fall prey to the seductive qualities that images host, and that can drive audiences to the acts of folly that the texts take such delight in describing. But for all the apparent thematic continuity between the earlier and later tales, the imperial authors' narratives are themselves products of a very different aesthetic (and religious) sensibility and a changed culture of viewing. Where they privilege the role of the artist and his own relationship to the work he has produced,[224] and play on the assumption that the distinction between the fashioned image and the living being can be overcome,[225] audiences of earlier times may have approached representations from a quite different perspective: for those who first looked on the Knidia, the goddess's marble form might have been not first and foremost an object of desire, but a mirror in which an audience of men, and still more markedly of women, too, could understand their own capacity to arouse eros through their bodies transfigured into works of art.

[222] For ancient accounts of the Knidia, and the youth who tried to make love to her, [Lucian] *Amores* 13–17; Pliny *HN* 36.20–21.
[223] Note particularly Ov. *Met.* 3.418–19, where the likeness of the reflection to a marble statue is underscored.
[224] For the anecdotes suggesting that Praxiteles used his own mistress Phryne as model, Ath. 13.590, and Havelock 1995: 3, 47–49.
[225] For this shift, see Osborne 1998: 234–35.

CHAPTER FIVE

The Image in the Text

PINDAR'S FIFTH *Nemean*, composed to celebrate Pytheas's triumph in the pankration, opens with some negative advertising: "I am not a maker of statues as to fashion idling *agalmata* standing on their bases" (1–2). The declaration prompts a scholiast to tell an explanatory anecdote. The parents of the victor Pytheas, he reports, went to Pindar to commission an ode to celebrate their son's triumph. Horrified at the price demanded by the poet (some 3,000 drachmas), they decided that they would do better to have a bronze statue made. But the athlete's parents suffered further indecision, and, returning to Pindar, they gave him the commission after all. The opening lines of the poem supposedly approve their choice, evoking the statue fixed to its pedestal by way of foil to the moving, sounding song that the encomiast has devised for his patrons (2–5).

The opposition set up in these opening lines, and the scholiast's fanciful recreation of the rivalry between Pindar and the *andriantopoios*, anticipate current views of why poets (ancient and modern both) choose to introduce visual representations into their verbal compositions.[1] Discussions regularly focus on the paragonal character of the device that pits the two media against one another, and showcases the struggle between the narrative impulse of speech and the fixed form of the crafted object.[2] While the model of two rival modes matches some of the scenarios traced out in the ancient texts, archaic and classical authors commonly construct a more intricate interplay between the artifact and song. Pindar's fifth *Nemean*, as my later reading of the piece will suggest, replaces the initial division with a symbiotic relationship between the statues and ode and shows how they mingle and exchange their roles and attributes. By the end of the performance, the poet has created a partnership that redeems the disparaged *agalmata* and demonstrates the song's dependence on a statue for its own future life. Nor is Pindar alone in using the properties of artifacts to enhance the merits of his

---

[1] The "verbal representation of visual representation" is the definition that Heffernan (1993: 3) gives to ekphrasis. I avoid the term "ekphrasis" here because this chapter will include many passages in the ancient sources that refer to, rather than describe, statues, and that present them in ways that do not conform to ekphrasis as currently understood.
[2] See particularly Mitchell 1986 and Heffernan 1993: 1–7 and passim.

product; authors both before and after him embed plastic representations in their works not so much to contest or challenge the image's claim as to harness its powers to their poetry or prose. The uncanny activities of statues explored in the previous chapters will reappear in this more bounded form: the object that can amaze, entrance, petrify, and generate love in its viewers, that can move, see, and even talk, lends its many dimensions to the text, transferring its affective and performative faculties to the words that describe and surround it, and granting to the more ephemeral composition something of its own material character.

I end with these exchanges between the statue and its verbal frame not only because they reaffirm the powers assigned to images so far, but also because they illuminate a critical dimension of textual appeals to sculpted works that earlier chapters have only glanced toward. For all its importance as a vehicle for epistemological, metaphysical, and emotional concerns, the statue more narrowly satisfies a reflexive end, permitting the composer of a song or speech to scrutinize his own activity and to hold that activity up for display; for image-maker read author, for statue the poem or address, and for statue-viewer substitute the reader or listener to the piece. Sometimes positive and sometimes negative paradigms for the act of composition and "reader response," the statue offers a device that can mirror back the surrounding work, commenting on its genesis, character, and lasting impact.

THE FUNERARY MONUMENT

Pindar's fifth *Nemean* presupposes that victor statues (the *agalmata* referred to in the opening lines) and odes have a common purpose: both aim to celebrate and memorialize the athlete's triumph in the games. The kinship assumed by the encomiast informs many other visual and verbal products of the archaic and early classical ages; songs and plastic representations similarly serve to commemorate the dead, to celebrate outstanding individuals among the living, and, most broadly, to promote memory and *kleos*. In one formulation, "for a hymn, a dirge, a victory ode, and an encomium, one may substitute a temple frieze, a gravestone, a victor statue, and an honorary portrait. All alike praise the *aretē* of the recipient through a 'far-shining memorial' (*tēlauges mnēma*) that confers 'undying glory' (*kleos aphthiton*) upon him or her."[3] But evidence from the archaic age suggests that visual and verbal media did not so much offer independent avenues of memory and praise

---

[3] Stewart 1990: 54. The tale told of Hipponax (Pliny *HN* 36.11–12)) neatly reverses this idea: the blame poet encounters the statue type that, in prompting abuse, most exactly replicates the function of his own particular product.

as more frequently form partners in a single enterprise. Accounts of the commemoration of the dead in epic song regularly harness the two kinds of memorialization to one another, showing how frequently each depends on the other and builds on its character and claims: no artifact without the speech that disseminates its message, and no verbal renown without some monument to spark it off.

The *Iliad* and the *Odyssey* feature a series of man-made objects explicitly designed to preserve the names and deeds of the dead. Located in the analphabetic heroic age, these monuments quite properly lack the inscriptions that might otherwise identify them as belonging to a particular individual and ensure his lasting fame. But the absence of writing in no way interferes with their efficacy, and each proves able to generate the audible acclaim, the continuous celebration in men's speech and the poet's song, that *kleos* expressly describes.[4] Agamemnon concludes his tale of the funeral rites on Achilles' behalf, and of the "great and perfect (*amumona*) grave mound" (*Od.* 24.80) heaped up for him,[5] with the promise of fame that the mound and the rituals performed in its vicinity can guarantee: "So, even now when you have died, you have not lost your name, but for all time there will be noble *kleos* among all men" (93–94).[6] More succinctly, Menelaus builds a *tumbos* for his brother, "so that his *kleos* might be unquenched" (*Od.* 4.584), and in a twist on the common scheme, Hector imagines the grave of an opponent whom he would slay as a source of *kleos* not for the dead, but for the victor in the encounter:

> And some day one of the men to come will say as he sails on the wine-dark sea in his well-benched ship: "This is the mound of a man who died long ago in battle whom glorious Hector killed." So he will speak some day and my glory will not ever be forgotten. (*Il.* 7.87–91)

The *sēma* cited by Nestor at *Iliad* 23.326–33 supplies the counterexample to this union of tomb and word: because the viewer cannot discern the precise function of the stump and stones standing in the ground, nor decide whether they served as a grave marker or as a racing goal set by men of old, the hero who may lie beneath is lastingly deprived of fame.

What allow the epic grave monuments to act as prompt and midwife

---

[4] But see Ford 1992: 131–71 for the countersuggestion that the Homeric poet deliberately devalues the physical marker and monument and calls attention to its obscurity.

[5] Note how the grave has assumed the properties, most particularly the excellence, of the hero.

[6] The tangible monument not only draws witnesses into the act of verbal commemoration, but guarantees that the celebration will continue on into future days; the funeral games that Thetis establishes for her son at the site of the grave will be cyclical events that keep his name ever fresh among generations to come.

to spoken commemoration are properties that depend on their material and visual nature. Funerary markers are first and foremost enduring objects: Homeric cairns and tombstones qualify as *empedoi*,[7] lasting fixtures in the landscape whose permanence finds a reiteration in the *kleos aphthiton* sung by the poet.[8] The choice to position Achilles' grave "on a jutting promontory by the broad Hellespont" (*Od.* 24.82) is also a considered one; visible and conspicuous (*tēlephanēs*, 83) from a great distance, it can better attract the attention of the wayfarer and impel him to pronounce the words of praise. Tombs, like *sēmata* of other kinds,[9] must be commanding presences,[10] landmarks "easily distinguished" from far and wide. The sailor whom Hector imagines passing by on board ship in *Iliad* 7.87–88 catches sight of one such carefully sited mound, and in remembering the occasion for its construction also celebrates its occupant. And in the meeting between the traveling witness in his well-benched vessel and the rooted tomb, the poet glances toward another function that the marker should fulfill: ideally it can provoke the broader dissemination of the information that it contains.[11]

Although Homeric representations of death and the commemoration of the deceased do not mirror any specific historical reality, several extant Dark Age and eighth-century monuments suggest an overlap between the world of the epics and that of the early audiences for the songs. The grandiose structure found at Lefkandi in Euboea (dated to the early tenth century, and not later than c. 950) must have been erected on behalf of a community leader, who was buried together with the pair of prestige-bestowing horses sacrificed on his grave; this literally palatial monument, so distinctive and visible, would have alerted the viewer to the exceptional nature of the man, proclaiming his wealth

---

[7] For the immobile stele, see chapter 3. For a discussion of the range of meanings covered by the term *empedos*, see Zeitlin 1996: 30–31.

[8] On the negation of decline and change that the term *aphthiton* describes, see Nagy 1979: esp. 175–89.

[9] Cf. *Il.* 2.318, 13.244, with Ford 1992: 143–44. As Sourvinou-Inwood (1995: 134) argues, when the grave marker assumes this commemorative role and is not evoked purely in terms of the physical object that constitutes it (in which case the poet uses the term *tumbos*), it is designated a *sēma*.

[10] Cf. Pind. *Ol.* 1.93–94, where Pelops's grave works in precisely this fashion: from the "much frequented *tumbos*" and altar with its many visitors, the poet moves instantly into "the fame of the Olympic festivals that shines from afar" (*to de kleos tēlothen dedorke*).

[11] Contrast the Sirens, who block the spread of *kleos*, and by immobilizing Odysseus would turn him, along with the white bones strewn on the beach, into commemorative markers of their own power. As several recent readings emphasize, the *Odyssey* itself deliberately disturbs many of the conventions that both it and the *Iliad* describe: Odysseus is the hero who may possess *kleos* quite independent of a grave, and whose fame can exist even while he lives.

and power, and would have guaranteed that his memory would be a lasting one. So, too, an impressive marker over a later Protogeometric grave, consisting of a huge prismatic stone measuring some 1.35 meters, would have generated and focused commemoration of the deceased; not surprisingly the structure is associated with significant ritual activity by subsequent generations.[12]

From the mid-seventh century on, the monument — whether it took the form of a vase, a built tomb, an unworked stone, a stele with or without sculpted decoration, a column, or a statue[13] — achieved far greater autonomy by virtue of the inscription cut onto its surface. Now the role of the ensemble as a force that activated and shaped recollection of the dead could be vastly expanded: besides recording the name, birthplace, and patronym of its inhabitant, the inscribed marker could additionally direct the viewer's response, and even supply him with the appropriate words of grief or praise.[14] But for all the novel possibilities that the written text opens up, the epitaph proves a conservative device, presenting itself as dependent on and even subordinate to its material support, announcing the virtues of the marker, and ascribing to itself many of the same attributes and functions. The symbiosis demonstrated in the Homeric songs becomes more intimate still as the inscription ties its commemorative and celebratory powers to those of the artifact.

In her detailed study of inscribed grave monuments from the archaic age, Christiane Sourvinou-Inwood establishes that in the great majority of cases the epigram includes at least one reference to the structure itself. Particularly common are the formulas "I am/This is the *sēma/mnēma* of *x*" or "*b* put up this *sēma/mnēma* for *a*"; or the term *sēma* or *mnēma* may more succinctly be followed by the name of the dead in the genitive case. Many of the texts not only name the physical artifact, but call the viewer's attention toward it, enjoining him to stop and look[15] and highlighting and spelling out the merits of the object to which they direct his eye. Where a statue or carved stele tops the grave, the beauty of the image may be noted in the inscription that styles the work an *agalma* or simply *kalon*.[16] So, too, the visibility of the *sēma*, its location in an especially prominent site, returns as a common motif,[17] and per-

---

[12] For these, see discussion in Sourvinou-Inwood 1995: 115–18, 140 n. 101.

[13] For these different possibilities, Kurtz and Boardman 1971 and Sourvinou-Inwood 1995: 142–43.

[14] Although not all archaic epitaphs contain praise formulas, many do, and clearly praise was perceived as an important if not indispensable element in the archaic epitaph; for this, Sourvinou-Inwood 1995: 172; Day 1989.

[15] E.g., *CEG* 19, 28, 68.

[16] E.g., *CEG* 18, 26, 161, 165.

[17] E.g., *CEG* 16, 39, 74, 136. Of course this visibility *does* belong to the monument: in

manence figures as another attribute that the epigram assigns to the monument of which it forms a part. Most elaborate is Kleoboulos's sixth-century epigram that privileges the enduring character of the bronze figure decorating Midas's tomb: "I am a maiden of bronze and I stand on the tomb of Midas. As long as water flows and tall trees grow, and the rising sun gives light, or the radiant moon, and rivers flow and the sea boils, here I shall remain on this sad tomb and tell passersby that Midas is buried here" (*GVI* 1171).[18]

Over and above the emphatic focus on its material support, the epigram may declare itself coextensive or consubstantial with the monument by speaking in its voice.[19] In the numerous instances in which the inscription announces itself the *mnēma* or the *sēma* of the individual — and in Jesper Svenbro's account, the standard phrase "This (*tode*) is the *sēma/mnēma* of *x*" should properly be read as an "egocentric" statement with the first person understood[20] — it assumes the persona of the tomb and/or of its decorative device.[21] Other formulas more implicitly presuppose the monument as speaker of the text: the stone may simply invoke the passerby without direct reference to itself,[22] address the dead,[23] or answer on behalf of the deceased the questions that the viewer puts to it.[24]

Neither primitive animism nor a confusion of the person of the dead with the grave marker explains this convention of the speaking monument.[25] Instead the practice follows naturally from the defining property that the inscription shares with the object it accompanies, its permanent presence at the site;[26] the monument takes on the speaker's part because neither the author of the epitaph nor the deceased can be there to fulfill the role. In asserting its "presentness," the text participates in the char-

---

Attica funerary *kouroi* were raised along the road east and south from Athens to Sounion, some even erected on tumuli.

[18] For other examples that stress the enduring nature of the monument and the eternity of the mourning that it therefore guarantees, see *CEG* 5, 89, 97, 136.

[19] As Rasche (1910: 8–9) establishes, monuments that speak for themselves predate monuments that speak for the dead. For examples, see Burzachechi 1962.

[20] Svenbro 1988: 33–52.

[21] But note that the declaration can also be read in less literal fashion, and the writing can proclaim itself the instantiation of the memory of the deceased.

[22] E.g., *CEG* 13.

[23] E.g., *CEG* 50, 69.

[24] On these, Kassel 1983: 10–11; Walsh 1991: 85. On occasion the individual who raised the monument speaks (*CEG* 136), or the reader speaks *in propria persona* (*CEG* 41, 53). The dead may also speak on their own behalf (*CEG* 80, 108).

[25] For critiques of these earlier views, Svenbro 1988: 50–51; Sourvinou-Inwood 1995: 164–67.

[26] For this argument, Svenbro 1988: 51–52.

acter of the grave structure whose chief merit lies in its stability and unmoving character, and on several occasions the inscription makes the fact of its complementary constancy the matter of a boast: the words accompanying the sixth-century statue of Phrasikleia remind the viewer that the dead will eternally be called *korē* (*CEG* 24), and the epigram on the early fifth-century tomb of the Aiginetan Mnesitheos presents itself as *akamaton*, or unwearied (*CEG* 108). So, too, Midas's bronze maiden will everlastingly declare her message to the passerby.

The very presentness of the text, its capacity to speak at any time, also determines the manner in which it seeks to perform its task and reveals another area of continuity between the inscription and the monument. In contrast to the "winged" words of the celebrant or poet, the epigram remains lastingly attached to its immobile base: "The reader moves, the stone does not, and the stone therefore needs a way to assert its presence and to capture its reader's attention."[27] As part of this attention-getting exercise, the writing first imposes itself on its audience visually rather than verbally. The mode in which the engravers place and cut the letters into the stone endows the text with the assertiveness of the raised mound, stele, or image; the stocheidon style introduced in the sixth century, and enhanced by the spatial arrangement of the inscription and the practice of painting the letters sometimes in red, or in red alternating with black, would promote the epigram's visibility, attracting the passerby, compelling him to stop and look.[28] Once an audience has been drawn to the site, the inscription might deploy other stratagems to keep him standing there. The stele of Mnesitheos (*CEG* 108) first greets the observer in friendly fashion (*chairete*), then bids him read, and further engages his curiosity by inviting him to learn "what man is buried here" before finally disclosing the requisite information.[29] If the role of the larger monument is not just to catch the viewer's eye but also to make him propagate news of the dead, then the epitaph can again lend its support: several bid the reader move on when his task is done, continuing a journey that itself allows the diffusion of memory of the deceased.[30]

Just as the text ascribes to itself the same merits and limitations that the monument possesses, it views its broader character in the terms that the grave marker has already established. Once the funerary rites are done, the tomb sealed, and the monument raised, the *sēma* becomes the

---

[27] Walsh 1991: 83.
[28] Carson 1996: 4.
[29] The inscription is discussed at length in Svenbro 1988: 57–65.
[30] E.g., *CEG* 13; cf. *Anth. Pal.* 7.318 for a play on the notion. For other examples, Walsh 1991: 79 and n. 8.

visible symbol for the new persona assumed by the dead, "and most emphatically for that part of his new persona that existed in the world of the living, that is, his memory."[31] Following the lead of the monument that physically and visually embodies that memory, rather than reproducing the deceased himself or herself, the inscription defines itself as a *sēma* or *mnēma*, the "sign" or "memory" of the dead as well as the literal marker of the grave. Frequently acknowledging itself as separate and detachable from its subject,[32] it even claims the attention and gestures of lamentation that can no longer be addressed to the physical remains.[33]

Few monuments better demonstrate these and other interfaces between artifact and text than the *korē* raised on behalf of Phrasikleia. Initially assuming the identity of the monument and attributing permanence both to the statue and to its own written message, the inscription also indicates the division between the absent maiden and the image, styling itself a substitute rather than identical with the deceased, embodiment not of her presence but of her memory; then, as the voice hovers between the statue and the dead, it suggests the existence of two distinct but closely kinned personas: "[This is/I am] the *sēma* of Phrasikleia. I shall forever be called maiden (*korē*), since in place of marriage this name is what the gods have allotted me" (*CEG* 24). But more striking still is the semantic whole that viewing and reading together build. The work of replacement that the monument silently but visibly effects

[31] Sourvinou-Inwood 1995: 120. As Day (1989) shows, the memory that endures is presented, both through the language of the epitaph and the iconographical conventions of carved stelae and funerary images, as a generic one; the dead is archetypically noble.

[32] Indeed, on many occasions the epigrams emphatically prohibit such a confusion with the dead. The common declaration that "*x* made me" patently reminds the reader of the material quality of the tombstone or image, or the inscription sharply differentiates between the *sēma* and the deceased by mentioning the two as separate entities (e.g., *CEG* 27). The tomb of one Prokleidas, dated to the second quarter of the fifth century, additionally uses its shifting tenses to open up a temporal breach between the gravestone and the now dead man: "The *sēma* here, beside the road, will call itself Prokleidas, who died while he was fighting for his country" (*CEG* 142). In no extant examples where the grave monument consists of a statue and an inscription does the name of the dead appear in the nominative; instead the *korē* or *kouros* is said to be the *sēma* or *mnēma* of the individual, rather than the individual him- or herself (for which Sourvinou-Inwood 1995: 165). In the case of the cenotaph, the metamorphosis of the physical body into a mere name on a tomb is particularly marked; so Pfohl 1967: no. 5: "This is/I am the *sēma* of Denias, whom the sea destroyed unseen."

[33] Note the complex interplay and shifting of the identities of the ego in *CEG* 159: "Whoever was not present when they carried me out in death, let him now lament me. [This is/I am] the *mnēma* of Telephanes." So, too, in *Iliad* 24.16 Achilles drags the body of Hector around the *sēma* of Patroklos, even though his dead friend's remains actually reside elsewhere.

(an image for a maiden) finds its analogue in the other exchange (the name *korē* for the missing nuptial rites) that the written words describe. So, too, while the stone image visually affirms the maiden's status as *korē* and the enduring nature of the title included in the text, the inscription's focus on the dead's *kleos*, first sounded in the name Phrasikleia, then reiterated in the term *onoma* ending the epigram, takes tangible shape in the closed lotus that the statue holds at its breast:[34] the flower, the symbol of the maidenhood that the girl will eternally enjoy, concretizes the message contained in the words, displaying both the source and the precondition of Phrasikleia's lasting renown.[35]

The funerary epitaph's symbiosis with the monument follows naturally from its particular character, its dependence on the artifact that gives it its support and frame. But the composers of epigrams are not alone in their constant references to a physical structure that can serve as the visible embodiment of an individual or collective *kleos*. For poets and orators engaged in the celebration and commemoration of individuals both dead and living, a tangible monument seems a necessary component in their compositions, and their songs and speeches glance repeatedly toward both real and notional objects which might preserve the reputation of their subjects. Cut free from an actual commemorative artifact, the poem or address most commonly makes good its lack by imagining its words a monument of a metaphoric kind, one that can appropriate and surpass the properties that a real-world counterpart might possess. So Simonides' lines recalling the dead at Thermopylae (531 *PMG*) style themselves a second *sēkos* (6) or precinct in place of the grave that actually held the bodies of the fallen, and Pindar erects a *lithos* by way of musical *sēma* for the dead Megas and his still-living son (*Nem.* 8.47);[36] in a parallel move, Perikles describes his words as a "most conspicuous tomb" and "uninscribed *mnēmē*" (Thuc. 2.43.2–3) as he strives to draw the Athenians' eyes away from the visible *dēmosion sēma* where their relatives lie interred. Statues, funerary and honorific both, supply a particularly ready source of paradigms and foils as eulogists set about this task of creating parallel and kindred "sites" for the propagation of glory.

VICTORY STATUES

As the anecdote pinned to Pindar's fifth *Nemean* illustrates, victory images recalling triumphs in the athletic games were no less critical to the

---

[34] The crown is ringed by other lotuses, alternately closed and half-open.
[35] For the lotus as symbolic of virginity, Stewart 1997: 115; for a different construction of the link between the flower and the maiden's *kleos*, Svenbro 1988: 26–29.
[36] Cf. *Nem.* 4.79–85, *Isthm.* 8.59–65.

athlete's enduring fame than epinician songs. The epigrams included on these statues' bases follow much the same patterns as those described for the funerary epitaph: they, too, speak in the voice of the image, promote its merits, and often differentiate the artifact from the living person of the athlete.[37] Like the inscribed grave markers, these statues with their epigrams reappear in the poetic celebrations composed on the winner's behalf, leaving explicit and implicit traces of their presence in the epinician odes that Pindar created. Much in the manner of those who memorialize the dead, the encomiast seeks to harness the attributes of the victory monument to his poetry, and by drawing on its design, iconography, and inscribed contents, grants it a critical role in the performance of the odes.

The most explicit instances of this embedding and appropriation involve the transformation of the poem itself into a statue, one that the encomiast's own musical talents have set up. In *Nemean 3*, Pindar introduces the youthful members of the *kōmos* waiting for the Muse by the riverbank as *tektones* eager to catch the harmonious strain from the arriving goddess (4). The poet himself shares the song that the Muse brings with the chorus and the lyre (11–12). The result of these mingled efforts is the fashioning of a decorative offering to adorn the victor's home, a *chōras agalma* or ornament of the site (13). Already the terms *tektones* and *agalma* might have turned an audience's thoughts to victory statues, but the reference to the agora in line 14 further concretizes the adornment, and defines and positions it more exactly: because Aristokleides has been victorious in the pankration, the song declares, he has not disgraced the central civic space of his home. This litotes obliquely asserts that, on the contrary, the victor's achievement has brought honor to the town square in the form of a monument; the metaphoric *agalma* has become the actual dedication decorating the city center, like the statue of Euthymos in the Lokrian marketplace, or Theagenes' statue in the agora of Thasos. Pausanias's later account of Aiginitan topography (2.29.6) allows us to understand just how precise a match Pindar has devised: in the agora of the island's leading town stood the hero shrine of Aiakos, its forefront supplying a natural site where athletic sculpture might be raised.[38] In more glancing fashion the poet reappears as the builder of a monument that adorns (*kosmein*) the victor's town (or more particularly the "broad avenues" his phrase describes) in *Nemean 6.46*, while in *Isthmian 1.14* the singer announces his readiness to construct (*teuchein*) for Herodotos an "honor (*geras*) of the four-horse chariot."[39] In these several instances, the act of poetic

---

[37] See the collection of Ebert 1972 and discussion in Kurke 1993 and Steiner 1993.
[38] As noted in Mullen 1982: 76.
[39] For other "concrete" uses of *teuchō*, see *Ol. 7.48* and *Pyth. 7.12*. *Geras* also frequently

composition can do more than create a song that doubles for the statue; it more directly resembles the sculptor's art when it succeeds in transforming the living individual into monumental form, and in *Nemean* 2.6–8 the returning victor figures as the artifact (*kosmos*) that embellishes his city.

No statue can stand without a base or pedestal, and several odes begin by constructing this firm and enduring support for the monument fashioned by the subsequent song of praise. In *Nemean* 2, Timodemos's portion of life has given him as an ornament, a *kosmos*, to Athens. This reification of the victor picks up on the conceit of the opening lines, where the poet already placed the necessary foundation stone (1–4): "From that point where also the Homeridai, the singers, start the majority of their stitched-together songs, from the prooimion of Zeus, so, too, this man has first received his foundation (*katabolan*) of victory of the sacred contests." To this neat synthesis of statue base, first win, and proem to the fabricated song corresponds the *kosmos* that is at once the victor-turned-commemorative image and the poem that celebrates his achievement. The same support appears as the opening gambit of *Pythian* 7, where a *krēpis* is set down to receive the Alkmeonid winning team: "The great city of Athens is the loveliest (*kalliston*) prooimion to cast down as a foundation stone of songs for the broad-strengthed clan of the Alkmeonids" (1–3). Again the object combines several functions: it serves as the base for the ode-to-come, implicitly presenting the song in the likeness of the monument that normally tops the foundation stone, and it recalls the actual equestrian dedications made by victors in racing events and frequently set up on the Athenian Acropolis.[40] The epithet used of the Alkmeonids looks forward to the particular merits of the *krēpis*, too, their own broad strength finding a visual match in the firm-rooted stone.

The expressions chosen by Pindar to represent these notional statues and statue bases also incorporate the other attributes that literal monuments ascribe to themselves. Just as the victory image demands the bystander's attention through its own striking appearance, repeatedly declaring in its accompanying inscription that it is "most beautiful to see," or more simply *kalon*, Pindar's musical artifacts are no less visually compelling. The terms *kosmos*, *agalma*, and *kalliston* attest to the ornamental and precious quality of the song-turned-artifact, its ability to delight the eye no less than the ear.[41] On occasions the poet replicates

---

figures as the actual prize the athlete received (*Ol.* 2.49, 8.11; *Pyth.* 5.31). When Pausanias describes what seems to be the Achaeans' failure to honor Oibotas with a statue after his victory, he begins by remarking that they gave him "no special *geras*" (7.17.13).
[40] For examples of these, Serwint 1987: 77.
[41] The same point goes more generally for other manufactured objects in the song—the

the sculptor's practice still more minutely. The readiest way for an artist to signal that his statue portrayed a victorious athlete was to include a representation of the fillet or headband bestowed on the contestant immediately after his win.[42] These sculpted wreaths, regularly decorated, painted, or even inlaid with precious stones, exactly correspond to the musical crowns that Pindar devises, and most particularly provide the model for the intricately worked (*pepoikilmenan*) *mitra* that the poet presents at the shrine of Aiakos in *Nemean* 8.13–16. Only when the articles have attracted the viewer's attention with their eye-catching beauty can they go on to declare their messages of praise; that, too, is the explicit purpose of the *krēpis* in *Pythian* 7 that makes the names of the victor and his city *epiphanesteron*, or illustrious (7).

Pindar, no less than the raiser of the statue, also ensures that the viewer of the monument he builds hears its words of praise. On many occasions the musical artifacts in the odes come complete with their own versions of the epigrams inscribed on actual victory-statue bases: these not only display the same information as their models, but actually mirror the original inscriptions in their location, form, and vocabulary.[43] In building this writing into his metaphoric *agalmata*, Pindar also replicates the purpose of the engraved notices: primarily designed to preserve the spoken victory announcement, which named the athlete, his father, and his city and might indicate the festival, event, and even age class in which the victor had competed, the messages included on statues and poetic artifacts alike turn the monuments into lasting reenactments of the moment when the herald proclaimed the winner as he stood to receive his crown.[44] And just as a variety of syntactic devices deployed in the victory epigrams serve to endow the monuments with the powers of speaking their subject's praise, presenting them as "oggetti parlanti," so Pindar introduces the same expressions and grammatical "shifters" to make his verbal artifacts act as prompts and generators of speech on the athlete's behalf.[45] On this particular count, the model of the statue serves the poet very well, allowing him to make good on the most fundamental claim of his art: by virtue of the speaking monument within the song, the poem becomes able to announce the

---

wreath forged by the Muses in *Nem.* 7.77–79, the treasure house of *Pyth.* 6.5–14, the great hall of *Ol.* 6.1–3.

[42] Hyde (1921: 155) observes that the fillet actually appears more frequently than the crown; see, too, Serwint 1987: 112–16.

[43] For this argument, Steiner 1993: 167–72.

[44] E.g., *Nem.* 8.15–16, *Ol.* 3.3–5, *Pyth.* 6.15. For the relationship between the inscription and the victory announcement, see Kurke 1993: 144–45.

[45] The expression "oggetti parlanti" I borrow from Burzachechi 1962. For details of this argument, see Steiner 1993: 176–80.

athlete's triumph into future generations, defeating the forgetfulness, ignorance, or willful negligence of its audience with its ceaseless declarations of the subject's glory.[46]

Many of the examples cited above suggest that Pindar robs the statue of its role even as he replaces it with his songs, and tints allusions to these alternate commemorative devices with the same "paragonal" quality marking several other references to monuments and memorializing artifacts in the odes.[47] But the metaphor of song as base already points to the possibility of a more cooperative venture, where verse and image complement one another and together build a fresh and more powerful whole. This is the scenario that *Nemean 5* describes as it, like so many other odes, takes its thematic cue from its opening conceit and ends by resolving the dichotomy that its prelude had seemingly created. The statues, declared silent and immobile at the start, appear in the early stages of the song to infect the poet and his exercise of his craft with their own unwanted properties: no sooner has the laudator embarked on the mythical portion of his praise than he finds himself brought to a sudden halt, immobile and speechless in his refusal to broach the fratricide that stains Aiakid history (*stasomai*, 16). Where earlier both stasis and silence were the portion of the images, the same condition now afflicts the singer seeking to fulfill his task.[48] In the middle of a second episode concerning the family of local heroes, Pindar recognizes that the wordsmith no less than the statue-maker works in a medium that can immobilize: the *dolos* with which Hippolyta wishes to "bind" Peleus consists of the lying word that, in terms evocative of poet and craftsman both, the woman fastens into a manufactured work: *pseutan de poiēton sunepaze logon* (29; cf. *Ol.* 6.3).

But as the poem nears its end, with the Aiakids now returned to their illustrious sphere and the encomiastic song itself revivified, the singer seeks to restore the more positive associations that images and language both possess, and prepares to show how each can serve the other. Drawing toward the final visualization of the piece, Pindar declares the need for an Athenian *tektōn* of athletes (49). The obvious target of the conceit is Menander, the trainer from Athens who groomed Pytheas for

---

[46] For odes guaranteed future life, see the closing of *Pyth.* 3, and *Isthm.* 2.45–48.

[47] So the notional stele is whiter than Parian marble (*Nem.* 4.81), and the *lithon Moisaion* is easier to set up (*Nem.* 8.47) than its real-world counterpart; in like fashion, the treasure house at *Pyth.* 6.12–14 escapes the damage of time and the elements.

[48] As Segal (1974: 400) notes, the Aiakidai themselves are similarly figured (*stantes*, 11). When the poet recovers his capacity for motion a few lines on, the statue seems again to have left its mark: as the singer makes ready to launch himself from his waiting pose (19–21), his stance recalls that of the victory monument, which frequently depicted the athlete poised and waiting for the competition to begin.

his triumph in the pankration and played artist to the "matter" of the athlete's body; but the term *tektōn* no less readily recalls both the *adriantopoios* of the opening line and the craftsman-poet, two individuals who serve the victor by transforming his win into the enduring stuff of images and odes. The *tektōn* also leads smoothly into the final motif where the chorus is requested to bear "grassy *stephanōmata* with the aid of the yellow-haired Graces" to Themistios, grandfather of the present-day laudandus (50–54). It was J. B. Bury who first suggested that the description involved not just the common elision between the wreath and song, but also more literally the crowning of an image of Themistios, sculpted at the time of his own athletic win and then set up in front of the shrine of Aiakos located in the town square.[49] The proposal is attractive on several counts; it both explains why the chorus receives the order not to stiffen (*mēketi rhigei*, 50), as though the dancing bodies risked momentary petrification from too-close contact with the static stone, and turns the conclusion of the song into a glance toward an actual ritual performed by the returning athlete, who might dedicate his wreath to statues raised for earlier athletes and ancestral heroes.[50] While the chorus's own dance steps and loud-voiced praise effectively display the mobility and sounding properties of the song, the ode-turned-ornament will hereafter enjoy all the durability and "presentness" that comes with its adhesion to the tangible structure of the monument; and encompassed by the moving bodies and vivifying act of praise, the victor statue might lose its defining stasis and appear a figure simply poised or resting (another meaning that the opening term *elinusonta* can carry) before a fresh athletic feat. The glance toward the ritual act also grants the performance of the ode its own recurrent and enduring character: by virtue of its link to the monument, it has a future life as part of the celebrations that regularly take place at the site of the statue and shrine.

In *Nemean* 8 the poet himself crowns the monument with the wreath, which again unites both the literal victory fillet and the epinician song: "A suppliant on behalf of this dear city and these citizens, I clasp the revered knees of Aiakos bearing a sounding, intricately worked Lydian headband, a Nemean *agalma* of the double furlong races of Deinias and his father Megas" (13–16). Although properly the shrine of Aiakos that stood at the center of the agora, here Pindar reimagines that *hērōion* in anthropomorphized form and makes his offering as though in the act of

---

[49] Bury 1890: 83 and 87; see, too, Mullen 1982: 162.
[50] Paus. 7.17.14. The more generalized practice involved the dedication of wreaths to heroes and ancestors; e.g., *Isthm.* 7.24 and *Ol.* 9.12. For dedicating the wreath to the city, *Nem.* 8.13–16.

supplicating and honoring an image. The *mitra* that he bears is simply an older term for the *tainia* or victory fillet, bound by the athlete about his head immediately after winning an event and figured by the maker of the monument. In a characteristic glide between the activities of singers and athletes, the "I" of the verse here mirrors the actions of the victor: according to the protocol of the Nemean games, Deinias would first have dedicated his official crown to Zeus before leaving Nemea, and then would have offered the *mitra* to Aiakos, the local hero, when he returned home.[51] Towards the ending of the ode, Pindar sets up fresh monuments of his own: at lines 44–48 he prepares to raise a *lithon Moisaion* for Deinias and Megas, styling the song a second commemorative object to take its place alongside the earlier monument and giving his piece all the stature and geographic centrality that the "image" of Aiakos enjoyed. Together the two metaphors again make the process of athletic success and its musical celebration a continuous one: Pindar's encomion of Deinias acts as an ornament for Aiakos, just as future songs in praise of other victories will serve as offerings to the monuments that the poet now sets up.[52] Without the artifact by way of paradigm and quite literal support, the ode remains a thing deracinated, confined to a single performance.

HONORIFIC STATUES AND THE ENCOMIASTIC ADDRESS

Already included in many of the Pindaric examples are references to the communal as well as individual gratifications that the monument, whether that of a dead or living man, can bestow. From the common attributes that statues and songs sometimes dispute, but no less frequently share, I want to turn to a comparison of their more public roles, and to their place within the communities that commissioned and played audience to these twin disseminators of praise. Composing encomia and erecting honorific statues to outstanding members of the city-state are parallel enterprises on several scores, both hedged by similar restrictions: in each instance the author and artist must conduct negotiations with the gods, patrons, and larger public for the work and satisfy the demands of a frequently heterogeneous clientele. The very act of raising a statue to a mere mortal, whether athlete, statesman, or general, smacks of heroization and/or apotheosis,[53] while too close an as-

---

[51] For this "double dedication," see Nisetich 1975: 62.

[52] That Pindar's own songs achieved the status they claimed for themselves a scholion affirms: *Olympian* 7, commissioned to celebrate the victory of Diagoras of Rhodes in 464, was, the scholiast remarks, inscribed in gold letters, and dedicated in the Temple of Athena Lindia on the island.

[53] As observed by Raschke (1988: 39–40).

simulation of the poet or speaker's laudandus with a legendary, mythical, or divine prototype risks violating the unbreachable boundary between gods, heroes, and men.[54] The patron and subject of the work must receive the praise that he has paid for and that is his due, but overly particularized or extravagant verbal and visual celebrations can generate *phthonos*, garnering envy, hostility, and disbelief in the broader audience.[55] By setting the repeated and preemptive references to these dangers included in the encomiastic discourse of the late archaic and classical ages alongside the conventions that contemporary statue-makers observe, I want to suggest fresh analogies and exchanges between the verbal and visual spheres. Not only must speakers, singers, and artists preserve similar decorums, but, more critically for my argument, a reference to a physical artifact within the poet or orator's piece can provide him with a paradigm for his own undertaking: displaying and adorning its subject much as the verbal tribute aims to do, the image in the text highlights the author's methods and success in performing his appointed task.[56]

No polis, the ancient authors suggest, was more sensitive to the risk of elevating both the living and the dead too high than democratic Athens,[57] and both the trends and the lacunae in the city's archaeological record can corroborate their account. Well-documented changes in the style of grave markers after c. 500 show the personal and political charge adhering to the funerary monument: neither free-standing sculpture nor relief stelae appear in Attic cemeteries until the closing decades of the fifth century (and when they do reemerge, the men depicted have lost the athletic and martial accoutrements that gave them their claims to elite status, power, and prestige in sixth-century representations); in-

---

[54] Hence Pindar's frequent reassertions of the distinction (e.g., *Nem.* 7.54–60, 6.1–11); cf. Simon. 542.14–20 *PMG*; Bacchyl. 14.1–11.

[55] E.g., Pind. *Pyth.* 7.18–19, *Ol.* 11.7, 2.95–98; Bacchyl. 13.199–200; Thuc. 2.35.2.

[56] For two illuminating, broad-based discussions of the overlap between praise poetry and images, see Svenbro 1976 and Vernant 1990a: 60–71. Each suggests that changing conditions surrounding poetic performance from the archaic to the early classical age transformed songs into public possessions that were "placed in the middle" of the space of the polis. In this particular regard, Vernant proposes an analogy between the poem and the statue: "Le poème 'déposé au centre' est rendu bien commun dans l'espace abstrait et permanent du groupe. Sous cette forme nouvelle . . . il est placé sous le regard de la cité, mis à la disposition du corps social, comme l'image figurée est faite pour être vue, et pour être vue par tous" ("The poem, 'placed in the middle,' is turned into a common good in the abstract and permanent space of the group. In this novel form . . . it is set beneath the city's gaze, placed at the disposition of the social body, just as the fashioned image is made in order to be seen, and to be seen by all," 61).

[57] Gauer 1968: 177–78 explores the point.

stead, individual Athenians are buried without sculpted monuments.[58] Those who died fighting on their city's behalf enjoyed nothing comparable to the *kouroi* that adorned the graves of aristocrats such as Kroisos; they gained only a place in the list of single names inscribed on the stone stelae annually erected in the Kerameikos.[59] Equally absent from civic and sacred sites were the athletic images that stood in the marketplaces, temples, and shrines of other fifth-century city-states. Although Athens could boast of its full share of victors in local and international competitions, these monuments to individual and particularized moments of success seem to have had no place in the democratic city's extant sculptural repertoire.

Nor need we rely on arguments from silence alone. Citizens who achieved prominence in the martial sphere and sought the signal honor of a monument while they were still alive encountered a resistance amply reflected in near-contemporary and later sources. Aeschines records details of the controversy that followed the victory at the battle of Eion on the Strymon in 475:

> There were men at the time, Athenians, who endured much toil and danger at the river Strymon, and conquered the Persians in battle. When they came home, they asked the people for a reward, and the democracy gave them great honor, as it was then esteemed: permission to set up three stone herms in the Stoa of the Herms, on condition that they not inscribe their own names upon them, so that the inscription might not seem to be in honor of the generals but of the people.[60] (3.183)

Even a common herm, barely anthropomorphized in form, was thought too bold an act of self-assertion when identified by the individual's name.[61] In the event, the lines composed for the monument, following Jacoby's reconstruction,[62] neatly reconcile their several constituents: eliding the difference between the *hēgemones* (mentioned explicitly only

[58] Cic. *Leg.* 2.64–65 suggests actual legislation to limit expenses on funerary monuments; however, popular disapproval may have been a powerful factor in promoting the changes.
[59] By way of reaction to these restrictions in the early fourth century, see the grave monument for the young Dexileos, dated to 394/93, with discussion in Osborne 1998: 15–16.
[60] See discussion of the incident in Osborne 1985: 58–64. As he notes, Aeschines may simply be reconstructing events on the basis of the inscribed monument rather than reporting what actually happened. Plutarch (*Cim.* 7.3–8.2) claims that even uninscribed, the monument represented an exceptional honor, and was only granted because the victory had been the first nondefensive victory the Athenians had won, and had allowed them to expand their territory.
[61] For the suggestion of the herm's particular association with democracy, see Osborne 1985.
[62] Jacoby 1945: 185–211.

once) and their men, they focus not so much on the merit of the generals who led the troops to victory as on the larger mass of the Athenians who showed themselves worthy to act as leaders to the rest of the Greeks.[63] Apparent, too, from the inscription is the civic purpose informing both this and other commemorative dedications: as the second stele cited by Aeschines declares, the monument was erected so that individuals viewing the herms in future days might be inspired to labor in common actions (*amphi xunoisi pragmasi*, 3.184). As in the case of the athletic images that Socrates discusses in his conversation with Kleiton,[64] the question the citizen asks of the monument is not what it does for the subject of the representation, but how it serves the broader audience and polis at large.

The distaste for honorific images seems to have persisted through to the end of the fifth century, and even on into the early years of the fourth; as Demosthenes points out, almost one hundred years elapsed between the raising of the statue of the Tyrannicides and the grant of an image to Konon in 394 following his decisive victory at the battle of Knidos (20.70). Sparta had its own cautionary story (albeit recorded only in a much later source) of a military victor who flouted convention and erected a celebratory statue on his own behalf.[65] After his defeat of the Athenians at Aigospotamoi in 405, Lysander dedicated an oversized bronze votive at Delphi, depicting himself crowned by Poseidon in the company of gods, heroes, and his sea captains (Paus. 10.9.7). The image confirmed the Spartans' suspicion of their general's overweening pride and, along with several other indicators of his excessive ambition, hastened his fall from political grace.[66]

Statesmen as well as military victors could find themselves caught up in the politics surrounding memorialization in plastic or pictorial form. Plutarch mentions that Themistokles commissioned an image of himself, one depicting him as "a person not only of noble mind, but of a most heroic aspect," but notes that the portrait he had made was set up in the private shrine of his favorite goddess, Artemis Aristoboule, rather than in a public place (*Them.* 22.2). Plutarch also preserves a second

---

[63] For this, Osborne 1985: 59–60.

[64] Cited on pp. 34–35.

[65] Although Gauer (1968: 177) suggests that Sparta was more tolerant of the honorary portrait than Athens. But note the prohibition against tombstones inscribed with the name of the dead (unless the individual had died in battle) that Plutarch attributes to Lykourgos (*Lyc.* 27.2).

[66] See discussion in Stewart 1990: 51; cf. the very similar story told of Pausanias's dedication of an inscribed offering at Delphi (Thuc. 1.132.2–4, with discussion in Steiner 1994: 78, 136).

tale that again seems to reflect the Athenian distaste for housing images of living (and dead) "first" citizens within their own civic space.[67] When Pheidias fashioned the Amazonomachy on the shield of Athena, he records, the statue-maker included in it

> both his own portrait among the reliefs, as a bald man lifting a stone high with both hands, and a very handsome one of Perikles fighting with an Amazon. And the position of Perikles' arm, which is holding a spear before his eyes, is cunningly contrived for the purpose of concealing the likeness, which is, however, perfectly plain from either side. (*Per.* 31.4)

The device, according to the author, contributed to the *phthonos* that Pheidias had already provoked among the Athenians and fueled the hostile rumors surrounding him and Perikles both. Although all eight mentions of these "cryptoportraits" have been shown to belong to the Hellenistic tradition of marvel literature,[68] Plutarch's story might seek to recapture and comment upon a properly fifth-century, and recognizably Athenian, sentiment.

Where images of historical individuals, some living, some dead, did exist, the fifth-century statue-maker chose not to attempt a too-singularized or portrait likeness. Instead, as I explored in Chapter One, he created a generic account that assimilated the particular personality to a familiar and idealized type, representing his subject in his public role and bringing out what he shared with the audience: the inspired poet, the perfect statesman, the exemplary general, each of whom offered the viewer a reflection of his own best virtues. The choice to subsume individuality may be not just a matter of style and technique, but a means of avoiding the hubris that overly specific characterization involves. Perhaps to a still greater degree than the name inscribed on the statue base, the personalized physiognomy and physique make the image into a portrait likeness, one that necessarily prohibits the larger audience from recognizing itself in and emulating this "everyman." The sources attest as much in reporting the hostile reactions that the too-prominently "named" visual representation could spark: because the artist Mikon included in his depiction of the battle of Marathon on the Stoa Poikile various historical individuals who could be identified by the scars and wounds incurred by their heroic deeds, the composition was held to

---

[67] Aeschines mentions a statue of Solon, set up as "a reminiscence and an imitation" of the statesman, and "showing his customary demeanor as he used to address the Athenian people" (1.25). But the statue stands not in the city that was Solon's chief concern, but in the marketplace of Salamis.

[68] Preisshofen 1974. The Hellenistic sources even invented the notion that if the supposed portraits were removed, the entire composition would fall apart.

detract from the glory of the less prominent individuals also fighting on their city's behalf.[69]

If democratic Athens was particularly scrupulous in regulating and superintending the forms and contents of its public monuments, then conventions surrounding victory images erected in other cities and at the sites of the games suggest the broader diffusion of these sensitivities. Although the statue formed one of the privileges of the athlete's win, and the quasi-heroic character adhering to a victory in one of the four crown games might of itself place the contestant beyond the limitations that mortals must usually observe,[70] there remained certain modesties that the laudandus and his image-maker were bound to practice. A passing remark in Lucian reports that "not even at the Olympic games are the victors allowed to set up statues greater than life-size, but the Hellanodikai take care that not one of them shall exceed the truth, and the inspection of the statues is more exacting than the examination of the athletes" (Pro eikonibus 11). Although the source is late, the comment jibes with a very early inscription that calls attention to the exact likeness of the statue to the victor, declaring the two equivalent in size.[71] Pliny's reference (HN 4.16) to the rule that only triple victors at Olympia had the right to "iconic" (iconicas) images points to another attempt to regulate and circumscribe; while the precise meaning of "iconic" remains a matter of dispute, and a properly portrait image may not be what the author has in mind,[72] the remark still indicates that statues offering a recognizably close match to the individual victor occupied a special and restricted niche. More commonly, the few extant victory statues and copies suggest, sculptors followed the vogue for generic and embellished representations and avoided the overly particularized.

Fresh indications of attempts to keep the individual's status within acceptable limits belong to the inscriptions engraved on the statue's base. Highly repetitive, they come complete with the requisite mention of the victor's city placed alongside his name and patronymic. The community may figure simply as the athlete's place of origin, but it also

---

[69] For a full list of sources, see Rouveret 1989: 153 n. 63. We might also compare the treatment of Greeks and Persians in Aeschylus's Persae, where in contrast to the barbarians, no individual Greek is named.

[70] The heroization already latent in the raising of a monument might even be realized after the victor's death, when a cult could be instituted on his behalf. E.g., Philippos of Kroton, Hipposthenes of Sparta, Polydamos of Skotusa, Diognetos of Crete, Euthykles of Lokris, Theagenes of Thasos. For discussion, Fontenrose 1968; S. Lattimore 1987; Serwint 1987: 19–24; Kurke 1993: 149–53.

[71] CEG 394. But note Hyde 1921: 45 for the proposal that several victory images were larger than life-size.

[72] For discussion of the different readings, see W. H. Gross 1969–71; Hyde 1921: 54–57.

frequently appears within more elaborate formulations that describe how the victor shares his glory with the city that launched him on his enterprise and makes the larger body of citizens participants in the glory he has achieved. Typically the epigram visualizes its subject granting his home his actual crown or the less tangible *kudos* that adheres to the talismanic prize.[73] An epigram dated to the first half of the fifth century celebrates one Theognetos who "crowned the city of good fathers" (Ebert 12 = *Anth. Plan.* 16.2), while the fourth-century monument of Dikon more plainly states: "I am Dikon son of Kallimbrotos, and I was victorious four times at Nemea, twice at Olympia, five times at Pytho and three times at the Isthmus. And I crown the city of the Syracusans" (Ebert 35 = *Anth. Pal.* 13.15). Preserving the same conceit, a much later epigram from Ephesos concludes its victory catalogue: "Accordingly I bestow *kudos* upon my father Eirenaios and my homeland Ephesos by means of immortal crowns" (Ebert 76B.9–10).[74]

That victory images were designed to serve collective as much as personal interests, the history and chronology of these monuments at Olympia affirms. A handful of statues raised in honor of athletes who had been victorious as many as two centuries before (that of the Spartan Chionis, for example, whose victory fell in the twenty-ninth Olympiad, or 664, but whose statue was the work of the artist Myron, whose floruit fell between 480 and 450)[75] reveal that the dedication of victory monuments was a competitive business in which city-states vied with one another and sought to outnumber and outplace the images set up by their particular rivals.[76] No differently from the other images and buildings (treasuries most prominently among them) that individual states commissioned and set up as declarations of wealth and power, athletic statuary played its part in the jockeying for status at panhellenic sites.

If honorific and commemorative images raised on behalf of the individual living and dead are closely circumscribed, then verbal encomiasts must plot a no less careful course among the potential perils surrounding their task. The toposlike stratagems that they employ to make palatable their subject's glory and to disarm an audience whom they imagine jealous or incredulous are familiar ones: in an apotropaic move, the speaker or singer acknowledges the risk of incurring *phthonos* head on, or attempts to legitimate the extravagant praise he will give by appeals to a divine witness or other honored authorities;[77] modesty is regularly

---

[73] For a close study of the formula, Kurke 1993: 138–49.
[74] Note Pindar's copying of the device at *Ol.* 5.1–8 (with Kurke 1993: 138).
[75] For Chionis, see Paus. 6.13.2, 3.14.3.
[76] Raschke 1988: 41.
[77] On these devices, see particularly E. L. Bundy 1986.

enjoined on the laudandus, together with warnings of the jealousy of the gods and the transience of all good fortune, while myths of characters punished for their inability to "digest their *olbos*" (Pind. *Ol.* 1.55–56) reiterate the caution. More subtle devices work to reconcile the laudandus and his achievements with the larger audience before whom the encomiast delivers his piece. The subject of the praise can figure as a public benefactor, whose exploits serve the polis at large, and just as the statue-maker dwells on the paradigmatic aspect of his model, so the speech or song that paints an individual in the colors of the ideal king, soldier, or citizen presents him in the guise of an exemplary everyman. Thucydides' Perikles famously takes this "genericizing" one step further in his Funeral Oration when he explains his preference for omitting all description of the actual deeds that the dead performed (2.35.1–2); in the encomion following his deliberately polemical opening, the speaker effectively replaces the individual subject with the city common to all that forms the chief matter of his praise.

But much more striking correspondences, and dissonances, too, can occur when the encomiast introduces a visual commemoration into his song or speech of praise. Using the example of the honorific statue as paradigm or foil for his enterprise, he decoratively declares his composition able to satisfy individual and collective demands. Leslie Kurke has already assigned such a positive mediating function to several of the metaphoric *agalmata* and offerings that Pindar so frequently introduces into his songs:[78] carefully positioned between the gifts and countergifts that circulate among an aristocratic elite, and the public works that adorn the city where they serve the interests of the people at large, the materialized ode together with the triumph it proclaims can become a "common benefaction bestowed on the city by the victor."[79] As so many testaments to the patron's civic-minded largesse, these artifacts also provide examples of his exercise of *megaloprepeia*, lavish public expenditure, and help to diffuse the hostility that his preeminence is bound to provoke.

Applied to the victory statues that, I have suggested, Pindar plants at strategic moments in the song, Kurke's argument illuminates another motive behind the poet's choice to include the monuments. Over and above the contribution that it makes to the celebratory powers of the ode, the artifact also signals that the poem, like the victory statue, exists on behalf of the city as a whole. So in *Isthmian* 1 the spokesman follows up his initial invocation of Thebes, prominently located at the opening of the song, by declaring his intention of fashioning (*teuchein*)

[78] Kurke 1991: 163–94.
[79] Ibid.: 170.

a *geras* for Herodotos by way of recompense for his victory in the chariot race (14). When this ornamental offering appears a second time, the private tribute has become a source of common benefit, an *agathon xunon* set up (*orthōsai*) by the poet "in return for toil" (45–46). The metaphoric artifact in *Nemean* 3 undergoes the same change in nature. The *agalma* erected by the composer and his chorus on behalf of the victor Aristokleides turns out to be no private dedication, but a statue destined for the agora at Aigina, whose communal glory and visible magnificence it will enhance. And when the poet comes with his musical wreath in hand to crown the image/shrine of the tutelary hero Aiakos, he is acting on behalf not of the victor alone, but "of this dear city and these citizens" (13–16), matching the public nature of the monument with the adornment that recapitulates its civic character. The statue bases set down at the start of several odes similarly seek to redistribute the glory of the win and, like the epigrams on actual victory dedications, introduce the city as a necessary partner to the achievement. The foundation stone supporting *Pythian* 7 records the name of Athens as well as that of the aristocratic Alkmeonidai (1–3) and binds the victorious house that has displayed its wealth and standing by a win in that most elite of events, the chariot race, to the city at large. United in a single ensemble, poem, victor, and monument all promote the glory of the citizens even as they embellish the civic space.

While Pindar uses statues to boost the cohesive and harmonizing powers of his art, Simonides includes the fashioned work in a song of praise for the Thessalian dynast Skopas (542 *PMG*) with a characteristically combative and even negative intent. No sooner does the poet introduce a monument that appears exactly to anticipate the laudator's task than he discards it and declares it inapposite, and goes on to build a more appropriate and useful "image" of his own. The changes that Simonides rings on his opening conceit also look to the larger agenda guiding his composition: seeking to situate his laudandus within a civic rather than a particularized or elite order, and to declare his necessary participation in the larger community over which he presides, he looks to modify a markedly aristocratic mode of representation with what might be styled a more "middling" one.[80]

But first for the statue that acts by way of prelude. There is no mistaking the artisanal quality of the conceit devised by Simonides to begin his composition:[81]

---

[80] On this "middling" mode, and Simonides' adherence to it, I. Morris 1996: 38–39.
[81] Svenbro (1976: 153–57) offers the most detailed account of the connections between the phrase and statue-making.

ἄνδρ' ἀγαθὸν μὲν ἀλαθέως γενέσθαι
χαλεπὸν χερσίν τε καὶ ποσὶ καὶ νόῳ
τετράγωνον ἄνευ ψόγου τετυγμένον.

Truly to become a good man is hard, fashioned foursquare in hands,
feet, and mind without censure.

But more problematic is the relationship of this opening declaration to
the remainder of the song. In his extended reading of the proem, Jesper
Svenbro argues that the artifact serves primarily to figure the unique
powers of poetry, and so to assure the patron of the high value of the
work he has commissioned: because *alatheōs* retains its archaic sense of
the negation of forgetfulness, someone who qualifies as an *agathos alatheōs* is an exemplary man "in the memory of men," an individual
who has entered the particular poetic domain of "non-oubli" or the
unforgotten. Together the conjunction of statuary and song forms a particularly powerful union that guarantees Skopas the permanence and
immortality that he seeks, as the two media join in moving the individual beyond the upsets brought by circumstance and change and place
him in the "dimension atemporelle" (atemporal dimension) reserved for
heroes and for gods. No rivalry here, but a perfect example of how the
fashioned image can model and substantiate the poet's claims.

Svenbro goes on to propose that we read the remainder of the poem
as an elaboration of its opening assertion, a programmatic statement of
the power of the poet to memorialize his laudandus for what he has
achieved even in the face of the changing lot of mortal men. But the
subsequent lines do not so much expand as alter the opening ideal, and
disturb the apparent tight collusion between word and image. When
Simonides paints his portrait of the individual who attracts his com-
mendation, his laudandus looks rather different from the exemplar presented in the initial phrase: now the poet celebrates the individual who
does nothing shameful willingly (28–29), who is a generally sound type
(36), and who knows the justice that benefits the city (35). Some have
read these sentiments as a revisionary treatment of the old aristocratic
virtue of *aretē*, and the setting forth of a radical new view of what it is
to be *agathos*;[82] but other commentators object to this account, noting
that a challenge to the values of a now-declining aristocracy ill accords
with a song that celebrates an individual belonging to precisely this topmost social sphere.[83] Instead, according to a very different interpreta-

---

[82] Gentili (1988: 65) talks of a replacement of "the ethic of absolute values" with "the
ethic of relative values . . . which moves from the lofty plain of aesthetic and agonistic
striving to the broader one of ethical and social commitment in a community context."
[83] Dickie 1978; Svenbro (1976: 142) further notes that Simonides would have been all the

tion, the opening statement and its rejection more simply cohere with a topos common in praise poetry, one that notes the impossibility of human perfection and introduces the sentiment by way of foil to those virtues that men can realistically attain.[84]

To unsnarl this tangle of readings, we need to look more closely at the artifact that figures so prominently at the head of the song, whose own attributes and properties serve as a frame for the remainder of the piece. First and foremost the poet calls attention to the object's fixed and unchanging nature as it stands firmly rooted to the spot where it is raised. The very sound and structure of the lines reinforce that impression of immobility: the assonant and ponderous *chi* in *chalepon* and *chersin*; the use of *t*'s and *g*'s (the one "expressive of binding and rest in a place," the other whose heavy sound "detains the slipping tongue")[85] in the parallel forms of *tetugmenon* and *tetragōnon*; and the design of the third line, where the poet places the two echoing terms as flanks to the expression *aneu psogou* as though to emphasize the fact that no flaw rocks the stability of this tightly compacted object.

A fresh reminder of the permanent and unmoving quality of the work belongs to *tetragōnos*. While the expression frequently carries a positive moral charge,[86] and initially goes to Simonides' presentation of the statue as an embodiment of all that is excellent, it could also possess associations of a different kind, which become critical later in the song. Although no contemporary text allows us to fix the precise significance of the term, in later "art historical" sources *tetragōnos* refers to the overly rigid, immobile, and ungainly character that viewers came to find in early statuary.[87] Themistius comments, "Before Daidalos, the execution not only of herms but also of other pieces was foursquare" (*Or.* 26.126), and Daidalos, of course, was celebrated for making his statues look more active and more mobile.[88] Suggestive, too, is the observation of Diogenes Laertius, who notes that the sculptor Pythagoras of Rhegion, a contemporary of Simonides, was known for pursuing *summetria* and *rhuthmos* in his works (8.47), qualities that would have set his images apart from their more blocklike and ponderous predecessors.[89] It seems likely enough that Simonides, whose carefully structured epi-

[84] So Dickie 1978, citing as parallels *Nem.* 7.54–60, 6.1–11, and Bacchyl. 14.1–11.

[85] Pl. *Cra.* 426d -427c.

[86] See pp. 42–43.

[87] For reading the term as a sculptural rather than a moral quality, see Svenbro 1976: 154.

[88] Cf. Thuc. 6.27.1; Paus. 2.10.7, 9.40.3.

[89] The trend continues into the period after Simonides' composition. First Polykleitos, and then Lysippos after him, were similarly praised for their mastery of *summetria*, and Pliny

grams so neatly complement the images they are designed to accompany, and whom the anecdotal tradition reports as a connoisseur of contemporary painting, stone-cutting, and statue-making techniques,[90] was familiar with these trends and would have imported them into his songs.

Read together with the remainder of the poem, the seemingly positive affirmations of stability, rootedness, and immobility at the start come to acquire a more negative or outdated aspect. Declaring unchanging perfection impossible to achieve, and the prerogative only of the immortals who enjoy precisely the permanence and immutability that the statue displays,[91] the poet then introduces a man who remains content with doing nothing base, and who shows himself as adaptable and resourceful (*mēd' . . . apalamnos*, 34) as the ever-changing conditions characteristic of his life demand.[92] The fixed and immobile image, representative of a style being rapidly superseded by something new, emerges as singularly ill-suited to the laudandus; instead, circumstances, and particularly leadership in polis life (35), call for a more fluid and dynamic paradigm, one that in its manifestation of *summetria* exhibits precisely that sound constitution or health (*hugiēs* 36) that the poem singles out for praise.[93]

But the design of the image carries with it additional implications. As several commentators have observed, the statue introduced at the start corresponds to nothing so much as the *kouros* of the late sixth century, which subsequent accounts would describe as foursquare and blocklike in style.[94] Again Simonides selects this statue type not only for its merits but for its limitations too, making it the model he will go on to amend and change. First among its several inconcinnities is the suitability of the *kouros* for the dead rather than living man. By way of signaling the funerary context of the image, Simonides inserts the expression *anēr*

---

contrasts the images of Lysippos with the "foursquare" and now outmoded pieces that fifth-century sculptors had produced (*HN* 34.65).

[90] Carson 1996 for this.

[91] Such declarations of permanence reappear in other songs of praise at precisely those moments when poets contrast the unchanging nature of divine existence with the vicissitudes characteristic of the ever-shifting human lot. This is noted by Dickie (1978).

[92] See Campbell 1982: ad loc. for discussion of the phrase.

[93] Health, as Chrysippus's citation of Polykleitos's canon would later make clear (B3 DK), depends on the achievement of *summetria*, the harmony that ideally exists between the different elements in the body. The statue-maker gives expression to this internal equipoise through his own practice of *summetria*, which guarantees that each external component of the human body stands in correct proportion both to its neighbor and to the whole.

[94] For the equation of the foursquare image and the *kouros*, see Svenbro 1976: 156; Rouveret 1989: 146; more generally Vernant 1990a: 61.

agathon genesthai ("to become a good man"), a phrase used elsewhere specifically to characterize those who have acquired glory, as well as commemorative monuments, through the heroic manner of their death.[95] While the *kouros*'s "atemporality" would serve as complement to the unchanging condition of the deceased, the subject of Simonides' song is very much alive, and his behavior must prove responsive to his present lot.

No less ripe for modification may be the heavy ideological charge that the *kouros* carried with it. It not only stood as the instantiation of all the ideals of *kalokagathia*, a visible statement of the aristocratic assumption that high birth, wealth, physical beauty, and moral excellence formed a single and cohesive whole, but it also directed its appeal to a very narrow clientele. Because of the high cost of marble works, the market for the statues was necessarily a restricted one, largely confined to aristocrats or "those wealthy and pushy enough to act like aristocrats."[96] While the virtues and wealth the *kouros* puts on show remain entirely appropriate for a dynast of Skopas's kind, and place him in the company he would presumably have liked to keep, Simonides wishes to make room for other of his laudandus's roles and merits (real or imagined), too. Still preserving the properly aristocratic virtues (the individual deserving of praise remains an *agathos*, and free from the taint of *aischra*), the paradigmatic man also shows his public-spiritedness as he dispenses "city-benefiting" justice (35). In contrast to the inwardly directed conspicuous consumption that the *kouros* represents, Skopas, as befits a public benefactor, spreads his largesse more broadly.

It is the task of the laudator to match the composition to the particular patron of the moment (so Pindar at *Ol.* 6.8–9) and to design a tribute that, like the statue, perfectly reflects his merits and achievements. Much more than the *kouros*, Simonides' finished song supplies the mirror image of its subject, displaying the same attributes as Skopas and audibly and visibly enacting the innovations it describes. The composition replaces the solidity and heaviness of the opening lines and of the figure they evoke with a more free-flowing and motion-filled form, liberating the rigid statue from its moorings and making its subject partake of the changing rhythms that are the common lot of men. The constant evocations of shifts and alterations, of travel over all the earth,

---

[95] Loraux 1986: 99–100. Herodotus's account of Kleobis and Biton perfectly exemplifies the convention: after their extraordinary feat of bringing their mother to the festival of Hera, the two brothers promptly died, and received eternal commemoration in the form of the possibly still-extant *kouroi*: "The Argives having made statues of them dedicated them at Delphi on the grounds of their proving themselves to be the best men" (*hōs andrōn aristōn genomenōn*, 1.31.5).

[96] Hurwit 1985: 198.

combine with the repeated enjambments, qualifications, conditions, and use of the future tense to promote a sense of openness and dynamism.[97] Modifications occur at the level of diction, too. If the opening conceit includes an echo of Homer's phrasing at *Iliad* 15.641–43, where the poet similarly describes an individual possessed of every *aretē*, with feet for fighting and a mind excellently "forged" (*etetukto*),[98] then the retrospective glance entirely suits the nature of the *kouros*, which models its bodily appearance after the Homeric warrior and also looks back to the glorious heroic age. But this is the world that Simonides' poem is in the act of replacing, and when an epic phrase returns at 24–25, it is followed by a line of gentle mockery that effectively explodes the grandiosity of what came before. For the rest, Simonides' language features terms found in very different and nonheroic contexts and that describe qualities lying outside the scope of the Iliadic world. The closing lines of the composition alert the audience to the developments that have gone on, both in the "body" of the text and in that of the initial artifact. Now patron and larger clientele can admire a work that preserves the merits of the introductory *kouros*, still beautiful in all respects and free from the admixture of anything base (*aischra mē memeiktai*, 39–40), but invested with all the additional attributes that a more dynamic, harmonious, and contemporary image can boast.

If Pindar and Simonides both draw on monuments as positive or negative paradigms for their task of praise, then Isocrates also punctuates his self-styled *epainos* for the dead Cypriot monarch Evagoras with references to statues, and deploys the images to achieve several different ends through the course of the address. A concern with relations between words and more concrete or visible forms of commemoration declares itself from the start. The eulogy opens by evoking the *taphos* where Evagoras lies buried, a grave whose prominence is reinforced by the offerings, athletic contests, and due funerary rites that his son has organized in an outstanding exercise of *megaloprepeia* (*Evagoras* 2). But these modes of memorialization, explicitly designated as displays that Evagoras might look upon (*orōnta* 2), still lack one essential element, the gift of verbal praise, which an orator alone can supply, and which uniquely guarantees that undying memory (*athanaton . . . mnēmēn*, 3) most desired by the dead. Like the poets before him, Isocrates has used the funerary monument and recurrent ritual celebrations that take place at its site to provide a frame or peg for his own act of commemoration, only then to declare the superior acceptability of his particular offering to the laudandus. So, too, the statement with which he

---

[97] Note, too, the synizesis in 23, 24, and 30, and the synecphonesis in 15.
[98] As suggested in Svenbro 1976: 153.

concludes the opening motif shows the writer's mastery of the conventions with which he works; a single phrase suggests language's capacity to concretize Evagoras's *aretē* in enduring form (*aeimnēston an tēn aretēn . . . poiēseien*) and recalls the unique efficacy of verbal praise, which, unlike the fixed *taphos* or localized funerary rites, can travel far and wide (*para pasin anthrōpois*, 4).

Through the course of the speech, another monument raised to Evagoras duly appears. After his financial cooperation with the Athenian general Konon, a partnership that brought victory to the city at the battle of Knidos, the Athenian people honored both individuals with the highest accolades, "and set up images where the statue of Zeus Soter stands, near to it and to one another, a memorial (*hupomnēma*) both of the greatness of their benefaction (*euergesias*) and of their friendship to one another" (57). The honorary portrait, raised in front of the Zeus Stoa in the Athenian agora, appears perfectly calibrated to its several constituents. It stands primarily as a testament to the civic-mindedness of Evagoras, who had already been granted the privilege of Athenian citizenship on account of the *megalas euergesias* he had bestowed on the city (54). But Isocrates' account also satisfies his more exclusive audience, the son and heir of the dead man, by including a reference to the aristocratic element in the partnership: since the two individuals acted through mutual *philia*, the personal bond of friendship that the monument also commemorates, the dynast and honorary citizen of the democratic polis are perfectly reconciled, just as they are in the speech itself.

A final, and more dismissive reference to portrait images at the closing of the piece rounds out Isocrates' sequence of monuments and returns in more explicit fashion to the assessment of the relative powers of verbal and other memorializing modes with which the encomion began: "I believe, Nikokles, that although portrait images of bodies are fine memorials, those images of deeds and thoughts which one might observe only in well-crafted (*technikōs*) discourse are worth much more" (73). Through his careful choice of terms, the eulogist has transferred to his words of praise the merits of the rejected *eikones*. While *technē* in Isocrates regularly refers to the rules governing the practice of rhetoric, the expression *technikōs* selected for this occasion also glances back to the artistry of the manufactured image that has just gone before. By way of confirmation of the elision he effects, the author then imagines the audience for the finely worked speech as one composed not of listeners, but of viewers (*theōrēseien*).

Isocrates goes on to refine the point he has already made. Because images can do no more than represent the visible body, displaying external beauty but neglecting to portray the "worthy deeds and *dianoia*" of their subject,[99] they necessarily fall short of the desires of the *ka-loikagathoi*, who "do not so much pride themselves on the beauty of their bodies as they desire to be honored for their deeds and their judgment" (74). Not only capable of displaying the inner as well as outer man, verbal eulogy trumps the artistic images on a second and equally familiar score:

> Images (*tupoi*) are bound to remain solely among those in whose city they were set up, but words may be published throughout Hellas, and having been spread abroad in the leisured associations (*diatribais*) of right-thinking men, are welcomed among those whose good opinion is more to be desired than that of all others. (74)

Here the timeworn topos of the immobile statue as foil for the peripatetic word (or text) has acquired a fresh dimension. The particular superiority of the verbal/written encomion lies with its ability not just to travel abroad, but also to find for itself an audience of those select and like-minded men best able to appreciate Isocrates' noble subject;[100] in this setting, Evagoras can garner fresh honor and renown among those with wealth enough to engage in leisured associations, men whose plaudits carry greater value than those of the heterogeneous group of citizens passing by the statue, or frequenting the grave erected in the public space.

To round out this litany of the verbal encomion's merits, Isocrates includes a third and final claim: while no one can make their bodily *phusis* resemble that portrayed in statues and paintings, individuals can "imitate the character of their fellow men and their thoughts and purposes apparent in the spoken word" (75). Once again, Isocrates has borrowed from the properties of the *eikones* to describe the virtues and impact of his own activity. As I noted earlier, portrait images raised in Greek city-states were designed to act in precisely the manner that Isocrates would deny to them, furnishing visual paradigms by which citizens might regulate not just their bodily appearance, but their conduct, *ēthos*, and broader "hexis," too. The exemplary and paideutic power of the artistic representation is even latent in the expression that Isocrates chose when dismissing the works in his previous remark: they are *tupoi*, the molds, impressions, or stamps that the author elsewhere cites in describing how students are modeled or fashioned by their teachers (*Against the Sophists* 18; *Antidosis* 194). Just as on these other occasions Isocrates imagines the pupil as the product of the craftsman's

---

[99] Here Isocrates plays on the familiar dichotomy between inner and outer that statues, as Chapter Two argued, so frequently serve to focalize.

[100] Cf. Thgn. 239–43.

hand, stamped by the *technē* that the teacher deploys, so here, too, he has used the seemingly devalued artistic idiom for the power that he would give to his address: the explicit purpose of the *Evagoras* is to supply Nikokles with an image of his dead father, internal as well as external, so that he may imitate the model as portrayed in speech.

IMAGING THE WORD

The self-referentiality that characterizes both Simonides' and Isocrates' verbal praise, where the modified or rejected image informs the nature and purpose of the surrounding composition, does not belong exclusively to the encomiastic genre. Instead authors more broadly deploy statues when they wish to explore the properties that they would ascribe to their own linguistic art and to highlight how the verbal *technē* displayed by the speech, song, or text works on its audience. In using the artifact as paradigm or analogue for the activity of *logos*, the sources also draw attention to the transfer or exchange of attributes, both desirable and more equivocal, that may result; the juxtaposition of images with speeches, arguments, and larger literary creations changes the nature of both parties, endowing each with the powers more usually associated with the other term, and sometimes confounding common assumptions about what words and plastic works can do.

The equivalence between a work of art and the larger discourse surrounding it may have an early sounding in the archaic age, rehearsed by a celebrated practitioner of *logos* and storytelling in all its positive and negative aspects. The wonderful brooch that the disguised Odysseus cites in his account of the clothing that he once wore holds up a mirror to the narrative in which it appears, revealing its character and signaling through the response it garners just how the speaker's own words should be received.[101] The verisimilitude of the artifact, and the proximity to visual reality that its closely observed details achieve, correspond to a story that embeds true elements within a fabricated whole,[102] and that comes prefaced by the reminder that its teller knows how to speak many "falsehoods made like to true things" (*Od.* 19.203). In accord with the other *sēmata* exchanged through the course of the conversation (most notably the transparent "dream" that Penelope recounts at the close of the dialogue), the all-too-proleptic brooch may not so much correspond to the actual object that Odysseus once wore,

---

[101] See chapter 1 for an earlier discussion of the brooch.
[102] So, too, the *poikilia* (228), the variegated or highly worked quality of the brooch, models the speaker's own skilled practice of his craft, his fabrication of a story made up of heterogeneous materials.

as be the beggar's means of alerting Penelope to his true identity and testing her response.

The description of the *thauma* that the ornament elicits, a combination of admiration for its technical virtuosity and pleasure at imagining that the scene depicted within it is actually played out before the viewer's eyes, also suggests how hearers both internal and external should react to Odysseus's tale: Penelope, and those listening to the rhapsode's song, should not believe all that they are told, but rather should marvel at the *technē* of the "artist" while recognizing the gap between his narrative and the lived reality. That the speech is no less "daidalic" than the self-described *daidalon* of the brooch (227), Penelope's own behavior at the conclusion of the beggar's speech can affirm: the persuasive power of the tale, and its evocation of the hero whom she thinks forever lost, elicits her longing to weep even as she apprehends the *sēmata*, the signifying markers that Odysseus has constructed and planted within his address (249–50). It is not so much that brooch and story beguile as that the modeled character of each combines artifice and reality to create a scenario different from that announced by its purely representational dimension.

The paradox declared at the start of Odysseus's virtuoso performance, that of words that imperfectly correspond to the truth they claim to represent, appears pegged to a more riddling artifact on a second occasion. Turning to the mythical portion of his song in *Olympian* 1, Pindar introduces Pelops,

> τοῦ μεγασθενὴς ἐράσσατο Γαιάοχος
> Ποσειδάν, ἐπεί νιν καθαροῦ λέβη-
>   τος ἔξελε Κλωθώ,
> ἐλέφαντι φαίδιμον ὦμον κεκαδμένον.   (25–27)

> with whom the mighty Earth-holder Poseidon fell in love when Klotho drew him out of the pure cauldron, distinguished by his shoulder gleaming with ivory.

The story behind this ivory addition, which turns the hero into an eros-inspiring artifact decked out in precious metal, is the very centerpiece of the controversy that Pindar will go on to address. According to one version of events, the gods (or Demeter alone) ate Pelops's original shoulder when Tantalus served up his son at a banquet he hosted for the immortals, and then replaced the missing part after reconstituting the dismembered body in a cooking pot; but in the alternate account that Pindar will supply, these culinary adventures and cannibalism are no more than pieces of malicious gossip spread about by a jealous neighbor after the youth's abduction by Poseidon, lies that obscure the ivory supplement's true origins.[103] Before filling in both the traditional and his own alternate tale, the poet pauses to remind his audience of the nature and powers of the *muthoi* with which he and other storytellers work:

ἦ θαύματα πολλά, καί πού τι καὶ βροτῶν
φάτις ὑπὲρ τὸν ἀλαθῆ λόγον
δεδαιδαλμένοι ψεύδεσι ποικίλοις
   ἐξαπατῶντι μῦθοι·

Χάρις δ᾽, ἅπερ ἅπαντα τεύχει τὰ μείλιχα θνατοῖς,
ἐπιφέροισα τιμὰν καὶ ἄπιστον ἐμήσατο πιστόν
ἔμμεναι τὸ πολλάκις·   (28–32)

> Yes, wonders are many, but then, too, I think, in the talk of men stories decked out with embroidered lies deceive beyond the true account. But Charis, who fashions all things sweet for mortals, by bestowing honor makes even what is unbelievable often believed.

Both the scholia and more recent commentators have endlessly tried to sort out the elements of Pindar's introductory visualization, and to determine whether these lines allude to the original story or already preview the poet's revisionary narrative.[104] No less problematic is the status of the more gnomic remarks at 28–32, which may look back to and critique what has been said before, or instead prepare us for the mendacious story that will appear several lines on. But absent from these readings is a recognition of the very close linguistic and thematic ties that link the first description of Pelops to the discussion of *muthoi* and *Charis* that comes after it, and of the purpose that this connection serves: using the so-called break-off passage to gloss the figure of the youth, Pindar invites his public to understand the embellished hero as exemplar of the equivocal powers possessed by all acts of skillful craftsmanship, whether artistic or verbal, and of the impact that they can have on their audience.

The term *thaumata* that stands at the head of the lines of reflection harks very directly back to the words just sung. A boy decked out with an ivory shoulder is every bit as much a *thauma* as the works of divine or marvelous artistry (Achilles' shield, Odysseus's brooch, Pandora and the animals on her crown among them) that earn the description in epic texts. Also carefully chosen to promote the continuity between the mat-

---

[103] The precise nature of these origins are left undisclosed by Pindar, although, as Köhnken (1983) and others suggest, he allows us to suppose it some kind of mark of the hero's favored status endowed on him at his birth. For the various options, and the differing versions of the myth, see the detailed accounts in Gerber 1982 and Howie 1983.

[104] Among recent treatments, Gerber 1982; Köhnken 1983; Howie 1983; Hubbard 1987.

ter of the myth and the commentary is *daidallein*, a verb that originally denotes technical activity involving the combination of precious metals and/or the attachment of metal inserts to other objects and surfaces, frequently of a less high quality.[105] The expression works here both literally and metaphorically: while *muthoi* are decked out with lies, Pelops, the term reminds us, emerges from the cauldron beautified by the precious ivory that has been fastened to the more prosaic matter of his body. As for the parti-colored or *poikilos* quality of those lies, that, too, harks back to the earlier portrayal on at least two counts: first, in adding the white ivory to the living figure (and the name Pelops may originally have meant "dark-face"), the gods have created precisely such a multi-hued and heterogeneous object; and second, the play of light that an object characterized as *poikilos* so frequently generates matches the sheen issuing from the shining (*phaidimos*) shoulder piece. The effect of the brightness and dazzle common to both the ivory addition and the variegated stories is the same; they suggest through their art the animation of the living or actual thing. Not surprisingly, the Charis whom Pindar makes responsible for these acts of wonderful artistry herself behaves in the manner of a craftsman: she models (*teuchei*) the sweetnesses that she bestows on mortals and uses in her transformation of the incredible into the credible that *mētis* (so *emēsato* at 31) which belongs to the artisans of archaic and classical song. The pleasure that Charis's creations also bring recalls the impact that the beautified Pelops had on his immortal viewer: among the *meilicha* that men enjoy are those furnished by erotic delight.

Beyond these particular parallels are the larger hermeneutic and ethical questions that verbal representations and the figure of Pelops jointly pose. A marked equivocation surrounds Pindar's assessment of storytelling in the "break-off" passage. While the negatively charged elaborate lies may be added on, covering over the original *logos* in dissembling fashion, the activity informing their creation does not inevitably carry the stigma of falsehood and *apatē*; instead, Pindar goes on immediately to redeem the acts of artistry he has seemingly rejected, introducing the divine, personified Charis with an adversative *de*, and presenting her as a wholly positive power who brings *timē*, devises *meilicha*, and has already appeared in relation to Hieron's delightful victory at line 18. These contrasting evaluations map exactly onto the alternate readings that the ivory shoulder bears, both of which Pindar has taken pains to compress into his rapid preview of the myth in lines 25–27.[106] Under-

---

[105] For detailed discussion, Frontisi-Ducroux 1975: 61, 73.

[106] As most commentators are forced to acknowledge, these lines offer a medley of the different tales: the cauldron and the shoulder would naturally put an audience in mind of

stood within the context of the false tale, the ivory feature functions as an addition or supplement, a work of artifice that replaces the original element much as *muthoi* cover over the true *logos*; although not deceptive in and of itself,[107] the shoulder piece both generates and helps make plausible the lying story that the jealous neighbor has devised. But as part of the "real" version that Pindar also heralds from the start, the ivory mark forms an integral part of the original body and, as suits a benefaction granted by the gods, inspires pleasure and sweetness in those who witness it. The poet's vocabulary and phrasing in line 27 (*elephanti phaidimon ōmon kekadmenon*) teasingly admits both possibilities. For Homer, the verb *kekasmai* means "to excel, surpass" and appears together with the attributes, whether mental or physical, that form an integral part of an individual. But in fifth-century Greek the expression more commonly accompanies the external objects, arms and armor among them, that men bear about their bodies, and refers to the act whereby they equip themselves with tangible attributes.[108] Similar questions of interiority and exteriority are generated by the structure of the line: is the ivory the source of the shoulder's gleam, as an initial reading would suggest, or is *elephanti* governed by the participle ("equipped as to his shining shoulder with ivory"), indicating that the element makes visible the radiance that already inheres to the youth?

These issues bear particularly closely on the agenda that *Olympian* 1 sets itself, in both its mythical and its more programmatic portions. Poets who draw attention to the business of emendation in which they are engaged, as Pindar patently does when he addresses Pelops at 36 and announces that he will speak in opposition to those who have gone before, risk being caught in a bind: even as they assert the primacy and veracity of their account, they inevitably signal their own act of substitution, opening themselves up to the charge that they behave no differently from the revisionary storytellers whom they critique.[109] But in ridding the ivory shoulder of its supplementary, secondary, representational nature, and in giving it the status of what is native and primary, Pindar grants his version of events that same originary status. Unlike deceitful taletellers, whose interest lies only in astonishing and beguiling

---

the story of cannibalism and its aftermath, while the adjective *katharos* joined to the cooking pot, the presence of the goddess Klotho, and the unequivocally positive terms used of the ivory addition suggest a revised account.

[107] Although to an audience familiar with *Od.* 19.562–65, the matter in which the addition is made might give pause.

[108] Gerber 1982: ad loc.

[109] So Stesichorus's Palinode, which uses its fashioned *eidōlon* deliberately to point out the manufactured and secondary nature of the revised account in which that double appears. See Bassi 1993 for this.

an audience, he does not use his medium to distort and embroider the truth, but rather strips away what others may have added on, and allows the "natural" person and *logos* to stand free of later accretions. Once Pelops's body and the myth belonging to the hero have been refurbished and restored, Pindar can resume his own act of verbal artistry. Turning back to his laudandus in the final moments of the performance, the singer declares that he will deck out (and the verb he chooses is naturally *daidallein*) Hieron in the folds of song (105). Much like the gods in the story that Pindar has "recovered," the encomiast uses his skill not to contrive a misrepresentation or secondary account, but to realize and externalize the beauty that already belongs to his subject. By virtue of the *sophia* that the closing line cites (116), Pindar's song makes its subject into a work of art that inspires *thauma*, delight, and even eros in its viewers.

In a fresh attempt to set straight what he considers another erroneous version of a myth, Gorgias would again include works of art in his text and create still more troublesome links and exchanges between the verbal and visual or plastic spheres. Long before statues figure explicitly in the *Encomion to Helen*, the address dwells on the "artifactual" quality of speech: *logos* assumes the form of a corporeal, palpable, and modeled object whose success depends on the *technē* used by the orator, poet, or writer in devising or fashioning it. Gorgias first introduces speech as a physical body characterized by *apatē* (8) and, after celebrating its varied capacities, returns to its twin fabricated and illusion-making character. The false word that persuades is molded (*plasantes*, 11),[110] and in legal contests the written argument devised by the fabricant's art (*technēi grapheis*) and "not spoken with truth" wins the day (13).

In the central portion of the discourse, the rhetorician concentrates on the effect of this *logos* on the listener's mind and soul, and still more emphatically gives to speech a reality like that of a physical substance that can charm, persuade, and actually change the *psuchē*'s makeup by its magico-medical imprint or *tupos*; the manufactured discourse now becomes manufacturer in turn, molding the matter of the soul just as it was earlier shaped by the speaker's or writer's craft, and making the unbelievable and unintelligible appear before the eyes of the audience — or more strictly, before those of their opinion or *doxa* (13). But speech, and the *peithō* that adheres to it, is not alone in working on a listener in this manner. Later, turning to the impact that objects of sight have on the faculties of viewers, Gorgias moves almost imperceptibly from the fears and pleasures that visible phenomena provoke to the identical sensations inspired by representations of the same: *opsis*, which transmits

---

[110] The verb is itself a richly loaded one; for one account, Svenbro 1976: esp. 200.

images (*eikones*) to the spectator, works on the soul by "stamping it with its sensation of objects" and engraves "on the mind images of the things one sees" (17). Nor are these interior *tupoi* and engravings the only artworks cited in the text. Equally able to prompt the sensations that a viewer registers are the finely crafted statues and *agalmata* that afford the eyes a divine delight (18). Whether listening to a well-crafted speech or looking at the products of a master artist's hand, the audience's soul responds to their physical presence and generates its own shapes and markings in turn.[111]

Through the repetition and recapitulation of terms and motifs used from the start of the address, Gorgias has connected not just two, but three tangible, affective, and seductive forces. Positioned behind the corporeal *logos* and objects of vision there stands the actual figure of Helen who opens the text, and whom Gorgias not only presents as a *sōma* (4) but also uses by way of paradigm for the active and reactive powers that belong to the other "bodies" he goes on to cite: anticipating the single-bodied *logos* with its godlike powers (*theotata*, 8), Helen has a divine beauty (*isotheon*) and physique that instantly charm those who look on her (4); the sensations of eros, *pothos*, pain, and fear (*phrikē periphobos*, 9) that she and *logos* both inspire return in the account of the impact on the mind of paintings and statues and their engravings, which similarly give rise to longing, pain, and ineffable delight (18).[112] Helen parallels verbal and visual representations on one further count: able to provoke powerful sensations in her viewers, she is worked upon in turn, and exchanging her active role for a passive one, she becomes both hearer and viewer: overmastered by persuasive speech and entranced by the sight of "Alexander's body" (19), she had no choice but to act as she did.

But Gorgias does more than make a general point about how Helen, and hearers and viewers of *logoi* and works of art after her, behave. At the end of the address, the sophist reveals his own *logos* as the prime practitioner of the process it has traced out, and includes its author among those who succumb to its charms: "I wished to write the speech as an encomion for Helen, but a plaything for me" (21). The terms *logos* and *grapsai* most obviously declare this piece akin to the compositions featured in the central portion of the text (particularly in section 13, with its reference to the *logos* that is written [*grapheis*] with skill), and so alert the audience to the persuasion and seduction it has worked on them and the *tupoi* it has left on the matter of their souls.[113] But the

---

[111] Note that the *eikones* that the viewer receives are called "exactly like speech" (17).

[112] See Buchheim 1989: 164 n. 19 for this parallelism.

[113] An additional link lies with the *ekplēxis* that occurs when the eye sees alarming visions

more striking expression *paignion* also situates the address very much in the frame that Gorgias has devised. A physical object, a plaything or toy such as a craftsman might fashion, the speech has by its close acquired the fixity that *logos*'s supremely light and mobile body (8) earlier eschewed. No less tellingly, a *paignion* also signifies the darling in whom the lover takes delight;[114] endowing his speech with seductive qualities (and note how earlier that incantation which is typical of speech could change what the mind saw by "mingling with it," *sunginomenē*, 10), Gorgias implies that he, like Helen, is not only master artist and generator of the images to which others succumb, but a body affected in turn. He, too, must respond to the pleasure and (sexual) charm that his and other *logoi* exercise, and in so doing offer himself as exemplar for those who play audience to his text. Images, whether those engendered by speeches, bodies, or visual representations, are potent objects of desire, whose artistry only increases their appeal.

Left ambivalent in all this is the larger issue of veracity that Gorgias's deliberately agonistic account only glances toward. Although the sophist, like Stesichorus in his Palinode before him, opens with the claim that his version presents the reality of the misconstrued affair (1–2), the speaker's own exposition rapidly calls into question the truth value of his retelling of the tale. His discussion will go on to reveal that the *logos* that persuades produces *apatē*, and that persuasion succeeds because it has first fashioned a false *logos* (8–14). If truth only lies with a reality that exists independent of *logos* (as Gorgias seems to suggest at 2), this text allows its audience no way of passing beyond the *eikones* that it and the phenomena it describes have conjured up. Instead the listener or reader can do no more than respond by adopting the attitude that Gorgias recommends elsewhere,[115] giving himself up to the pleasure that comes with a conscious and willing surrender to the artistic tricks being practiced on him and admiring the facility or *dexiotēs* (so Ar. *Ran.* 1009) of the author. Whether this facility works on the audience to good or ill effect — and *pharmaka*, as Gorgias's own description at 14 makes clear, can operate in both modes — the encomium leaves unresolved.

While Gorgias alludes to statues and paintings only in passing, and chooses to insert the attributes of artifacts into his description of his address, Euripides makes the self-standing work of art central to his own revisionary account of the slandered queen. Where an earlier chapter highlighted the "statuesque" character of both Helen and the *ei-*

---

and causes the viewer to run away (16); so Gorgias's novel style is said to have stunned (*exeplēxe*) the Athenian audience (A4 DK).

[114] So Ar. *Eccl.* 922.

[115] B23 DK, cited p. 90.

dōlon that figures her nature and history, I want now to turn to the dense interplay between the activities of these two plastic images and of the *logos* both internal to and framing the drama. To witness the actions and nature of the doubled protagonist is to recognize how works of linguistic artistry affect their audiences, and to wonder at both the costs and the benefits of the pleasures that visual and verbal representations bring.

For the audiences internal and external to the play, the two fashioned figures not only double for one another but, in a fresh act of "gemination," also model the workings of *logoi* in a drama where almost every narrative comes complete with its pair, leaving hearers incapable of distinguishing truth from falsehood, of determining the original from the revised account.[116] Alongside the contending versions of Helen's own history that have attached themselves, one to the person of the *eidōlon*, the other to the queen, other tales and countertales appear. Perhaps the *logos* that Zeus gave birth to Helen when in the form of a swan is true or *saphēs*, or perhaps the event happened altogether otherwise (*Hel.* 17–21); two *logoi* concerning the fate of the Dioskouroi circulate (*duo d'eston logō*, 138), stories whose dual syntax matches the one-in-two quality of the twins and their twofold fate after death. The motif continues throughout the play, forming part of its constant returns to the phenomenon of doubling: speakers question whether Menelaus is genuinely dead or merely believed so (132, 309), single names denote different things (588, 491–99), and every statement made by Helen in the scene where she dupes Theoklymenos carries a double entendre.

The very existence of these conflicting accounts and multiple meanings harks back to a theme already sounded in Gorgias, and in Pindar before him. *Logos* (or *muthos*, depending on the author's sympathies) exists as a device that corresponds to the *eidōlon* or work of art because it, too, can represent and replace and stand at one remove from the reality it claims to describe; fashioned, refashioned, and divided into two contending versions in the hands of skilled practitioners, its persuasive powers may exist independent of its relation to an original truth.[117]

---

[116] Walsh 1984: 98–99.

[117] Read against Gorgias's *Encomion*, the phantom of Euripides' *Helen* displays fresh analogies with language and its workings. It, too, is a thing at once corporeal, plastic, ethereal, and an "empty seeming" (*kenēn dokēsin*, 36), parallel to the *doxai*, which, according to Gorgias, "are exactly like speech" (17). Identical to speech in nature and impact are also the *eikones* introduced by Gorgias, the matter with which the mind must go to work, and Euripides' drama effectively stages the scenario that Gorgias had conceived: characters in the drama are bound to construct their version of reality on the basis of the *logoi* that they hear, and of the two more literal *eikones* they confront—the double, and a Helen characterized as a second work of art.

But where Pindar purges the linguistic art of its power to mislead, and Gorgias celebrates its capacity to do the same, Euripides takes a more equivocal view. Because the *eidōlon*'s history and behavior conform to the earlier canonical *logos* of the "real" Helen, the living woman and her tale in the play become the imperfect copies, departures from the traditional version, both marked by difference and by their fabricated nature.

The scenario, stories, and speeches peculiar to *Helen* are not alone in taking their character from the presence of the *eidōlon*; using the creation and action of the phantom as a paradigm for his own production of a fiction compounded not just of words but of visible images, too, the playwright equates his drama and its impact on his audience with the workings of the manufactured double on those who witness it.[118] The nexus of relations that Euripides devises again recalls that which Gorgias had earlier created: the plastic image, the person of the queen, and the play that encompasses both all show themselves fabricated and fabricants in turn. Most patently, the three phenomena are self-styled works of representation, issued from a master craftsman's hand. Just as early episodes in the play introduce Helen and her double as mimetic artifacts, the products of the shape-making skills of Zeus and Hera, so drama comes invested with this same "fashioned" character. Through the device of the play-within-the-play staged by Helen to bring about her and Menelaus's flight, Euripides most patently exposes the craft that goes into theatrical creation and shows how its producer and director must be a skilled maker of *eidōla*. The construction of the cenotaph, the verbal duping of Theoklymenos, and the several other elements of the queen's plot all attract the vocabulary that was earlier applied to the manufacture of the double; Helen's devices are similarly described as *mēchanai* (813, 1034; cf. 610), and, like the image fashioned by divine skill and artistry, they, too, depend on their maker's exercise of her *sophia* (1049) and *technē* (1091, 1621; cf. 930).[119] And should the audience miss the links between the miniaturized production onstage and his own activity, Euripides underscores the theatrical quality of what Helen sets before them and its parallelism with the larger drama in which it belongs: so Menelaus critiques the "shopworn" character of his wife's ruse (1056), which includes the hackneyed stratagems found in this and other escape dramas, and he marks the moment when he undertakes the

[118] As Downing (1990: 9) has cogently argued, the *eidōlon* "provides the clearest opportunity for the self-reflexive representation of the dramatist's own *apatē* within the play itself," with *apatē* understood as "a consciously produced fiction deliberately divorced from a concrete reality." Note, too, Walsh 1984: 101.

[119] For detailed discussion, Downing 1990: 11–12.

dramatic role that Helen has traced out for him, declaring that he will perform his "deceptive *oiktos*" (1542) in a "fictitious manner" (1547).[120] Fresh reminders of the fictive and contrived quality of what the playwright stages belong to those "metatheatrical" moments (among them 164–66, 947–48, 996–97) when Euripides nods toward the role-playing actors behind his protagonists.

If several characters within the play replicate the business of the dramatist, displaying their capacity to manufacture images, tell fictional stories, and generally practice the *apatē* that results from the artist's skillful exercise of his craft, then other individuals reflect back Euripides' spectators and their response to the visual and verbal impressions, the *morphai* and *eikones*, set before them. The *eidōlon*, Helen, stories, and theatrical representation are not only the fictional products of another's shape-making skills but also, following Gorgias's earlier scheme, fabricants that "mold" their witnesses in turn and elicit their cognitive and emotional responses. The double, possessing the beauty and seductive powers that adhere to Helen's body, persuades all those who set eyes on it of its reality, and has occasioned the ten-year bloody strife on which the chorus and the queen repeatedly dwell. Confronted with the no less convincing person of the living Helen, individuals find their visual and mental powers thrown into confusion, and they must either accept the reality of both the queen and the *eidōlon* (118) or suppose their internal faculties impaired (580–81). For all its patent fictionality, Helen's "production" succeeds in convincing those who attend its visual representations and hear the role-players speak their words, and it overcomes the skepticism that Theoklymenos and his men vainly try to exercise. While Euripides makes his own audience complicit in the deceptions that the image-generating protagonists in the drama have devised, the question of the theatergoers' own response to his production remains an open one. His reminders of the *technē*, *mēchanai*, *doloi*, and *poiēsis* that went into the creation of *Helen* notwithstanding, has the audience, too, succumbed to its persuasive impact and *apatē*, and accepted, as least for as long as the play lasts, its revisionary account of the renegade queen?

Also posed, and in more direct fashion than in Gorgias's text, is the larger moral and epistemological charge informing this *apatē*.[121] Can the seductive and illusion-producing powers of drama, and of the representations that it puts onstage, act to good effect, ultimately bringing about the reward of the virtuous (Helen and Menelaus) and the punishment of the bad (Theoklymenos)? Might Gorgias's contention, that to yield to

---

[120] Note, too, 1589, where the sea journey is dubbed a "deceit."
[121] See particularly Downing 1990 and Walsh 1984: 104 for this.

the poet's deception is the mark of the sensible man, be realized in the greater degree of self-knowledge and wisdom that some of the characters achieve as a result of the tricks practiced on them? Or should an audience focus rather on the pain and suffering provoked by the *eidōlon* and other *doloi* filling the text (e.g., 1103, 1130, 1322) and remember the censure that the chorus appears to address to the contrived and self-conscious quality of Helen's beauty (1366–68)?

While acknowledging the negative powers that go along with works of artifice and deception, Euripides ultimately vindicates his activity on the grounds of the pleasure and release from pain that words, artistic images, and other products of poetic skill afford. In the ode to the Mountain Mother, the chorus describes how its own activity of music, dance, and song, here mirrored in the performance of the Charites and Muses, transforms pain into pleasure (1341–52) and brings about the very effect that Gorgias had assigned to *logos*, the removal of *lupē*, grief, and its replacement with joy (*charan*; cf. *Encomion* 8). It comes as no surprise to find Aphrodite, dubbed fairest of all divinities, appearing in this context (1348–49) and presiding over the very moment when the Mother laughs and experiences *terpsis* in place of her former distress. The mastermind behind the story that the play narrates, and the ultimate practitioner of "*apatai* and devious inventions" (1103), the goddess also offers a model for the common manner in which artistic and literary creations work, their parallel generation of desirable images that afford an almost divine delight. Exposing the illusory quality to these creations may also come at too high a price: perhaps continued belief in the *eidōlon* is preferable to the painful recognition that the carnage-filled Trojan War had been waged to no purpose.

Euripides' choice of theme, as so many readings acknowledge, is deeply implicated in the drama's time and place. Performed in 412, in the aftermath of the crushing defeat suffered by the Athenians in Sicily, *Helen* both offers pleasurable escapism and, less comfortably, suggests parallels between the city's grand and ultimately futile venture and the Trojan War pursued for a phantom's sake. Through the figure of the *eidōlon*, Euripides signals the power of images, both plastic and verbal, to beguile an audience and to generate their own seductive "reality." As Thucydides' accounts of the debates preceding both the Sicilian venture and the other actions undertaken in the course of the Peloponnesian struggle seek to illustrate, *logos*, and the manifold visual as well as auditory delights that lie with its skillful exercise, played no small role in setting the city on its ill-chosen and precipitous course. In a polis where citizens attending the Assembly have become, in the demagogue Cleon's own self-serving description, "spectators of *logoi*," and where they are undone by the *hēdonē* that they derive from hearing and being viewers (*theatai*) of well-turned speeches (3.38.4, 7), the power of spectacles that appeal both singly and in combination to an audience's ears and eyes has become a source of acute anxiety.

As Thucydides' (or Cleon's) words additionally suggest, in politics no less than in the literary domain, the boundary between artistic and verbal representations remains a fluid and permeable one, and nowhere more than when a speaker, writer, or dramatist seeks to delight and persuade his audience with his display of craft. Rather than setting the two media in the paragonal relationship privileged by modern writers and critics, the ancient sources and practitioners of *logoi* more readily break down the divisions and invest each medium with the other's powers: both words and visual images arouse their spectators' emotions, moving, beguiling, and prompting an emotional and kinetic response. The tricks and stratagems supposedly deployed by the politicians of late fifth-century Athens form the natural corollary to the exchanges between the two spheres. Just as words have become objects that attract the eyes of the audience, and in which the skilled *theatēs* takes delight, so, too, the person of the speaker offers a view-worthy spectacle in and of itself. Breaking with tradition, Cleon is credited with having first introduced gesture into demagogic oratory, with wearing his cloak girt up about him in a flamboyant manner and waving his arms and hands about as he spoke his piece.[122] Using body as well as voice, he becomes that moving, speaking image of the myth-maker and poet's imagination.

I close with this focus on the power of words to generate images and of representations to embody words because it at once emphasizes the continuities in the material treated so far, looks forward to the changes that the epilogue will take up, and suggests one final observation about the statues featured in this study. From very early on, the Greeks chose to set their visual representations within a milieu of speech and text. Statues designed for votive and funerary purposes displayed inscriptions on their bodies and their bases, divine images came encompassed by the act of prayer, and victory monuments contained visual directives for the redelivery of the announcement of the win. The very question of an artifact's capacity to "presentify" rather than merely to replicate often depended on its possession of speech, or its ability to respond to the words addressed to it. Poems, speeches, and other literary forms imagined themselves in the shape of speaking artifacts, objects that could realize the same syntheses and combinations of word and image as

---

[122] For this account, Arist. [*Ath. Pol.*] 28.3; cf. *FGrH* 115 F 92; Plut. *Nic.* 8.3; Cic. *Brut.* 28.

many of the statues themselves. In the arrangements they devise, the archaic and classical sources achieve much closer and bolder unions than would the authors of later antiquity, who generally practice this boundary-crossing only within the increasingly self-conscious and marked device of *ekphrasis*, the placement and description of works of art within literary compositions. But on one score the Hellenistic and imperial texts remain true to the earlier model. Perhaps matching the role occupied by the real-world statues that continued to stand throughout the public and private spaces of Greece, authors imagine images as talking points. The objects not only speak, but more frequently still provoke discourse on the part of their viewers, inspiring conversations that can touch on topics that range from philosophy, to aesthetics, to politics, love, and beyond. It has been my aim throughout to reconstruct some of these exchanges, and to suggest that images acted as so many visual cues to which ancient audiences responded in speech and text.

Lucian's Retrospective

THE INTERACTIONS between images and texts that the last chapter traced would continue on through the Hellenistic and into the imperial age, acquiring ever more formalized and sometimes polemical forms. Callimachus, Theocritus, and the composers of the countless meditations on real and notional works of art that make up the *Greek Anthology* insert statues into their poems to demonstrate the now similar, now contrasting properties and powers of their compositions, and to construct relations both symbiotic and antagonistic between the *eikōn* and the surrounding *logos*. So, too, the different spheres continue their mutual borrowings as rhetoric claims for itself the capacity vividly to present scenes to the hearer's eyes (through the device of *enargeia*), while the "art historians" who first appear in the Hellenistic age recognize that statues and paintings can express and incite feeling no differently from texts. But rather than summarize these and other developments, I end with two paired works that gather together many of the strands that went into thinking about images in the archaic and classical ages, and that redeploy them in an entirely novel setting. Composed in the second century A.D., by a Syrian-born author writing in praise of a Roman emperor's Greek mistress, Lucian's *Eikones* and *Pro eikonibus* both help to recapitulate the themes covered in the previous chapters and chart the extent to which the wholly new political and social conditions of the age have given the archaic and classical topoi a radically changed significance.[1]

An unknown woman of extraordinary beauty passes through the streets of an ancient city; a bystander stands transfixed at the sight, all powers of motion and speech momentarily lost. Later, relating the encounter to his friend Polystratus, Lycinus — Lucian's mouthpiece here — finds that the incident has beggared his verbal powers. Mere words alone cannot manifest (*emphanisai*) an *eikōn* or portrait that matches the language-defying perfection of what he has seen, and on this occasion he must seek a different descriptive mode (*Eikones*, 3). Already the

---

[1] While art historians have made heavy use of the first of the texts for their discussions of the statues cited there, the two dialogues have otherwise attracted little critical attention. For exceptions, see Romm 1990, and particularly Goldhill forthcoming, whose reading I cite extensively here.

term *eikōn* intimates the device that Lycinus will adopt for the remainder of this and its pendant dialogue. Not just a portrait or an image, *eikōn* also refers to a statue,[2] and following that expression Lycinus will proceed verbally to "sculpt" a representation of the supremely beauteous spectacle. Challenged by Polystratus to produce his account, he makes his intentions plainer: he will call to his aid the sculptors of old "in order that they might fashion (*anaplaseian*) me the woman."

But statues and their powers are very much in the air even before Lycinus introduces his master conceit. In the opening lines of the *Eikones*, the protagonist compares his encounter with the unnamed beauty to the experience of seeing the Gorgon: "Just as it says in the myth, I was struck stiff with *thauma* and almost became a stone instead of a human." Fresh mythical references frame Polystratus's response:

> Heracles! That is an extraordinary spectacle you are talking of, and a terribly potent one, if a mere woman could strike Lycinus from his senses. For you experience that readily enough with boys, so that it would be quicker to move all Sipylus from its base than to draw you away from your beauties, and keep you from standing open-mouthed, and often teary-eyed, too, just like the daughter of Tantalus. (*Eikones* 1)

These two disparate myths of petrifaction not only tell the reader that he is in the company of members of the cultural elite (Niobe is not directly named, but is identified only through the geographic marker and parentage that an educated audience would recognize), but also remind him of the complex dynamics involved in viewing, and the power play that goes on between the two parties to so charged a visual encounter. Lycinus's "stiff" condition self-mockingly registers the erotic component to his gaze, and the deliberate misconstrual of the Niobe myth, here cast as the lithified victim of a frustrated passion, confirms that the individual who turns the viewed into a source of erotic stimulation becomes objectified in turn.[3] Nor does vision travel in one direction alone, as Lycinus's rejoinder to Polystratus's wish to see this woman makes clear:

> You may be very certain that if you get but a distant view of her she will strike you dumb and more motionless than a statue. But if she were to look at you as well, what device could drag you from her? She will bind you and lead you off wherever she wishes, just as a magnet does to iron. (*Eikones* 1)

---

[2] See Price 1984: 177 for a useful discussion of the term at this period. The *eikōn* can also, of course, refer to a simile, and Lucian's play on the term recalls Alcibiades' own at Pl. *Symp.* 215a.

[3] As noted in Goldhill forthcoming.

For all her "to-be-looked-at-ness," the target of this gaze has given up none of her agency, and through their exchange of glances viewer and viewed assume the same monumentalized form.

Reworking not only the myths but also the attendant themes familiar from much earlier texts, Lucian has adapted them to the particular situation in which his spokesman finds himself. This paragon of loveliness, as we will go on to discover, is none other than the mistress of the emperor Verus, whose skillful negotiation of her public role the more directly encomiastic portions of the dialogue will recognize. Her position is marked by both the passivity and the power that Lycinus's introduction balances: at once the dependent object of her lord's favor and affections, she is also a source of patronage in her own right, whom those seeking advancement in court society would do well to cultivate. To look on and speak about the consort of the most powerful individual of all demands quite literal circumspection,[4] and as the opening suggests and the *eikōn* conceit goes on to illustrate, an oblique approach offers the safest stratagem. Just like the Gorgon who can be neither directly viewed nor verbally detailed in her living form, and who may only be described in verbal or visual accounts when she has been transformed into an artistic image or artifact,[5] so, too, Panthea (whose name is long postponed, and is finally released only via an appeal to another "representation," this time textual, of the classical age[6]) must be portrayed through the *eikones*, which are myths and plastic images both.

Those plastic images are then brought onto the scene, each one a familiar and celebrated work by a fifth- or fourth-century artist — Praxiteles, Pheidias, Alkamenes, and the rest. Lycinus's choice of material for his latter-day *eikōn* respects the canonical status that the statues and sculptors of the high classical and early Alexandrian ages had long since achieved, and promotes the larger agenda framing the composition of this and other works belonging to the so-called Second Sophistic. In a self-conscious attempt to encourage a renaissance of classical Greek culture, members of the educated elite in the empire turned back to the fifth and fourth centuries B.C., and revived the Attic Greek used by the authors of the earlier ages for their own compositions. But even as

[4] A point already brought out by Herodotus's tale of the Lydian Gyges and Candaules' wife at 1.8–12.

[5] So Frontisi-Ducroux 1995: chap. 5.

[6] At *Eikones* 10, following Polystratus's revelation that the woman "has the same name as the beautiful wife of Abradatas," a character in Xenophon's *Cyropaideia*, Lycinus observes the impact of that earlier author's powers of representation: "It makes me feel as if I see her when I reach that place in my reading." As Lucian's audience is supposed to remember, the initial description of the heroine in Xenophon's text (5.1.4–7) is itself framed as an ekphrasis.

Lycinus appeals to classical precedents and declares himself dependent on the models they supply, he emerges as more than a slavish imitator. Borrowing features from the individual images and recombining the different statues' parts, the encomiast produces a hybrid artifact that resembles nothing that has gone before. The procedure exactly suits the relation to the classical past that Lucian more broadly seeks to achieve: desiring to recover the distant and only partially transmitted cultural heritage, he also wishes to demonstrate his independence from a potentially oppressive paradigm.[7]

Nothing better speaks the broken nature of the transmission of this classical model than the fashion in which Lycinus presents the images that he cites. First to be described is the notorious Aphrodite of Knidos, which Polystratus, remembering his visit to its shrine, dubs "the fairest of the creations of Praxiteles"; Lycinus then follows up his remark by alluding briefly to the story of the man who fell in love with the marble goddess (*Eikones* 4). On several counts the two protagonists (and Lucian behind them) unwittingly show themselves practitioners of a mode of viewing particular to members of a postclassical elite Greek culture. The aura of a work now derives not from its function and religious charge, its capacity to instantiate this or that living goddess, but from the individual artist who had created it; no statue enters the text without the attendant name of its producer, now as important as the representation itself. Polystratus's visits, and his repeat visits for a second look, to the different places where these images are found put him in the company of other educated travelers of the age, who perform Grand Tours of the cult sites of Greece in order to see the famous works of art displayed there. The titillating story that adheres to the Knidia only enhances her touristic appeal and encourages the viewer self-consciously to monitor his response to her allure.

That the image has been stripped of its presentifying role and turned into a work of art invested with a purely "secularized cult value,"[8] the closing of the second dialogue underscores. For all Lycinus's initial desire to recover the *archetupon* of his subject (*Eikones* 3), and Polystratus's subsequent declaration that he will produce an *eikōn* that is "an imitation after the archetype" (*pros to archetupon memimēmenē*, 15), the two speakers play a teasing game that finally refuses both art and language the power to make the real woman visible. Indeed, Lycinus will end by declaring an attempt to return to the antecedent reality quite foreign to his enterprise. He counters Panthea's objection

---

[7] I return to this correspondence between the hybrid image and the discourse itself below.
[8] Camille 1989: 341 for this.

to her hubristic equation with goddesses in his encomion by asserting that she has misunderstood the terms of his comparison or simile (now *eikōn* in its linguistic sense): he has likened her not to the deities themselves, who lie quite beyond the powers of "human imitation" (*Pro eikonibus* 23) and do not reveal themselves to men's sight, but only to their sculpted likenesses. He has fixed his eyes not on an archetype as it originally seemed but on an imitative account in fashioning his picture. The *eikōn* that earlier claimed to match the ineffable vision of beauty now turns out to be an act of ekphrasis narrowly defined, and all that can be recovered are the images produced by the Masters of old. Nor does this paragon of beauty ever figure as a living participant in the conversation. Lacking even a name for the first portion of the dialogue, her absence becomes even more marked in the second part of the diptych, where Polystratus describes Panthea's own scrutiny of Lycinus's portrait and gives her response in reported speech; requiring a mouthpiece, this woman so vaunted for the quality of her voice has become the dumb statue cited in the two friends' opening exchange.[9]

But perhaps the "real" Panthea was never there all along. Her initial appearance already has the quality of a work of (self-)representation, as she shows herself in "splendid pomp" (and *paraskeuē* in *Eikones* 2 also carries the sense of something prepared and plotted in advance), attended by eunuchs and maids as befits her more-than-private station, and holding up a bookroll that is described as open at its middle (9);[10] apparently discussing the contents of the work with one of her escorts, she takes care to smile so as to display the glorious teeth that inspire Lycinus to his highest flights of admiration (*Eikones* 2 and 9). In his careful diagnosis of his reaction to the spectacle that Panthea has offered, and the "speaking out" — the basic meaning of the term *ekphrasis* — that her appearance has prompted, the author of the address in her praise responds in kind: he views her as a work of art, and his subsequent dismembering of the fifth- and fourth-century statues that he cites

[9] The realm of secondary representations in which Panthea is made to dwell affects others besides the woman herself. Through the act of ventriloquism that he must perform in the second dialogue, Polystratus himself enters into the mimetic game, assuming a role other than his own and lending his voice to the "absent presence." A fresh piece of substitution and a new form of mimetic play end the text, as Polystratus prepares to relate Lycinus's words back to the offended party. Now he is invited to take on the role of replacement, to act the part of the absent Lycinus before Panthea (29), just as he assumed the role of Panthea before his friend.

[10] As the heroine of Anthony Trollope's *The Eustace Diamonds* points out on several occasions, a woman wishing to be thought educated should know more than the opening lines of a text.

will correspond to his parceling out of the various elements of Panthea's living form into detachable body parts.[11]

If Panthea engages in a self-fashioning in the first dialogue, then the second introduces her as a skilled reader of the images that others have devised. The imagined confrontation between the original and the copy that another has made and set up for view not only revisits a situation favored by Hellenistic and later epigrammists, where the subjects of the works observe and comment on representations of themselves,[12] but also reveals that composing a visual or verbal encomion is every bit as delicate a deed as it was in classical times, fraught with dangers old and new. Lycinus, as the reader would rapidly understand, has created his *eikōn* to celebrate and praise Panthea, to enhance still further the fame of a woman already *aoidimos* (*Eikones* 10);[13] but she, recognizing that the artist bent on flattery can easily generate false images, fears that Lycinus might have devised just such a misrepresentation, and through his hubristic exaggerations produced something that generates *phthonos*. For all the author's attempt to meet her charge by claiming that praise relies on exalted rhetoric rather than strict accuracy and by seeking to distinguish between an encomion and a self-serving flattery, the *agōn* (*Pro eikonibus* 29) between the plaintiff and defendant remains unresolved at the second dialogue's end. As the dispute reveals, questions of who actually controls and diffuses the public image of a person, and whom that image is designed to benefit (its subject, its creator, or the broader public for the work?), are critical ones, able to reflect and negotiate the relative positions of the two parties to the exchange.[14] Within the imperial world, the act of praise is in itself a bid for power, and a potential means of determining the mode in which those beyond

---

[11] This dismemberment also goes to the erotic element in the experience as the amorous viewer fetishizes the desired body, investing its accessory objects or attributes with erotic significance (for this, Brooks 1993 and Pacteau 1994). Treating each element in turn corresponds to a haptic desire to touch each one.

[12] Note particularly *Anth. Plan.* 16.160, 162, 169; Alciphron *Epist.* 4.1

[13] Goldhill (forthcoming) notes that the term only appears once in Homer, used by Helen of herself and Paris (*Il.* 6.358). But equally significant might be the use of the expression in Herodotus at 2.135.5, here applied to the most famous of Greek courtesans, one Rhodopis, who traveled to Egypt to ply her trade and supposedly built a pyramid with her earnings.

[14] For further remarks on this issue, see Goldhill forthcoming. It is also instructive to read these questions against the then-current practice of imperial image-making. Alexander was the first Greek potentate whom we know to have carefully monitored his representation in plastic form, and by Augustan times at least, he was reported to have given Lysippos sole rights of portraiture (Plut. *Mor.* 335a–b); the Roman emperors, to a greater or lesser degree, also exercised control over their portraits, particularly in numismatic form. But, as Price (1984: 172–74) argues, ruler images in the Greek East were largely set up on local initiative, and imperial involvement may have been considerably less pronounced.

the immediate court circle will view the object of the celebratory account.

Not that Lucian's two statue-makers would grant any disjuncture between the attributes of the "real" Panthea and those displayed by the *eikōn* that both she and they have fashioned. Lycinus, taking his cue from the divine builders of Pandora, who similarly cobble together heterogeneous features and turn from the surface of their vessel to its depths, first models the exterior of his image, then hands it over to Polystratus for the addition of the appropriate internal properties. The visible body possesses all the allure of the archetypal manufactured woman, and of the sensual representations created by the sculptors of the late fifth and fourth centuries. From the Knidia the Panthea *eikōn* borrows its liquid and winning gaze (*Eikones* 6), and from other seductive goddesses the garment nicely calculated to reveal its bodily charms; its delicacy of texture suggests a virtual transparency, and it "clings close where it should" while floating in the air at other points (7). Lycinus then invites no lesser artists than Polygnotos and Apelles to furnish the blush that contributes so powerfully to the image's charms (7), and draws his work to a close by summoning to the image's side the same Charites (now in company with the Erotes) who attended Pandora so many centuries before.

But, as Polystratus goes on to argue, Lycinus has only furnished half the picture: all he has done is to praise Panthea's *sōma* and *morphē*, while "the virtues of the soul, which are unseen, need also to be included" (*Eikones* 11). He begins by endowing the *eikōn* with a voice for singing and speaking proper Attic speech (a "gift" that the Pandora image also receives), and then passes on to her *paideia*, *sophia*, *sunesis*, and other intellectual, ethical, and spiritual attributes. In all this, as Polystratus also signals at the start of his contribution (11), his chief concern is with making the two portions of the *eikōn*, its external appearance and its unseen interior, coherent and harmonious reflections of one another. The portrait image that he fashions, he explains, will resemble neither those women whose pleasing bodies belie the worthlessness of their souls (Pandora once again, but the negative exemplum here), nor Egyptian temples, all loveliness and ornamentation without but housing a monkey or cat for a deity within,[15] nor Helen, who appears as foil later in the dialogue (22).[16] The text concludes with Poly-

[15] Frequently Egyptian divine images themselves offer Greek writers examples of a problematic split between appearance and essence: how can a deity masquerade in the likeness of a cat, dog, or ass?

[16] Helen lurks in several ways behind the text. According to an anecdote familiar from many sources, when Zeuxis agreed to create a picture for the city of Kroton, he had the

stratus proposing that the two artists join their portraits together, "the *eikones* that you modeled of her body, and the pictures that I painted of her soul" (23), to form a single and cohesive whole, and to set the work in a book so that men both now and hereafter might experience the same *thauma* that the sight of Panthea first aroused.

The sudden transformation of an *eikōn* into a text (an image reading now becomes an image read) plainly tells the reader what he has known all along: that composing an encomion and fashioning a statue are parallel enterprises that can mingle, exchange, and contest their terms. Lucian's turn to the realm of the statue-maker has meant both a self-reflexive meditation on his own activity and his foray into the time-honored debate surrounding the relative merits of images and words. Most patently, the dialogues employ the vocabulary of craftsmanship and sculpture to speak of their own rhetorical enterprise. Even before we know that Lycinus will deploy statues to formulate his account, Polystratus has charged him with "modeling (*anaplattōn*) a miracle-working kind of beauty (*teration ti kallos*)" (*Eikones* 2). Shortly afterward the metaphor becomes quite literal. Declaring his inability to do as Polystratus bids (to "display the *eidos* of his beauty in words"), Lycinus summons as helpers the craftsmen of old in order that they might "model" (*anaplattein* again) the *eikōn* for him. In the remainder of the dialogue, speech acquires powers—reminiscent of those which Gorgias once ascribed to his own and other persuasive *logoi*—that give to it the role of the statue-maker's crafting hand and tools: it is *logos* that undertakes the task of adorning (*metakosmein*) and fitting together (*suntithenai* and *harmozein*) the disparate parts of the final work; and it achieves that quality of *eurhuthmia* highly prized in ancient discussions of classical statuary (5). In his own additions to the work already set up, Polystratus refers on several occasions to Lycinus's act of *plastikē* and styles himself painter to his friend's statue-maker. The partnership the two speakers achieve recalls the cooperative venture that ancient image-making involved.[17]

The parallels between plastic and verbal creation continue into the second dialogue of the pair. Through the message she conveys via Polystratus, Panthea acknowledges her laudator's "modeling" (*to plasma*

---

town assemble its most beautiful maidens, and took one portion of his depiction from each (so Cic. *Inv. rhet.* 2.1; Pliny *HN* 35.64, cf. 66; Dion. Hal. *Vett. cens.* 1). Helen, from the epic texts on, is also the constant object of the desiring gaze and is chiefly described in terms of the effect that she has on others; from the first, she, too, comes surrounded by verbal, visual, and plastic representations of herself.

[17] Praxiteles, Pliny tells us, had his own artist of choice with whom he worked (*HN* 35.130–33); the artist would add the final touches to the image, painting both face and body in brilliant tones and contributing to the overall impression of liveliness.

sou, Pro eikonibus 10) but bids Lycinus redo the work. For all the fact
that the eulogy has already gone into public circulation, much as a
statue-maker's image would be set up for general display, the author
still retains the liberty to correct and refashion what he has done, both
to rewrite (*metagrapsai* at 8 recalls the artist's activity, too) and to "re-
shape" (*metarrhuthmein*, 14) the *logos*. In evoking a precedent for the
task she asks the speaker to undertake, Panthea cites the actions of the
most famed of fifth-century sculptors. According to the anecdote she
relates (found here alone, and perhaps invented for the purpose of the
argument), Pheidias hid himself behind a door to hear the criticism that
viewers would address to his celebrated Zeus at Olympia: "Then, when
the spectators had left, Pheidias locked himself up once more and cor-
rected and reshaped (*metarrhuthmein*) the *agalma*" (14). A second verb
also does double duty for the *logos* and *agalma* both: the composer, like
the sculptor, must "set up again"/"revise" (*epanorthoun*, 14) the work
he has devised. Correct and pleasing proportions and a general aesthetic, and perhaps ethical rectitude, should belong to creative ventures
of all kinds, whether the craftsman works in words or in the harder
matter of stone or bronze.

Polystratus, for all his part in the construction of the image, shows
himself in sympathy with Panthea's critique. He also urges his friend to
undertake an act of revision, conflating the kindred arts as he advises
Lycinus to "refurbish (*metakosmein*) the *biblion*" (*Pro eikonibus* 12).
His recognition of the faults of the encomion, he notes, came about
when he confronted the finished product, not so much as would do an
auditor and reader of a written text, but as a connoisseur who trains a
practiced eye on a work of art; on an initial hearing he found nothing
amiss, but adopting a different stance, that which belongs to the viewer
of a statue or painting, he registers its several deficiencies: "I experienced just about what we all experience when we look at things. If we
see them very close up, under our very eyes, we can discern nothing
accurately (*akribes*), but if standing off we look at them from the right
distance (*summetrou*), everything is revealed clearly." Of course, Lucian
has neatly turned this fresh appraisal into an additional compliment for
the object of his praise: even from the optimal viewing point, that which
allows the clearest and most accurate look (a Platonic as well as Stoic
conceit), Panthea shows to advantage.[18]

Because the finished statue, no less than its mode of creation, so
closely jibes with the written piece, the author who inserts a real or
notional image into his composition must select his object with great
care; in both its attributes and its technique the artifact reflects back the

---

[18] See Goldhill forthcoming for this.

surrounding discourse, manifesting the poet's or orator's generic and stylistic choices in microcosmic fashion.[19] Within the *Eikones* and *Pro eikonibus*, the two fictional image-makers implicitly debate and validate Lucian's preferred mode of composition. Lycinus begins by presenting the satirist's own agenda as he outlines his projected enterprise. While looking to the statues most emblematic of a classical aesthetic, those images made by Pheidias, Alkamenes, Praxiteles, and their kind, he nonetheless aims through his work of graft and synthesis to present something quite novel; he would play innovator and not mere copyist, and he deliberately sets out in quest of what is hybrid and "particolored" (*summiges kai poikilon, Eikones* 5). When Polystratus joins in the game, he initially places himself in a different literary camp.[20] Posing as the strict traditionalist, he wants his description to adhere to existing "canons," and he intends to avoid the variegated manner of his friend in order to display his portrait as something prepared "according to the ancient *plastikē*" (12). But from behind the scenes, Lucian makes Polystratus depart from his stated program and forces him to comply with the satirist's own: he, too, must resort to hybridization when he attempts to describe his subject's *paideia*, and, finding no single archetype adequate, he combines a series of heterogeneous precedents (16). The *eikōn* that emerges comes to supply a perfect match for the discourse itself. Very much in step with the statue that presents a bold amalgam of existing types, building out of earlier elements something entirely new, this encomion infuses life into the timeworn panegyric mode and reworks the standard topoi into a variegated multiform quite distinct from any classical speech of praise.

But for all that the two dialogues take their cue from the *eikōn* embedded in their midst, Lucian never allows the plastic representation to displace *logos* and its claims. Like Isocrates, Dio Chrysostom, Aelius Aristides, and other speakers both earlier and contemporary, Lucian follows up Simonides' familiar quip ("Pictures are silent poems, and poems are speaking pictures," Plut. *Mor.* 346f) and sets the respective powers of verbal and plastic representations in agonistic as well as com-

---

[19] As Romm (1990) has shown, this is very much what Lucian is about in other dialogues where he draws from the sculptor's studio and depicts his activity in these borrowed clothes. By way of declaring his preference for "an aesthetic based on pliancy and recombination rather than on fixity of outline" (ibid.: 75), the satirist sometimes opts to work in clay rather than less malleable metal, and his readiness on this and other occasions to dismember and recombine even the most vaunted of classical works (and for the sculptors of old, read the fifth- and fourth-century orators held up for emulation by Lucian's contemporaries) signals his simultaneous familiarity with a hallowed tradition and freedom from its constraints.

[20] As signaled in ibid.: 89–90.

plementary relations. An early threat to the descriptive capacities of the statue appears in Lycinus's departure from his stated agenda. Trying to conjure up Panthea's complexion, he has to turn not to a visual artist but to a verbal one, and to call on Homer, dubbed "the best of *grapheōn* [writers/artists]"; only the Homeric simile describing Menelaus's bloodied thighs in the likeness of ivory tinged with crimson can exactly convey the quality and shading of his subject's skin (*Eikones* 8). Of course the joke, apparent to the educated reader, depends not only on Homer's having had recourse to a verbal *eikōn* (the poet "likened" the thighs) to describe a visual effect,[21] but also on his use of a work of art by way of vehicle within his conceit: the thighs stained with blood recall the *agalma* that a woman is fashioning to serve as a cheekpiece for horses (*Il.* 4.141–45). Poets, and other writers, too, reappear in Polystratus's emendations and additions to the *eikōn* that his friend has put on display, and now words are expressly summoned as the medium through which he proposes to reveal those internal qualities deemed "invisible" (12). In his summation of the enterprise at the close of the *Eikones*, Polystratus again plays on the two meanings of the term *graphein* as he suggests joining in one Lycinus's plastic images and "those *eikonas* that I painted/wrote (*egrapsamēn*) of her soul" (23). While not explicitly privileging the "graphic" mode, Polystratus renews his challenge to the capacity of the image to supply a fully rounded portrait: for all its possession of exterior and interior, can the statue effectively project its subject's invisible and inner qualities, or can only the painter's — or more critically, the writer's — *eikones* (as Isocrates had much earlier affirmed in his *Evagoras*) achieve that feat?

Polystratus also makes a second and still more weighty claim on behalf of the Panthea image fashioned out of words. Comparing it to the works of Apelles, Parrhasios, and Polygnotos, and to objects "made of wood and wax and colors," he declares that once placed within a book, this *eikōn* will enjoy a longevity superior to that of the painted and plastic goods (*Eikones* 23). The remainder of the two dialogues actually bears out this surprising claim. For all their seeming durability and the hardness of the matter in which they are made, the statues of the classical age prove less resistant to attack and change than the discourse currently being shaped before an audience of contemporary and latter-day listeners or readers. While Lycinus can dismember and fragment the cultural icons of old with impunity, he has, so far, resisted Panthea's attempts to impose similar modifications on his work, and he distances himself from Pheidias's example of emendation here. Even should Panthea prove victorious in this *agōn* (the votes, the end of *Pro eikonibus*

[21] Goldhill forthcoming.

remarks, have yet to be cast), Lycinus's misdirected efforts will abide for all to wonder at.

On this particular score, Lucian's dialogues emerge as prescient in ways he could not anticipate. Either wholly lost or visible in no more than fragments or the copies and reworkings of the imperial age, the statues that he cites exist chiefly in ancient and modern textual accounts, and whatever wonder they provoke has come to depend on the power of words to call them up. But even transformed into literary and rhetorical topoi and subordinated to the controlling hand of the text, the dimensions of the image so central to archaic and classical responses still glimmer through these dialogues: whether affirming or denying the objects their presentifying, paralyzing, petrifying, seductive, and revelatory capacities, Lucian acknowledges that only works of art can begin to encompass the most beautiful woman on earth, and suggests that hearers and readers must become viewers in order to experience both the dangers and the delights that exposure to such a figure involves. And no less in keeping with the earlier material that I have explored, the Panthea image also proves inextricably bound up with the larger political and cultural environment surrounding subject and "artist" both. Using the statue as a vehicle for constructing and describing the power relations between different social spheres, as well as the literary agenda that the author pursues, Lucian exhibits anew the multivalent nature of the object, and its readiness to assume the meanings that successive generations have placed on it.

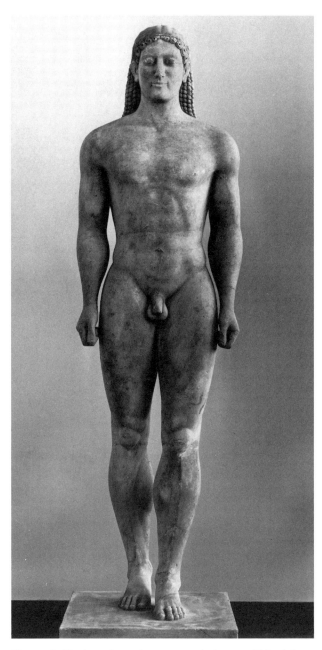

Figure 1. Kroisos from Anavyssos, Attica, c. 530. Athens
NM 3851. Photo courtesy of Hirmer Verlag.

Figure 2. Group made by Geneleos and dedicated by [. . .]arches from the Heraion at Samos, c. 550. Berlin and Samos (Vathy) Museum, Samos 2546. Photo courtesy of Deutsches Archäologisches Institut, Athens.

Figure 3. "Charioteer" from Motya (W. Sicily), c. 480–470. Marsala. Museo Archeologico. Photo courtesy of Malcolm Bell.

Figure 4. Diadoumenos of Polykleitos, Roman copy, from Delos, original c. 430. Athens NM 1826. Photo courtesy of Alinari/Art Resource, N.Y.

Figure 5. Warriors A and B from the sea off Riace Marina (Italy), c. 460–440. Reggio Calabria, Museo Nazionale. Photos courtesy of Erich Lessing/Art Resource, N.Y., and Alinari/Art Resource, N.Y.

Figure 6. The tyrannicides Harmodios and Aristogeiton by Kritios and
Nesiotes, Roman copy, original 477/76. Naples, Museo Nazionale G 103–4.
Institute negative no. 58.1789, photo by Bartl. Photo courtesy of Deutsches
Archäologisches Institut, Rome.

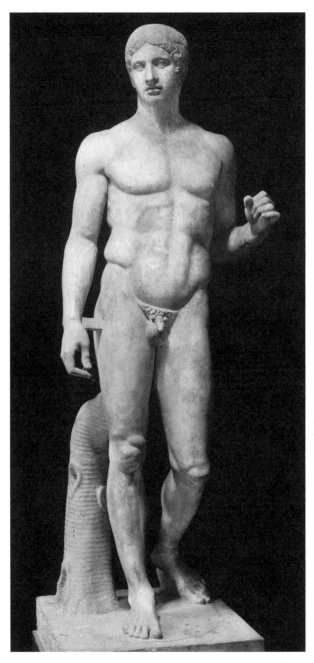

Figure 7. Doryphoros of Polykleitos, Roman copy, from
Pompeii, original c. 440. Naples, Museo Nazionale 6146.
Photo courtesy of Alinari/Art Resource, N.Y.

Figure 8. East pediment of the Temple of Zeus at Olympia, c. 470–457: central group of Pelops, Zeus, and Oinomaos. Olympia Museum. Photo courtesy of Hirmer Verlag.

Figure 9. Temple of Athena Nike Parapet, Nikai and bull, c. 420–400. Athens, Acropolis Museum, ACR 972 and ACR 2680. Photo courtesy of the Alison Frantz Collection, American School of Classical Studies at Athens.

Figure 10. Nike of Paionios from Olympia, c. 420. Olympia Museum 46–8. Photo courtesy of Hirmer Verlag.

Figure 11. The cone of Apollo Aguios on a drachma from Ambracia, 2d century B.C. Photo courtesy of the American Numismatic Society.

Figure 12. Zeus from Cape Artemision, c. 450. Athens NM Br. 15161. Photo courtesy of Hirmer Verlag.

Figure 13. Grave stele of Aristion, made by Aristokles, from Velanideza, Attica, c. 510. Athens NM 29. Photo courtesy of Alinari/ Art Resource, N.Y.

Figure 14. Gravestone of Ktesileos and Theano, from Athens, c. 410–400. Athens NM 3472. Photo courtesy of Hirmer Verlag.

Figure 15. Gravestone of Hegeso from the Kerameikos cemetery in Athens, c. 400. Athens NM 3624. Photo courtesy of Alinari/Art Resource, N.Y.

Figure 16. Attic black-figure amphora attributed to Group E from Vulci, c. 540. Side A. MMA 41.162.143. Photo courtesy of the Metropolitan Museum of Art.

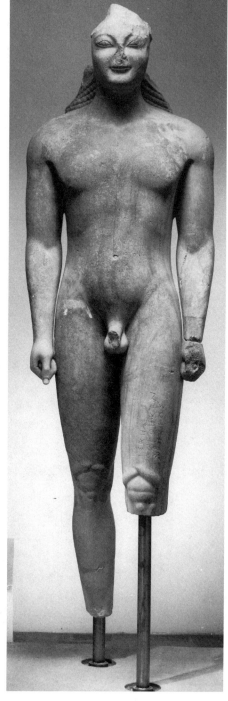

Figure 17. Colossal *kouros* dedicated by Ischys from the Heraion at Samos, c. 570. Samos (Vathy) Museum 81.89. Photo courtesy of Deutsches Archä-ologisches Institut, Athens.

Figure 18. Attic red-figure kylix with victorious athlete attributed to the Kiss Painter, c. 500. Baltimore B5. Photo courtesy of the Johns Hopkins University Archaeological Collection.

Figure 19. Attic red-figure cup attributed to the Antiphon Painter. Berlin 2314. Photo courtesy of Antikensammlung, Staatliche Museen zu Berlin — Preussischer Kulturbesitz.

Figure 20. *Korē* from the Athenian Acropolis, c. 520–510. Athens, Acropolis Museum 675. Photo courtesy of the Alison Frantz Collection, American School of Classical Studies at Athens.

Figure 21. "Peplos" *korē* from the Athenian Acropolis, c. 530. Athens, Acropolis Museum 679. Photo courtesy of the Alison Frantz Collection, American School of Classical Studies at Athens.

Figure 22. "Lyons" *korē* from the Athenian Acropolis, c. 540. Lyons Museum (torso and head) and Athens, Acropolis Museum 269 (legs). Photo courtesy of the Alison Frantz Collection, American School of Classical Studies at Athens.

Figure 23. Temple of Athena Nike Parapet, Sandal Binder, c. 420–400. Athens, Acropolis Museum 973. Photo courtesy of the Alison Frantz Collection, American School of Classical Studies at Athens.

Figure 24. Temple of Athena Nike Parapet, Athena (seated) and Nike, c. 420–400. Athens, Acropolis Museum 989. Photo courtesy of the Alison Frantz Collection, American School of Classical Studies at Athens.

Figure 25. Nike and youth, Athenian white-ground "bobbin," c. 460. MMA 28.167. Photo courtesy of the Metropolitan Museum of Art, Fletcher Fund, 1928.

Figure 26. East pediment of the Temple of Zeus at Olympia, c. 470–457: Hippodameia. Olympia Museum. Photo courtesy of the Alison Frantz Collection, American School of Classical Studies at Athens.

Figure 27. West pediment of the Temple of Zeus at Olympia, c. 470–457: Deidameia and the centaur Eurytion. Olympia Museum. Photo courtesy of the Alison Frantz Collection, American School of Classical Studies at Athens.

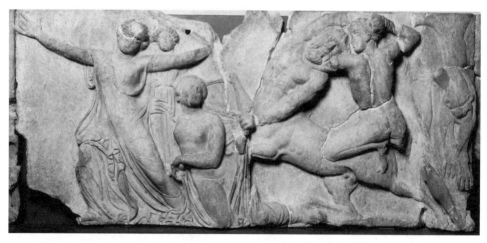

Figure 28. Centauromachy from the temple of Apollo at Bassai/Phigaleia, c. 400. BM 303. Photo courtesy of the Trustees of the British Museum.

Bibliography

Arrowsmith, W. 1973. "Aristophanes' *Birds*: The Fantasy Politics of Eros." *Arion*, n.s. 1: 119–67.

Babut, D. 1975. "Héraclite et la réligion populaire," *Rev. Ét. Anc.* 77: 27–62.

Barkan, L. 1986. *The Gods Made Flesh: Metamorphosis and the Pursuit of Paganism.* New Haven and London.

Barletta, B. 1987. "The Draped Kouros Type and the Work of the Syracuse Youth." *AJArch.* 91: 223–46.

Bassi, K. 1989. "The Actor as Actress in Euripides' *Alcestis*." In J. Redmond, ed., *Women in Theatre*, Themes in Drama no. 11, 19–30. Cambridge.

———. 1993. "Helen and the Discourse of Denial in Stesichorus' Palinode." *Arethusa* 26: 51–76.

Baxter, T.M.S. 1992. *The Cratylus: Plato's Critique of Naming.* Leiden.

Bell, M. 1995. "The Motya Charioteer and Pindar's *Isthmian* 2." *Memoirs of the American Academy in Rome* 40: 1–42.

———. 1996. "Il canto del choreutes. Un bronzo greco dal Gianicolo. Appendice. Una dedica ad Apollo dal Gianicolo." *Acta Instituti Romani Finlandiae* 16: 77–99.

Belting, H. 1994. *Likeness and Presence: A History of the Image before the Era of Art.* Trans. E. Jephcott. Chicago and London.

Benveniste, E. 1932. "Le sens du mot *kolossos* et les noms grecs de la statue." *Rev. Phil.* 6: 118–35.

Bérard, C. 1986. "L'impossible femme athlète." *Annali dell' Istituto universitario orientale di Napoli* 8: 195–202.

Berger, J. 1972. *Ways of Seeing.* London and Harmondsworth.

Bettini, M. 1992. *Il ritratto dell'amante.* Turin.

Bevan, E. 1940. *Holy Images: An Inquiry into Idolatry and Image-Worship in Ancient Paganism and in Christianity.* London.

Blackman, A. M. 1924. "The Rite of Opening the Mouth in Ancient Egypt and Babylonia." *Journal of Egyptian Archaeology* 10: 47–59.

Boardman, J. 1978. *Greek Sculpture: The Archaic Period.* London.

Boegehold, A. L. 1996. "Group and Single Competitions at the Panathenaia." In J. Neils, ed., *Worshipping Athena: Panathenaia and Parthenon*, 95–105. Madison, Wis.

Bohringer, F. 1979. "Cultes d'athlètes en Grèce classique." *Rev. Ét. Anc.* 81: 5–18.

Bonfante, L. 1989. "Nudity as a Costume in Classical Art." *AJArch.* 93: 543–70.

Bonner, C. 1950. *Studies in Magical Amulets Chiefly Graeco-Egyptian.* University of Michigan Studies, Humanistic Series 49. Ann Arbor and London.

———. 1956. "The Sibyl and Bottle Imps." In R. P. Casey, S. Lake, and A. Lake, eds., *Quantulacumque: Studies Presented to Kirsopp Lake*, 1–8. London.

Bourdieu, P. 1990. *The Logic of Practice*. Trans. R. Nice. Stanford.

Breckenridge, J. D. 1968. *Likeness: A Conceptual History of Ancient Portraiture*. Evanston, Ill.

Brett-Smith, S. C. 1994. *The Making of Bamana Sculpture: Creativity and Gender*. Cambridge.

Brillante, C. 1988. "Metamorfosi di un'immagine: Le statue animate e il sogno." In G. Guidorizzi, ed., *Il sogno in Grecia*, 17–33. Rome and Bari.

Brooks, P. 1993. *Body Work: Objects of Desire in Modern Narrative*. Cambridge, Mass.

Bruneau, P. 1975. "Situation méthodologique de l'histoire de l'art antique." *Ant. Class.* 44: 425–87.

Buchheim, T. 1989. *Gorgias: Reden, Fragmente und Testimonien*. Hamburg.

Bundy, E. L. 1986. *Studia Pindarica*. Berkeley.

Bundy, M. W. 1927. *The Theory of Imagination in Classical and Medieval Thought*. Urbana, Ill.

Burkert, W. 1963. "GOHS: Zum griechischen 'Schamanismus.'" *Rh. Mus.* 105: 36–55.

———. 1985. *Greek Religion, Archaic and Classical*. Trans. J. Raffan. Cambridge, Mass.

Bury, J. B. 1890. *The Nemean Odes of Pindar*. London.

Burzachechi, M. 1962. "Oggetti parlanti nelle epigrafi greche." *Epigraphica* 24: 3–54.

Buxton, R.G.A. 1980. "Blindness and Limits: Sophokles and the Logic of Myth." *JHS* 100: 22–37.

Camille, M. 1989. *The Gothic Idol: Ideology and Image-Making in Medieval Art*. Cambridge.

Campbell, D. A. 1982. *Greek Lyric Poetry*. 2d ed. Bristol.

Carson, A. 1982. "Wedding at Noon in Pindar's Ninth Pythian." *GRBS* 23: 121–28.

———. 1996. "Writing on the World: Simonides, Exactitude and Paul Celan." *Arion*, 3d ser. 4: 1–26.

Castriota, D. 1992. *Myth, Ethos, and Actuality: Official Art in Fifth-Century B.C. Athens*. Madison, Wis.

Caughie, J., and A. Kuhn, eds. 1992. *The Sexual Subject: A Screen Reader in Sexuality*. London and New York.

Childs, W.A.P. 1988. "The Classic as Realism in Greek Art." *Art Journal* 47: 10–14.

Clader, L. L. 1976. *Helen: The Evolution from Divine to Heroic in Greek Epic Tradition*. Leiden.

Clark, T. J. 1984. *The Painting of Modern Life: Paris in the Art of Manet and His Followers*. Princeton.

Clerc, C. 1915. *Les théories relatives au culte des images chez les auteurs grecs du IIme siècle après J.-C.* Paris.

Cohen, B. 1993. "The Anatomy of Kassandra's Rape." *Source* 12: 37–46.

———. 1997. "Divesting the Female Breast of Clothes in Classical Sculpture." In A. O. Koloski-Ostrow and C. L. Lyons, eds., *Naked Truths: Women, Sexuality, and Gender in Classical Art and Archaeology*, 66–92. London and New York.

Cohen, D. 1991. *Law, Sexuality and Society: The Enforcement of Morals in Classical Athens*. Cambridge.

Collard, C. 1991. *Euripides' Hecuba*. Warminster.

Connelly, J. B. 1993. "Narrative and Image in Attic Vase Painting: Ajax and Kassandra at the Trojan Palladion." In P. J. Holliday, ed., *Narrative and Event in Ancient Art*, 88–129. Cambridge.

Cook, A. B. 1914. *Zeus: A Study in Ancient Religion*. Vol. 1. Cambridge.

———. 1940. *Zeus: A Study in Ancient Religion*. Vol. 3. Cambridge.

Corbett, P. E. 1970. "Greek Temples and Greek Worshippers: The Literary and Archaeological Evidence." *BICS* 17: 149–58.

Cormack, R. 1997. *Painting the Soul: Icons, Death Masks and Shrouds*. London.

Courtney, E. 1980. *A Commentary on the Satires of Juvenal*. London.

Crowther, N. 1985. "Male Beauty Contests in Greece: The *euandria* and the *euexia*." *Ant. Class.* 54: 285–91.

Dahl, E. 1978. "Heavenly Images: The Statue of St. Foy of Conques and the Significance of the Medieval 'Cult-image' in the West." *Acta ad archaeologiam et artium historiam pertinentia* 8: 175–91.

Day, J. 1989. "Rituals in Stone: Early Greek Grave Epigrams and Monuments." *JHS* 109: 16–28.

De Angeli, S. 1988. "Mimesis e Techne." *Quaderni urbinati di cultura classica* 28: 27–45.

Dean-Jones, L. 1994. *Women's Bodies in Classical Greek Science*. Oxford.

Delcourt, M. 1957. *Héphaistos ou la légende du magicien*. Bibliothèque de la Faculté de Philosophie et Lettres de l'Université de Liège 146. Paris.

Deonna, W. 1930. "L'image incomplète ou mutilée." *Rev. Ét. Anc.* 32: 321–32.

———. 1935. "Les yeux absents ou clos des statues de la Grèce primitive." *Rev. Ét. Grec.* 48: 219–44.

Depew, M. 1997. "Reading Greek Prayers." *Cl. Ant.* 16: 229–58.

Detienne, M., and J.-P. Vernant. 1978. *Cunning Intelligence among the Greeks*. Trans. J. Lloyd. Atlantic Highlands, N.J.

Dickie, M. 1978. "The Argument and Form of Simonides 542 *PMG*." *Harv. Stud.* 82: 21–33.

Dodds, E. R. 1951. *The Greeks and the Irrational*. Berkeley.

———. 1960. *Euripides' Bacchae*. 2d. ed. Oxford.

d'Onofrio, A. M. 1982. "*Korai e kouroi* funerari attici." Istituto Universitario Orientale. *Annali del Seminario di Studi del Mondo Classico. Archeologia e Storia Antica* 4: 135–70.

Donohue, A. A. 1988. *XOANA and the Origins of Greek Sculpture*. Atlanta.

Dover, K. J. 1970. *Aristophanes: Clouds*. Oxford.

———. 1978. *Greek Homosexuality*. Cambridge, Mass.

Downing, E. 1990. "*Apate, Agon* and Literary Self-Reflexivity in Euripides' *Helen*." In M. Griffith and D. J. Mastronarde, eds., *Cabinet of the Muses*, 1–16. Atlanta.

Drees, L. 1968. *Olympia: Gods, Artists and Athletes*. London.

duBois, P. 1988. *Sowing the Body: Psychoanalysis and Ancient Representations of Women*. Chicago.

Ducat, J. 1971. *Les kouroi de Ptoion*. Paris.

———. 1976. "Fonctions de la statue dans la Grèce archaïque: *kouros* et *kolossos.*" *BCH* 100: 239–51.

Durante, M. 1968. "Untersuchungen zur Vorgeschichte der griechischen Dichtersprache: Die Terminologie für das dichterische Schaffen." In R. Schmitt, ed., *Indogermanische Dichtersprache*, 261–90. Wege der Forschung, Band 165. Darmstadt.

Ebert, J., ed. 1972. *Griechische Epigramme auf Sieger an gymnischen und hippischen Agonen. Abhandlungen der sächsischen Akademie der Wissenschaften zu Leipzig*, Philhist Kl. Band 63, Heft 2. Berlin.

Ellis, J. 1992. "On Pornography." In J. Caughie and A. Kuhn, eds., *The Sexual Subject: A Screen Reader in Sexuality*, 146–70. London and New York.

Elsner, J.A.S. 1992. "Visual Mimesis and the Myth of the Real: Ovid's Pygmalion as Viewer." *Ramus* 20: 154–66.

Elsom, H. E. 1992. "Callirhoe: Displaying the Phallic Woman." In A. Richlin, ed., *Pornography and Representation in Greece and Rome*, 212–30. Oxford.

Faraone, C. A. 1987. "Hephaestus the Magician and the Near Eastern Parallels for the Gold and Silver Dogs of Alcinous (*Od.* 7.91–94)." *GRBS* 28: 257–80.

———. 1991a. "The Agonistic Context of Early Greek Binding Spells." In C. A. Faraone and D. Obbink, eds., *Magika Hiera: Ancient Greek Magic and Religion*, 3–32. New York.

———. 1991b. "Binding and Burying the Forces of Evil: The Defensive Use of 'Voodoo Dolls' in Ancient Greece." *Cl. Ant.* 10: 165–205.

———. 1992. *Talismans and Trojan Horses: Guardian Statues in Ancient Greek Myth and Ritual.* New York and Oxford.

Ferrari, G. 1990. "Figures of Speech: The Picture of *Aidōs.*" *Métis* 5: 186–200.

Ferri, S. 1960. "Nuovi contributi esegetici al 'canone' della scultura greca." In *Opuscula, studi classici e orientale* 11: 122–58. Florence.

Fontenrose, J. 1968. "The Hero as Athlete." *California Studies in Classical Antiquity* 1: 73–104.

———. 1978. *The Delphic Oracle.* Berkeley.

Forbes Irving, P.M.C. 1992. *Metamorphosis in Greek Myths.* Oxford.

Ford, A. 1992. *Homer: The Poetry of the Past.* Ithaca, N.Y.

Foucault, M. 1985. *The Use of Pleasure. The History of Sexuality*, vol. 2. Trans. R. Hurley. New York.

Fraenkel, E. 1962. *Aeschylus: Agamemnon.* 3 vols. Oxford.

Francis, E. D., and M. Vickers. 1981. "Leagros Kalos." *PCPS* 207: 96–136.

Freedberg, D. 1989. *The Power of Images: Studies in the History and Theory of Response.* Chicago and London.

Frischer, B. 1982. *The Sculpted Word: Epicureanism and Philosophical Recruitment in Ancient Greece.* Berkeley.

Frontisi-Ducroux, F. 1975. *Dédale: Mythologie de l'artisan en grèce ancienne.* Paris.

———. 1991. *Le Dieu-masqué.* Rome.

———. 1994. "Athéna et l'Invention de la Flûte." *Musica e storia* 2: 239–67.

———. 1995. *Du masque au visage: Aspects de l'identité en Grèce ancienne.* Paris.

———. 1996. "Eros, Desire and the Gaze." In N. B. Kampen, ed., *Sexuality in Ancient Art,* 81–100. Cambridge.

Gauer, W. 1968. "Die griechischen Bildnisse der klassischen Zeit als politische und persönliche Denkmäler." *JDAI* 83: 118–79.

Geffcken, J. 1919. "Der Bilderstreit des heidnischen Altertums." *Archiv für Religionswissenschaft* 19: 286–315.

Gentili, B. 1988. *Poetry and Its Public in Ancient Greece from Homer to the Fifth Century.* Trans. A. T. Cole. Baltimore.

Gerber, D. 1982. *Pindar's Olympian One: A Commentary.* Toronto.

Gernet, L. 1981. *The Anthropology of Ancient Greece.* Trans. J. Hamilton and B. Nagy. Baltimore and London.

Gigon, O. 1935. *Untersuchungen zu Heraklit.* Leipzig.

Gill, C. 1990. "The Character-Personality Distinction." In C. Pelling, ed., *Characterization and Individuality in Greek Literature,* 11–31. Oxford.

Gill, D. 1974. "*Trapezomata*: A Neglected Aspect of Greek Sacrifice." *Harv. Theol. Rev.* 67: 117–37.

Golden, M. 1988. "Male Chauvinists and Pigs." *Echos du monde classique/ Classical Views* 32, n.s. 7: 1–12.

Goldhill, S. 1998. "The Seductions of the Gaze: Socrates and His Girlfriends." In P. Cartledge, P. Millett, and S. von Reden, eds., *KOSMOS: Essays in Order, Conflict and Community in Classical Athens,* 105–24. Cambridge.

———. Forthcoming. "The Empire of the Senses: Crossroads in the History of the Eye." In T. Siebers, ed., *The Body Aesthetic: From Fine Art to Body Modification.* Ann Arbor.

Gombrich, E. H. 1961. *Art and Illusion: A Study in the Psychology of Pictorial Representation.* New York.

Gordon, R. L. 1979. "The Real and the Imaginary: Production and Religion in the Graeco-Roman World." *Art History* 2: 5–34.

Gosling, J.C.B. 1973. *Plato.* London.

———. 1975. *Plato: Philebus, Translated with Notes and Commentary.* Oxford.

Graf, F. 1985. *Nordionische Kulte.* Bibliotheca Helvetica Romana 21. Zürich.

———. 1997. *Magic in the Ancient World.* Trans. F. Philip. Cambridge, Mass.

Griffith, M. 1983. *Aeschylus: Prometheus Bound.* Cambridge.

———. 1995. "Brilliant Dynasts: Power and Politics in the *Oresteia*." *Cl. Ant.* 14: 62–129.

Gross, K. 1992. *The Dream of the Moving Statue.* Ithaca, N.Y. and London.

Gross, W. H. 1969–71. "Quas iconicas vocant: Zum Porträtcharakter der Statuen dreimaliger olympischer Sieger." *Gött.-Nachr.* Phil.-hist. Kl. 3: 61–76.

Halbertal, M., and A. Margalit. 1992. *Idolatry.* Trans. N. Goldblum. Cambridge, Mass.

Hallett, C. H. 1986. "The Origins of the Classical Style in Sculpture." *JHS* 106: 71–84.

———. 1995. "*Kopienkritik* and the Works of Polykleitos." In W. G. Moon, ed., *Polykleitos, the Doryphoros, and Tradition,* 121–60. Madison, Wis.

Halperin, D. 1990. *One Hundred Years of Homosexuality.* New York and London.

———. 1992. "Plato and the Erotics of Narrativity." In R. Hexter and D. Selden, eds., *Innovations of Antiquity*, 95–126. London and New York.

Hanson, A. E. 1990. "The Medical Writers' Woman." In D. Halperin, J. J. Winkler, and F. I. Zeitlin, eds., *Before Sexuality: The Construction of Erotic Experience in the Ancient Greek World*, 309–38. Princeton.

Harrison, E. B. 1965. *The Athenian Agora*. Vol 2. *Archaic and Archaistic Sculpture*. Princeton.

———. 1985. "Early Classical Sculpture: The Bold Style." In C. G. Boulter, ed., *Greek Art: Archaic into Classical*, 40–65. Leiden.

Hatt, M. 1993. "Muscles, Morals, Mind: The Male Body in Thomas Eakins' *Salutat*." In K. Adler and M. Pointon, eds., *The Body Imaged: The Human Form and Visual Culture Since the Renaissance*, 57–69. Cambridge.

Havelock, C. M. 1965. "The Archaic as Survival versus the Archaistic as a New Style." *AJArch.* 69: 331–40.

———. 1995. *The Aphrodite of Knidos and Her Successors*. Ann Arbor.

Heffernan, J. 1993. *The Museum of Words*. Chicago.

Henrichs, A. 1993. " 'He Has a God in Him': Human and Divine in the Modern Perception of Dionysus." In T. H. Carpenter and C. A. Faraone, eds., *Masks of Dionysus*, 13–43. Ithaca, N.Y.

Himmelmann, N. 1990. *Ideale Nacktheit in der griechischen Kunst*. JDAI Ergänzungsheft 26. Berlin and New York.

Hirschle, M. 1979. *Sprachphilosophie und Namenmagie im Neuplatonismus: Mit einem Exkurs zu "Demokrit" B142*. Beiträge zur Klassischen Philologie, Heft 96. Meisenheim.

Howie, J. G. 1983. "The Revision of Myth in Pindar Olympian One: The Death and Revival of Pelops (25–27, 36–66)." *Papers of the Liverpool Latin Seminar* 4: 277–313.

Hubbard, T. 1987. "The Cooking of Pelops: Pindar and the Process of Mythological Revisionism." *Helios* 2: 3–21.

Hupperts, C.A.M. 1988. "Greek Love: Homosexuality or Pederasty?" In J. Christiansen and T. Melander, eds., *Proceedings of the Third Symposium on Ancient Greek and Related Pottery*, 255–65. Copenhagen.

Hurwit, J. M. 1985. *The Art and Culture of Early Greece, 1100–480 B.C.* Ithaca, N.Y.

Hyde, W. W. 1921. *Olympic Victor Monuments and Greek Athletic Art*. Washington, D.C.

Jacoby, F. 1945. "Some Athenian Epigrams from the Persian Wars." *Hesperia* 14: 157–211.

Jakobson, R. 1987a. "Two Aspects of Language and Two Types of Aphasic Disturbances." In K. Pomorska and S. Rudy, eds., *Language in Literature: Roman Jakobson*, 95–114. Cambridge, Mass.

———. 1987b. "The Statue in Puškin's Poetic Mythology." In K. Pomorska and S. Rudy, eds., *Language in Literature: Roman Jakobson*, 318–67. Cambridge, Mass.

Jameson, M. 1993. "The Asexuality of Dionysus." In T. H. Carpenter and C. A. Faraone, eds., *Masks of Dionysus*, 44–64. Ithaca, N.Y.

Jay, M. 1993. *Downcast Eyes: The Denigration of Vision in Twentieth-Century French Thought*. Berkeley and Los Angeles.

Kahn, C. H. 1979. *The Art and Thought of Heraclitus*. Cambridge.

Kampen, N. B., ed. 1996. *Sexuality in Ancient Art*. Cambridge.

———. 1997. "Epilogue: Gender and Desire." In A. O. Koloski-Ostrow and C. L. Lyons, eds., *Naked Truths: Women, Sexuality, and Gender in Classical Art and Archaeology*, 267–77. London and New York.

Kannicht, R. 1969. *Euripides: Helena*. 2 vols. Heidelberg.

Kassel, R. 1983. "Dialoge mit Statuen." *ZPE* 51: 1–12.

Kerferd, G. B. 1981. *The Sophistic Movement*. Cambridge.

Keuls, E. 1978. *Plato and Greek Painting*. Leiden.

Köhnken, A. 1983. "Time and Event in Pindar O. 1.25–53." *Cl. Ant.* 2: 66–76.

Kötting, B. *Peregrinatio religiosa: Wallfahrten in der Antike und das Pilgerwesen in der alten Kirche*. Münster.

Krieger, M. 1991. *Ekphrasis: The Illusion of the Natural Sign*. Baltimore.

Kris, E., and O. Kurz. [1934] 1979. *Legend, Myth and Magic in the Image of the Artist*. New Haven.

Kroll, J. H. 1982. "The Ancient Image of Athena Polias." In *Studies in Athenian Architecture, Sculpture and Topography Presented to Homer A. Thompson*. *Hesperia* suppl. 20: 65–76. Princeton.

Kurke, L. 1991. *The Traffic in Praise: Pindar and the Poetics of Social Economy*. Ithaca, N.Y.

———. 1993. "The Economy of *Kudos*." In C. Dougherty and L. Kurke, eds., *Cultural Poetics in Archaic Greece: Cult, Performance, Politics*, 131–63. Cambridge.

———. 1995. "Herodotus and the Language of Metals." *Helios* 22: 36–64.

———. 1999. *Coins, Bodies, Games, and Gold: The Politics of Meaning in Archaic Greece*. Princeton.

Kurtz, D. C., and J. Boardman. 1971. *Greek Burial Customs*. Ithaca, N.Y.

Kyle, D. G. 1987. *Athletics in Ancient Athens*. Leiden.

Laqueur, T. 1990. *Making Sex: Body and Gender from the Greeks to Freud*. Cambridge, Mass., and London.

Lattimore, R. 1962. *Themes in Greek and Latin Epitaphs*. 2d ed. Urbana, Ill.

Lattimore, S. 1987. "The Nature of Early Greek Victor Statues." In S. J. Bandy, ed., *Coroebus Triumphs: The Alliance of Sports and the Arts*, 245–56. San Diego.

Lazzarini, M. L. 1976. "Le formule delle dediche votive nella Grecia arcaica." *Memorie dell'Accademia Nazionale dei Lincei*. Classe di Scienze Morali, Stor. Filog. Serie 8.19: 47–354.

Leclercq-Neveu, B. 1989. "Marsyas, le Martyr de l'Aulos." *Métis* 4: 251–68.

Leftwich, G. 1987. "Ancient Conceptions of the Body and the Canon of Polykleitos." Diss., Princeton University.

Lippold, G. 1950. "Die griechische Plastik." *Handbuch der Archäologie* 3.1. Munich.

Lissarrague, F. 1990a. *The Aesthetics of the Greek Banquet*. Trans. A. Szegedy-Maszak. Princeton.

————. 1990b. "Why Satyrs Are Good to Represent." In J. J. Winkler and F. I. Zeitlin, eds., *Nothing to Do with Dionysos? Athenian Drama in Its Social Context*, 228–36. Princeton.

————. 1990c. "The Sexual Life of Satyrs." In D. Halperin, J. J. Winkler, and F. I. Zeitlin, eds., *Before Sexuality: The Construction of Erotic Experience in the Ancient Greek World*, 53–81. Princeton.

Lonsdale, S. 1989. "If Looks Could Kill: παπταίνω and the Interpenetration of Imagery and Narrative in Homer." *CJ* 84: 325–33.

L'Orange, H. P. 1982. *Apotheosis in Ancient Portraiture*. New Rochelle, N.Y.

Loraux, N. 1982. "Mourir Devant Troie, Tomber pour Athènes: De la gloire du héros à l'idée de la cité." In G. Gnoli and J.-P. Vernant, eds., *La mort, les morts dans les sociétés anciennes*, 27–43. Cambridge and London.

————. 1986. *The Invention of Athens: The Funeral Oration in the Ancient City*. Trans. A. Sheridan. Cambridge, Mass.

————. 1993. *The Children of Athena: Athenian Ideas about Citizenship and the Division between the Sexes*. Trans. C. Levine. 2d ed. Princeton.

————. 1995. *The Experiences of Tiresias: The Feminine and the Greek Man*. Trans. P. Wissing. Princeton.

McDonnell, M. 1991. "The Introduction of Athletic Nudity: Thucydides, Plato and the Vases." *JHS* 111: 182–93.

MacLachlan, B. 1993. *The Age of Grace: Charis in Early Greek Poetry*. Princeton.

Malten, L. 1961. *Die Sprache des menschlichen Antlitzes im frühen Griechentum*. Berlin.

Mango, C. 1963. "Antique Statuary and the Byzantine Beholder." *DOP* 17: 53–77.

Mark, I. S. 1979. "Nike and the Cult of Athena Nike on the Athenian Acropolis." Diss., New York University.

Massenzio, M. 1969. "Cultura e crisi permanente: La 'xenia' dionisiaca." *Studi e materiali di storia delle religioni* 40: 27–113.

Meiggs, R., and D. M. Lewis. 1969. *A Selection of Greek Historical Inscriptions to the End of the Fifth Century*. Oxford.

Merkelbach, R. 1973. "Ein Fragment des homerischen Dionysos-Hymnus." *ZPE* 12: 212–15.

Métraux, G.P.R. 1995. *Sculptors and Physicians in Fifth-Century Greece*. Montreal and Kingston.

Meuli, K. 1975. "Die Gefesselte Götter." In T. Gelzer, ed., *Gesammelte Schriften* 2: 1035–1197. Basel and Stuttgart.

Mikalson, J. D. 1983. *Athenian Popular Religion*. Chapel Hill, N.C.

Mitchell, W.J.T. 1986. *Iconology: Image, Text, Ideology*. Chicago.

Moret, J.-M. 1975. *L'Ilioupersis dans la céramique italiote: Les mythes et leur expression figurée au IVe siècle*. Geneva.

Morris, I. 1996. "The Strong Principle of Equality and the Archaic Origins of Greek Democracy." In J. Ober and C. Hedrick, eds., *Dēmokratia: A Conversation on Democracies, Ancient and Modern*, 19–48. Princeton.

Morris, S. P. 1992. *Daidalos and the Origins of Greek Art*. Princeton.

Mullen, W. 1982. *Choreia: Pindar and Dance*. Princeton.

Mulvey, L. 1992. "Visual Pleasure and the Narrative Cinema." In J. Caughie and A. Kuhn, eds., *The Sexual Subject: A Screen Reader in Sexuality*, 22–34. London and New York.

Nagy, G. 1979. *The Best of the Achaeans: Concepts of the Hero in Archaic Greek Poetry*. Baltimore.

Neale, S. 1992. "Masculinity as Spectacle." In J. Caughie and A. Kuhn, eds., *The Sexual Subject: A Screen Reader in Sexuality*, 277–87. London and New York.

Neer, R. 1995. "The Lion's Eye: Imitation and Uncertainty in Attic Red-Figure." *Representations* 51: 118–53.

Neils, J., ed. 1992. *Goddess and Polis: The Panathenaic Festival in Ancient Athens*. Princeton.

———. 1994. "Phylai and Festivals in the Light of *Demokratia*." *AJArch*. 98: 284–85.

Nilsson, M. P. 1967. *Geschichte der griechischen Religion*. Vol. 1. 3d ed. Munich.

Nisetich, F. J. 1975. "Olympian 1.8–11: An Epinician Metaphor." *Harv. Stud*. 79: 55–68.

Nochlin, L. 1991. "Women, Art, and Power." In N. Bryson, M. A. Holly, and K. Moxey, eds., *Visual Theory: Painting and Interpretation*, 13–46. Cambridge.

Nock, A. D. 1972. *Essays on Religion and the Ancient World*. Edited by Z. Stewart. 2 vols. Cambridge, Mass.

Nussbaum, M. 1986. *The Fragility of Goodness*. Cambridge.

Oakley, J. H., and D. Sinos. 1993. *The Wedding in Ancient Athens*. Madison, Wis., and London.

Oehler, K. 1984. "Democrit über Zeichen und Bezeichnung aus der Dicht der moderne Semiotik." in L. G. Benakis, ed., *Proceedings of the First International Conference on Democritus*, 1: 177–87. Xanthi.

Onians, R. B. 1988. *The Origins of European Thought*. 2d ed. Cambridge.

Osborne, R. 1985. "The Erection and Mutilation of the Hermai." *PCPS*, n.s. 31: 47–73.

———. 1987. "The Viewing and Obscuring of the Parthenon Frieze." *JHS* 107: 98–105.

———. 1988. "Death Revisited, Death Revised: The Death of the Artist in Archaic and Classical Greece." *Art History* 11: 1–16.

———. 1994a. "Looking On—Greek Style. Does the Sculpted Girl Speak to Women Too?" In I. Morris, ed., *Classical Greece: Ancient Histories and Modern Archaeologies*, 81–96. Cambridge.

———. 1994b. "Framing the Centaur: Reading Fifth-Century Architectural Sculpture." In S. Goldhill and R. Osborne, eds., *Art and Text in Ancient Greek Culture*, 52–84. Cambridge.

———. 1996. "Desiring Women on Athenian Pottery." In N. B. Kampen, ed., *Sexuality in Ancient Art*, 65–80. Cambridge.

———. 1997. "Men without Clothes: Heroic Nakedness and Greek Art." in M. Wyke, ed., *Gender and the Body in Mediterranean Antiquity*, *Gender and History* 9: 504–28.

———. 1998. *Archaic and Classical Greek Art*. Oxford and New York.

———. 1999. "Sculpted Men of Athens: Masculinity and Power in the Field of Vision." In L. Foxhall and J. Salmon, eds., *Thinking Men: Masculinity and Its Self-Representation in the Classical Tradition*, 23–42. London.

Overbeck, J. 1868. *Die antiken Schriftquellen zur Geschichte der bildenden Künste bei den Griechen*. Leipzig.

Pacteau, F. 1994. *The Symptom of Beauty*. London.

Padel, R. 1992. *In and Out of the Mind*. Princeton.

Parker, R. 1983. *Miasma: Pollution and Purification in Early Greek Religion*. Oxford.

———. 1996. *Athenian Religion: A History*. Oxford.

Pfohl, G. 1967. *Greek Poems on Stones*. Vol. 1, *Epitaphs: From the Seventh to the Fifth Centuries*. Leiden.

Philippson, R. 1929. "Platons Kratylos und Demokrit." *Philologische Wochenschrift* 30: 923–27.

Picard, C. 1933. "Le cénotaphe de Midéa et les "colosses" de Ménélas." *Rev. Phil.* 7: 341–54.

Platnauer, M. 1984. *Euripides: Iphigenia in Tauris*. Reprint. Bristol.

Pollitt, J. J. 1972. *Art and Experience in Classical Greece*. Cambridge.

———. 1974. *The Ancient View of Greek Art: Criticism, History and Terminology*. New Haven and London.

———. 1985. "Early Classical Greek Art in a Platonic Universe." in C. G. Boulter, ed., *Greek Art: Archaic into Classical*, 96–111. Leiden.

———. 1986. *Art in the Hellenistic Age*. Cambridge.

Preisshofen, E. 1974. "Phidias-Daedalus auf dem Schild der Athena Parthenos? Ampelius 8, 10." *JDAI* 89: 50–69.

Price, S. 1984. *Rituals and Power: The Roman Imperial Cult in Asia Minor*. Cambridge.

Quirke, S., and J. Spencer. 1992. *The British Museum Book of Ancient Egypt*. New York.

Ramnoux, C. 1959. *Héraclite, ou l'homme entre les choses et les mots*. Paris.

Rasche, G. 1910. "De Anthologiae Graecae epigrammatis quae colloquii formam habent." Diss., Münster.

Raschke, W. 1988. "Images of Victory: Some New Considerations of Athletic Monuments." In W. J. Raschke, ed., *The Archaeology of the Olympics: The Olympics and Other Festivals in Antiquity*, 38–54. Madison, Wis.

Raven, J. E. 1951. "Polyclitus and Pythagoreanism." *CQ* 45: 147–52.

Reeder, E. D., ed. 1995. *Pandora: Women in Classical Greece*. Baltimore and Princeton.

Richardson, N. J. 1974. *The Homeric Hymn to Demeter*. Oxford.

Richter, G.M.A. 1961. *The Archaic Grave Stones of Attica*. London.

———. 1968. *Korai: Archaic Greek Maidens*. New York.

———. 1970. *Kouroi: Archaic Greek Youths*. 3d ed. London.

———. 1984. *The Portraits of the Greeks*. Abridged and rev. ed. by R.R.R. Smith. Ithaca, N.Y.

Ridgway, B. S. 1970. *The Severe Style in Greek Sculpture*. Princeton.

———. 1981. *Fifth-Century Styles in Greek Sculpture*. Princeton.

———. 1993. *The Archaic Style in Greek Sculpture*. 2d ed. Chicago.

Robert, L. 1960. "Recherches épigraphiques." *Rev. Ét. Anc.* 62: 316–24.

Robertson, C. M. 1975. *A History of Greek Art.* Cambridge.

Romano, I. B. 1980. "Early Greek Cult Images." Diss., University of Pennsylvania.

Romm, J. 1990. "Wax, Stone and Promethean Clay: Lucian as Plastic Artist." *Cl. Ant.* 9: 74–98.

Rose, H. T. 1956. "Divine Disguisings." *Harv. Theol. Rev.* 49: 62–72.

Rosen, S. 1983. *Plato's Sophist: The Drama of Original and Image.* New Haven and London.

Rosenmeyer, T. G. 1955. "Gorgias, Aeschylus and *Apatē.*" *AJPhil.* 76: 225–60.

Rouveret, A. 1989. *Histoire et imaginaire de la peinture ancienne.* Paris.

Roux, G. 1960. "Qu'est-ce qu'un *kolossos*?" *Rev. Ét. Anc.* 62: 5–40.

Russell, D. A. 1992. *Dio Chrysostom: Orations VII, XII and XXVI.* Cambridge.

Saïd, S. 1987. "Deux noms de l'image en grec ancien: Idole et icône." *Comptes rendus de l'Académie des Inscriptions et Belles Lettres* 31: 309–30.

Saintillan, D. 1996. "Du festin à l'échange: Les grâces de Pandore." In F. Blaise, P. Judet de la Combe, and P. Rousseau, eds., *Les métiers du mythe: Hésiode et ses vérités*, 316–48. Paris.

Sartre, J.-P. 1966. *Being and Nothingness: An Essay on Phenomenological Ontology.* Trans. H. E. Barnes. New York.

Schneider, L. A. 1975. *Zur sozialen Bedeutung der archaischen Koren-statuen.* Hamburg.

Schuhl, P.-M. 1952. *Platon et l'art de son temps.* Paris.

Schweitzer, B. [1932] 1963. "Xenokrates von Athen. Beiträge zur Geschichte der antiken Kunstforschung und Kunstanschauung." In B. Schweitzer, *Zur Kunst der Antike. Ausgewählte Schriften*, 105–64. Tübingen. [Originally published in *Schriften der Königsberger gelehrten Gesellschaft*, Geisteswissenschaftliche Klasse 9:1–52].

———. [1940] 1963. "Studien zur Enstehung des Porträts bei den Griechen." In B. Schweitzer, *Zur Kunst der Antike. Ausgewählte Schriften*, Band 2, 115–67. Tübingen.

Seaford, R. 1995. *Reciprocity and Ritual: Homer and Tragedy in the Developing City-State.* Oxford.

Sedgwick, E. K. 1985. *Between Men: English Literature and Male Homosocial Desire.* New York.

Segal, C. P. 1974. "Arrest and Movement: Pindar's Fifth Nemean." *Hermes* 102: 397–411.

———. 1993. *Euripides and the Poetics of Sorrow: Art, Gender, and Commemoration in Alcestis, Hippolytus, and Hecuba.* Durham, N.C. and London.

Serwint, N. J. 1987. "Greek Athletic Sculpture from the Fifth and Fourth Centuries B.C.: An Iconographic Study." Diss., Princeton University.

Shapiro, H. A. 1981. "Courtship Scenes in Attic Vase Painting." *AJArch.* 85: 133–43.

———. 1989. *Art and Cult under the Tyrants in Athens.* Mainz.

———. 1992. "Eros in Love: Pederasty and Pornography in Greece." In A. Richlin, ed., *Pornography and Representation in Greece and Rome.* 53–72. Oxford.

Sharrock, A. R. 1992. "The Love of Creation." *Ramus* 20: 169–82.

Simon, E. 1983. *Festivals of Attica: An Archaeological Commentary*. Madison, Wis.

Sissa, G. 1990. *Greek Virginity*. Trans. A. Goldhammer. Cambridge, Mass.

Sissa, G., and M. Detienne. 1989. *La vie quotidienne des dieux grecs*. Paris.

Smith, P. 1981. *Nursling of Mortality: A Study of the Homeric Hymn to Aphrodite*. Frankfurt.

Solomon-Godeau, A. 1988. *Sexual Difference, Both Sides of the Camera*. New York.

———. 1993. "Male Trouble: A Crisis in Representation." *Art History* 16: 286–312.

Sörbom, G. 1966. *Mimesis and Art*. Upsala.

Sourvinou-Inwood, C. 1994. "Something to Do with Athens: Tragedy and Ritual." In S. Hornblower and R. Osborne, eds., *Ritual, Finance, Politics: Athenian Democratic Accounts Presented to D. M. Lewis*, 269–90. Oxford.

———. 1995. *"Reading" Greek Death*. Oxford.

Spivey, N. 1996. *Understanding Greek Sculpture: Ancient Meanings, Modern Readings*. London.

Stehle, E., and A. Day. 1996. "Women Looking at Women: Women's Ritual and Temple Sculpture." In N. B. Kampen, ed., *Sexuality in Ancient Art*, 101–16. Cambridge.

Steiner, D. 1993. "Pindar's 'Oggetti Parlanti.'" *Harv. Stud.* 95: 159–80.

———. 1994. *The Tyrant's Writ: Myths and Images of Writing in Ancient Greece*. Princeton.

———. 1995a. "Stoning and Sight: A Structural Equivalent in Greek Mythology." *Cl. Ant.* 14: 193–211.

———. 1995b. "Eyeless in Argos: A Reading of *Agamemnon* 416–19." *JHS* 110: 175–82.

———. 1996. "For Love of a Statue: A Reading of Plato's *Symposium* 215a–b." *Ramus* 25: 89–111.

———. 1998. "Moving Images: Fifth-Century Victory Monuments and the Athlete's Allure." *Cl. Ant.* 17: 123–49.

Stewart, A. 1978. "The Canon of Polykleitos: A Question of Evidence." *JHS* 98: 122–31.

———. 1982. *Skopas in Malibu*. Malibu.

———. 1983. "Pindaric *dike* and the Temple of Zeus at Olympia." *Cl. Ant.* 2: 133–44.

———. 1986. "When Is a Kouros Not an Apollo? The Tenea 'Apollo' Revisited." In M. A. del Chiaro, ed., *Corinthiaca: Studies in Honor of Darrell A. Amyx*, 54–70. New York.

———. 1990. *Greek Sculpture: An Exploration*. New Haven.

———. 1997. *Art, Desire, and the Body in Ancient Greece*. Cambridge.

Stieber, M. 1994. "Aeschylus' *Theoroi* and Realism in Greek Art." *TAPA* 124: 85–119.

Sutton, R. F. 1992. "Pornography and Persuasion on Attic Pottery." In A. Richlin, ed., *Pornography and Representation in Greece and Rome*, 3–35. Cambridge.

Svenbro, J. 1976. *La parole et le marbre: Aux origines de la poétique grecque.* Lund.

———. 1988. *Phrasikleia: Anthropologie de la lecture en Grèce ancienne.* Paris.

Tersini, N. 1987. "Unifying Themes in the Sculpture of the Temple of Zeus at Olympia." *Cl. Ant.* 6: 139–59.

Van Straten, F. T. 1995. *Hiera Kala: Images of Animal Sacrifice in Archaic and Classical Greece.* Leiden.

Vermeule, E. 1981. *Aspects of Death in Early Greek Art and Poetry.* Berkeley.

Vernant, J.-P. 1980. *Myth and Society in Ancient Greece.* Trans. J. Lloyd. Atlantic Highlands, N.J.

———. 1982. "La belle mort et le cadavre outragé." In G. Gnoli and J.-P. Vernant, eds., *La mort, les morts dans les sociétés anciennes,* 45–76. Cambridge and Paris.

———. 1983. *Myth and Thought among the Greeks.* London.

———. 1990a. *Figures, idoles, masques.* Paris.

———. 1990b. "Figuration et image." *Métis* 5: 225–38.

———. 1991. *Mortals and Immortals: Collected Essays.* Ed. F. I. Zeitlin. Princeton.

———. 1996. "Les semblances de Pandore." In F. Blaise, P. Judet de la Combe, and P. Rousseau, eds., *Les métiers du mythe: Hésiode et ses vérités,* 381–92. Paris.

Vernant, J.-P., and F. Frontisi-Ducroux. 1988. "Features of the Mask in Ancient Greece." In J.-P. Vernant and P. Vidal-Naquet, eds., *Myth and Tragedy in Ancient Greece,* 189–206. Trans. J. Lloyd. New York.

Versnel, H. S. 1987a. "Greek Myth and Ritual: The Case of Kronos." In J. N. Bremmer, ed., *Interpretations of Greek Mythology,* 121–52. London.

———. 1987b. "What Did Ancient Man See When He Saw a God? Some Reflections on Graeco-Roman Epiphany." in D. van der Plas, ed., *Effigies Dei,* 42–55. Leiden.

von Leutsch, E. L., and F. G. Schneidewin, eds. 1958. *Corpus Paroemiographorum Graecorum.* Hildesheim.

Walsh, G. B. 1984. *The Varieties of Enchantment.* Chapel Hill and London.

———. 1991. "Callimachean Passages: The Rhetoric of Epitaph in Epigram." *Arethusa* 24: 77–105.

West, M. L. 1966. *Hesiod's Theogony.* Oxford.

———. 1978. *Hesiod: Works and Days.* Oxford.

White, N. P. *Plato: Sophist.* Indianapolis and Cambridge.

Willers, D. 1975. "Zu den Anfängen der archaistischen Plastik in Griechenland." *Mitteilungen des Deutschen Archäologischen Instituts, Athen.* Beiheft 4.

Wilson, P. 1999. "The *aulos* in Athens." In S. Goldhill and R. Osborne, eds., *Performance Culture and Athenian Democracy,* 58–95. Cambridge.

Winkler, J. J. 1990. *The Constraints of Desire: The Anthropology of Sex and Gender in Ancient Greece.* New York.

Wollheim, R. 1980. *Art and Its Objects.* 2d ed. Cambridge.

Wünsche, R. 1979. "Der 'Gott aus dem Meer.'" *JDAI* 94: 77–111.

Xanthakis-Karamanos, G. 1980. *Studies in Fourth-Century Tragedy*. Athens.

Yunis, H. 1988. *A New Creed: Fundamental Religious Beliefs in the Athenian Polis and Euripidean Drama*. Hypomnemata 91. Meisenheim.

Zanker, P. 1995. *The Mask of Socrates: The Image of the Intellectual in Antiquity*. Berkeley and Los Angeles.

Zeitlin, F. I. 1994. "The Artful Eye: Vision, Ecphrasis, and Spectacle in Euripidean Theatre." In S. Goldhill and R. Osborne, eds., *Art and Text in Ancient Greek Culture*, 138–96. Cambridge.

———. 1996. *Playing the Other: Gender and Society in Classical Greek Literature*. Chicago.

Index of Passages Cited

Subject Index

Achilles, 21–22, 98, 150n.59, 169
Admetus, 149, 151, 191–93, 199, 206
Aeschylus, 102; *Agamemnon*, 49, 137, 144, 149n.50, 180; *Choephori*, 7; *Seven against Thebes*, 105; *Theoroi* or *Isthmiastai*, 45–50
Aethlios of Samos, 91
agalmata, 6n.9, 16, 27, 82n.14, 83–84, 121–22, 137, 235
agalmatophany, 135
agalmatophilia, 185, 194n.35, 199, 204
Agamemnon, 253
aglaos, 214
Agrigento, 180
aidōs, 206.69, 206–7, 230, 232–33, 236–37
Aineas, *eidōlon* of, 23
Ajax, 170–71
Alcestis, 149–51, 192n.29
Alcibiades, 132–33, 200–201, 216n.105
Alexander, images of, 175n.158, 300n.14
Alkamenes (sculptor), 50n.147, 92, 297, 304
Alkmaion of Kroton, 43
Alkmene, death of, 6
altar, importance of, 113n.135
Altis (sacred precinct of Zeus at Olympia), 17, 18n.49
Amasis (Egyptian pharaoh), 126–29
Amazonomachy, 59
Amazons, 248
Anakreon, 38–39, 216
anatithēmi, 115n.144
anatomy. *See* realism
Anchises, 97, 97n.72, 235
ancient Near East, consecration of statues in, 114–15, 115n.145
Andromeda, 197
angeion, 125
animation, of statues, 45–50, 90n.44, 114–20
anointing, of statues, 112
apatē, 44–50, 286, 288, 291–92. *See also* craftsmanship; *technē*
Aphrodite, 97, 97n.73, 163, 163n.104, 169, 186n.5, 189n.17, 235; Knidian, 175, 192n.30, 250, 298
Apollo, 97, 99–100, 99n.79, 169–70; Apollo Aguios, 81; Apollo Karneios, 81; Delian, 106n.102
apotropaia, 173, 176, 179
apotumpanismos, 161n.98
archaizing, in cult statues, 91–92n.49, 91–94

Archermos, 243
archons, Athenian, and oath rituals, 10
Ares, 163, 163n.103, 164
Argive Heraion, 93, 103
Aristeas, disappearing corpse of, 7
Aristogeiton, and Harmodios, 29–30, 37–38, 219–22
Aristophanes: *Nubes*, 129–30; *Peace*, 108, 112, 165; *Ploutos*, 172, 180
Aristotle, 35, 41n.126, 119
Arnobius, 82n.12, 112
Artemis, 81, 86n.31, 87, 103; Artemis of Ephesos, 107; Artemis Ortheia, 86; Artemis Phakelitis, 111; Artemis Soteria, 85, 107, 178
Astylos of Kroton (athletic victor), 8, 18
Athena, 94n.62, 97–99, 103–4, 104n.95, 158–59, 186n.5, 187, 189n.17, 189n.18, 195–96, 200; Athena Lemnia, 102; Athena Parthenos, 101–2; Athena Polias, 91, 101n.86, 105n.98, 108–10, 135n.1, 176; Athena of Siris, 175
Athenaeus, 86n.31, 110–11, 118
Athens: Acropolis, 113; City Dionysia, 107; conventions of memorialization in, 265–70; Hephaisteion, 113; Parthenon, 93, 101–4, 246–48; social norms of desire in, 208–11; Temple of Athena Nike, 58, 241; Temple of Hephaistos, 175
athletes, 223–27, 226n.147, 229, 229n.154
athletic images, 8–9, 17–19, 17n.48, 222–34, 259–65, 270–71
athletic victors, 223–24, 229n.155, 230–34, 259–65
audience, theatrical, 47–48, 50, 52, 53n.151, 172n.144, 176–77, 177n.168, 291–93. *See also* viewers

baituloi, 82n.12
base, of statue, 158–59, 257, 261, 273
Bassai, Temple of Apollo, 58, 93, 247–48
bathing, of statues, 109–11
Baxter, Timothy, 72–73
beauty, 76n.199, 102, 211, 213–15, 261–62, 286; of beloved, 194–98, 295–96, 299; Plato on, 130–33; and truth, 61–62, 74–77
Beazley, J. D., 227n.149
Bell, Malcolm, 31, 230–31, 231n.165

356 • Subject Index

Harmodios and Aristogeiton, 29–30, 37–38, 219–22
Harrison, E. B., 31n.85
Hatt, M., 199n.45
Hector, 253
Hecuba, 51–53
Hekate Epipyrgidia, 92
Helen, 6, 49–50, 137, 137n.7, 144, 144n.32, 163n.104, 301n.16; and double, 54–56, 71–72, 193–94, 199; in Euripides, 288–92; in Gorgias' *Encomion*, 286–88
Hephaistos, 21–22, 24–25, 30, 116–18, 139, 142–43, 162, 166–68, 166n.122, 187, 187n.7, 189n.18, 202
Hera, 87, 110, 162, 191n.25, 235; Samian, 86n.31, 91, 110–11, 135n.1
Heracles, 171
Heraclitus, 121–22
Hermes, 81, 82n.13, 86, 134, 168, 168n.133; Hermes Perpheraios, 83, 107; Hermes Propylaios, 92
herms, 92, 133–34, 267–68
Herodotus, 6–7, 43–44, 105, 126–29, 160, 220n.118
heroes, 219–22, 220n.119
heroization, risk of, 266–71
Hesiod: *Theogony*, 24, 78, 161, 164; *Works and Days*, 24, 71, 116–18, 126
hidruō, 115n.144
Hierocles (Alexandrian Neoplatonist), 123
hieroō, 115n.144
Himmelmann, N., 220n.119
Hipparchos, 216, 219, 221
Hippocratic corpus, 27–28, 42
Hippolytus, 53–54
historical individuals, representations, 37–39, 37n.106, 61–62, 61n.171, 269. *See also* portraits and portraiture
hobbling, of cult images, 165–68
Homer, image of, 38
Homeric Hymns, 80, 95–97, 100
homosexuality, 210–11, 214–27
homosocial relations, 223, 223n.125
Hope, 190n.22
Horai, 189n.17
Hugh of St. Victor, 194n.35
Hyde, W. W., 229n.155, 262n.42

iconoclasm, 120–25, 127
iconophilia. See *agalmatophilia*
idealization, 32–35, 32n.88, 37–39, 61n.171, 250, 258n.31
ikelos, 22, 25n.63
Ilioupersis, 59
Ilissos grave relief, 153n.70
image, self as, 51–52

images. *See* athletic images; cult images; funerary monuments; *korai; kouroi*; portraits and portraiture; statues; votive images
immobility, 136–40, 146–47, 151–52, 275–76
imperial images, 300n.14
inanimation, of statues, 136–45
inscriptions, 19–20; of athletic images, 17, 17n.48, 19, 228–29, 229n.156, 270–71; funerary, 11–13, 147, 154, 156, 214n.94, 255–59 (*See also* funerary monuments); of *korai*, 237–38, 238n.189; of *kouroi*, 214, 217–18; of Kritios and Nesiotes' Harmodios and Aristogeiton, 221; votive, 14–16
Iphthime, *eidōlon* of, 23
Isocrates, 278–81
isonomia, 43–44
ivory, 196, 196n.38, 282–85, 285n.106

Jakobson, R., 3n.1

Kahn, Charles, 122
kalokagathia, 277
keimai, 151
kekasmai, 285
Keuls, E., 57n.158, 65n.179
Kleobis and Biton, story of, 7, 7n.16, 8n.17, 277n.95
kolossoi, 6n.9, 9–11, 49, 137, 137n.7, 140, 159n.91. *See also* statues
korai, 13–14, 14n.36, 15, 15n.40, 16, 151–56, 234–38; Peplos, 93; of Phrasikleia, 13–14, 257–59. *See also* statues
kouroi, 12–13, 13n.32, 29, 151–56, 152n.66, 212–18, 276–78; of Apollo, 99–100, 99n.79; of Kleobis and Biton, 277n.95. *See also* statues
Kresilas (sculptor), 58
Kris, E., 11n.26
Kroll, J. H., 91
Kronos, 161, 161n.96, 162, 162n.101, 164–65, 186n.5
Kurke, Leslie, 128n.189, 272
Kurz, O., 11n.26
Kyrene (Libya), 9, 180

Laodamia, 193, 193n.31
Lapith maidens, rape of, 246–49
laudandus, 271–72, 286. *See also* statues; texts
laws: concerning sexual conduct, 210, 216, 224; sacred, 113, 118, 140
Leagros, 224, 224n.130, 226
Lefkandi (Euboea), 254–55